LAND OF PARADOXES

SUNY Series in Israeli Studies
Russell Stone, editor

LAND OF PARADOXES

Interest Politics in Israel

BY
YAEL YISHAI

STATE UNIVERSITY OF NEW YORK PRESS

Published by
State University of New York Press, Albany

For information, address State University of New York Press,
State University Plaza, Albany, N.Y., 12246

Production by Marilyn P. Semerad
Marketing by Bernadette LaManna

Library of Congress Cataloging-in-Publication Data

Ishai, Yael.
    Land of paradoxes : interest politics in Israel / Yael Yishai.
        p.   cm. — (SUNY series in Israeli studies)
    Includes bibliographical references and index.
    ISBN 0-7914-0725-X (cloth). — ISBN 0-7914-0726-8 (pbk.)
    1. Pressure groups—Israel. 2. Israel—Politics and government.
I. Title.   II. Series.
JQ1825.P359I84   1991
322.4′3′095694—dc20   90-10193
                                                             CIP

10   9   8   7   6   5   4   3   2   1

For my mother

Contents

List of Illustrations

List of Tables

Preface

This book is about interest politics in Israel, an old-new country imbued with political paradoxes: It is ruled by potent political parties and an intrusive state machinery; it is inhabited by a vociferous population reflecting a tremendous cultural and demographic variety. The book surveys economic organizations, professional associations, and trade unions. It looks at the settlement movements and immigrant associations, two manifestations of the ongoing process of nation building. Included, too, in the list of organizations examined are cause groups, usually more associated with contemporary issues in Israel politics.

The conventionally used term "interest group"—taking in as it does under its rubric such varied organizations as the Israel Manufacturers Association, Peace Now, and the Union of Ethiopian Immigrants—may appear to be arbitrarily used. The similarities between an association of industrialists and their counterpart merchants justify their being lumped together under one analytical concept. But how can one account for a discussion comparing Gush Emunim, with its nationalistic-neomessianic message, and the Israel Medical Association? The starting point of this book, therefore, is the premise that interest groups, of all types and shapes, are characterized by certain attributes that distinguish them from other forms of political organizations. This distinction is particularly important in Israel, where the boundaries separating the numerous components of the polity have tended to be blurred. Historical processes, national mores, patterns of political behavior, and the distribution of resources have contributed to this lack of clarity. For example, Takam, a settlement movement whose early members belonged to the founding fathers of Jewish settlement in the prestate era, is associated with the Labor party; the aforementioned Gush Emunim is regarded as a spearhead of the pro-Greater Israel political parties. The Israel Medical Association is perceived as a trade union, but one that is also intertwined in the political web of Israeli society. The extremely high involvement of the state and its organs in countless spheres of social and individual life also casts serious doubts on the valid application to Israeli politics of the universal meaning of the term "interest groups."

The major contention of this book is that the extent of linkage between interest groups and the power structures in Israeli society—i.e., political parties and state organs—is an empirical question that renders necessary a scientific examination. It is further argued that one cannot generalize and reach conclusions about the autonomy of interest groups in the Israeli polity unless organizational, behavioral, and normative-ideological aspects of their behavior are probed. It is further assumed that although specific types of organizations may be termed "interest groups," subdivisions within this broad category should be distinguished in order to promote an understanding of their interaction with their broader environment. Consequently the first objective of this book is to make an analytical distinction between interest groups and other political actors. The definition of interest groups used here is rather lax, pertaining to those associations whose aim is to influence public policy. Yet the characterization is not so lax as to include every particpant in the political process. Not included are local authorities, government agencies, military establishments, and the like—not because they do not have an "interest," nor because they exert no influence on the political process. These organizations are excluded because of their too obvious, readily visible identification with the political establishment. Therefore they do not qualify as interest groups. Although the definition is not too restrictive, it is confined to groups having a formal organizational basis; transient and sporadic protest activities are omitted.

The definition of the universe available for investigation has implications for the objectives of this book, which are threefold: to present data on a so-far neglected aspect of Israeli politics, to put Israel in a comparative political perspective, and to look into the special characteristics of Israel as a democracy under pressure.

The Israeli political science agenda has been slow to accord interest group politics the attention paid to other aspects of the polity: the political parties, the electoral system, and protest behavior. The book tries to provide a substantial amount of basic information about the whole range of interest groups that concern themselves with national policy—from those concerned with jobs to those preoccupied with peace and war, from advocates of women's rights to proponents of improving the quality of Israel's environment. The picture of Israeli interest groups that emerges offers (so far) the only source of information regarding this important aspect of the country's politics. Such information, however, would lose much of its value if it were not examined in a comparative perspective, thus enabling the use of models and concepts derived from perceptions of the experience of other countries. Although Israeli politics has been said to be unique, different, and in many respects even aberrant, it is nevertheless not so deviant as to preclude comparison. The comparative aspect of the study is of particular importance to the third objective, which may be first in importance.

The fundamental assumption of this book is that the independent, autonomous activity of interest groups is a *sine qua non* for a democratic regime. It is the essence of liberty and freedom. Dispersed political power is an essential (though by itself not sufficient) condition for democracy, which in Israel today is still extremely precarious. The reasons for this vulnerability have been widely alluded to: Israel is a party-democracy in which political power is disproportionately concentrated in the hands of political parties and their agents in the state administration. Major national decisions are arrived at not through the regular democratic process of bargaining, but rather in literally smoke-filled rooms of the party machinery. Additional weak points characterize Israeli democracy. The role of the ultra-orthodox parties is magnified because of their pivotal role on the political map; to some, the country may appear to resemble a theocracy where religious minorities impose their tenets on a largely secular majority. Israel has been depicted, too, as a "garrison democracy" professing little tolerance of dissent. Legitimation of differences is not anchored in law and practice. Deviation from the mainstream is denounced and derogated. Hatred of the country's non-Jewish minorities and a rigid stand on issues concerning the Arab-Israeli conflict have been identified as detrimental to democracy. The fact that Israel defines itself as a Jewish state, its critics note, also impedes progress toward a fully Western-style democracy.

This book does not plead the cause of innocence for Israeli democracy, which probably has many deficiencies. But it does judge it by a yardstick that enables a distinction among three forms of regimes: extreme party regimes, in which democracy is tilted toward the authoritarian end; corporatist regimes, in which a fundamental partnership operates between political authorities and public organizations; and pluralist regimes, where dissent and variety are acknowledged and legitimized. Israel is not expected to fit ideally with any of these patterns, which nevertheless serve as excellent ideal types of variations against which sound comparisons can be made. The discussion of interest group politics, thus, may not only add facts to a largely missing body of knowledge, it may also contribute to an appreciation of the role played by these associations in the Israeli democracy. Interestingly enough, opinions regarding this role tend to be polarized. Many Israelis are concerned over the growing influence of pressure groups on public life. The presumed ability of Gush Emunim to push the government into approving more settlements in the occupied territories or the success of the Manufacturers Association in blocking the relaxation of import barriers are not favorably viewed. Situated at the other end of the pole are those who depreciate the impact of interest groups on the political process, which, as they see it, is monopolized by political parties and state agencies. The attempt to understand the role of interest groups in Israeli politics vis-à-vis political parties and the state constitutes, therefore, the major objective of this work.

The writing of the book was not only an intellectual endeavor. It has also been an exciting experience of meeting people, on both sides of the political fence: policy makers and policy takers. I am highly indebted to the many interest group leaders and senior government officials who spared time and effort to explain to me the intricacies of public associations and public policy making. Their hospitality, patience, and good will have turned this research project into an enriching human experience.

I acknowledge with gratitude the essential financial support provided by a grant from the Israel Foundation Trustees that enabled me to gather and analyze the data. I alone am responsible for the shortcomings of this book. Still, it is in a way a product of collective effort. My students at the University of Haifa contributed more than they probably recall. I owe a great deal to my research assistant, Haim Ben-Nun and to my English editor, A. M. Goldstein, whose intelligence, efficiency, responsibility, and professional competence greatly aided in the completion of this work. finally, I am most grateful to my family for their consideration and forebearance, to my husband Ori, my children Michal, Tammi, Eran, and Yuval, their spouses and children, who provide constant living proof of the merits of human diversity and association.

INTRODUCTION

Israeli Interest Group Politics in a Theoretical Perspective

The Hebrew word for "group" *kvutza*, means a few people; it also connotes the first form of cooperative settlement established in Palestine in the early days of the Zionist endeavor. The founders of Degania, the first *kvutza*, chose this word for their commune because they wished to maintain a small, cohesive, and intimate social unit, having little in common with giant economic organizations. The word "interest" has no Hebrew equivalent. It is so alien to the Jewish culture that it has not been incorporated into the language. Yet in Israel, as in other industrialized democracies, interest groups are part and parcel of political life, some of these groups exerting enormous influence on its course of development.

Israel so far has received scant attention in the burgeoning literature on interest groups. The neglect can be explained, in part, by the fact that the country has been considered a typical party-state, in which effective political power is heavily concentrated in the hands of the political parties. Israel has also been perceived as being ruled by an extremely potent, intrusive state machinery, whose scope of activities and involvement in citizens' affairs rank among the highest in the democratic world. Thus concentration on partisan battles, electoral preferences, coalition rivalries, and the state apparatus has provided little insight into the role of interest groups in the Israeli political system. There is, therefore, a dire

1

need to deal with this important aspect of political activity, present in every democratic society. This book represents an attempt to meet the need for a comprehensive analysis of Israeli interest group politics. The emphasis will be on the national political arena and on the interaction among government, political parties, and associations in shaping policy. In the process of analysis an attempt will be made to assess the applicability to the Israeli scene of prevailing theories on interest group politics in the literature describing Western industrial democracies. The purpose is not only to place Israel mechanically in one (or more) of the rubrics of interest group theories. An additional intention is to examine their utility in explaining such a complex polity as Israel. The state has repeatedly been described as a unique political phenomenon (Sartori 1966, 1976), but its uniqueness lies only in the *combination* of characteristics that are present in other configurations. This study addresses itself to this particular blend.

The rapid proliferation in Israel of a wide variety of interest groups, along with their increasing interaction with government institutions and with political parties, has added an important new dimension to the politics of contemporary Israel. The emergence and growing importance of interest groups suggest that the Israelis have not lagged behind their counterparts in developing "the art of association" within the context of a liberal democracy. One of the distinctive aspects of the development of interest group politics in modern Israel, however, is that it has often displayed elements of integration with authoritative institutions, namely, the state and political parties. Historically, associations were part of the process of nation building rather than a channel for expressing individual concerns and demands. The highly politicized nature of Israeli associational life is observable not only in the interest groups' goals but also in their organizational and behavioral attributes. The noisy arena of interest group activity, which has developed within the context of an omnipotent party system and a Leviathan state, make Israel a suitable case study. Accordingly the phenomenon of Israeli interest groups will be analyzed in the light of the three major trends identified in the interest group literature: pluralist, corporatist, and elitist. Each of these configurations has been predominant in different historical periods, under varying political circumstances, and in certain social and economic sectors.

One of the major objectives of this book is to study the emergence of these three configurations in Israel in terms of their behavior as either competing or complementary means of structuring interest representation. Much of what will be presented in the chapters to follow will attempt to explain three very striking aspects of the development of interest group politics in modern Israel: first, the growing tendency for adversary politics despite intensive mobilization efforts by the authorities, a remnant of the prestate era; second, the paucity of semi-official statutory bodies enabling state-group cooperation despite a high degree of concentration and monopolization in the group arena; and third, the tenacious adherence of voluntary associations to collective-oriented norms despite behavior that largely reflects pluralistic practices. All three aspects conflict with key hypotheses and assumptions that are prevalent in the major theories of associational development and group politics. Most students of interest groups agree that under circumstances of mobilization, groups refrain from adversarial politics and, instead, lend their share to the national effort; that under conditions of centralization and concentration interest groups become formal partners to authoritative policy making; and that in liberal societies, individual demands are legitimately pursued.

The discussion of interest groups in Israel will be preceded by a comparative examination of the leading theories of group politics. An attempt will be made to identify the characteristics of each of the configurations, to examine their relevancy to the Israeli setting, and to elaborate their implications.

The Three Models of Interest Group Politics

By simple logical construct, it appears that the relationship between interest groups and governing institutions can follow any or a combination of three broad patterns: first, the governing institutions are subject to the will of interest groups; second, the governing institutions share power and authority with organized public contenders; and third, the governing institutions are in fact "governing"—that is, imposing their will on voluntary associations. Official policy makers can thus choose to be responsive and to yield to public inputs, to incorporate them into the process of decision making, or largely to ignore them. Jack Hayward described these options as follows:

> First there are attempts to persuade, manipulate, cajole or coerce interest groups into conformity with official policy, presented as the dictate of the general, national or public interest. Secondly, there are attempts by the interest groups to persuade, manipulate, cajole or coerce the official decision makers

into action or inaction which may be persented as in conformity
with the public interests "as a whole". Finally, there are attempts
to promote cooperation between the interest group spokesmen
and the official policy makers by coordinating or "concerting"
their activities within a formal or informal consultative system
so as to achieve a consensus which can be presented as in the
public interest. (1966: 1–2)

Analysts of interest politics, whether those of Western
societies (e.g., Wilson 1987; Keeler 1987; Hayward 1979) or non-
Western societies (e.g., Bianchi 1984) have focused their attention
on the first two of the three configurations, pluralism and corporatism. The classification of interest politics into two major
types leads to inconclusive findings. Several authors have made
further distinctions within these two categories, such as pressure
pluralism and clientele pluralism (Keeler 1987; Atkinson and Coleman 1989). Most students of interest politics, however, have ignored the third variation of associational politics, elitism, which is
prevalent mainly in party-democracies. This book will attempt to
fill the lacuna by adding to the list of configurations the elitist
model of democratic interest politics. Although broad schemes
suffer from obvious limitations—they are over-simplified and are
merely rough approximations of complicated realities—they do
offer analytic generalizations that aid in explaining the nature of
group politics in a specific societal context. Adding the Israeli case
to those that already have been studied can provide tentative
answers to the questions posed above. Thus, tentative conclusions
regarding interest politics in general, as well as in the Israeli context, can be derived.

The pluralist configuration: influence from below

Modern pluralism started out as a conceptual reaction to the
concentration of power in the formal institutions of the state. Its
proponents argued that public associations form the core of
politics, and they do not derive their power from any other source.
Pluralists believe that a rich associational activity represents liberty, equity, and a meaningful life in society. They echo Alexis de
Tocqueville in positing that the absence of voluntary associations
mediating between citizens and state was the prime cause of the
French Revolution, just as their presence in nineteenth-century
America was a vital feature of democracy in that country. Modern
pluralist analysis, whose initial leading proponents were David
Truman (1951) and Robert Dahl (1961), assumes that civil society
is made up of a plethora of diverse, fluctuating, competing groups
of individuals with shared interests. Politics is regarded as com-

petitive and contentious rather than either consensual or integrative. The backbone of pluralism is polyarchy, a regime exhibiting a relatively high tolerance for oppositions and affording relatively widespread opportunities for influencing the conduct of the government. Pluralism and polyarchy coexist, since the institutions of polyarchy are sufficient to ensure that autonomous associations, of considerable variety and number, will play an important role in the political life of a country (Dahl 1971). Both the merits and the inevitability of autonomous associations were noted by Robert Dahl who described their essence as follows:

> The advantages of organized cooperation make organizations desirable. Indeed, the existence of relatively autonomous political organizations is necessary to the practice of democracy on a large scale. Finally, the rights necessary to the existence of polyarchy make independent organizations legally possible. That they are desirable and possible makes them inevitable. It takes only the first feeble flickering of freedom for independent organizations to spring to life when the controls of an authoritarian regime are relaxed: witness Italy, Austria, Germany, and Japan after their regimes collapsed at the end of World War II, Czechoslovakia in 1968, Poland during the rise of Solidarity. (1984: 234)

The essence of pluralism is a well-defined boundary between interest groups and the political decision-making process. Interest groups are seen as working from outside the institutions of government in order to influence the formal actors involved in governmental policy making. The underlying assumption is that "there is a high probability that an active and legitimate group in the population can make itself heard effectively at some crucial stage in the process of decision" (Dahl 1956: 5145). The pluralist arena is ever changing, since interest groups confront both each other and the government in shifting patterns of competition. A natural dynamism creates a diversity of groups whose ability to appeal to the many concerns of each individual is a guarantee that no one interest will monopolize power. The dynamism of a pluralist society is, presumably, a safeguard against the abuse of power that might flow from uncontrolled pressure on policy makers.

The corporatist configuration: shared influence

In the pluralist model, interest groups play the most visible role in shaping politics; by contrast, the most powerful actor in the corporatist model is the state. The reintroduction of the concept of corporatism into the vocabulary of contemporary political science was said to be "the most remarkable feature of western political thought during the past two decades" (O'Sullivan 1988: 3). The corporatist paradigm provided a new perspective on many aspects of interest group politics. It shied away from the "free market" advocacy of pluralism. Its main departure from the traditional pluralist approach can be summed up in the words of Collier and Collier: "It takes as a starting point the role of the state in shaping interest representation" (1979: 967). In the pluralist paradigm, the state is expected to play at most a passive role in determining the mode of interest group activity. The corporatist paradigm is based on the assumption that the state will act as an "architect of political order" (Anderson 1979) and will, therefore, profoundly affect group dynamics. The state is not "an arena for which interests contend or another interest group with which they must compete"; it is, rather, "a constitutive element engaged in defining, distorting, encouraging, regulating, licensing and/or repressing the activities of associations" (Schmitter 1982: 260).

Phillipe Schmitter, the leading authority on corporatist modern politics, has elaborated ideal-type conceptualizations of pluralism, state corporatism, and societal corporatism as alternative patterns and strategies for structuring interest representation; each has a very different consequence for the organization of groups, for their modes of interaction with the state, and for their degree of political interest. State corporatism is basically a defining element of the anti-liberal, authoritarian state. It is associated with the tight subordination of subunits to central power and the repression of sectional needs. Societal corporatism is embedded in political systems with relatively autonomous centers of power, ideological diversity, and "layered" or "pillared" political subcultures (Schmitter 1974: 22). The two types of corporatism are distinct from each other: they are products of different social, economic, and political processes. They are vehicles for different power relations, and they are purveyors of different policy consequences.

Corporatism is not a simple mode of orchestrating traditional interests. It involves the formal recognition by the state of the social power of "strategic actors" (Magagna 1988: 421) that have passed the "threshold criteria," i.e., those interest groups that have sufficient power to directly affect outcomes in specific arenas of national policy. These groups may claim a legitimate share of power as a function of their social—in most cases economic—role. Corporatism is not tantamount to mere government consultation with organized interest groups. It connotes "integrated participation"; that is, formal rights granted by the state to influence governmental decisions through routine participation in policy-making bodies (Olsen 1983: 148). This distinction is particularly relevant to the difference between "hard" corporatism and "soft" corporatism ("dilution" in Jordan and Richardson's words, 1987: 102). The latter entails only parts of the original concept, whose analytical boundaries were provided by Schmitter in his 1974 path-breaking article. In this volume, "corporatism" does not follow the "undiluted" scheme offered by Schmitter and his colleagues; rather it adopts Olsen's (1983) version, which focuses on the aspects of "integrated participation."

The elitist configuration: influence from above

In hindsight the elitist pattern of politics is incompatible with democratic theory and practice, since it emphasizes the preponderant power of political authority vis-à-vis ordinary or, for that matter, organized citizens. A deeper review of the elitist model of interest group politics reveals, however, that it may also appear under conditions of formal democracy. The Jacksonian idea that every citizen is capable of influencing the functions of government is a peculiarly American concept. Its main thrust is that the political involvement of organized groups is good for society because it makes democracy more meaningful and authorities more responsive to public demands. It is also good for the individual because it enables each person to develop a sense of civic responsibility as well as to advance individual goals.

Given this heritage, it is not surprising that the expansion of grassroots autonomous political associations is a desirable goal for democratic societies. In many respects, however, this belief is irrelevant or inapplicable to other societies. In actual practice, not many countries, apart from the United States have approximated the pluralist model of associational activity. For others, especially those undergoing far-reaching transitions, the elitist model has had more utility. The elitist model does not imply that organized participation is totally subdued by those in power. Rather, it indicates that society, including its organized associations, is highly penetrated by the elite and that citizen organizations appear to be more mobilized than challenging (Huntington and Nelson 1976).

A process of mobilization is likely to occur when the elite makes an effort to involve masses of the population in politics. If a structural change in political and economic institutions is designed, it will be necessary to incorporate as many people as possible in the political process. In order to assure stability, however, this participation has to be under elite supervision. The mobilization of social forces into politics in periods of rapid change is essential for forestalling national decay. By socializing individuals and groups into the existing value system and by inducing them to endorse national goals, the elite not only preserves its own power and sustains its own leadership. It also provides a belt of security for a transitional society. As Huntington remarked:

> In a sense, the top positions of leadership are the inner core of the political system; the less powerful positions, the peripheral organizations and the semi-political organizations are filters through which individuals desiring access to the core must pass . . . . These institutions impose political socialization as the price of political participation. (1968: 22, 83)

In elitist configurations, the heroes of politics are the political parties or, to be more precise, one particular party that is "identified with an epoch; when its doctrines, ideas, methods, its style, so to speak, coincide with those of the epoch" (Duverger 1954: 308). The "epoch" manifests great variety. The Congress party of India adopted an epoch of liberation from colonial rule; the Socialist party in Sweden was identified with an epoch of social welfare; the French Radical party incarnated political radicalism, and Israel's Mapai, the predecessor of the Labor party, espoused Zionist-socialism as its major epoch. All these parties socialized public associations in their efforts to live up to their epoch and to implement the goals set by it. Their relationships with interest groups were fashioned in the framework of what has become known in the literature as "party penetration of society."

Political parties are known for "colonizing" the state machinery; but under elitist circumstances, they are also prone to penetrating social organizations. This development implies that there are party ties to other organizations, enabling parties to influence mass opinion and behavior in a variety of ways (Ware 1987: 196). Many European parties, for example, demonstrate features of social penetration. The Dutch parties offer an extreme example in this respect, situated as they were at the apex of a host of organization (Houska 1985: 13), but there are also other democratic states in which this practice was habitual. In Italy, for example, many interest groups were captured by either the Christian Democrats (DC) or the Communists and subordinated to the interest of their political controllers (Hine 1987). The "cradle to the grave" approach induced the organizational embrace of prospective voters in an environment in which the party was involved in some way in most aspects of the citizens' lives. Social penetration by political parties is the main cause and the major outcome of the elitist model of interest group politics.

Each of the models of interest group politics is associated with structural and behavioral characteristics, which, when combined, produce the respective model. Under particular consideration as distinguishing variables among these models are the following: the organization of the group arena, the role of the political parties, the role of the state, the internal organization of groups, groups' interaction with the state, groups' strategies, the role of groups in the policy process, and the outcomes of their activity.

Organization of the interest group arena. In pluralist configurations, the proliferation of groups in the national arena is extensive. Moreover, the number of groups representing the same sector tends to be large, as groups constantly organize and disband. According to Truman (1951), groups are formed in response to changes in their immediate environment. The "wave effect" will trigger the formation of associations in response to the rise and success of another interest group. The need to counterbalance rivals is also a major catalyst of group formation. Consequently, alliances between or within sectors do not constitute a common pluralist feature. The name of the game is contest and race for power. Given the many effective resources available, the great diversity of social interests, and the low barriers to access, groups tend to form quickly and easily when the need emerges to press their demands on public officials.

In contrast to the large number of associations under pluralism, the corporatist society is characterized by a limited number of interest groups, each monopolizing their own domain of interest. In the "hard" version of corporatism, the groups are hierarchically ordered, and the peak associations are granted official status in the decision-making process (Offe 1981: 213). In democratic corporatism, the hierarchy is not enforced from "above" and groups are not instruments of the state. Rather, they develop from "below"; that is, from the gradual evolution of "Interassociational demands and intra-organizational processes" (Schmitter 1981). Groups are free to enter into cooperative relations with the government and, in principle, are free to terminate such ties. The structure of the interest group map in the corporatist model is determined by the functional contribution of interest groups to society. Competition among interest groups is minor. Instead, there are continuing attempts to forge mutual accommodation and collaboration by emphasizing the interdependence of various social segments. It is often the case for ostensible rivals, such as labor and business, to cooperate in an attempt to present a common front when interacting with the state. Under a corporatist structure, the interest group arena will thus tend to be concentrated, harmonious, and monopolized.

In the elitist model, the number of interest groups on the national level is irrelevant, since all associations branch from the same tree—the political party (or parties) in whose hands power is concentrated. A high proliferation is likely to occur in a multiparty system when power is held by more than one party, each with its own clan of interest groups acting to implement its objectives. In elite societies, the extent of centralization on the national level is also bound to be reflected on the interest group level. The higher the centralization, the less likelihood there is of group fragmentation. But if, as the case appears to be in Holland, there is more than one party representing a social sector (e.g., several Catholic parties), then the associations are likely to be fragmented along the same lines. Interaction among interest groups on the national level tends to be high within the "political family," i.e., among interest groups affiliated with the same political party. Interaction tends to be nearly nonexistent or even adversarial among associations aligning themselves with rival political camps.

The role of the party. Classic pluralist theory, such as presented by Almond and Powell (1966), regards the group-party nexus as essential to democratic practices by prescribing a different function for each in the political process. Interest groups, according to this theory, are responsible for articulating demands; political parties are in charge of aggregating these demands into manageable policy options. Key (1961) viewed alliances between interest groups and political parties as inescapable in political systems having competing parties, although associations remain free to choose their contacts with parties and are not linked to them institutionally or otherwise. Parties mediate between interest groups and political authorities. A clear demarcation between the two organizations is, however, a hallmark of pluralism.

Under corporatism, the role of political parties is diminutive. This model of interest politics has been said in fact to undermine party-government relations (Berger 1981). A well-known corporatist practice is the cooperation of interest groups with government agencies in the formation and administration of policies. It often happens that these arrangements are so well developed that one traditional function of the parties, the articulation of interests, becomes considerably reduced. It is precisely the decline of parties and the inability of the legislature to aggregate interests that give rise to corporatist structures. Corporatism represents, in the view of its proponents, the "short circuiting" of the party system as groups establish direct contact with the government (Wilson 1987: 36). The effort made by parties to conquer the marginal voter in order to represent multiple interests further removes them from the centers of power. As a result, power shifts to the extra-parliamentary arena. Parties are too weak to integrate their followers in a unitary will, to screen demands, and to propose realistic alternatives for the conduct of the modern polity (Pizzorno 1981: 268). One result may be that an interest group will utilize its experience in forging policies and turn itself into a political party.

Interest groups and political parties in elitist configurations interact in the form of what LaPalombara has termed "parentela relationship" (1964: 306). "Parentela" denotes consanguinity, lineage, or kinship. A *parente* is a member of one's family and is entitled thereby to special consideration and unique privileges. In modern politics, parentela involves a relatively close relationship between certain associational interest groups, on the one hand, and the politically dominant party, on the other. The conditions for the development of a parentela relationship are the existence of a hegemonic party, one unchallenged by serious rivals, and its willingness to act on behalf of its kin group. Parentela also requires that associations succeed in finding a place inside the party, although this can be done mainly through a basic commitment to the party's ideology.

The role of the state. The role of the state in the pluralist configuration is minimized. It does not articulate any national or collective interest except as the consequence of group activity. There is no such a thing as "national interest," because the goals of society amount to the sum total of the interests of all groups. Group pressure is the one and only determinant of the course of government policy. The liberal state has in fact been depicted as a mere cash register that totals up the resource credits of competing groups (Nordlinger 1981: 152). It suffices with balancing and reconciling conflicting demands; it is active as a broker and mediator, working out and facilitating the acceptance of policy compromises on the part of the competing groups.

In corporatist regimes, the state plays a crucial role. The more the state performs regulative and integrative functions, and the more it is involved in its citizens' affairs, the more it requires the cooperation of organized associations. The corporatist state, therefore, confers legitimacy upon functional groups, whose role in society is indispensable. The state formally acknowledges national interest groups by licensing and granting them representational monopolies. These privileges are presumably granted in exchange for observing certain controls on their selection of leaders, on their articulation of demands, and on their supporters (Schmitter 1974). The state agrees to devolve upon or share with interest groups much of its decisional authority; nevertheless it controls the political process. Although consultation and participation are guaranteed the associations, the allocation of parliamentary seats, the overall and more precise formulation of the agenda, and the direction of the deliberations are far more influenced by the state than by private interests (Nordlinger 1981: 171).

In the elitist model, the state is colonized by the party; therefore it has no autonomous role in regard to interest politics. The state administration is staffed by party recruits; the state's policy is determined by partisan institutions; the state's ideology and raison d'etre are guided by the ruling party's ideology. The bureaucracy does not represent an instrumental meritocracy, unblemished by patronage; rather it operates under the aegis of the party. Concomitantly bureaucrats demonstrate patronizing attitudes toward interest groups, regarding them as agents of the authorities. In the eyes of government officials, the citizens tend to be more like subjects than legitimate adversaries.

Organization of internal group structures. In pluralistic systems, the internal organization of interest groups is characterized by a great measure of autonomy and independence. Governments or political parties play no role in the organizational life of interest groups. The group solicits its own financial resources, and is not funded by official sources. Low-density group membership reflects its voluntary nature. In the absence of compulsory techniques, the group has to provide incentives to its rank and file, usually in the form of selective benefits (Olson 1968). One of the inducements for membership is the ability of each individual to participate in the life of the group and to influence its internal process of decision making (Wilson 1973). Organization is largely decentralized, enabling members of branches or subsections to participate actively. The internal life of an interest group reflects the political attributes of the external environment in which it operates. Under pluralist circumstances, there is thus more of an inclination toward internal democracy than there is in other forms of interest group politics; there is no external interference with the nomination of candidates; internal divisions of opinion are common, and opposition is legitimate. Challenging the authorities usually does not lead to an eventual breakup of the association. Since internal adversaries are granted a voice in the group's political life, they also have an undisputed right to have their claims heard in the process of intragroup policy making.

This is not the case in corporatist systems, the chief attribute of which is government sponsorship of group resources; the state provides associations with funds for their activity. In pure corporatist structures, the state also interferes with the selection of their leadership. Its involvement in the internal affairs of groups is in exchange for recognition and the acquisition of the right to "integrated participation." In hard core corporatist structures membership in interest groups is mandatory because of legal decrees. In softer versions, membership is induced by social pressure or practical necessity. Density of group membership is an effective way to identify a corporatist structure. Another important element of corporatism is internal group cohesion, which is indispensable. In its absence, the mutual state group relationship is discontinued. Discipline is essential for a group's accepting the accords hammered out by its leadership in interaction with the state (Crouch 1983). The inability of the leaders to sustain these accords undermines the whole system of corporatist cooperation. Because of the necessity of maintaining associational discipline, the degree of internal democracy is not very impressive. The lack of internal democracy is manifested in the paucity of internal opposition, in the denial of access to contenders, and in the general absence of adversarial intra-organizational politics. A threat to the stability of corporatist arrangements is, however, always present. Close relations of a narrow group leadership with the state's bureaucracy may exclude grassroots participation and trigger membership resentment. An overturning of the association's leadership by disfavored constituencies may result (Schmitter 1983).

Interest groups operating in elitist configuration are likely to demonstrate a high dependence on party financial and manpower resources. The dividing line between party and group leaders is blurred. The group may select leaders for party institutions from among its members; the party, in turn, is highly involved in the nomination of the association's executive and other governing bodies. Since the party is the source of power, there is little tolerance of opposition within the group. Formal procedures are not strictly adhered to (what's the use?). There are no serious challenges to the group leadership. In fact, major divisions rarely appear, and serious internal tensions do not surface. If controversy nevertheless arises, the usual consequence is a split, since an elitist system is not capable of absorbing dissent. Proliferation of interest groups may follow, with factional divisions forged along internal partisan cleavages. The organizational structure of interest groups under elitist configuration thus tends to be centralized and cohesive.

Groups' relationship with the state. The key word in the relationship between interest groups and the state in a polyarchy is "access." Liberalism as a theory postulates that national authorities are susceptible to demands exerted by any segment of society and the ears of the decision makers are attuned to their advocacies. Access is assured by virtue of the philosophical tradition that presupposes the participation of citizens in the act of government. Although representative democracy made individual participation obsolete, and thereby removed the individual from the core of power, the "slack resources" (to use Dahl's term) available to each and every citizen guarantee them the right to be heard, i.e., to have access to the centers of power.

The hallmark of corporatism is the participation of private associations in the formal process of government. The legitimacy of this participation is derived from the assumption that the delegation of public policy functions to private interest organizations represents an attempt to utilize the collective self-interest of social groups to create and maintain a generally acceptable social order (Streeck and Schmitter 1985: 16).

In an elitist configuration, interest groups amalgamate with the state, since the polity at large tends to be clustered around political parties. One possible form of amalgamation, especially in states adhering to democratic rules of government, is the direct representation of interest groups in decision-making bodies. This political strategy was in the past associated with authoritarian corporatist regimes; in the democratic context, however, representation takes place not through the direct recruitment of associational representatives to the legislature, but through the ballot, when the parties contest for the people's vote.

Strategies of action. In pluralist societies, groups attempt to influence authorities from the outside. The underlying feature of pluralist strategies is their variety. In fact, all channels of access are widely open, and all means of trying to influence the authorities are acceptable so long as they remain within legal bounds and do not violate the democratic rules of the game. The list of strategies of action is almost endless. It includes the establishment of contacts with the administration, with elected legislative representatives, and with all those who are willing to listen to the group's demands. One common strategy under pluralist configurations is direct action taken by individual citizens operating within the confines of nonassociational groups. For their part, interest groups devote much effort to mobilizing public opinion and broad participation. Marches, demonstrations, and rallies typify pluralist behavior. Strikes are also viewed as a legitimate strategy for blocking undesirable policies. The means of action employed by interest groups thus extend from ordinary dealings with government officials and parliamentary delegates to unstructured activity undertaken by loosely organized individuals. In order to modify the government's position or policy, some groups also undertake what is referred to as "protest" politics. In his seminal study of French interest politics, Wilson makes a distinction between pluralist politics and protest politics: the former is the institutionalized, orderly form of interaction between interest groups and state; the latter expresses frustration and ideologically motivated behavior (1987: 18–25, 39–44). In the context of the present work, both strategies are included in the pluralistic model. Protest may be regarded as one more strategy in the arsenal of pluralistic groups, regardless of its motivation or participants, as long as it is confined to the limits of legal behavior. Both protest and institutionalized strategies lead to a continuous process of bargaining between associations and public officials, which is the hallmark of pluralism.

The key word for corporatist strategies is coordination. Groups do not bargain with authorities, nor do they exert pressures. It is not only that cajoling is conceivably immoral in a harmonized society, it simply is an unnecessary device. Almond and Powell suggest that "the general rule is that the interests [of associations] will be articulated through those channels which are most available and those which seem most likely to bring the demands to the attention of the relevant decision makers" (1966: 75). Under corporatism, the availability of joint interest group–state forums is self-evident. The institutionalized links between interest groups and government make all other strategies and means of influence superfluous. There is no need to lobby, to mobilize public opinion, to establish intermittent contacts with government officials, to court legislators or local representatives, to demonstrate, to protest, or for that matter to forge close links with political parties. Under corporatism, regular, institutionalized consultation is designed to achieve agreement, which is the blueprint for corporatist arrangements. The council, committee, board, or any other forum that brings together representatives of interest groups and the government administration constitutes a major channel of action for associations.

In the elitist model, strategies are narrowly focused. Interest groups gain access to the political process through the parties with which they are associated in a parentela linkage. Rational behavior dictates that the political parties, being the major—if not the sole—source of power, be chosen both as targets of influence and as transmitters of demands to the bureaucracy (which is, as may be recalled, also penetrated by the parties). The parties' role is ubiquitous: as the sole mediators, as the policy makers, and as the gatekeepers of the public demands. There is more to choosing the party as a target than rational calculation, however. In the elitist model, the strategies of pressuring, cajoling, and prodding the government are simply not practiced, since the society at large is united around the objectives promulgated by the party. Gone is the usual image conjured up with "pressure" and "lobby," of narrow interests threatening the integrity of society and putting at risk the fulfillment of its collective goals. Interaction with the authorities in the elitist configuration is not carried out through bargaining; rather, it demonstrates a process of integration between the tree (the party) and its branches (associational groups).

Interest groups in the policy process. The role of associations in the policy process has been subject to theories of agenda setting. In pluralist configurations, interest groups play a crucial role in the stage of initiation. They bring issues to the attention of decision makers, who tend to be responsive and yielding. In corporatist configurations, initiation of policy alternatives emanates from the state; however, no binding policy can be formulated unless cooperation with organized citizens is secured. Although the state crystallizes policies, interest groups are permitted full-fledged participation. They, furthermore, play an active role in implementing authoritative decisions. Cooperation between state and associations minimizes the need for elite responses. Under elitist circumstances, the public is a passive spectator. Hopes for influence are based on the elite's own ability to assure formal agenda status.

The integration of interest groups and the ruling elite precludes responsiveness as a political practice.

The outcomes of group activity. A distinction needs to be drawn between the micro-outcomes pertaining to the organization of interest groups and the macro-outcomes in regard to society at large. It appears that all three models of interest group politics prescribe structures that are geared to achieving the same macro-goal: the aim of pluralism (in its classic version) is to achieve social equilibrium with the fluctuating acquiescence of numerous contenders; corporatism is noted for its contribution to attaining stability, which is indispensable in an era of economic crisis and governmental overload (Schmitter 1981); finally, the goal of elitism is to establish a political balance, which is essential for the fulfillment of national or social goals. The variation among the different models thus pertains not to their macro-goals, but to the means by which these goals are achieved.

The major determinants of outcomes in pluralist systems are the resources available for group action. The list of these resources is innumerable: among others, numbers, votes, organization, money, expertise, information, social status, a positive public image, access to the mass media, control over economic resources. The intensity of the members' preferences, their dedication to the cause of the group, and their propensity to create a "nuisance impact" (Milbrath 1967) constitute important factors in determining group success. Although some groups control a disproportionate share of some resources, the diversity and widespread distribution of resources make for a noncumulative pattern of "dispersed inequalities" (Nordlinger 1981: 151). It is not necessary in pluralist systems to belong to the party or to have an integrated linkage with the source of power. It is necessary, however, to amass the largest possible amount of power in order to survive the race and to win the competition. Whether or not the arena is in effect open to all contenders is an acute problem, one that is widely dealt with by critics of the pluralist theory (e.g., Bachrach and Baratz 1962; McConnell 1966; Schattschneider 1975; Lowi 1979). For the purpose of this discussion it suffices to note that the accumulation of resources is the best predictor of success (Gamson 1968).

The functional role of groups in society provides the key to understanding their integration in the policy process in corporatist configurations. The state does not demonstrate benevolence by sharing its power with outsiders, let alone devolving part of its authority. It shares power because the functional contribution of groups is invaluable for the act of governance. The role of functional contribution in shaping relations between the state and interest groups has been emphasized in the literature (e.g., Brenner 1969). The expansion of government activity in the welfare state, on the one hand, and the need to lessen the scope and intensity of economic strife, on the other, prompted corporatist arrangements. The major economic groups, the professional associations, and other select organizations became the beneficiaries, enjoying the privileges of integrated participation.

In elitist models, interest groups play a modest role in the policy process since they are subject to the influence of the party, the major purveyor of national goals. The right to participate in the process promulgated by the party, be it liberation from colonial rule, the establishment of a welfare society, the consolidation of Catholic rule, or bringing Jews from their countries of exile and anchoring them on their own land, is a reward in itself. All demands are processed within the "family." In elitist configurations, the veto power of organized associations is extremely weak, since it is inconceivable that the latter would dispute the elite and challenge a decision geared to the attainment of nationally accepted goals. There is little encounter with the authorities; integration between parties and interest groups precludes such an option. If resources do not count, then what are the determinants of the success of an association? Influence is secured mainly by adherence to collective goals, to the calling represented by the party. The larger the contribution of an association to the fulfillment of these goals, the greater will its prospects be of obtaining more of the assets and commodities distributed by the elite.

Table 1.1, at the risk of some simplification, succinctly summarizes the three models of interest group politics. Because of their divergent emphases, each model presents a different perspective as well as different insights into group politics. The variables presented in the table may serve as a guideline for the discussion to follow.

The Israeli Political Environment

The purpose of this book is not only to locate Israel somewhere on the elitism-corporatism-pluralism triangle, but also to understand the possible factors that may have tilted the interest arena toward one or another of the models or may have produced the specific blend characterizing contemporary Israel. The hypothetical factors involve changes in (a) the political structure; (b) the socioeconomic environment; and (c) the value structure.

Table 1.1
Comparative Attributes of the Three Models of Interest Group Politics

	Pluralism	Corporatism	Elitism
Organization of the group arena	proliferation	concentration	mirrors the partisan make-up
Role of political parties	mediation	—	domination
Role of the state	"cash register"	pervasive	colonized by party
Internal group structure	autonomous	dependence on state	dependence on party
Group interation with state	confrontation	cooperation	co-optation
Group strategies	bargaining	coordination	integration
Groups in the policy process	initiation	implementation	submission
Determinants of outcomes	group resources	functional contribution	adherence to collective goals

Changes in the political structure

Israel started its political life as a genuine "party-state," in which parties played a decisive role in both the country's political and social life. Many spheres of social activity were entrusted to the political parties or, at least, were largely dependent on political-partisan decisions. Whether or not a similar scope of party-politicization has endured to date will be examined in the succeeding chapters. Two prominent changes, however, are noticeable in the party domain. First, the Israeli party system has been crystallizing into three major blocs: a left-wing bloc, a right-wing bloc, and a religious bloc. These blocs (especially the religious camp) may now be internally divided; but the forming of the Labor party (1968) and the establishment of the Likud (1973) produced two major poles around which splinter parties have clustered. The bipolarization of Israel's political system both intensified the electoral contest and somewhat blurred the lines between the two contenders. The growing importance of the media in the elections campaign also contributed to the development of "catch-all" techniques (Mendilow 1988).

A second, and even more pronounced change, lay in the decline of dominance in the Israeli party system. For a full generation, beginning in the prestate era, Israel was ruled by a classic dominant party—Mapai (later the Labor party)—whose impact on the political, social, and economic life of the country was profound. Although the electoral attainments of this ruling party gradually declined, its grip on centers of power was so tight that the country was shocked to learn on May 17, 1977, that the party had been ousted from government and replaced by its arch-rival—the Likud. The "upheaval" of 1977 was the watershed of Israel's political life: it revolutionized the composition of the elite, it enabled the recruitment of new constituencies into the political process, it introduced new values into policy programs; and it changed or, as suggested by Schweitzer (1984), it reflected a change in the contents of the political agenda. Post-1977 Israel was different (Seliktar 1986). The shift may have marked "more of the same"; on the other hand it could also have signified a structural change in the polity, the outcomes of which have not yet been fully or finally determined.

Changes in the socioeconomic arena

By any criteria, Israel has undergone striking social and economic changes in the relatively short period of time since its establishment. In 1947, when statehood was declared, the country's half a million Jews could count only a handful of households among themselves that enjoyed the privileges of affluence that were already visible in other Western societies. The most important element that shaped Israel's development, growth, and economic structure in the years to follow was the addition of population. Israel became known as "a country of immigrants, established for and run by immigrants" (Ben-Porath 1986: 47). The state's raison d'etre was—and is—to ingather, retrain, and forge into one nation Jewish immigrants from all over the world. Economic growth and a rising standard of living were by-products of this population increase. The rate of economic development in its first two decades was astonishing: national income rose an average 9 percent annually, while the population increased 4 percent in the first decade and 3 percent in the second. Israel's rapid growth, both of population and of per capita product, leading to a high rate of gross national product, was said to be a unique phenomenon unequaled elsewhere (Syrqyin 1986).

These record growth rates, which changed the economic structure of the young country, came to an end in the mid-1960s, when Israel encountered a severe economic crisis. The dramatic victory in the Six Day War of 1967, however, injected resources into the economy and invigorated the country's growth once again. The war was a watershed, not only for Israel's foreign policy and its domestic sociopolitical make-up, but also for its economy. The average annual growth from 1968 to 1972 (11.5 percent) even exceeded that of the former period. Mass immigration from Western societies and the Soviet Union added technologically educated and trained manpower to the Israeli economy. The spectacular upsurge in living standards was manifested in the indicators of private consumption per capita, which grew almost consistently. Although the 1973 October war slowed down economic growth and eventually led to severe problems of inflation, in the 1980s, Israel was no longer a developing society. It had joined the ranks of the industrialized states.

Changes in the value structure

In the first twenty years of statehood, Israelis were preoccupied with fundamental problems of survival. Surrounded as the country was by hostile neighbors, it had to cope with external threats and incessant belligerency. The intransigence of the neighboring Arab countries produced a deep sense of insecurity, which left its imprint on all walks of life. The economy, the educational system, the ideological setting, and even family affairs were all subject to the "conflict." At the same time, however, Israel carried the banner of the welfare state, providing for the needs of many citizens who were greatly underprivileged when it came to the basic commodities of the affluent society. It was not until the late 1970s that the rise in the standard of living was shared by large portions of the population.

During the country's formative years, the economic burden was heavy, despite the dramatic growth in the national product. The Israelis' order of priorities was clear-cut: their major concern was security, next in importance came their material needs. The Six Day War introduced changes in this regard and by the 1970s, Israel was already portraying symptoms of a postindustrial society, namely, restructuring of the labor force, expanding educational opportunities, and increasing information resources (Dalton, Beck and Flanagan 1984). To begin with, the farming sector began to feel this restructuring as its labor force declined from 17.6 percent of the nation's total in 1955 (*Statistical Abstract* 1968: 260) and fell steadily to 4.6 percent in 1988 (*Statistical Abstract* 1989: 338). Concomitant with the country's adoption of advanced industrialism, a marked shift to the service sector occurred. Israel has passed Daniel Bell's (1973) threshold for postindustrialism—half the labor force is employed in the tertiary sector. These industrial-economic trends paralleled an expansion in educational opportunities, particularly at the university level. The proportion of the population attending institutions of higher education increased by a factor of 41.5 between 1948–49 and 1987–88. The population growth factor over the same period was 5.0 (*Statistical Abstract* 1988: 638; 31). This increase in educational opportunities was accompanied by a concomitant rise in information resources, including the installation of television, which began operating in 1968.

The changes in Israel's political, economic, and ideological systems are presented in figure 1.1. At its inception, Israel was a genuine party-democracy, to which the elitist model is most applicable. The changes in the party system and the relative perceived decline in the power of the parties may have produced a change in interest group politics bifurcating into two directions: Israel's economic development encouraged the participation of functional groups in the policy processes and triggered the emergence of corporatist patterns; its economic affluence generated a change of values by pushing Israel toward the pluralistic pole on the interest group configuration. The underlying question is whether this analytical co-variation between the interest-political model and the change identified indeed prevails. The answer to this question will be provided by distinguishing among three major categories of interest groups, each of which represents a different configuration. Tracing the structural and behavioral characteristics of each of these interest group categories will enable the understanding of changes over time, as well as trends of interest politics in contemporary Israel.

Interest Group Models and Types of Groups

Classification of interest groups abound. Almost any study of a national configuration of interest politics offers its own distinction among types of associations. In all these taxonomies, two categories stand out: groups seeking to advance the material benefits of their members and groups seeking to advance an idea or a value to which they adhere (Stewart 1958; Finer 1958). among the former, the classic economic interest groups can be identified: trade unions, employer associations, organizations of farmers, and professionals guilds. This sectional category also includes groups

Fig. 1.1. Process of Sociopolitical Changes and Model of Interest Group Politics

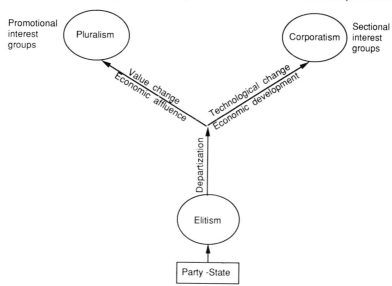

of handicapped desirous of gaining a larger portion of the national pie and other categoric groups like students or tenants, and immigrant associations. The common denominator of all such groups is their defense or advancement of material personal benefit. Sectional interest groups comprise the traditional political configuration referred to by the early admirers of democracy, such as John Stuart Mill and Alexis de Tocqueville. These groups demonstrate the freedom of individuals to organize in order to defend or promulgate their own interests. The importance of the sectional interest groups especially manifests itself during periods of economic change, when their contribution to the growth of the economy and to technological development is vital. Their functional role in society is the major reason for their inclusion in the policy process.

The division of the interest arena between material and non-material associations is universally applicable. In Israel, however, as well as in other party-democracies, party-oriented associations may also be identified within this category. This distinction, or overlapping characteristic, is lacking in the literature. For example, trade unions are usually linked to a political party; yet organizations of workers are usually classified as sectional groups fulfilling vital roles in a country's economy. An economic group they are indeed, but their partisan affiliation distinguishes them from other sectional interest groups. In the case of Israel, the party-affiliated groups also include the farming sector; the other associations in the sectional category are the business groups and "others," consisting of residual associations.

The second major analytical category consists of promotional groups, also known as "issue-oriented groups" or "cause groups." A promotional group, as distinct from a sectional group, advocates a goal that, in the long run, is not evaluated in material assets. The hard core of the promotional category are public interest groups; that is, groups that seek a "collective good, the achievement of which will not selectively and materially benefit the membership or activists of the organization" (Berry 1977: 7). These include the environmental groups, consumer organizations, and the like. Sports associations (those not established for profit purposes) and welfare groups seeking to aid society at large (such as the Cancer Society) or to provide assistance to the underprivileged or to erase poverty and misery are also included among the promotional interest groups.

The emergence of issue-oriented groups has been attributed to the growing opportunity provided by pluralist regimes for mobilizing new constituencies into the political process and for dealing with issues that political parties have failed to absorb. Berry observed that promotional groups contribute to democracy by representing citizens and presenting policy preferences:

> Like all interest groups, public interest lobbies form a linkage element between citizens and governmental elites. In their lobbying they articulate what they perceive to be the issue positions of certain sectors of society. What is particularly noteworthy about the advocacy work of public interest groups is that they represent constituencies that have been chronically unrepresented or underrepresented in American politics. (1977:288)

Thus promotional associations have come to represent an expanding participation in political life. The diffusion of these groups is also linked to changes in the distribution of power. They constitute a countervailing force to the traditional business groups and organizations. They challenge corporations and they combat the big economic associations, despite their undeniable inferiority in regard to organizational resources. Public interest activism,

Vogel has argued "succeeded in significantly narrowing the boundaries of managerial discretions. Many corporate abuses were reduced and those that continue are now less likely to go unchallenged. In sum, public interest groups are to the last decade what the trade union movement was to the thirties and the muckrakers were to the Progressive Era: the driving force behind increased restrictions on corporate prerogative" (1981: 607). Promotional associations, then, herald a change in the traditional division of power in industrialized countries. Their emergence in the Israeli society is expected to mark the transition from elitism to pluralism, from the materialist era to post materialism.

A hypothesized relationship between environmental factors, a model of group politics, and the three types of associations is presented in figure 1.2. Party-affiliated interest groups are expected to demonstrate Israel's elitist strands, the economic organizations are expected to portray Israel's corporatist elements, and promotional associations are expected to mirror new winds blowing in the Israeli polity. The present study of interest groups in Israel sets out to verify this model and to examine the interrelationships of its variables.

Fig. 1.2. Models of Interest Politics by Environmental Attributes and Types of Groups

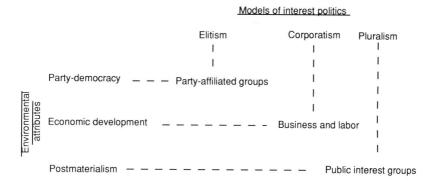

The Data and Methodology

The objectives were to examine interest politics in Israel and the role played by associations in shaping public policies. The research was confined to interest groups on the national level that have acquired a measure of institutionalization. The operational test for organizational viability was registration in the phone direc-

tory of one of the country's three major cities—Tel Aviv,
Jerusalem, or Haifa. Only national headquarters were included in
the list. Bearing in mind the size of Israel (a land area approx-
imating that of the United States state of New Jersey and a population of four and half million) and its urbanization (approximately
72 percent of the population resides in the major metropolitan
areas), it was assumed that the vast majority of interest groups had
their offices located in one of the three big cities. In fact, over 90
percent were located in Tel Aviv, the largest economic and commercial metropolitan area of Israel. The search in the telephone
directory was based on common words incorporated in the names
of interest groups: committee, union, council, association, society,
federation, etc. Other groups, listed under different titles or just
under an acronym (such as Malraz, the Council for the Prevention
of Noise and Pollution) were identified by informants. One interest group—Peace Now—was included in the study although it
had not acquired the symbol of institutionalization—registration
in the phone directory—at the time the empirical research was
conducted. Its inclusion was deemed necessary, however, because
of its influence on political life. The groups selected for this study
comprise only a part of the associational universe in the country.
Many neighborhood associations and self-help groups were excluded. Some were not involved in "politics," i.e., in the determination of public policy; some were ephemeral entities. Many
others, though, are due scholarly attention, which hopefully be
granted them in the future.

   Most of the findings of this study are based on four sources.
First, mail questionnaires were sent to the headquarters of 277 interest groups during the winter of 1988–89; a total of 162 replied (a
response rate of 58.5 percent). Second, interviews with leaders of
62 interest groups were conducted by the author in 1987 to 1989,
unveiling important facets of Israeli group life. Wilson (1987: 10)
has noted the strong negative connotations of the word "pressure"
in the French context. In Israel, not only is "pressure" totally rejected as a title (although, as will be shown below, much less as a
practice), but leaders of associations would not even accept being
labeled as "groups." The manufacturers, the physicians, and the
metal industry workers do not admit being organized within a
"group." The label, furthermore, is unacceptable to Gush
Emunim, and other issue-oriented associations, which would
much rather endorse the term "movement." The subjects of the
research, therefore, were approached as, and the questionnaires
referred to, "public organizations" rather than interest groups.
Having surmounted this difficulty in terminology the interviews

ranged in length from one hour to a series of consecutive meetings, altogether lasting a couple of hours, with the major interest groups in each analytical category. Representatives of all the larger interest groups of repute in Israel—Histadrut, Manufacturers Association, Bar Association, Medical Association, Peace Now, Gush Emunim, just to name a few—were included among the interviewees. The groups that responded to the questionnaire (and the representatives interviewed) were divided into four broad categories and further broken down into a classification of nine types, given in table 1.2. (A list of all interest groups represented in the study is found in Appendix A).

Table 1.2
Membership Affiliation of Interest Group Respondents

Type of group	Number
Sectional Groups	
Trade union	22
Business group	23
Professional association	19
Farmers organization	15
Categoric group	17
Immigrant association	12
Total sectional groups	108
Promotional Groups	
Public interest group	22
Welfare association	19
Sports or cultural group	13
Total promotional groups	54

The questionnaire (see Appendix B) was designed to probe the following features:

• The structure of the national interest group arena; the degree of cooperation or competition on the associational level.

• The relationship between interest groups and political parties in regard to finance, leadership selection, electoral campaigning, and contacts.

• The organizational attributes of interest groups, their year of founding, membership size, density of membership, budget resources, internal elections, patterns of internal democracy, degree of organizational centralization and cohesion.

- The relationship between interest groups and agencies of the state, namely the bureaucracy and Israel's parliament, the Knesset. The questionnaire investigated the independence of associations from state organs and the frequency and purpose of their contacts with official bodies and persons.

- The strategies of influence characteristic of interest groups, covering the whole spectrum from direct action (street demonstrations and strikes) to institutionalized participation in joint state-group committees or councils.

- The role of interest groups in the policy process.

- Finally, the views of interest groups on the outcomes of their activities, and the presumed reasons for these outcomes. Opinions were also sought on the general contribution of interest groups to Israel's political life in particular and to society in general.

Most of the questionnaire consisted of closed-ended questions. The open-ended conversations with group activists during the interviews supplied the basis for the general evaluation of interest group politics in Israel.

The third source of information came from forty-one interviews conducted with senior officials in thirteen government ministries (taking part were twelve directors-general and twenty-nine deputy directors-general). The administrators not serving as directors-general were chosen on the basis of their functional role in the ministry and their responsibility for domains having important relevance to interest group activity. The interviews, conducted from November 1988 to June 1989, lasted from at least an hour to three hours (the latter in three separate one-hour meetings). These interviews contained six closed-ended questions, the aim of which was to investigate the attitudes of top government bureaucrats toward interest groups (the questions are presented in Appendix C). Most of the interview was devoted to open-ended questions regarding patterns of policy making in Israel. Not one senior official who was requested to devote a portion of his or her scarce time for the purpose of scholarly research refused to do so.

The fourth source of information was provided by a study conducted by the author in 1984–85. Its results were published in a Hebrew-language book with the title *Interest Groups in Israeli Politics: The Test of Democracy* (Yishai 1987a). Since the methodological questions faced by the present study are different from those referred to in the earlier work, the latter provided a source of examples rather than a source of systematic data. Exemplificative material was also provided by publications issued by interest groups and by Israel's daily press, which reports extensively on the activities and structures of national interest groups.

The Plan of the Book

The ensuing ten chapters of this book are devoted to an analysis of interest group politics in Israel. The first chapter describes and analyzes the particular characteristics of the Israeli interest group arena, including the historical and contemporary role of political parties; the economic and political powers of the state, and the domestic socioeconomic and ideological divisons that have brought about associational activity. In chapter two, the universe of groups is described in line with the taxonomical categories of interest group theory. A review of the historical development of the major interest groups in the country is presented, with special emphasis placed on the national structure of the group arena in terms of concentration or atomization-proliferation. Chapter three looks into the linkage between groups and political parties. The analysis focuses on three variations of this relationship: groups within parties, groups acting as parties, and groups acting upon parties. The subject of the fourth chapter is the state and its relations with interest groups. First, the historical development of the formal legal basis of interest groups is examined. This is followed by a discussion of the attitudes of senior officials (representing the state) and of Knesset members toward voluntary associations. Chapter five considers the organizational attributes of interest groups in Israel: the degree of concentration of associations, the relationship between groups in the national arena, their autonomy insofar as being free of state/party resources, and their internal democracy. The sixth chapter presents the mirror image of the topic of chapter four: the relationship of interest groups with the state. The analysis deals with the access of associations to decision-making forums (i.e., the government and the Knesset), their participation in joint state-group bodies, and their integration in the policy process through direct representation in national authorities. Chapter seven delves into the various strategies and methods of influence of interest groups; the techniques used by groups in order to promote their interests are probed, and a rough distinction is made among the three major strategies: bargaining, coordination, and integration. The eighth chapter examines the role of interest groups in the policy process. The discussion centers on their role in initiating policies, on their contribution to implementation, and on their submission to authoritative decisions. It also probes the elite responsiveness to their demands. Chapter nine looks at consequences. This is done by evaluating the views of association activists regarding their influence (i.e., their ability to exercise a veto) and their perceived determinants of this influence. A summary chapter, reviewing the major findings of the study, attempts to understand the Israeli case, to place it in a time perspective, to identify the possible causes of trends over time, to impart to Israel a comparative perspective, and to re-evaluate interest group theory in view of the Israeli case.

This book is thus about interest groups in Israeli politics, and their adjustment to their surroundings. Environmental changes on the Israeli scene are readily identifiable. The Interest group arena is expected not only to reflect these changes but perhaps also to precipitate their pace. One major problem confronting Israeli society, however, is the simultaneous occurrence of socioeconomic and normative transformations. The country entered an era of rapid economic development while encapsulated by a party regime; it had developed a yearning for new values while engulfed by a comprehensive economic upsurge. Fundamental problems of security, affluence, and identity required concomitant solutions rather than a sequential, compartmentalized treatment. The convergence of problems highlighted the paradoxes of the Israeli polity, which were caused not only by an incongruence between vision and reality but also within vision itself. Israel strives to be a Jewish state while declaring itself a democracy based on universal principles of equality; it preaches turning swords into plowshares, but it worships power. The path chosen by interest groups may indicate how Israel has coped with the paradoxes of its polity. Interest politics is not expected to fit neatly into one of the theoretical rubrics but rather to expose the ambiguities of the system. the deviation from theory does not necessarily refute its validity. Rather, it may indicate that Israel faces a serious problem of coherence, emanating from the paradoxes characterizing its polity. Interest groups provide a prism through which the intricacies of this polity can be examined.

CHAPTER ONE

The Israeli Polity:
Party, State, and Society

The high partisanship of the Israeli polity left its imprint on the country's interest group system. Within the framework of a formal democracy political parties offered a comprehensive umbrella that covered all aspects of society and introduced a strong elitist flavor into associational life. Accompanying the partisanship of the first two decades of the state's existence was the emergence of a new policy actor, the state's bureaucracy. Called into being by the government's role in fulfilling national functions, the state's involvement in the citizens' affairs introduced a series of new factors into the interest group arena. The centralization trends that were making their presence felt in the economy were counterbalanced, however, by the growing heterogeneity within Israeli society, which produced an environment congenial to pluralism. This chapter will probe the three faces of the Israeli polity, which gave rise to the unique combination of the three configurations of interest politics.

Israel as a Party State: The Source of Elitism

All leading Israeli political scientists (Akzin 1955; Gutmann 1977; Galnoor 1982; Arian 1985) agree that Israel is a "party-state" in which effective political power is heavily concentrated in the hands of political parties. This may not be unique to Israel, since "party-government" is believed by many to be the essence of representative or parliamentary democracy. But in Israel, the term means not only government-by-party but also the presence of nine characteristics that distinguish a party-democracy from other

types of democratic regimes. In a party-democracy political parties play a major role in the provision of social services, they are
agents of mobilization, they control nominations to political offices, they establish a highly disciplined organizational structure,
their leaders hold responsibility to the party rather than to the people, and they penetrate the bureaucracy. In a party-state politics
enjoys a high salience, and the partisan elite is insulated from
public pressures. The upshot of these characteristics ends the list:
in a party-democracy the parties fulfill a vital role in the policy
process; their influence is decisive in determining the course of the
nation.

Parties as providers of social services

In Israel the political parties fulfill social functions parallel to
those maintained by the state. The origins of their functional role
in the socioeconomic domain go back to the prestate era, when the
parties carried the major load of building the Jewish homeland. So
broad were their activities that they seemed at times to over-
shadow the purely political activities of formally governing
bodies. The political parties sponsored agricultural movements,
industrial and construction enterprises, recreational activities, and
welfare services. This prominent socioeconomic role carried over
into the early days of statehood. The Israeli atmosphere of those
days was vividly described by Akzin:

> A person who subscribes to the party's daily newspaper, is
> given medical care in a party-sponsored clinic, hospital or con-
> valescent home, spends his evening in a party club, plays
> athletic games in the party's sport league, gets his books from
> the party's publishing house, lives in a village or in an urban
> development inhabited solely by other adherents of the party
> and is accustomed to look to the party for the solution of many
> of his daily troubles—is naturally enveloped and surrounded by
> an all-pervasive partisan atmosphere. (1955: 520)

The establishment of the state was expected to narrow considerably the social role of the political parties, since many of their
functions were, of course, transferred to the state, although at an
uneven pace (Etzioni 1962). The parties, however, have retained
some of their past role in providing social services. They no longer
do so directly but through extensions that serve their interest, such
as women's organizations and economic enterprises. This feature
is particularly conspicuous in the health domain, which has re-

tained to date many of its partisan attributes. As will be shown later, the Histadrut (Israel's trade union movement) owned General Sick Fund (*Kupat Holim*) practically monopolizes the provision of medical services in some spheres, especially in primary care. The parties' imprint is seen, too, in the nationally state-controlled media communication network. To a varying degree, they still stand at the apex of an interconnected network of organizations and institutions that they control. The direct social-action role of Israeli political parties has thus acquired the force of habit. It is perpetuated by inertia more than by a preplanned design.

Yet Israel of the 1980s is very different from the state of the 1950s. To recapitulate Akzin's description, many changes have taken place: the number of party-owned newspapers has considerably declined; party-affiliated publishing companies are on the verge of bankruptcy; a large proportion of Israelis take their vacations outside the country; party membership itself is reportedly declining (Arian 1985: 106); by and large, residence is heterogeneous in terms of partisan affiliation; finally "problems" are solved either by psychiatric services or by the state's welfare agencies. Even in the health services, the temple of partisanship, there has been a constantly growing demand for private medical care, and a concomitant increase in private medicine, owing to the failure of the public (mostly partisan) health services to respond adequately to increasing demands. Nonpartisan health funds (such as Maccabi) have also significantly increased their membership. The glass is thus only half full: the parties still fulfill social functions, but the trend is clear. In this respect, Israel today is less of a party-state compared to its past.

Parties as agents of mobilization

Political mobilization (also referred to as socialization) is considered a major function of political parties (Almond and Powell 1966). In a party-state, however, the load that parties bear in performing this function is remarkably high. Mobilization can be performed by socializing the individual. It can also be carried out by penetrating wider clusters of citizens—specific age groups, occupational categories, ethnic communities, and social organizations. This latter was precisely the pattern adopted by Israeli political parties. The leading party in the early statehood period, Mapai, carried the major load, but other political parties followed suit by utilizing a variety of techniques for mobilizing different segments of the population.

As has been noted by Medding (1972: 20), three basic strategies are employed to incorporate constituencies into a political party: noncompetitive penetration, in which a social group formally affiliates itself as a body to the party; competitive penetration, which is the case when a number of parties compete for the control and direction of social sectors; and attenuated penetration, or the targeting of efforts at individuals rather than organized or semi-organized groups. All the early Israeli political parties, but especially Mapai, proved extremely successful in fulfilling aggregative and integrative roles. Mapai incorporated diverse social forces, such as professionals and blue-collar workers, that were otherwise opposites in interests and in goals. It brought together different elements: close-knit communities, functional groups, economic interest groups, and primordial groups as well as individuals. By using a rich repertoire of strategies, including ideological appeals, policy promises and not the least the distribution of rewards, the party successfully welded these groups into one large inclusive constituency.

This mobilization process enabled the avoidance of major problems confronting a society in transition, in particular class and ethnic polarization. The bitterness and force of these cleavages were attenuated for a long period of time because of the integrative role played by Mapai, the country's dominant party. Making itself available to most sections of the Israeli society, Mapai fulfilled a major socializing function, as well as enhanced its own control over important junctions of power. Mapai, though, was not the only party that acted as a successful agent of mobilization. Most of the political parties tried to appeal to all groups throughout the country, and most succeeded in incorporating elements from almost all segments of the population. The role of political party as agent of mobilization, like its role as a provider of social services, has also been attenuated. The mass immigration that characterized the first years of statehood has long been absorbed into the body politic. Other targets of mobilization are less susceptible than in the past to party influence. Alternative frameworks for professional associations and other occupational groups are more readily available.

Nominations to political office

One of the characteristics of a party-state is the making of public policy by persons who are elected to governmental positions exclusively on the basis of their political party affiliation

(LaPalombara 1987: 211). In Israel this is precisely the case. The Israeli electoral system, a proportional representation system in the extreme, does not allow much freedom to individual iniatives. Although Israelis enjoy free access to party channels and can try to get themselves elected to the party's institutions, their enunciations invariably reflect the party's voice once they are elected (Galnoor 1982: 36). The major reason is the nomination system to the electoral lists.

The method by which Israel's political parties nominate legislative candidates has been the subject of criticism because of its generally centralized and oligarchical tendencies. Until the 1980s the most usual practice was for the leadership of the party to turn over the preparation of an electoral list to a small nominations committee, which reported to the party's central committee (Sager 1985: 50). Although the nominations committee did take into consideration the party's constituencies in terms of faction, region, ethnic orgin, age, and (to a limited extent) gender,— the process was controlled from above. Despite the acknowledgement of social diversification the centralized system of making up a list concentrated the power of nominations in the hands of a small group of party leaders. Party loyalty was stressed as the main quality of a candidate. This feature of Israeli politics has been one of the major triggers in the drive to change the electoral system.

What seemed an iron-clad nominations system did undergo considerable change in the mid-1980s. The Likud was the first party that transferred the power of deciding the composition of the Knesset list from a small oligarchic committee to a large (though perhaps not less oligarchic) forum—the party's center, composed of more than 2000 members. Other parties were forced to follow suit and grant their wider institutions the authority to compose the party list. Yet no popular control over the selection of parliamentary representatives has been introduced. The rank-and-file party membership—let alone the constituency at large—is not a partner to the nominations process, which is still controlled by party headquarters.

Internal party organization

In a party-democracy the party has a centralized and cohesive organizational structure, it has authority over its members, and it can effectively compel its representatives to behave according to its prescriptions. Israeli parties have indeed maintained a centralized and hierarchical organizational structure. Centralization has had the following manifestations:

- centralized modes of financing, including acquisition of party club houses, supply of campaign funds and current expenses;

- central recruitment of candidates for local party offices;

- increasing receptivity to central guidance by maintaining an ongoing "rapport" with local activists (Yanai 1981: 206).

These centripetal devices granted the party a whip over its branches. authority was practiced, too, through disciplinary measures meted out to the parliamentary faction. Party discipline is an ever present reality in the Knesset, with each party, through one of its offices, seeing to the attendance and voting of its members. Party discipline is reinforced by the delegates' dependence on party leaders for reelection. The unchallenged right of the party over committee assignments and Knesset regulations also spurs party command. A member of Knesset's right to participate in important legislative debates is strictly controlled by the party's offices. A member at variance with his or her party's position is not likely to be chosen to speak. Another important aspect of group discipline is manifested in submitting motions. Knesset regulations permit a member to submit any number of motions or bills. Their chances of being considered, however, depend very much on the party. Every party requires clearance of its representatives' initiatives. The practice also applies to questions, which are assigned to different members after being formulated by the party's leadership. The most conspicuous manifestation of discipline, however, is in regard to legislative voting. For instance a Member of Knesset may ask the party's permission to abstain from a Knesset vote, but this will not likely be granted in a close contest or on a matter of great principle (Sager 1985: 141). Furthermore, absence from the chamber during a vote may earn the MK the censure of the party, much as would an abstention. One common practice employed by recalcitrant members is to speak out freely on the issue but to vote for the party's position. There have been (rare) instances in which the problem was declared to be one of "conscience"; in such cases, party discipline was lifted and voting became a matter of individual choice. For example, in a debate on a measure restricting women's right to an abortion, MK Sarah Doron (Likud) was granted permission to abstain on the grounds of conscience.[2]

Maverick behavior in the Knesset was in the past a rare occurrence. There were only a few cases in which an MK dared to defy the party. The ardent dove Lova Eliav (Labor Alignment) once voted against a supplementary budget and also abstained in a no-confidence motion in 1971.[3] He later withdrew from his party and formed his own list. By the 1980s, however, breach of discipline was somewhat more common. Ezer Weizman, then Likud, voted against the government owing to policy differences regarding the peace process; a group of thirteen alignment MKs voted against the 1981 bill to apply Israeli law in the Golan (Yishai 1985a). They were reprimanded by their party's leadership. Although the chains that bind party discipline may be weakening, they are sufficiently strong to compel members to act in accordance with the party's preferences. Parliamentary discipline is not a unique Israeli phenomenon; it is typical of all parliamentary systems of government. Knesset members, however, also vote as their respective party dictates for good reason: their political future is practically at the mercy of the central party institutions.

Responsibility of partisan office holders

Important office holders are individuals elected by their party's institutions. They are responsible to the voters not as individuals but as representatives of the parties under whose label they were elected. "Responsibility" is given a critical test when the party leader quits office. Is resignation instigated by public pressure or, alternatively, are the party and its institutions the cause of forfeiting office?

Withdrawing from political office is not a common practice in Israeli politics. There were, however, seven major incidents in which a prime minister or a foreign minister resigned during an incumbency. David Ben-Gurion, Mapai's leader and prime minister, was the first to resign (in December 1953), on personal grounds.[4] Next was Moshe Sharett whose resignation (in August 1956) as foreign minister was prompted by Ben-Gurion, who wanted to clear the scene before the planned Sinai Campaign by removing the dovish Sharett. In the Knesset debate which followed Sharett's resignation, the prime minister conceded that he had had policy differences with Sharett and that he had reached the conclusion that because of the tense security situation there had to be maximum coordination between the defense ministry and the foreign ministry (Ben-Gurion 1971: 489–496). Ben-Gurion himself quit office again (in July 1961). His reason was also tied to party politics: Mapai's refusal to yield to his demands regarding the investigation of the "event," the so-called Lavon Affair (Yanai 1969).[5]

The most famous resignation of a political celebrity in Israel was that of Prime Minister Golda Meir (in April 1974), following the Yom Kippur war. Her act provides an illuminating example of the party's impact on leadership positions. In her memoirs Meir wrote:

> The more I spoke with my friends on the ongoing party dispute and the more I analyzed this dispute the more I realized that I cannot go on like this. I have reached a point where it was apparent that without the support of the whole party (the majority was on my side all the time) I could not have acted as its leader. The time came when I told myself: "This is it. I shall resign and others will have to try and form a coalition. There is a limit to what I can swallow, and I have certainly reached this limit." (1975: 331)

The importance of "the support of the *whole party* (emphasis mine) in Meir's decision to quit office was indicative of her source of power as well as the target of her responsibility. Meir did not resign because of the public protest that was staged after the 1973 war; nor did she seem perturbed by the marked decline in her party's support in the 1973 elections.[6] Meir's major concern was the partial support of her party membership for her course of policy (see also Dayan 1982: 735) even though, by her own testimony, the preponderant majority did remain faithful to her leadership.

Four other resignations of top national leaders occurred after Meir's withdrawal from office. Yitzhak Rabin resigned from premiership (in March 1976) after the exposure of a foreign-currency bank account; Ezer Waizman, defense minister under Menachem Begin's premiership, quit office (on May 1980) on account of disagreements over the peace process (Weizman 1981). Moshe Dayan quit his (foreign) ministerial position (on December 1981) for the same reason: opposition to the political course adopted by the Likud government. Lastly, Menachem Begin's resignation as prime minister (in 1983) remains a mystery to date. In any case, it is unlikely that it was instigated primarily by public pressure or discontent. Partisan leaders are thus induced to quit their national posts not because of public demand, but because of intra-party disagreements and rivalries.

Parties' penetration of the bureaucracy

A crucial aspect of the politicization of public policy is the partisan impact on a country's civil service. No direct data exist on the political affiliation of Israeli state bureaucrats, but those familiar with the situation seem to have agreed that there was a considerable over-representation within ministries of the party in charge, which increased the longer this party was in control and the higher the level of managerial rank (Etzioni 1962). In the late 1950s steps wee taken toward the universalization of the civil service, the examination system being expanded as a basis for recruitment and promotion. The state explicitly prohibited senior officials from being members of parties' central bodies, taking part in a demonstration aimed at political objectives, or participating in the campaign activity of any political party competing for Knesset representation. Despite the various measures, much partisanship still informed the state bureaucracy. As one moved up the ladder of power in the administrative hierarchy, the prevalence of nonprofessional considerations grew, the political affiliation of a candidate being one of the determining factors for acceptance. Indeed, the top echelons of the bureaucracy were also regarded as a jumping board for political posts. When Israel was founded, many politicians became senior officials overnight. Subsequently joining the ranks of the bureaucracy proved to be an effective channel for a political career. Increasingly more political positions were occupied by former senior civil service officials and high-ranking military officers (Peri 1986). A majority of ministers in the Rabin cabinet of 1974, for example, had previously held executive military or civilian administrative positions (Galnoor 1982: 212).

The crumbling of the Labor party's dominance did not affect the spector of administrative politicization. When the Likud rose to power, it did commit itself to eradicating party penetration of the civil service. Indeed, many officials remained in office although the party in government had changed. It soon became evident, however, that the Likud was following in the footsteps of its predecessor. At present the picture remains ambiguous. It is not easy to identify with certainty which appointments were—and are—motivated by political considerations and which by professional standards. Indicators used to measure the incidence of each pattern reveal that only 28 percent of the newly created 3,500 civil service positions filled during 1984 were done so as a result of tenders; 41 percent were filled neither by tenders nor through the government employment office; 23 percent were formally exempt from tendering; and 7 percent were filled by temporary workers (Sharkansy 1988: 11). These data, equivocal as they are, demonstrate a measure of politicization of the civil service. Nevertheless efforts are being made to curb such politicization. A committee appointed by the Israel state commissionaire recommended that civil servants be banned from membership in party centers and other bodies responsible for the nomination of candidates to the Knesset. If a law to this end is adopted, only a handful of administrators could be nominated without tenders, based on the minister's discretion.

Allegations of "political appointments" were made in 1989. Although providing no direct evidence for the political motivations behind the appointments, the state comptroller did have a "sound ground to suspect" that party affiliation was the reason for many nominations. Numerous examples show that the practice is widespread among government ministries, regardless of political camp. Members of parties' central committees, ministers' personal aides, and even their former chauffeurs have been appointed to positions within a ministry or on boards of government companies. The state comptroller (1989: 629–642) found that between 1986 and 1988, 61 percent of all directors appointed to government companies as representatives of the public were members of a particular party's central committee. There were numerous government companies in which every director appointed to represent the public was a partisan activist. The circumstantial evidence thus describes a pattern that departs markedly from the standards of Western democracies.

The salience of politics

Israel is a highly politicized society. Its voting percentage is among the highest in the democratic world. Party membership, although declining, is also impressive. The major feature of politicization of this society, however, is its high political "temperature." As far back as 1955, Akzin referred to the "more than usual intensity with which ideological differences are regarded by the politically active segments of Israel's population." He wrote:

> In Israel politics is not looked upon as a sport or a game in which adherence to the rules of the game is often deemed more important than the stake itself. In Israel it is the stake that matters, and the stake, of course, is power—power not only for the sake of the privileges and prestige which it carries in its wake . . . but also for the sake of the political doctrine which the respective party seeks to advance. Because of this approach, politics in Israel is taken extremely seriously and a militant adherent of a party considers himself a warrior in the war of righteousness against evil. (1955: 510)

In the early years of the state, political debate was characterized by mutual recrimination and personal assaults.

Tolerance of opposition was very low, and the inter-party clash very bitter. There was not much inclination to compromise. The heated political climate of Israel in its formative years may have cooled off, but politics still enjoys a high salience, compared to other Western democracies. The importance of politics in Israeli life bears empirical manifestations, as well. Czudnowski (1970; see also 1968: 883–886) has defined the index of salience as the ratio between the rank order of goals sought through political action and that of goals sought through economic, social or other non-political action, measured by a scale on which goals are rated according to the subjective preferences of individuals or groups. The higher the value attached by individuals or groups to the goals they seek through political action, the greater is the salience of politics. In Israel the salience of politics ranks extremely high because both the demand for and supply of resources in large sectors of the country's social and economic life were dominated by political motivations and handled by political organizations. The absorption of immigrants, national security, and settling the land became personal and collective goals of first priority. These goals, though, were mostly achieved through public investment and services supplied by party-controlled organizations—the Histadrut, the Zionist Federation, or even the state bureaucracy.

The insulation of the political elite

The prolonged control of parties generated paternalistic attitudes on the part of the elite. This added another layer to the structure of party control. Paternalism, although imbued with concern for the masses, also incoporated an element of disdain for those who were outside the inner circles of power. Paternalism was embedded in the political history of Israel. It was an outcome of the heroic process of nation building. Amos Elon has described the moral corruption resulting from this exaggerated "parental care":

> The paternalism of the veterans grew naturally from their role as a self-proclaimed pioneer elite. Like many former revolutionaries who have grown old in office they came to believe not only in their own irreplaceability, but in the infallibility of their judgment as well. Veteran Israeli leaders still habitually display an aristocratic contempt for what they disdainfully call the "masses" or the "man in the street". The socialists among them are often more disdainful of "the street" than the non-socialist, for the early idealism of the former has been corroded by their many years in office. Their political experience has taught them that only organized power matters. They are notoriously insen-

sitive to public opinion that is not formalized as an ideology, as
a political party . . . . (1971: 311)

The paternalistic attitude, coupled with a conspicuous insen-
sitivity to nonpolitical inputs, was both a cause and an outcome of
the traits of the party-state. In recent years, with the physical ex-
haustion of the founders' generation, this attitude has considerably
diminished. Yet traces of the old-fashioned paternalism are still in
evidence, stimulated by the enduring partisan influence on
political life.

Parties as policy makers

The foregoing implies that political parties were major actors
on the policy arena. Analyses of public policy rarely deal with the
direct role that parties play in the policy process. When a party
assumes office, its platform influences the national agenda (Rose
1984 57-60). The various planks, however, account for only a
small proportion of the government's agenda. In a party-state, the
role of the party in the actual process of authoritative decision
making is much more substantial. Party institutions elaborate
policy alternatives. Their decisions bind party representatives in
the government and in the legislature. In a party-state, decisions
about which policy alternatives will be made official are made not
independently by office holders, but within the forums of the
political parties of which they are members (LaPalombara 1987:
211).

In Israel reality is more complicated than the picture posited
in the theory. Investigation of internal party processes has revealed that many important decisions were formulated by the formal governing institutions and never reached party bodies. (Medding 1972; Arian 1985) Foreign policy as a whole was put on the
party's agenda only post factum, after a decision was made by the
government or, in most cases, after a decision had already been
implemented. The decision to launch a preemptive attack on Egyptian forces in Sinai (1956) or to go along with Sadat's peace initiative (1977), at least in its inceptive stages, were thus decided on
with little party involvement. In contrast, economic policy decisions were often made within the ruling party's executive bodies.
The process often constituted an elaborate bargaining procedure,
involving the party's top leaders in the government, in the
Histadrut (while the Labor parties were in office), and in other partisan sectors.

The role of parties in formulating national policy is, overall, also in decline. Factional strifes, which in the past resulted from ideological dissension over principles of politics, tend now to focus on personal rivalries. The parties' agenda consists mainly of organizational affairs rather than of policy issues. An event that occurred in the late 1980s provides a good example. The Peace Plan put forth by Israel's unity government in 1989, which proposed holding of elections in the occupied territories, was debated in partisan forums only after it was formally endorsed by the government. The purpose of the debate in the Likud was to place "constraints" on the cabinet ministers and to terminate the peace initiative. The government, however, overruled these constraints by taking another vote which reaffirmed its previous position. The Likud's decision (made on July 5, 1989) to halt the peace initiative remained only on paper. The government's policy remained unchanged despite blatant party opposition. In the Labor party, evasion of decisions taken by elected party institutions is in most cases unnecessary, since such resolutions are largely manipulated by the party's leadership (Aronoff 1977). In contemporary Israel political parties may ritually debate policy issues but the real power lies elsewhere.

The increase in the number of ministers following the establishment of the National Unity government further diminished the impact of Israeli political parties on policy making. In fact major decisions were debated and endorsed not even in the government as a whole, but in a "kitchen" or "inner" cabinet consisting of the prime minister and a few other senior ministers. The ruling parties' position may have been anticipated in the process of formulating policy, but by no means were they a major catalyst. In fact, the number of relevant public and private agents taking part in policy formation is constantly growing.

The Powerful State: Incentive to Corporatism

The state of Israel is among the more pervasive political organizations in the democratic world. It was founded by people who were brought up in countries where a "statist" political culture prevailed and where statehood ranked prime. As Elazar put it: "Their expectations were that a proper state must be a reified one, that is, one standing outside of and above its citizens and existing independently of them. Such a state . . . was viewed as a major instrument for social change and, accordingly, was expected to be comprehensive in its approach to its citizens, prepared to intervene in every aspect of life in order to bring about the necessary changes" (1986: 186). Although some politicization of the bureaucracy has been evident, it is not totally captured by political parties; it is a separate political entity whose influence is amply felt in all walks of life. Intervention in citizens' affairs has had clear economic and legal manifestations.

The economic dimension

Although the economy grows more sophisticated and has also been somewhat liberalized in recent years, it is still very much under state direction and control. The economic sector is theoretically free, but in actuality it is largely influenced by the government through a tight network of restrictions, permits, orders, monetary measures and the like. The state's involvement in the country's economic activity is manifested in the following indicators

Public expenditure. It is common to assess a government's involvement in the economy by means of the proportion of national resources represented by government spending. Israel scores very high on this measure. There is more than one version of the volume of national resources spent by the government. According to the International Monetary Fund (IMF) Israel was in first place among Western democracies in 1980, with governmental expenditure amounting to 76 percent of gross domestic product (GDP). Ireland and Iceland were a distant second and third with 51 and 41 percent, respectively. Israeli sources show figures substantially above those of the IMF report. Budget outlays by the government ranked between 80 and 85 percent of GDP for fiscal years 1978 to 1982. the Israel Central Bureau of Statistics reported that when a wider criterion was applied—i.e., spending by "government, local authorities and national institutions"—the expenditure amounted to between 95 and 105 percent of the GNP during fiscal years 1977 to 1981 (Sharkansky 1988: 4). Spending more than the nation's product is possible because governmental bodies receive substantial resources that do not figure into the calculations of the official GNP. The funds available through these means are subject to wide political manipulation, including the financing of political parties.[7]

Defense expenditure. Apart from repayment loans (which constitutes some 40 percent of the budget), defense expenditure is the largest single item in the state's budget. Israel, surrounded as it is by hostile enemies, has had to devote a large and increasing share of its resources to defense. Its economic activities are thus conducted under the shadow of preparedness for overt or covert war. Before the Six Day War, in June 1967, the share of defense expenditures in the GNP was 8 to 10 percent; in 1968 to 1972 it rose to approximately 22 percent; and following the October 1973 war, it jumped to 28 to 29 percent of national product. After the Lebanon war (1982 through 1984) the budget devoted to defense stabilized at around 20 percent of the GNP. Defense expenditure has been noted to be the most important deviation by Israel from the "normal" pattern of resource utilization present in other democracies. the comparative data are indeed striking. Israel's 20 percent annual military expenditure contrasts markedly to the 1 to 6 percent that is typical of most Western countries (Doron and Tamir 1983). The danger that the economy may someday not be large enough to support higher levels of defense expenditure has been an ever-present Israeli dilemma (Ben-Porath 1986: 61). The enormous share of defense expenditure in the national income is another—and perhaps a major—source of the state's strength. It is also, however, one of the reasons for its excessive involvement in the country's economic life.

Patterns of employment. A disproportionally high share of the employment in Israel is devoted to public services (Ofer 1967). Comparative data indicate that in 1984 Israel ranked second among European countries in the proportion of the labor force employed in public services (*Budget Proposal* 1987: 34). The Israeli cabinet has declared numerous hiring "freezes" for the public sector. During those freezes, though, ministers have used special contracts or temporary employment to evade the formal restraint requirement. The public sector always managed to continue its uninterrupted growth. The state has decisive influence on those employed by other sectors, as well. It determines welfare payments, salaries, and the degree to which wages and other items are linked to the cost-of-living index. Furthermore, employment policy is virtually controlled by the state. The Employment Service Law (1959) nationalized the labor exchanges and placed them under the supervision of the ministry of labor. Employers are obliged to hire workers through the national agencies. The creation of a virtual monopoly in supplying manpower to the economy enabled the state to apply socioeconomic criteria in determining priorities for employment and relief for unemployment (Halevi and Klinov-Malul 1968: 69). The government has also deliberately influenced the volume of employment by granting various privileges to firms that enagage a specific number of workers. This incentive has had an indirect impact on the economy by singling out large enterprises for preference over small ones and labor-intensive firms over capital-intensive ones.

Subsidies and transfer payments. As a welfare state Israel expends large sums on subsidies and transfer payments, whose share in the 1987 national budget was approximately 19 percent. This is a huge sum by any international standard. Even Sweden, which ranks high in the Western world in its scope of public expenditure, expends (proportionally) half the Israeli figure (*Free Economy* 1988). Subsidies and transfer payments are targeted at both consumption and production. Essential goods and services, such as dairy products, bread, poultry, and public transportation were heavily subsidized by the state. Subsidies were designed to lower the prices that affect the consumer price index and, through it, wages. Another type of subsidy, however, was aimed at maintaining income and increasing output. In recent years, serious efforts have been made to cut or at least to minimize government spending on subsidies for food and public transportation.

Subsidy of production is earmarked for industry and services. Direct financial inducements were used as a basic means of encouraging exports. The primary method involved the rate of the currency exchange, but there were also other forms of subsidy, such as participation in costs and investments. In the early years of statehood, the foreign exchange policy was highly discriminatory: there were multiple exchange rates based, inter alia, on the influence of the group demanding special privileges. Although an outright discriminatory policy is no longer in force, transfer payments continue to form a major source of state influence over economic affairs.

Taxation. Taxation is a principal instrument of economic policy (Wildavsky 1975). The high rate of the Israeli state's involvement in economic affairs has produced a heavy tax burden, which is both direct and indirect. In the early 1950s, taxes accounted for three-quarters or more of total internal receipts (Halevi and Klinov-Malul 1968: 187). Israeli economists have noted that the share of indirect taxes is much greater in Israel than in other developed countries, and this is strange in view of the state's past strong socialist orientation. In fact, the low share of property taxes has been an irritant to the more leftist parties.

Export/import policy. Export is regarded as a major means of economic independence, essential for political reasons. Since the state's inception, attention has been focused on expanding exports. The government's attempt to encourage export has many repercussions on the extent of its economic involvement. To begin with, export industries were given high priority in national development programs and in the development budget. In 1980, some 98 percent of the credits adminstered by the central bank (outside the framework of the government's budget) subsidized export-related activities. Direct and indirect financial aid were granted to export-oriented industries. In addition, severe bureaucratic restrictions were put on imports. Strict control of the quantity and composition of imports was maintained, primarily through a highly complicated licensing system. Although the government's control of imports has been relaxed, there are still areas in which the freedom to import is severely limited. These restrictions take the following forms:

- a high level of taxation in the form of customs duties, purchase taxes, and special levies designed to limit the volume of imported commodities;

- administrative restrictions on import through licensing;[8]

- cumbersome procedures for releasing imported goods for marketing, causing importers both inconvenience and superfluous expense;

- a growing resort to standardization as a means to limit import (*Free Economy* 1988)

The government itself is also involved in the direct import of goods and services, amounting to about a third of the country's total imports.

Investments. Investment policy provides one of the paradoxes of the Israeli economy. On the one hand, encouraging private investment has been an important policy goal for many years. A law for the encouragement of investment has been in force since 1950. "Approved" investments enjoy far-reaching tax concessions, subsidies, and capital grants. But private investments are largely controlled by the state through a complicated network of bureaucratic procedures. Reportedly, for example, investors in a hotel enterprise are required to obtain approvals from no fewer than fourteen different government ministries.[9] Government infrastructure investment in transport, communications, and public utilities also interfere with private investment.

Credit market. The state controls the supply of money through the Bank of Israel (established in 1954), which is responsible for the

of emergency, which has been in force ever since. There are three separate mechanisms for exercising emergency powers in Israel:

1. The Defense Emergency Regulations of 1945, promulgated by the British Mandatory government; these comprise the most drastic and most controversial method.

2. Emergency Regulations issued by government ministers under Section 9 of the Law and Administration Ordinance of 1948, based on a grant of authority from the legislature; these regulations are valid only for three months unless extended by the Knesset.

3. Regular legislation, whose period of validity depends on the existence of a state of emergency or whose functioning is in some way affected by the emergency; such legislation enables the government to exercise "emergency-type" measures subject to judicial review. The most widely used law is the Emergency Powers (Detention) Law, 1979 (Shetreet 1984; Bracha 1980).

The reasons for the declaration of emergency were quite obvious. Israel was and continued to be engaged in a war with the neighboring Arab states and the Palestinians of the West Bank and the Gaza Strip, with most of the state's population residing until 1967 within artillery range of hostile military forces. State authority in exercising the emergency legislation has been almost unlimited. Although in practice the use of emergency powers has fallen far short of what could be done legally, some of the broad powers available have been utilized. A leading legal scholar (Rubinstein 1980: 224) cited an example whereby the state is authorized to engage in a host of activities incompatible with civil rights, such as opening mail when necessary "for reasons of security and defense."

Emergency authority has apparently been used to enforce economic and financial laws; it has not been restricted to combating security dangers. In 1985, for instance, the National Unity government invoked Section 9 of the Emergency Regulations to enact a broad-ranging economic recovery program. The regulations established strict controls on prices, wages, taxes, and other economic indicators.[13] The unusual use of emergency powers was justified on the grounds that inflation and the continued economic crisis constituted a threat to national survival. Another example of the non-security use of emergency powers is the proliferation of return-to-work orders in labor disputes, especially in "vital public services" (Mironi 1983: 26–27). In 1960, striking El Al pilots were ordered to resume work. However, such orders remained sporadic until 1977. After the Likud assumed power, the use of emergency regulations to force public employees back to work became almost routine in labor relations.

The most broadly applied regulations have been the censorship provisions, which to date form the legal basis for control of the media. All press publications require licensing. The censure may prohibit publication of any material prejudicial to defense, public safety, or public order. This provision was defined by the Israeli Supreme Court as "a drastic and draconic directive, issued by a colonial regime which is incompatible with fundamental concepts of democratic state regarding the freedom of speech and the freedom of expression" (quoted by Segal 1988: 159). It has been pointed out that the authority to prohibit the publication of newspapers granted an unlimited authority to a government administration and did not subject its power to any meaningful restrictions or effective supervision (Negbi 1985: 19). Censorship, however, is softened by a voluntary arrangement under which most newspapers submit preprinted material for review. Proposed excisions can be appealed to a committee of three representatives of the press, whose unanimous decision is final. Censorship of theaters was lifted on August 7, 1989, for a trial period of two years; that of movies remains intact.

Emergency rules are thus means of intrusion into many spheres of life. Their power is immense because they may be promulgated by individual cabinet ministers, not only by the government at large. Since 1976, a minister may be granted authority to enact emergency regulations, and to date, this has been granted to fourteen ministerial portfolios.[14] In recent years, ministers have been granted limited, one-time authority covering the matter at hand, rather than a comprehensive authority.

Despite this gloomy picture on the whole, the use of emergency powers by the government has attenuated over time. Many powers have remained only on paper and have not been utilized. Democratic reality has mitigated the exigencies of security (Negbi 1987). The scale has tipped more in the direction of due process of law than in the direction of defense considerations, with the role of the courts in preserving civil rights having considerably expanded. The continuing use of emergency powers in non-security domains (such as the economy), however, demonstrates the power of the state, which has been attempting to adhere to democratic norms and safeguard the country's precarious security at one and the same time.

Social and Ideological Diversity: The Stay of Pluralism

The foregoing discussion indicates that Israel is a party-democracy in which the power of the state looms large, overshadowing the grassroots political participation that is essential for the practice of pluralism. Israel, however, has also been described as a noisy democracy, verging on anarchy (Sharkansky 1987: 11). The "noise" emanates from the political ideological and the socioeconomic divisions that have crisscrossed Israel. These divisions have served as a buffer against an overpowering party and state system. At least five factors have mitigated the centralization of power and its monopolization either by party or by the state: political diversification, territorial democracy, individualistic orientations, ethnic pluralism, and religious diversity.

Political diversification

Israeli voters, as a rule, have not tolerated the centralization of power but disperse their choices along a relatively wide spectrum of competitive, mutually restricting parties. Political divisions are evident on every issue, be it economic, religious, or security. Not one single issue is sufficient to rally a simple majority behind a single leader or party. Admittedly Mapai (subsequently the Labor party and then the Alignment) served for a whole generation as a dominant party, but its proportion in the electorate seldom exceeded one third. Only once, in 1969, in the elections to the 7th Knesset, did the Labor party, consisting of Mapai and Achdut Haavoda, win more than 45 percent of the votes. The Israeli party system was described as highly fractionalized, in which the majority of parties win less than 5 percent of the votes. In the past, not more than two parties (and usually only one) have gained more than 15 percent of the vote (Gutmann 1977: 126–128).

Fractionalization is accompanied by blatant factionalism, with most parties driven by deep internal strife based on ideological dissensions, personal animosities or socioeconomic cleavages (Yishai 1981). Since the early 1970s, though, the Isreali polity has demonstrated centripetal tendencies. The establishment of the Alignment (comprising the Labor party and Mapam) enabled the parliamentary unification of the Zionist-socialist bloc. The right-wing parties followed suit by forming, in 1973, the Likud (Tarrow and Levite 1983). The Israeli polity gravitated toward the center with each of the two major blocs winning (in 1984 and in 1988) about a third of the total vote. The two major blocs nevertheless continue to be a coalition of smaller subdivisions, which have been compared to "semi-feudal principalities" (Elon 1971: 292). As a result, a process of disintegration has also taken place among political camps. The Alignment crumbled as Mapam withdrew from cooperation with its counter-socialist party. In the religious camp (attracting some 20 percent of the Israeli electorate), no fewer than six parties presented lists in the 1988 elections.[15] Intra-party factionalism is also very much in evidence in parties that have traditionally had a reputation of being centralized and unified. Chief among them is Herut, which is plagued by deep factional divisions over succession to its veteran leadership. The Liberal party has been struck so hard by internal divisions that state courts have often been requested to mediate between hostile factions. Even Mapam, a noted centralized party, was deeply divided over its former alignment with the Labor party. In short, the Israeli political system may be moving toward the center, but centralization does not erase pluralistic manifestations. There is still a lot of noise in the political arena, where parties bitterly fight one another (and among themselves) and where numerous offshoots enter the political fray with very few legal or other restrictions.

Another aspect of political diversification occurs within the elite: namely, the differentiation and specialization of elites and their growing segregation. The elite in the 1980s were no longer a homogenized body, restricted only to small groups and maintained by semi-oligarchical principles. The uniform establishment (*Mimsad*) has given way to a continuous process of differentiation and segmentation on the basis of economic, educational, occupational, and ethnic criteria. As Eisenstadt (1985: 404) has put it: "Each such elite was indeed granted maximum autonomy within its special institutional arena. Before all of them—or almost all of them—there opened up far-reaching opportunities of advance, careers and attainment of high standard of life. At the same time they became more and more dissociated from one another." Relations between elites were no longer hierarchical and dependent, but more egalitarian. This development, Eisenstadt claims, produced a concomitant gradual atrophy of the political process in the central political framework. New leadership was recruited from different social strata, and the common background of the ruling elite became much less evident. These changes, which took place against the background of rapid economic growth and social mobility, provided a congenial environment for the pluralistic features of interest group configurations.

Territorial democracy

Another important manifestation of pluralism in Israel has been termed "territorial democracy" (Elazar 1986: 41–56). According to Elazar, who applied this phrase, the whole idea of Zionism was based on territoriality, since its major objective was to ingather the exiles, who were dispersed among numerous territories, and turn them into one nation, rooted in one territory. The cult of the land and the centrality of its settlement in both ideology and practice wore also manifestations of the yearning for territory. The process of nation building in the old-new land culminated in the establishment of the state in 1948 and the implementation of political democracy, i.e., the attainment of sovereignty and full citizenship. Since the process was dominated by political parties it bred the elitist features of society. But territoriality also served as a hotbed for pluralism. This "territorial democracy" originated in the prestate days, but is gaining momentum in contemporary Israel. The manifestations of territorial democracy are as follows:

• Territorial units comprise people with different ideological orientations and different political affiliations; put differently, residents of a territory do not all vote for the same party.

• Territorial units are allowed by the state to maintain their unique way of life and are given wide leeway to conduct their own affairs.

• Territorial democracy can be used to secure political power or influence for any group that happens to reside in a particular area at a particular time. Localities thus provide an expression of specific facets of citizens' goals.

Israel is moving rapidly toward a territorial democracy, owing to the upgrading of the territorial element in politics. Elazar has suggested that the place to look for the direction of political innovations in contemporary Israel is the local arena, "where despite the many restraints placed upon local government, politics function somewhat freer from the constraints of the countrywide political system" (1986: 253). Whether or not the territorial dimension provides the central theme in Israel democracy remains an open question. It does, however, add a strong pluralistic flavor to the political scene.

Individual orientations

To argue that Israel is characterized by individualistic orientations is, at a first glance, inaccurate if not totally fallacious. The

Israeli society has been described as fostering collectivist values (Eisenstadt 1967), in which unity was sacrosanct. Many political parties, putatively established on the basis of social divisions, incorporated the term "unity" in one of its grammatical forms in their titles. For example, the faction that withdrew from Mapai in the 1940s (Faction "B") was termed "To the Unity of Labor." One of the founding fathers of socialist Zionism, Berl Katzenelson, devoted much of his advocacy to the cause of unity. He perpetually underscored its importance. Schism, which characterized Jewish society in the Diaspora, was perceived to be disastrous. Because of their divisiveness, the Jews originally lost their national sovereignty and were dispersed among the nations for two millennia. Schism also prevented concerted efforts at bringing about a national revival (Katzenelson 1946: 105).

There is another side to the coin, however: the individual orientations deeply rooted in the Jewish tradition. Amos Elon, a leading analyst of Israeli society, referred to "the almost religious addiction [of the Israelis] to an extreme form of self-reliant, sometimes widely anti-social individualism" (1971: 297) that breeds comparatively low unanimity of both spirit and behavior. A rich diversity of norms, beliefs, rules, and customs produced "atomization"of society, which counterbalances any attempt at homogenizing it by manipulative means (Hareven 1988).

Individualism is also manifested in a deep suspicion of authority. Israelis may honor the state, but at the same time they are wary of control. The attitude of Jews to authority has traditionally been skeptical. In the Diaspora, they obeyed the law and conformed to the rules because obedience was essential for survival. It was accompanied, however, by disdain toward authority. A strong measure of this attitude has endured in contemporary Israeli political culture. Civic discipline has been documented as "'Every Man' doing 'whatsoever is Right in His Own Eyes'" (Sprinzak 1986). This phenomenon defines an orientation that does not regard adherence to the rule of law as a fundamental value, but as a form of behavior, which may, or may not, be adopted upon consideration of utility. It is, of course, a type of behavior that provides a hotbed for the development of anarchy.

The anarchistic strain has been said to run constantly through Israeli life. Its origins are numerous: the classical susceptibility of outsiders in a gentile society; the hostility of the Jew to the imposing, often unfavorable authority; and philosophical theories. The initiators of the Jewish settlement endeavor in Palestine wished to forge a new society in line with a nineteenth-century libertarianism, a society that was associated with a minimum of coercion and a maximum of voluntary engagement of free individuals. Perhaps the deeply inherent suspicion of any form of government shielded the citizens from the pincers of party and state.

Demographic dimensions of pluralism

According to Truman (1951), it is social diversification that induces the proliferation of groups under the pluralist configuration, on condition that variation is legitimated and acknowledged. In Israel both conditions prevail. Diversity is profound, manifesting itself in two major cleavages: ethnic and religious. This diversity has generated processes evident in melting-pot societies, where variation is molded into a dominant pattern, which nevertheless does not erase distinctions.

The ethnic cleavage. On the surface Israel is a homogeneous society, since over 80 percent of its population are of the Jewish faith, speaking the same language and sharing common historical heritage. The uniformity is deceiving, however, since this society is crisscrossed by an exceptionally wide ethnic variety.

Israeli Jews are divided into two major, albeit loosely defined, ethnic groups: Sephardim and Ashkenazim (definition being based on country of origin: Asia-Africa or Europe-America). Except for stereotypical generalizations, these terms are misleading owing to the many differences within each of these groups. Among the Sephardim one can identify the Yemenite Jews from the deserts of Aden, who are well versed in Jewish tradition, side by side with the Jews from Algiers, whose close affiliation with France "westernized" their lifestyle and blurred the difference between them and their fellow Jews born in mainland France. Among the Ashkenazim variety also looms large: Jewish peasants from the countryside in Rumania, as well as past inhabitants of Chicago, London, and Ottawa. The ethnic variety is amply demonstrated in the *Annual Statistical Abstract* which enumerates no fewer than forty-six countries of origin (beside "other" countries) in six continents. The largest ethnic group (originating from Morocco) constitutes no more than 13.5 percent of the population (*Statistical Abstract* 1988: 76).

The distinction between the two communities had some external manifestations, such as color of skin and form of dress. But the major expression of plurality was—and is—in economic differentials. Sephardic Jews have lower levels of income, housing, education, and employment status than their Ashkenazie counterparts. Although in the period of economic prosperity after the Six Day

War many Sephardim succeeded in "jumping over the fence" and joining the mainstream of society, those who did not felt a sense of discrimination more strongly than ever (Galnoor 1982: 57). Apparently time alone has not eroded the ethnic differentials. The Sephardim have, it is true, increased their share in political representation (Yishai 1984), but the economic gap between the Ashkenazie haves and the Sephardie have-nots has persisted into the second generation. Bernstein and Antonovsky (1981) found that the ethnic gap was in fact exacerbated among native-born Jews.

The cumulative sense of deprivation and alienation over the years has been increasingly channeled into the political sphere. The ethnic dimension of pluralism, which has its origins in the diversity of the social web, has been expressed in recent years both in the party and in the group arena. The demographic diversity of the Jewish population sustains Israel's pluralistic character mainly because a broad legitimation for social alternatives exist among the Ashkenazie mainstream. The majority does not claim exclusivity or dominance but acknowledges the alternatives (Shuval 1989).

The same does not pertain to the Arab-Jewish cleavage. Although the coexistence of the two communities is verbally legitimized, their physical and social separation, as well as the exigencies generated by the Arab-Israeli conflict, have impeded pluralistic arrangements. Relationships between Jews and Arabs are determined more by domination than by accommodation (Smooha 1978). The rise of extremism in both groups following the Palestinian upheaval in the occupied territories (December 1987 onwards) has further contributed to the deepening of the cleavage, which as of this writing has not been settled within the framework of pluralistic values or structures.

The religious cleavage. One of the nation's major goals is to disengage ethnicity from its social fabric and to mold all Jews into one people. This is not the case regarding the religious cleavage, which is highly institutionalized in the form of separate educational systems, judicial systems, and residential areas. In fact, separation is highly desired by the ultra-orthodox, who have undergone a process of cultural and social introversion (Shilhav and Friedman 1985). The cleavage between the religious and the secular also undermines social uniformity, although some hold that there is no clear-cut distinction between orthodox and secular Jews (e.g., Deshen 1978). A common definition differentiates between those observing all religous commandments, those observing some of them (such as visits to the synagogue on the High Holidays), and those who are completely nonobservant. Only a few, however, do not circumcise their infant sons or bury their dead in a nonreligious service.

Because of an unclear definition of orthodoxy, estimates of the size of the religious community are only tentative. Galnoor (1982: 51–52) claims that the observant and the ultra-orthodox comprise a quarter of the population; another quarter is totally secular, and the remaining half is partly observant. The wide spectrum on which Israeli Jews are situated does not prevent disputes between the polar extremes—disputes that are often deep and bitter. Disagreements pertain to fundamental legislative issues as well as to the modus operandi of daily life. There is much friction over the arrangements of the famous status quo, preserving the religious equilibrium as it was in 1947 (Rubinstein 1967). Since the advent of the Likud to power the religious community started to gain political benefits. The Knesset passed religiously inspired legislation, such as canceling El Al flights on the Sabbath (Saturday), changing the Anatomy and Pathology Law to prohibit postmortem operations without the written consent of the family, and amending the abortion law to prevent state permission for socially motivated cessations of pregnancy. Nevertheless, two major issues of contention remain untouched: these are the Law of Return, stipulating a definition of Jewishness, and the observance of the Sabbath. Attempts to incorporate into civil law an orthodox definition of Jewishness and to widen the scope of religious practice on the day of rest have triggered intensive group reaction. Despite the political accommodation between most religious and secular Jews, the division is real and the danger of societal disintegration ever present.

Both the ethnic and the religious cleavages, in addition to the others, provide grounds for the proliferation of interest groups seeking political redress of their grievances. Their relevance to pluralism, however, emanates from their contribution to the heterogeneity of Israel's social web and to the legitimation of variety.

Conclusions

This chapter has demonstrated the three strands of the Israeli polity. In the past the prominence of political parties was unchallenged. The nine indicators for a party-state reveal the extent to which political institutions were practically controlled by partisan elites. The list of symptoms is inexhaustible: political parties replaced state bureaucracies in providing social services, not only to the needy population of newcomers, but to veteran Israelis as well; political parties had played a crucial role in mobilizing the growing Israeli constituency; no one could be elected to a political office without having been endorsed by the members of political party institutions; and party discipline was strictly imposed. Leaders did resign from their office, but owing to internal party pressures not because of public demand. The influence of parties extended also to the bureaucracy whose members controlled the citizens' daily affairs. The salience of politics enabled the elite to insulate itself from the people and entertain a paternalistic attitude. The result of this process was a dominance of party's influence, although it was confined mainly to economic policy. Changes, however, did take place: the provision of social services has gradually been removed from partisan control; the mobilization undertaken by the parties is much less effective than in the past; the power to nominate is, and will in the foreseeable future still be, controlled by the party, but the circle of those participating in the selection process is constantly growing. In August 1989, for the first time in Israeli history, primaries were held for the nomination of Likud candidates to the Histadrut elections. The close competition between the two major political blocs—the Likud and the Labor Alignment—is one of the reasons for the continued strict party discipline. But back benchers, anticipating the approaching change of the electoral system, allow themselves more freedom than in the past. Office holders are still responsible to their respective parties rather than to the electorate, but there is a growing awareness of the decisive importance of the public mood. Measures are being taken to bar the politicization of the civil service; the curtain that veiled the "system" and shielded it from public scrutiny has been lifted.

Politics is still extremely salient, with both politicians and the ordinary citizen preoccupied with the alternative of peace or land. Some parties, though, are blurring their ideological proclivites in order to appeal to and catch the vote of broader constituencies. Important policy decisions are still arrived at not by party forums but by party representatives, whose major consideration is the benefit of their party.[16] Yet political parties are no longer alone on the scene; neither do they enjoy the glory of the past. One of the best indicators for the decline of the political party derives from a study that looked at the "index of democracy" in Israel. The findings of this research reveal that political parties enjoy the least trust among all Israeli political institutions, with only 2.1 percent of the population expressing "complete" trust in them, as against 52.1 percent that voiced "no trust" or "almost no trust" (Peres 1987). The picture that emerges is thus ambiguous. Israel is still a party-state in many respects, but at the same time other centers of power are gradually emerging. One of the most important centers is the state.

The "state" of Israel is not indistinguishable from political parties. It has its own machinery, its own set of rules, and its own norms of behavior. Even though politicization of the bureaucracy is evident, state officials are not puppets dancing to the music of their respective parties. In fact, the state is still prodigious. Although some steps have been taken toward relinquishing some of its authority, the state still penetrates deeply into the lives of its citizenry. In the early days of statehood, the government's pervasive role in the country's economic affairs was both an ideological tenet and a practical necessity, for only the state could cope with the combined challenges of defense, mass immigration, and economic development facing the newborn nation. The state did this through holding tight control of the economy and through exerting a large measure of influence on other spheres of life. As a result, it gained enormous power. Did the state share some of the burden with interest groups in order to withstand the enormous challenges? This is one of the main questions guiding this study.

Finally, pluralism manifested itself in two forms: in individual orientations, and in demographic diversity. Under the surface of unity, Israel bubbles erratically. It is an ever-changing society with strong individualist strands. Admittedly, there are constraints on pluralism unfamiliar to the Western observer. Israeli society was described as being basically "tribal" and not "national." Tribalism manifests itself in "integrated clusters of people linked together by bonds of blood, religion, birth, cult, faith, and myth (Oz 1979: 153), rather than in a common tradition based on linguistic heritage. The sense of a "people who shall dwell alone" tightened the attachment to the community, but within this community there is not only strict adherence to the formal structures of polyarchy (i.e., an independent judicial system, free elections, and due process of law), but there also exists a social and political climate that breeds the legitimation of diversity. This legitimation sustained the establishment of interest groups and legitimized their activity.

CHAPTER TWO

The Universe of Interest Groups

Interest groups in Israel have been part and parcel of the national effort. The whole structure of the *yishuv*—the prestate Jewish community in Palestine—was based on voluntary arrangements; but organized interest groups were evident from the early days of Zionist settlement. Farmers, workers, teachers, and doctors each formed associations to defend their respective interests and to promote national objectives. The dynamics of associational organization proceeds to date. During the winter of 1988–1989 fashion industry entrepreneurs organized themselves into an interest group;[1] the members of one-parent families (comprising 10 percent of all families in Israel) also formed an association, declaring their intention to advance legislation protecting their rights.[2] A group of women calling themselves "Women in Black" organized to protest Israel's continued occupation of the West Bank and Gaza Strip. These are but the latest examples, as of this writing, of the rich associational activity in the contemporary Israeli polity. The universe of interest groups includes strange bedfellows: the giant Histadrut, Israel's Labor Federation, alongside the Society for the Protection of Cats, with its dozen members. All, however, share a common denominator: they are organizations dedicated to influencing public policy in order to promote some common interest. By regarding the government as capable of providing their needs, be they material or ideological, they all are engaged in political life. A short delineation of their attributes is the subject of this chapter.

Party-Affiliated Groups

Trade Unions: The Histadrut

The Histadrut, Israel's general federation of labor, can hardly
fit the simple category of trade union. It is, to be sure, an organization of salaried workers, but it is also a giant economic empire. In
1986, the Histadrut economic affiliates produced more than 70
percent of the country's agricultural crop, 17 percent of its industrial output, and some 12 percent of all building and construction. Of total domestic output, the Histadrut accounted for some
20 percent by itself. According to estimates, one in four Israelis
works in a Histadrut-affiliated company or service. Under these
circumstances, it is awkward to define this organization simply as
a "trade union." Furthermore, owing to its magnitude and diversity, the Histadrut could hardly be termed a "group" at all: it includes some 85 percent of the Israeli population. Because, too, of
the variety of issues it handles, the Histadrut is not really an "interest" association. Yet it is practically the only body in Israel that
represents the interests of labor; it is the only spokesman for the
employed salaried worker.

From its inception, in 1920, nearly three decades before the
establishment of the state, the Histadrut was not targeting its activities at narrow trade unionist goals. The purpose of the
Histadrut "was more to create conditions beneficial to the development and organization of a new, privileged working class rather
than to protect the interests of an existing underprivileged one"
(Eisenstadt 1967: 38–39). One of its aims was, clearly, to gain
power for the labor movement. Perhaps, though, its primary function was to help build the political and economic institutions
necessary for the acquisition of Israel's national sovereignty. The
Histadrut is, then, a unique interest group, which has been
described as "the most important, most original, most problematic
institution bequeathed to the state of Israel by the yishuv" (Safran
1973: 127).

In addition to campaigning for fair wages and working conditions, the Histadrut from the beginning took on an educational
role—to train workers for new jobs, to provide schools for their
children, and to provide cultural activities to the public at large.
The Histadrut also fulfilled the role of a mutual aid society. The
social activity of the Labor Federation predated its inauguration.
As far back as 1911, a voluntary health insurance plan was installed, to provide much-needed medical care that eventually grew

into a comprehensive health service. The Histadrut Sick Fund (Kapat Holim) runs a large network of clinics, pharmacies, hospitals, and other health-related services that cover, by means of an insurance scheme, some three-quarters of the Israeli population. As will further be shown, a large variety of cooperatives (among them the settlement movements), women's organizations, sport clubs, and cultural bodies are also linked to the Histadrut. It was its activities in the field of economic enterprise, however, that made the Histadrut unique among other free labor organizations. The early Histadrut leadership believed that the only way to guarantee a strong working community was by means of an advanced, productive economy. To that end, it established *Hevrat Ovdim* (the Workers Company) to provide employment in the labor economy (Sharkansky 1979: 75).

Trade union activity is one of the Histadrut's major functions. Israel counts some forty-three national professional and occupational trade unions, four of which were formed in the early 1920s (Farmers, Clerks, Engineers, and Postal Workers). A Trade Union Department was opened in 1941, to coordinate the activities of the Histadrut and the national trade unions, to negotiate labor disputes, and to formulate national wage policy. The inability of the central Histadrut institutions at the time to deal with the increasingly variegated and complex trade union problems was the reason for setting up the department. There is a special subdivision for "academics," a group that has continuously been a source of organizational strain because of its demands for higher wage standards. Local plant committees come under the jurisdiction of local workers councils, which serve as the extensions of the Histadrut in urban localities.

The Histadrut's growth has been steady. The year it was founded (1920), 87 delegates, representing 4,400 members, attended the first convention. Almost seventy years later, in 1989, the membership has grown to 1,630,000. About two-thirds of the Jews (and half of the Arabs) in the country are members of the Histadrut, either directly or by being the spouse or child of a member. Membership in the Histadrut is open to "all men and women workers eighteen years of age and above who live on the earnings of their own labor without exploiting the labor of others," as its manifesto puts it. There are no religious, national, or ideological barriers to membership in the Histadrut. Arab workers are full members.[3] Membership in a trade union comes into effect only after the individual has joined the Histadrut and paid his or her dues. "Closed shop" is not permitted. All workers in an "organized

work place" are represented by the union, whether they join the
Histadrut or not, and about 1 percent of the wages of nonmembers
is deducted for this service. On the other hand, many Histadrut
members do not belong to a trade union; for example, those in kibbutzim and moshavim, housewives, students.

The institutional framework of the Histadrut (see figure 2.1)
has changed little since its inception. A general convention (some
1500 delegates) is elected every four years by a simple proportional
system. Voters are presented with lists affiliated with political parties. Before adjourning, the convention elects a council (501
members) which then elects an executive committee (189 members)
from among its members. Between conventions, the executive
committee possesses the highest authority, among others, to elect
a secretary-general and to approve the central executive committee
(39 members in 1988), which is the Histadrut's cabinet. It is the
central committee (consisting only of members of the party that
won the majority of votes to the national convention) that effectively rules the giant organization and speaks on its behalf. It is
responsible for the day-to-day implementation of policy and decisions made by an even smaller circle of leaders.

Fig. 2.1. Organization of the Histadrut

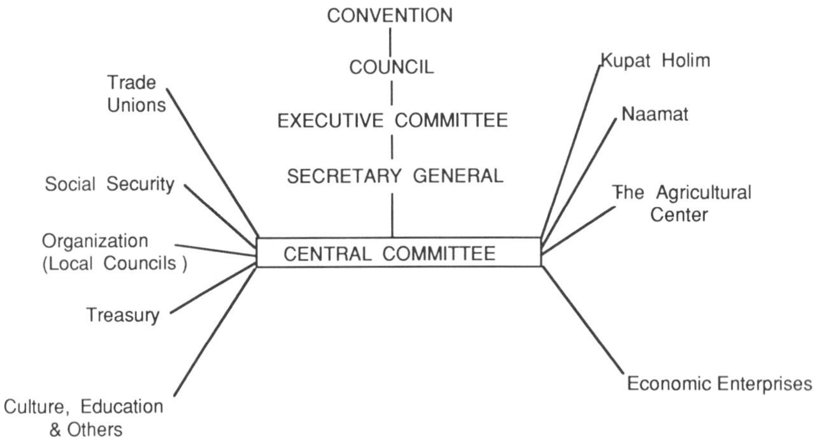

The Histadrut is not a federation of subunits, but a centralized
cohesive association. The institutional hierarchy, the centralized
system of dues collection, and the division of authority consolidate the concentration of power. Histadrut membership

reflects a cross section of the general population, from blue-collar manual workers, living on income supplements of the National Insurance Institution, to affluent professionals, dwelling in prosperous suburbs. This comprehensiveness is a mixed blessing. It does turn the Histadrut into the biggest and one of the most influential groups in the country, enjoying as it does a large financial and manpower pool from which it can extract resources. At the same time, however, the Histadrut faces threats to its integration, bitter internal divisions among its subunits, and long-lasting centrifugal tendencies (dealt with in chapter 4) that may be critical to its future development.

Aside from the Labor Federation, Israel has three other, marginal, trade unions: the National Workers Federation, established in 1934 as an extension of the Revisionist Movement (subsequently Herut); the Federation of Agudat Israel Workers; and the Federation of the Poel Mizrachi, an extension of the National Religious party. All three of these labor associations are extremely marginal and play no role in national economic politics.

Farmers associations

Israeli farmers are not individuals employed in agriculture but "settlers," and farming has not been a vocation but a destiny and a calling. Settlement of the land was one of Zionism's fundamental tenets; toiling the soil was a means both of individual redemption and of national revival. Agriculture was the climax of the occupational revolution envisaged by the founding-fathers of the *yishuv*. The exiled Jews had been restricted for centuries to occupations approved by Gentile authorities, mainly in trade and crafts. Promulgators of Zionism believed that becoming a pioneer (i.e., a farmer) would transform the returned exiles into a totally new, productive people. Returning to the land did not only serve the individual pioneer; it also furthered the collective goals of nation building. For the founders of Jewish nationhood in Palestine, coming back to (*eretz*) Israel was embodied in a return to its soil. That act provided a means of both remedying a historical injustice and building a future. Presumably, the revival of the nation could not possibly have happened without toiling the land and constructing Jewish settlements. Most of the Jews in Israel remained urban dwellers, but agriculture became associated with the highest ideals of the country.

It was against this ideological background that the farmers' associations organized. The earliest trace of a farmers' group goes back to 1883, when the vineyards growers formed the first organized interest group in Palestine. They were followed by citrus plantations growers. The activity and raison d'être of these groups were not significantly different from those of other farming groups in democratic societies. New forms of agricultural settlements, including the kibbutz and the moshav, emerged only in the 1920s, but they went on to serve as an example of Israel's "inventiveness and adaptation" (Arian 1985:29). The literature describing this unique social experience, the cooperative settlement, is voluminous. Cooperative settlements have been founded on the basis of communal ideas, mutual guarantees, and participatory democracy. Daily management is exercised by each agricultural unit, but questions of principle are determined by the kibbutz/moshav movement, which is also represented in the policy process.

The kibbutz movements have encountered dramatic changes, perhaps the major one being a shift from agriculture to industrial production. Kibbutz industry includes, at present, some 360 enterprises. The marked rise in the standard of living also has had impact on various aspects of kibbutz life. From the organizational perspective, the kibbutz movement has undergone several modifications. In the early days of statehood, there were three kibbutz movements (Hever Hakvutzot, Hakibbutz Hameuchad, Hakibbutz Haartzi) that were affiliated with three separate parties in the Labor camp. One split and two mergers produced two kibbutz movements—Takam, affiliated with the Labor party, and Hakibbutz Haartzi, affiliated with Mapam, further to the left. Despite these changes, the kibbutzim all adhere to the principle of cooperation, their common ideology enabling the formation of a Kibbutz Movement Alliance, which serves as a roof organization loosely coordinating the two movements.

The moshav movement, established in 1930, was also founded on the cooperative principle, although decentralization is much more evident, both on individual and collective levels. The moshav movement underwent a rapid growth, the number of units increasing from 60 in 1948 to 270 in 1988, mainly owing to the mass immigration in the 1950s. Settling the newcomers in moshavim was the product of a deliberate, official design. The kibbutz did not appeal to the newcomers: Of nearly one million immigrants in the first ten years, less than 2 percent went initially to kibbutzim. By 1954, as many as half of the new immigrants, most with no previous agricultural training, were being taken from the ship directly to the farm. Years later, the decision to do this came in for much criticism, but the policy has also been viewed as going beyond pragmatism: "The need to provide housing and work, to meet food shortages and to close defensive gaps in sparsely settled areas make the daring decision seen in retrospect to have been almost inevitable" (Shimshoni 1982: 112–113). The dramatic increase in size had repercussions for the cohesion of the moshav movement, which now, for all practical purposes, is split between the veteran units, inhabited by old-timer Israelis of European origin and so-called "new" moshavim, mainly those founded in the early 1950s and settled by immigrants from Arab-speaking countries. Although the moshav movement has retained its integrity and is not threatened by imminent fractionalization, the divisions between the two sections—the veteran moshavim and the so-called new moshavim—are often the cause of internal tensions.

Besides the major moshav and kibbutz movements, there are other settlement organizations, all of which were founded on the basis of affiliation with political parties (see table 2.1). There are religious kibbutzim and moshavim linked to the National Religious Party (NRP) and there are settlement organizations linked to the ultra-orthodox Poalei Agudat Israel. Right-wing parties also have their own settlement movements, all of which enjoy direct access to state-owned resources. In one case, however, a kibbutz movement outlived the party that sponsored it (the Liberal party). All settlement groups affiliated with the Histadrut cooperate within the framework of a roof organization—the Agricultural Center, which represents 650 agricultural settlements (385 moshavim and 265 kibbutzim). This center is predominant in the country's agriculture, since it produces 84 percent of Israel's farm products.

Economic Groups

Business associations

The relationship between business and government has emerged as one of the central issues of contemporary politics. According to the pluralist theory, business is one (albeit a major) actor in the political arena, exerting pressures in order to enhance its share in the national pie (Vogel 1987). The role of business in the political process has also attracted attention among proponents of the corporatist theory (Atkinson and Coleman 1989; Cawson 1985, 1986). By virtue of its functional role in society, the business

Table 2.1
Political Parties and Affiliated Settlement Movements (1987)

Party	Movement	Number of settlements	Population (thousands)
Labor party	Takam	161	74.0
	Tnuat Hamoshavim	253	89.3
Mapam	Kibbutz Artzi	83	41.1
Herut	Moshvei Herut	17	4.0
Liberal party	Hitachdut Haikarim		
NRP	Kibbutz Dati	17	7.4
	Moshvei Poel Mizrachi	79	30.4
Poalei Agudat Israel	kibbutz movement	2	1.4
	moshav movement	10	3.7
Independent Liberal party	Kibbutz Haoved Hatzioni	5	2.1
	Moshvei Haoved Hatzioni	26	6.7
	Haichud Hahaklai	48	15.6

Source: *Statistical Abstract of Israel* 1988: 52–53.

sector is an ideal partner of the state and, therefore, is a permanent, stable actor in the policy arena. Even the pluralists do not
assume that business is "just another interest group"; they realize
that it disposes of disproportional influence. Business has been entrusted with the power to decide whether (and where) to invest in
the new processes that are vital to the future prosperity of the
whole community (Lindblom 1977). In a seminal study of tariff
policy in the United States, Bauer, Pool, and Dexter (1968) provided empirical proof of the power of business in democratic
societies. Critics of the pluralist theory take this approach one step
farther: they assume that government is subservient to the interests of big business, and that the relationship between these two
major actors is structured in such a way as to minimize the risk
that the state will adopt policies that will inadvertently hurt
business activity (Wilson 1985: 1). This was not the case in the early years of Israel's statehood. In Israel of the 1950s, the term
"business" carried negative connotations because it was associated
with traditional Jewish occupations in the Diaspora. The Zionist
revolution focused on agriculture, on return to the land, not on
commerce and industry. Within a short period, however, business
groups emerged as the pivot for modernization. A rise in their
political influence was a natural result.

Business associations in Israel are organized within the
framework of two roof organizations, representing the interests of
the entire economic sector of the country. The most prominent of

the two is the Coordinating Office of the Economic Organizations, comprising fifteen organizations from various economic branches. It is dominated, however, by four major associations: the Israel Manufacturers Association, the Chamber of Commerce, the Center of Contractors and Builders, and the Farmers Union.

The Israel Manufacturers Association (MA). The organization of industrialists antedates the state. It was established in 1921 by middle-class Jewish immigrants who arrived in Israel after World War I and invested their money in small industrial enterprises. Severe competition in a limited market and, especially, the growing militancy of the labor movement following the establishment of the Histadrut (1920) induced organizational activity in the fledgling business sector. During the prestate era the objectives of the Manufacturers Association were threefold: First, the association acted as a pressure group protecting the industrialists' interests vis-à-vis the hostile British authorities. Second, the association confronted the powerful Histadrut in wage negotiations and labor disputes. Third, the manufacturers challenged the major goal of the prestate era: They offered "machine Zionism" as an alternative to the collectivist socialists' pro-land orientation. The MA attempted to divert both national resources and values from the cult of the soil to industrial production. In the late 1930s, the obstacles to this goal seemed insurmountable. During the second World War, however, rapid industrial development took place, the effect of which was to consolidate the MA and legitimize its objectives (Beilin 1988). Over the course of forty-odd years of statehood, the Manufacturers Association has accumulated further resources and turned into one of the most important interest groups in the Israeli political system. The MA's abundant resources are partly responsible for its prominent position. Its relatively high annual budget (in 1988, 1.450 million shekels), a well-staffed organization, and the expertise of its administrative workers have contributed to the association's efficiency. A wide membership and a cohesive organizational structure also constitute major assets. The Israel Manufacturers Association, however, is not a comprehensive group, since it includes only the entrepreneurs of the private sector and not firms associated either with the Histadrut or the government, such as the Israel Aviation Industry. Even without some of the country's largest employers, it is the private sector, with 94.6 percent (in 1987) of the establishments and 68.7 percent of the employees, that is preponderant in the economy (*Statistical Abstract* 1988: 419).

The MA is organized along functional lines, with five professional units: Chemistry and Pharmaceutics, Food, Electronics and

Software, Metal and Textile, and a General unit. There are also functional units for communication and public relations, labor and human resources, economy and foreign trade. A budgetary unit is responsible for the MA's financial affairs. The administrative units are headed by hired staff members, who act under the surveillance of elected committees. The MA's wide-ranging membership, harboring possible conflicting interests, is not detrimental to the association, the major reason for its internal cohesion being the structure of its central bureau, which represents all sectors. Another important element is the MA's leadership, which enjoys national fame. The MA now numbers some 1000 members, whose recruitment has been influenced by technological and economic changes over the years.[4]

The success of the MA was not only a product of its organizational competence; it also resulted from the interface between its objectives and those of the state. Indeed, the high institutionalization of the Manufacturers Association may have spurred the adoption of industrial productivity as a major policy objective.

The Chamber of Commerce. The Chamber of Commerce is a roof organization for numerous nonmanufacturing-sector associations: e.g., Real Estate Agents, the Union of Department Stores, and Importers of Cars. Established in 1919, the chamber initially faced severe difficulties in acquiring social legitimacy. One of the major objectives of the Zionist movement was to overturn the traditional occupational structure of Diaspora Jews, which was based mainly on trade and crafts, and to replace it with so-called "productive" work, mainly in agriculture. The industrialists had no difficulty in persuading the public they, too, contributed to the productivity of the Jewish community and delivered their share to the renaissance of the nation. For the tradesmen, this task was a relentless one, their image having been tainted by their association with the *luftgeschaeft*, derogated in favor of the new occupational aspirations.

The organizational structure of the Chamber of Commerce is similar to that of its counterpart in industry. There are some 1500 dues-paying members, organized by functional subunits. Exclusion from membership is based on the size of trade. The chamber is generally open only to the larger commercial businesses. Beginning in 1987, the chamber expanded its membership by incorporating various associations: the Truck Drivers, the Travel Agents, and other free-enterprise groups. Like its counterpart, the chamber has not encountered any grave disciplinary problems and acts with unanimity to promote its members' interests. Again, like the MA, the top chamber's leadership also consists of nationally known figures, members of the inner-circle "establishment." It attracts members by offering a variety of services, including marketing surveys, computer instructions, judicial assistance, and professional counseling in international commerce. The influence of the Chamber of Commerce has considerably increased during the last decade, owing mainly to the proficiency of its leadership. Its place in national politics, however, does not match that of the MA.

The Center of Contractors and Builders (CCB). The associational activity of those involved in construction also dates back to the 1920s. The establishment of the Center of Contractors and Builders provides another proof of Truman's "wave theory," which depicts the formation of one interest group as a reaction to the organizational activity of its counterpart. The unionization of the construction workers indeed triggered reciprocal activity in the business sector. The CCB confines itself to the private sector, which thus excludes the giant Histadrut construction company, Shikun Ovdim. Even so, CCB members controlled 88.8 percent of the construction market in 1987 (based on the building area; see *Statistical Abstract* 1988: 462). Its major organizational units are not based on functional criteria but rather on territory and magnitude. Formally power is divided among the branches, but the real rivalry is between the big contractors, who dominate the market (with 63.7 percent of buildings completed in 1987; *Statistical Abstract* 1988: 476), and builders who handle smaller-scale projects. The Center of Contractors & Builders attempted to jump on the wagon of other business groups by propagating their role in building the country and proclaiming their contribution to society. Their success in this regard was limited.

The Farmers Union. The Farmers Union represents the private agricultural sector in Israel. By virtue of its political-economic orientation, it is also a part of the business world. In the past, this union's political affiliation with right-wing parties hindered the establishment of a national agricultural front. The private farmers joined forces with the business associations because of their ideological and economic proximity. The Farmers Union is a fairly small organization; its 5000 members, scattered around the country, comprise but 1.7 percent of the total rural population (*Statistical Abstract* 1988: 53). Its share in the national economy is minuscule. Its power is derived from the historical role played by private farmers in the settlement endeavor that took place in prestate Israel.

Coordinating Office of the Economic Organizations. These four business associations—the Manufacturers Association, the Chamber of Commerce, the Center of Contractors and Builders, and the Farmers Union—formed the basis of the Coordinating Office of the Economic Organizations, the roof organization representing business groups in Israel. The four first joined forces in the mid-1950s in an Employers Unit for the purpose of coordinating activities. Having realized that separate activity reduced their influence, the members of the unit decided to coordinate more closely.[5] In 1966, cooperation among the four business groups was formalized with the establishment of the Coordinating Office, which claims to represent the business sector as a whole. The office may be considered "comprehensive" (Coleman and Grant 1985: 468), drawing its membership from most business sectors and addressing the general problems facing business in Israel. Since by its very nature this wide-ranging membership possess conflicting interests, the Coordinating Office adopted regulations enabling it to maintain diversity and yet to claim unity at one and the same time. The original four associations represented by the office have grown to fifteen (listed in its regulations). It is a typical peak organization with membership restricted to organized groups rather than individual firms or members. Each member group retains its separate set up, even though it is integrated into the office. The division between the small groups and the big ones, in terms of membership rather than in terms of power, is evident in the regulations. The Presidents' Committee, responsible for formulating the office's policy, consists of representatives of the "big four" alone, i.e., the Manufacturers Association, the Chamber of Commerce, the Center of Contractors and Builders, and the Farmers Union. In effect, the office is dominated by the manufacturers; however, the smaller groups may veto decisions by the leadership in the council, where they form a majority.

So far this complex organizational device has not been put to the test. The broad base of the office, covering a wide spectrum of economic activity (from agriculture through industry and finance to hotels and shoe repairing), of necessity causes it to restrict activity to a defense of collective interests. In domains in which a conflict of interest prevails (such as tax benefits to the manufacturers vs. tariffs on imported goods), the office declines to express an opinion and does not act on behalf of any group among its members. To safeguard its cohesion, the Coordinating office is reluctant to raise its voice even in matters on which the majority—but not all—of its members are united.

Much of the office's leadership's time is devoted to building sufficient internal unity to enable it to deal effectively with the Histadrut's demands on the wage front. When acting to this end, the office is under no threat of a split. Indeed, not one single organization has ever threatened to withdraw. Although the manufacturing industry and financial interests may have different perspectives and priorities with regard to monetary policy, exchange rates, and other macroeconomic questions, no open controversy has ever erupted—for the simple reason that the office avoids handling these issues. In fact, the office has declined to develop a fully institutionalized organizational structure (there are only a few hired workers) and operates on a low burner; still, it successfully represents the business sector on wage policy—its one, though extremely important, domain of economic activity. It is this benefit attached to membership that is evidently greater than the modest investment. The limited scope of the office's activities leaves much of the political activity to the individual associations, which operate outside the confines of the office and utilize independent channels to influence government decisions. Each has its own network of contacts with officials and members of Knesset and, in matters affecting its business sphere, totally ignores the roof organization.

The "third" sector. Until the 1980s the Coordinating Office monopolized the business sector, but in 1983 another actor entered the scene: the organization of the self-employed, called Lahav—representing twenty-five different associations. Lahav crosscuts other associations: it represents the small artisans, who also belong to the Association of Artisans and Small Industry, as well as self-employed lawyers, members of the Bar Association. Lahav's goal is to protect and promote the interests of a sector in the economy that is not represented either by the Histadrut (as are salaried workers) or by the Coordinating Office, which looks out for employers. Lahav's constituency has no stake in wage negotiations, but is eager to influence economic policy. The association's declared goal is to "widen the triangle of state-workers-employers to include a third sector—that of the self-employed whose voice in the policy process has remained unheard." So far Lahav has not been successful in securing formal representation. Among all employees in 1987, the proportion of the salaried work force reached 79.1 percent (*Statistical Abstract* 1988: 341), which leaves but a small proportion to the self-employed. The organization's request to join the Coordinating Office was turned down, as the employers were not eager to share their power with a newcomer on the associational scene. The validity of the corporatist law of closure has thus been confirmed. Since the influence of Lahav is still limited to trivial issues (such as property tax rate for shopowners in municipalities), the political interests of the business community seem to be fairly unified in one peak association that is more active than visible. The formation of Lahav has not introduced a competitor to the Coordinating Office. It is, in fact, difficult to envisage the association of the self-employed as an "opponent"; rather, it is a kind of adjunct, trailing behind its big brother on the road to influence. The failure of Lahav to join the prestigious business club proves that the characteristics of the business sector in Israel are congruent with the corporatist model: its constituent units are organized into a limited number of singular, non-competitive, and centralized categories.

Professional associations

Israel is highly professionalized in the sense that a high proportion of its (Jewish) labor force is university graduates. An overwhelmingly socialized economy controlled by the state has led to most professionals being employed in the public sector. This has produced a considerable unionization of professional organizations. The status of academics in Israel was influenced also by their contribution to the process of nation building. Before independence professionals were denied social status and recognition. Leaving one's profession to become a worker or a pioneer was regarded not as a sign of failure but as an act of heroism and selfless devotion to the national cause (Ben-David 1970: 203). During statehood, however, as the economy developed, occupational differences became increasingly important. The growing differentiation has led to the development of three types of professional associations: unions, associations that are both "professional" and unionized, and organizations focusing solely on professional issues.

The first category includes, for example, the elementary teachers, the social workers, and the microbiologists. These organizations are full-fledged unions bargaining on behalf of their members for higher wages. They operate under the aegis of the Histadrut, and are represented in its bodies. The wage policy worked out between the Labor Federation and the government applies to members of these unions. The oldest and largest among professional associations in the country is the Teachers Federation (numbering, in 1988, some 65,000 members). The federation organized in 1903 in order to protect the interests of the teachers; its principal goal was, however, to disseminate the revived Hebrew language and culture. For forty-five years, the Teachers Federation retained its autonomous organization status until, in 1948, it bowed under continuous pressures and was finally incorporated into the Histadrut. The federation has nevertheless maintained some measure of autonomy regarding its professional affairs.

Other professional associations such as the Union of Social Workers constitute an organizational unit within the Histadrut Trade Union Department. They, too, however maintain a relative degree of autonomy. The Engineers Federation, for example, a large and prosperous group, is one of the more autonomous unions. With some 40,000 members, playing a vital role in Israel's industrialized economy, the engineers were able to negotiate their own wages and even to affect organizational reform in the Histadrut regulations legitimizing their autonomy. Their power derives also from the fact that a parallel Engineers Bureau operates outside the Histadrut, focusing on professional affairs. The threat to withdraw from the Labor Federation and join their colleagues in the independent professional association enabled the engineers to obtain a large measure of autonomy vis-à-vis central Histadrut institutions.

The Israel Medical Association (IMA) is the only association outside the Histadrut that fulfills both union and professional functions. The IMA grew from a small group of seven doctors (organized in Jaffa in 1912) to a large association of some 12,000 physicians. The variety of specializations they represent and the abundance—some would say surplus—of physicians in the country (many of whom studied and practiced medicine in foreign countries), put a heavy burden on their professional association. Incorporating over 95 percent of the country's salaried physicians, the IMA has monopolized representation of physicians' interests in wage negotiations, physicians' salaries being determined on a national basis. In the past a bitter conflict took place between the Medical Association on the one hand and the combined forces of the Histadrut and the government on the other. The latter refused to negotiate with the doctors and asked them to join the Histadrut. The IMA, however, obtained the support of the whole medical profession and retained its autonomy. The association has proved to be a tough, militant negotiator. Doctors' strikes and work stoppages are a recurrent event in the Israeli health-services scene. As a professional association, the IMA imposes an ethical code on its members and determines professional standards for expertise, in which latter area it was granted state recognition. It jealously safeguards these activities from outside interference, insisting on the application of "pure" professional standards.

The third category includes groups such as the Bar Association, the Dentists Federation, and the Bureau of Accountants, which focus merely on professional issues. These associations were not unionized because of the occupational status of their members, the majority of whom are employed in the private sector. Most of these associations enjoy a measure of corporate autonomy. The Israel Bar Association is the only voluntary group in the country granted full statutory recognition. The corporate status of the lawyers was inscribed in a Knesset law (1961). It allows them important powers of internal legislation and jurisdiction in matters of professional practice. The law requires, for example, that every practicing lawyer be registered in the bar, and pay fixed dues. The Bar Association is responsible for the lawyers' professional affairs including licensing and ethical conduct. It is not involved in trade union activity, which is carried out by a small Lawyers Federation (some 2,000 members of the country's total 10,000 lawyers), which operates under the auspices of the Histadrut.

The Bar Association presents a unique case. It has been granted recognition in spite of past ideologically based opposition to special privileges for professional workers. None of the other groups has been conferred with full legal status, although many are officially incorporated into some aspects of policy-making regarding professional issues.

Other Sectional Groups

Immigrant associations

Ingathering of the exiles has been one of the major functions of the Jewish state. Since the proclamation of its statehood, Israel has absorbed over 1.9 million Jewish immigrants. The Law of Return, giving the right to all Jews to immigrate and to automatically acquire citizenship upon arriving in Israel, accentuated the national commitment. The process of immigration is widely discussed in the media and documented by official sources, since its scale is regarded as a major indicator of both the strength of the nation and the fulfillment of ultimate Zionist ideals. The immigrants are of very varied backgrounds and from numerous countries of origin. The most recent group to arrive in Israel in a large-scale immigration from the Soviet Union, which has opened its gates for the exit of Jews after many decades of severe restrictions. From another corner of the world came the black Jews from Ethiopia. A dramatic rescue airlift from the Sudan in 1984, termed Operation Moses, brought to Israel some 8,000 Ethiopians, who joined the 4,000 already living here.

Immigrants have traditionally organized themselves into interest groups. The number of such groups having an official status register with the ministry of immigrant absorption tends to fluctuate. In 1988 the list consisted of nineteen immigrant associations. Most of them were established in the early 1950s, with the major waves of immigrants who arrived after independence. Changes in the volume of immigration, countries of origin, and sociopolitical context have influenced the structure of the interest group arena. The goals of the immigrant associations are bifurcated. On the one hand, they aim at representing the interests of their members in dealing with government and national absorption agencies on matters affecting their integration. On the other hand, these groups also attempt to extend to their members and prospective members advice, guidance, assistance, and services in order to facilitate their integration. Some associations, such as the Latin American Immigrant Union, have extended their goals to include the initiation of *Aliya* (immigration). The immigrant associations are, thus, not strictly pressure groups, since they also act on behalf of the state in fulfilling important functions inherent in the welfare state. Indeed, in practice emphasis is placed on socializing and absorbing the immigrants more than on their demand for economic goods and services.

The associations vary considerably in their structure and activities. One of the most well organized is the Association of American and Canadian Immigrants in Israel, which represents a community of 60,000 North Americans (with a membership of over 16,000) through one national and five regional offices. A national convention is held every two years. A detailed constitution describes the group's goals and organizational structure. The association offers a broad spectrum of social services, particularly for new arrivals, but also for veteran immigrants. In recent years it has expanded its activity to issues pertaining to the quality of life in Israel, such as consumerism and the environment.

A striking feature of immigrant associations is their proliferation. As reported by Korazim (1988), between 1986 and 1988 about ten groups of Ethiopian Jews created their own associations, each one claiming to represent their community. The tendency to fractionalization is even more conspicuous among the Russian immigrants. A community of some 200,000 Jews from the USSR (in 1988) is represented by no fewer than thirty associations and groups. These people were divided among themselves while still in Russia by their political affiliations and personal rivalries; these took organizational form in their new country. There are also numerous associations based on geographic region. The Immigrant Association of Georgia represents a community of 38,000 Jews. There are also associations speaking on behalf of the Jews from Caucasia and Buchara. Attempts to coordinate among the numerous fractions and to establish a roof organization that would represent the interests of the whole Soviet community in Israel have so far been abortive. The common base of language, culture, political socialization, and problems facing the immigrant from the Soviet Union have not been a sufficient incentive for an alliance. Fragmentation and adversary relations continue to date, even among Jews from the Russian Republic.

Some attempts at coordination between immigrant associations have been successful, however, at least on a partial basis. The Council of English Speakers serves immigrant associations from North America, Australia, the United Kingdom, and South Africa. The function of this council is mainly to provide general information on rights, benefits, and available services. On a national basis, a Council of Immigrant Associations was formed for the purpose of serving as an umbrella body for all groups operating under the auspices of the Jewish agency. This council, which is loosely organized, attempts to forge a united front vis-à-vis absorption authorities, and to defend the rights of the newcomers. The leading actor in the council and its initiator, the Association of American and Canadian Immigrants, reported on difficulties in introducing a measure of coordination into the so-far highly proliferated arena of immigrant associations.

Categoric groups

This section includes groups whose members share a problem for which they seek solution through a change of public policy. The problem may be caused by virtue of a handicap (the Handicapped of the Israel Defense Forces IDF), by virtue of personal problems (Society for the Protection of the Rights of Men), or by a particular social status (the Students Union). All the groups under this category seek material benefit for their members and do not wish to redeem society as a whole. Membership is composed only of those having a direct personal and material stake in the cause a group promotes. Some associations, such as the Society for the Protection of Individual Rights (namely the rights of homosexuals), also aspire to achieve broader community recognition and legitimacy.

Israel can count some thirty organizations of handicapped persons or those acting on behalf of the handicapped (the latter to be discussed under the promotional category). People with a wide variety of illnesses from many disastrous events are represented, among them those whose health was impaired in the Holocaust and those once imprisoned in Soviet detention camps. All the horrors and suffering of the Jewish people in recent history are reflected in the titles of the associations of the handicapped in the country. An example of a categoric group is Yad Labanim (Memorial to the Sons), the association of bereaved parents and widows of soldiers and victims of Israel's wars. Yad Labanim was established in the midst of the War of Independence for the purpose of sanctifying the dead. Now, forty years on, it is largely involved in promoting and defending the material interests of its members. At the same time this group promulgates national goals by attempting to safeguard the values for which the victims of Israel's wars presumably fought and died.

Associations of the handicapped demonstrate a high degree of proliferation. For example, five organizations deal with the problems of the deaf: the Association of the Israeli Deaf, the Association of Difficult Hearing, the Educators of Deaf Children, the Parents of Deaf Children, and the Youth of Silence. A similar diffusion obtains among the victims of the Nazi persecution and of Soviet oppression. In 1980, a roof organization was established encompassing the majority (twenty-six of thirty) of the associations of the handicapped. The roof organization attempts to coordinate activities and to forge joint strategies. It is the spokesman for the handicapped in the administration; it also attempts to lobby legislators. Nevertheless, the degree of coordination it experiences is rather loose, with rivalry for scarce resources generating internal tensions and impeding concerted action.

The Students Union is another categoric group. In contrast to many student associations in democratic (and, for that matter, nondemocratic) countries, Israeli students are generally not proponents of social change. The major preoccupation of these 65,000 individuals (in 1988) is with tuition, grants, and loans. That is to

say, they are concerned with the material aspect of acquiring a
higher education rather than with revolutionizing society. One has
to remember that the average Israeli student, having undergone a
long period of compulsory and often additional voluntary military
service is older and more mature than his or her Western counterpart. The indifference of Israeli students to public affairs has been
documented in a scholarly research (Shapira and Etzioni-Halevy
1973). For our purposes, it suffices to note that the Student Union,
which is a federation of local unions in the country's seven universities, is a sectional group seeking to advance its members' material
interests. it competes for benefits lavishly dispensed by a patronizing state.

Promotional Groups

Public interest groups

During the 1960s Western societies encountered a revolution
of participation. Flower children rejected the materialistic values
of the technological society; students challenged the institutions of
higher education; the underprivileged staged protests to eradicate
social injustice; consumers organized to protect their rights vis-à-
vis big business; women declared war on inequality; and en-
vironmentalists challenged corporations to relieve humanity of
dreadful atmospheric dangers and to restore the qualities of
nature. The upsurge of these demands marked the era of "new
politics."

Israeli "new politics" took a different form. In Israel the color
green brings to mind the color of the PLO flag. Students are busy
fulfilling their duties in between their forty-five to sixty days of annual reserve service. Women are supposed to serve the nation by
increasing their birth rate in order for the nation to cope with the
ever-present demographic danger. Nonetheless, promotional
groups are active on the Israeli scene although they certainly fall
short of emulating their Western equivalents: There is no parallel
to Ralph Nader's consumer "raiders" or to Common Cause in the
Unites States or the "greens" in most European countries. Nor do
Israeli citizens chain themselves to the fences of military camps in
order to protest nuclearization; feminists are not at war with male
chauvinists, and the underprivileged have generally not set fire to
public sites. Despite their not being given to such extreme activism, promotional groups in Israel do portray the unique

features of Israeli democracy, focusing on environmental protection, on consumer affairs, on promoting civil rights (including female rights), on propagating religious values. The most influential groups, however, are involved in presenting proposals for alternative solutions to the lingering Arab-Israeli conflict.

Environmental groups. Alvin Toffler (1982: 151) described environmental groups as "the leading edge of the future in a three-way political and economic battle." In many—in fact in most—European free countries, the ecologists have turned their movements into political parties, attempting to influence the national agenda through parliamentary channels. In Israel, environmental issues were pushed to the bottom of this agenda. The quality of life is of secondary concern compared to the preservation of life, which is endangered by the precarious security situation. The exigencies of absorbing mass immigration also hinders serious consideration of ecological issues.

The activity of the ecological groups—the Council for a Beautiful Israel, the Council for the Prevention of Noise and Pollution (Malraz), and the Society for the Protection of Nature—has been influenced by these considerations. The first two associations share some organizational attributes: they are elite organizations with minimal rank-and-file activity. The founder of the Council for a Beautiful Israel, set up in 1968, was a member of Knesset, noted for his environmental concern. The council was manned by professionals: architects, educators, lawyers, and other public figures. On paper it targeted its activities on three major objectives: applying professional knowledge to repair environmental damage, recommending strategies for improving the quality of life, and intiating programs to deepen environmental awareness among the public. In actuality it was content to launch educational campaigns in schools, factories, gas stations, and the other institutions that were presumably conducive to raising environmental consciousness. Malraz was also initiated by members of the elite. Established in 1962, a year after the first environmental law was enacted by the Knesset, it, too, is promoted by professionals—lawyers, economists, physicians and engineers. It regards itself as a "watchdog" on the authorities, a trigger for the implementation of ecological legislation and enforcement of the standards necessary for maintaining a clean, noiseless environment. The two environmental councils lack both a strong organizational basis and membership support. Although the former claims to have nationwide membership, most of its affiliates are only sym-

pathizers endorsing its objectives. For its part, Malraz has practically turned into a one-man organization, headed by an ambitious though capable lawyer, and totally lacking mass support.

The Society for the Protection of Nature presents a different
character. The oldest and the most active of the environmental
groups, and the largest—it claims what is for Israel a huge
membership of 45,000—it was founded in the early 1950s by a
handful of nature lovers and university students, during one of
Israel's most stormy periods. The country was then plagued by a
severe economic crisis and political uncertainty; it had to cope
with enormous difficulties, both from external threats and
domestic instability. The founders of this organization may have
sought a refuge in nature, but they also had other goals in mind
which determined the group's future course: to increase Israelis'
love of their country and to acquaint them with its mountains,
valleys, and rivers.

The Society for the Protection of Nature is highly institutionalized. With sixteen branches and seventeen subdivisions, it
carries on a wide variety of activities. One of these is the operation
of field schools (in 1986, twenty-five in number), scattered all over
the country, which serve as centers for touring and hiking.
Although the society is a mass-based organization, most of its
members belong to the upper echelons of society: approximately
60 percent of the society's members are university graduates, compared to only 14 percent in the general population (Amir and Stern
1974). A typical member (some one-third of the total) is either a
student or a teacher. The society only seldom challenges the
authorities. It is more active in inculcating a love of the country
than in pressuring the powers that be to pay more heed to environmental issues. This aspect of its activity will be discussed further.

Two more groups should be mentioned although they promote human rather than physical ecology. One Nation, a
Beautiful Nation was established in 1977, in the aftermath of the
political upheaval that year, when the country was embroiled in a
deep ethnic and political rift. Its major purpose was to restore
brotherhood in the Jewish community. The second group—Good
Eretz Israel—was formed three years later by "do gooders"
wishing to disseminate the values of tolerance, good manners, and
comradeship among their fellow citizens. Both groups aimed at
fostering courtesy, mutual understanding and aid, love of
mankind, tolerance of any human being. Improving relations between Jews and Arabs residing in Israel was not, however, one of

their goals. Although the two groups were committed to invigorating "national pride, patriotism and unity of its [Jewish] people," (Manifesto of One Nation, a Beautiful Nation) they failed to attract much public attention; nor have they had any influence on public life. The importance of these groups lies in the strategies they pursue, which are geared to socializing the Israelis into already accepted, though much less practiced, values, rather than to facing down the ruling authority. Environmental groups are loosely organized under a roof association called Life and Environment, headed by a former MK specializing in ecological issues.

Consumer associations. Consumer activity is characterized by a relatively wide diversity. Five or six associations protect and promote the interests of the Israeli consumer, in a society in which awareness of consumers' rights ranks extremely low. The largest two organizations are the Consumers Council and the Consumers Authority. The Consumers Council was established by the government in 1966 as an adjunct of the ministry of industry and commerce. The Israeli Consumers Council represents consumers in government committees and in small claims courts. It is also active in releasing information regarding the quality of consumer goods. The council, however, is greatly politicized, although a capable director has thus far been successful in thwarting completely partisan domination. The council's board of directors is nominated by the ministers in charge (the minister of industry and commerce and the minister of finance), and their considerations have been tainted with much political flavor.

The Consumers Authority, the other large association, operates under the auspices of the Histadrut. It is, in fact, a department in its executive committee, its board of directors consisting of representatives of trade unions, workers councils, women's associations, and other Histadrut-affiliated bodies. Conspicuously absent are the representatives of the Histadrut's economic enterprises, including the marketing conglomerate (Hamashbir Latzorchan) whose activities should be scrutinized by the Consumers Authority. Their absence reduces the authority's effectiveness in controlling prices and inspecting product quality.

In addition, there are four small consumer groups, representing various social sectors.[6] The proliferation of consumer associations is without any proportion to the substance of the issue in the Israeli society and, for that matter, to the impact of their activity. Rather it was caused by power rivalries between the Histadrut and state agencies and by the personal ambitions of individuals, all of

which bear little relationship to patterns of consumerism in the
society at large.

Civil rights associations. The Civil Rights Association is one of the
most structured, most effective public interest groups in the country. It was established in 1972 by prominent figures in the Israeli
legal and judicial establishment, including professors from two law
faculties. The Civil Rights Association, which has a branch in each
of four major cities, showed particularly rapid growth in the late
1980s, owing to what its adherents saw as the deterioration of civil
rights in the occupied territories. The association concentrates on
specific complaints of a breach of civil rights, but it also acts as a
lobby, trying to influence legislation and policy making. It deals
extensively with freedom of faith, with inter-racial relations, and
with all other issues pertaining to human rights in a democratic
law-abiding society.

The Civil Rights Association is the only interest group in
Israel striving to protect individual rights. Numerous groups,
however, promote the rights of women, even though—or particularly because—Israel lags behind other Western societies in the
manifestations of female assertiveness. The state is committed to
equality between the sexes, and female pioneers have contributed
their share to toiling the land, drying the swamps, and making the
desert bloom, but the political and economic status of women in
contemporary Israeli society is an indication of gender inequality.
A variety of women's interest groups have attempted to cope with
this inequality and to protect women's rights. They have also
fulfilled mobilization roles to integrate women into the political
process.

Women's associations in Israel may be classified on the basis
of their militancy and attitude toward the feminist revolution. One
cluster of women's interest groups consist of those that do not aim
at far-reaching social change and suffice with promoting the
female's traditional roles. WIZO (Women's International Zionist
Organization) is a typical example of this type of group. It
operates day-care institutions, provides vocational training, maintains women's clubs, and offers leisure activities. WIZO does not
carry the banner of the feminist revolution but confines its activities to improving the lot of women in society. The old-time
division of labor between men and women is acknowledged,
though not encouraged. Other groups belonging to this category
are women's organizations affiliated with political parties,
especially in the religious camp (a vivid example being Emuna,
which is associated with the NRP).

Further along the militancy spectrum are associations whose goals are more radical, but whose strategies are moderate. Naamat, the Histadrut-affiliated women's movement, is a good example. It was founded in the early 1920s as the Council of Women Workers, to encompass the small group of women pioneers. In 1976, the name of the organization was changed to Naamat (which in Hebrew means pleasantry) in order to mitigate the association with "labor." Naamat wanted to attract middle-class women who were members of the Histadrut but who shied away from activity in its female section. Today Naamat numbers over 700,000 women from all walks of life; every woman in the Histadrut is automatically a member of Naamat. Like WIZO, Naamat also caters to the daily needs of women. It operates a network of child-care programs and offers a wide range of vocational courses and social clubs. It is more concerned, though, with developing the woman's understanding of political issues and social affairs. Naamat has actively lobbied for women's rights legislation to enhance equality between the sexes. As part of the Histadrut, however, Naamat is constrained by the trade union department, which is dominated by men. Naamat's advocacies have not been revolutionary, as reflected in the slogan adopted by this, the largest women's association in the country: it asked men "To Give Her a Hand"; the house chores, in other words, remain "her" exclusive responsibility.

At the other end of the political spectrum may be grouped the associations affiliated with feminist ideology: Woman to Woman, Center for Assistance to Victims of Sexual Abuse, and various fringe militant women's associations, all of which experience a common suffering: chronic shortage of resources. They are the least institutionalized of the female interest groups, being characterized by a loose organizational structure. The feminist movement, established by immigrants from the United States in the early 1970s, attracted a small nucleus of activists, who, dedicated as they were, generally failed to awaken the dormant self-awareness of Israeli women.

Women's groups find it difficult to coalesce because of their divergent orientations. For example, Women Against Offensive Advertisement fiercely attacked Naamat for compromising on an anti-feminist media ad sponsored by the Histadrut that depicted women as "merchandise." In the 1980s, though, a roof organization for women's groups, called the Shedula (the Lobby), aimed at providing a coherent, coordinated framework for the female voice in Israeli politics. Although the Shedula has jumped into the rough water of politics, its impact has been limited. The high fragmentation characterizing the women's group arena may be both a result and a cause of their vulnerability in political life.

Interest groups and defense policy. Israel is a nation at arms in which questions of war and peace acquire prime importance. Defense issues dominate the agenda to the extent that the 1988 elections were described as a "referendum on territories."[7] Until the 1967 war, group activity regarding Israel's security was practically nil. Consensus was—or seemed—unbroken, and no imminent alternative was available for official policy. Only after 1967 did organized public participation emerge on issues of war and peace. The interest groups concentrating on defense offer two alternatives: hawkish and dovish.

The Six Day War was an igniter that sparked intensive group activity. In that short war, Israel gained control of a territory that was 3.6 times larger than its own area, and inherited a population of 1.5 million Arabs. The erosion of the Green Line (the border demarcating Israel from the Jordanian-controlled Judea and Samaria and the Egyptian-controlled Gaza Strip) had not only military consequences but also deep emotional implications. Public opinion in Israel is deeply divided between those advocating the retention of territories, preferably by applying Israel's sovereignty, and those demanding the return of parts or all lands captured in the war. The hawks sustain their argument by the imperatives of defense and the rationale of geo-strategy. The advocates of Greater Israel believe that the state has a divine right over the lands and also that their return will impair Israel's security. The doves' advocacy rests mainly on considerations of realpolitik, coupled with moral stance. The proponents of withdrawal argue that forceful occupation of a large, hostile population is both unfeasible and undesirable; that occupation distorts and corrupts Israel as much as it is rejected by the Arabs themselves. The two strands of opinion have given rise to two major interests groups: Gush Emunim and Peace Now.

Gush Emunim, the major advocate of the retention policy, was preceded by the Land of Israel Movement, a fairly organized group that urged the prompt annexation of the territories occupied by Israel after the Six Day War. LIM was founded in 1967 by Laborites critical of the alleged moderate stand of their party regarding the future borders of Israel. The group was extremely resourceful in terms of leadership. Among its activists were noted writers (including the national poet Natan Alterman, and the first Israeli Nobel Laureate Shmuel Yosef Agnon), politicians, professors, and businessmen. Eventually, however divisions according to partisan affiliation, lack of operative strategy, and personal rivalries dwindled the group's resources. After the National Unity government was dismantled in August 1970, the LIM's Labor party members broke away from the movement. In the 1973 elections, LIM merged with the fledgling Likud and lost its status as an interest group.

Gush Emunim (literally the Bloc of Faithful), as LIM's heir and successor, is the most passionate and renowned proponent of the concept of a Greater Israel. Its superior resources, deeper penetration, and wider expansion distinguishes it not only from LIM, but to some extent also from every other comparable organization in Israel's political milieu of promotional interest groups. Gush Emunim was officially founded on February 4, 1974, by young orthodox middle-class activists. The group's structure appears to have been rather loose. It never institutionalized; it did not issue membership cards or collect fees on a fixed basis; it did not have a regular publication. In fact it was not even registered as a formal association. With the passage of time some institutionalization was achieved when the organization acquired office space at a permanent address and set up four departments (political, financial, settlement, and information). Quantities of oral and written propaganda began to be disseminated, and Gush branches were opened throughout the country (Yishai 1987b: 119). Gush Emunim institutionalized reluctantly, however, in fear that the price would be the loss of one of its major assets: individual motivation and enthusiasm. At the same time, however, organization was essential to carrying out its major goal: the settlement of the lands it preached to retain.

The Likud's ascent to power gave rise to great expectations and relieved Gush Emunim from its organizational dilemma. These expectations, however, soon changed into deep disappointment as the Likud began what was seen as a retreat: returning a major piece of land (the Sinai) for peace (with Egypt). The unexpected political realities provoked Gush Emunim into reshaping its organizational structure. As a means of confronting these realities, it branched into two subsections: Yesha and Amana. The founding of Yesha (the Hebrew acronym for Judea, Samaria, and Gaza) came in consequence of the Camp David accords. The peace process hit Gush Emunim hard, for the government that had conceded to Egypt and was willing to yield up territories included Gush supporters. The organization's vulnerability was publicly exposed when it failed to stop the retreat from Sinai, even though a public

interest group was founded to this end. The pace of settling the remaining territories also ran far below expectations, partly because
a supposedly supportive government was actually dragging its
feet. Despite these unfavorable circumstances, the growing
number of Jews residing in the occupied lands spurred organizational activity. Yesha was formed ostensibly as a municipal
framework, but in effect it continued to propagate the Gush
Emunim message in other ways. Yesha started out as the Association for the Advancement of Population and Absorption in Judea,
Samaria and Gaza. It was instigated by the Forum of Heads of
Councils, all of whose members were activists in Gush Emunim.
At present, Yesha numbers more than 130 settlements, inhabited
by some 75,000 settlers. It is highly institutionalized, with a well-
structured organizational framework and, like its predecessor, is
the major proponent of Greater Israel in ideal and practice.

The second section, Amana, is a settlement organization.
Founded in 1977, the intention was to institutionalize the function
regarded most important by Gush Emunim leaders: erecting
Jewish settlements all over the occupied territories. The formation
of a settlement organization was a strategy for sharing in the abundant resources streaming from state-run bodies. From personal
and ideological perspectives, Amana is almost indistinguishable
from its parent Gush Emunim. The two associations have close
manpower, funding, and other organizational connections. In
1987, nine of the eleven members of Amana's secretariat were at
one time or another activists in Gush Emunim. Amana has provided funds for Gush activities and implemented its policies. In practice, however, Amana is engaged mostly in planning and implementing settlement activity. The political lobbying and the
ideological socialization are performed by the same people but in
their capacity as Gush members.

The intensification of the uprising in the territories, the intifada, gave rise to a further proliferation of hawkish groups, most
of which, however, act on behalf of their own members and thus
do not qualify as public interest groups. Despite the high fragmentation, the hawkish roost is characterized by a high degree of cohesion and esprit de corps. The interest groups advocating the
hawkish alternative are united by their dedication to the idea of
Greater Israel, which has overshadowed divisions based on
demographic or economic attributes.

The doves were somewhat belated in their appearance, as well
as less homogeneous and less organized than their hawkish
counterparts. The land-for-peace option hardly seemed viable in

the wake of the Six Day War, and only a few individuals were willing to engage in "peace activity." The Movement for Peace and Security was founded in July 1967, but it failed to muster sufficient organizational resources for an enduring existence. Its activists, mainly faculty members of the Hebrew University of Jerusalem, apparently lacked organizaitonal skills. Still, the group did pose an ideological alternative (Isaac 1976).

The demise of the Movement for Peace and Security did not silence the dovish voice. Following President Sadat's visit to Jerusalem on November 19, 1977, Peace Now was established by students and staff of the Hebrew University who were high-ranking army reserve officers. In a public letter printed in the daily press of March 8, 1978, the organization's founders urged Prime Minister Begin to choose the path to peace. Peace Now could not be considered a regular protest group in that it was not formed to bring an end to an ongoing war (as were its United States counterparts during the Vietnam War); nor did it target its efforts on the accelarated militarization of the region, as did its European anti-nuclear counterparts. Rather, Peace Now propagated a policy option: willingness on the part of Israel to negotiate territories in return for peace. Since the eruption of the *intifada*, Peace Now has advocated an open dialogue with the Palestinians (i.e., P.L.O.), based on mutual recognition and abandonment of terror, and is regarded as the spokesman of the dovish mood in the Israeli polity. The movement has encountered some organizational difficulties and, in fact, has chosen to remain unstructured. Until the late 1980s, it never established bureaucratic bodies, had an elected leadership, or dispensed membership cards. It was not until 1989 that Peace Now started to undergo a process of institutionalization.[8]

The scope of Peace Now's support is hard to determine. Over the years, some 200,000 people have signed Peace Now petitions; its demonstrations are said to have attracted up to 100,000 participants (Bar-On 1985: 75). Despite this seemingly impressive success, Peace Now has suffered from a major disadvantage: compared to Gush Emunim, its level of internal cohesion is rather low. Peace Now provides a clear position as to what Israel should not do—it should not forcibly control 1.5 million hostile Palestinians. It is equivocal as to what should be done instead. Should Israel return all conquered lands or parts of them, and if so, to whom, when, and under which circumstances? These questions are not clearly answered by Peace Now, whose leadership has chosen ambiguity in order to mobilize the widest possible constituency willing to trade land for peace. Its vagueness proved detrimental in that it triggered fragmentation in both directions. Those opposing dialogue with Arafat thought that the movement was going too far in appeasing the Palestinians. Recalcitrants on the "left" side of the spectrum believe that Peace Now has failed to counter the authorities and that it portrays only half-hearted opposition to the continued events in the territories.

Dovish radicalism has contributed to the proliferation of peace groups—some thirty-six in all.[9] They advocate a variety of solutions to the Israeli-Palenstinian conflict, some based on the prompt, unconditional withdrawal of all Israeli forces from the territories to more or less the pre-1967 boundaries, and others based on less radical actions.[10] These protest groups endorse the establishment of an independent Palestinian state alongside Israel. The size of these groups and their impact on policy remains meager.

One cannot conclude the discussion of peace groups in Israeli politics without reference to the Lebanon war protest movement. Some dozen groups, including Peace Now, adamantly protested the war and demanded the retreat of the Israeli defense forces from the Lebanese territory. Some of these groups (e.g., Parents against Silence and Yesh Gvul, in Hebrew, "There is a Border/Limit") were better equipped with organizational resources. Most, however, had only a rudimentary structure; they never institutionalized and faded away even before the war was over (Yishai 1985b). None of these groups is included in the present research (except for Peace Now, which was not founded to protest the Lebanon war); but their appearance on the scene, against the background of a bloody war, reveals the change that has swept Israeli society. The significance of these groups lies far beyond their organizational activity. The unprecedented breaking of the rule of silence while the guns were roaring demonstrated that an era of new politics had forced its entry and taken hold of the country. The period of "Israelis of silence" had passed.

Charity groups

Israel might appear to offer an inhospitable environment for voluntary groups because it displays a major condition regarded by social scientists as blocking the development of such organizations: a tradition of central power. As Ralph Kramer, a leading expert on Israeli voluntary activity, has noted, "The outstanding feature of the Israeli power structure is the influence concentrated

in a few, highly centralized bureaucratic and political institutions"
(1981: 89). This has had the effect of inhibiting the creation of
large-scale voluntary services. The resultant lack of grassroots participation has also been described as one of the prominent features
of Israel's political culture (Fein 1967). Secondly, it has been widely believed that the state is responsible for solving almost any
social problem. The over-reliance on the state is a common feature
of most new nations. Elon observed that the Jews have waited a
long time for their sovereignty and eventually fought for it; the
demands on their government, therefore, are exorbitantly high:
"The government is expected to achieve—short of turning men
into women and women into men—practically everything else
from peace, prosperity, and the pursuit of happiness to high
wages, low prices, comfort, liberty, order, . . . even love, especially from the foreign press" (1971: 290). Thirdly, the practice of performing social functions within small units is largely absent. As
earlier described, a large volume of social services, including
medical care, child care, and care for the elderly, among others,
was provided by political parties and their extensions. The near
monopolization of this domain in the past greatly diminished the
space left for nonpartisan charity organizations. Finally, a major
prerequisite for the development of large-scale voluntary activity
was also missing in the early days of statehood: this is a middle
class with sufficient discretionary time and income for voluntary
activity. The defense burden, the economic hardships, and the
need for an overwhelming proportion of the population to adjust
to a new country, a new language, and a new culture, and often to
undergo occupational changes, as well, all greatly militated
against charity activity within the framework of voluntary
associations. The time, money, and energy available were severely
limited. In any case, most of the "participation space," that is, the
discretionary time available for voluntary work, was preempted
by political and religious groups rather than by social service agencies.

Yet there were also some conditions fostering the charity
associational activity. One was the sense of mutual responsibility
and of reciprocal guarantee, a basic feature of Jewish society. It is
corroborated by religious tenets and commandments to "help thy
brother." It is also a product of the hardships encountered by the
Jews when dispersed among the nations. Voluntarism geared at
collective values was also nurtured during the prestate era, when
authority was vested in informal bodies; these invigorated the
sense of reciprocal obligations. In recent years, with increased af-

fluence, the social role of a volunteer has been turning into a source of prestige and a channel for political mobility, as is the case in other Western societies (Kramer 1981: 93). Charity interest groups concentrate on health issues, and they represent interests of the handicapped, and the underprivileged. The two most prestigious, well-funded associations are the Cancer Association and the Heart Society. They were initiated mainly by professionals, and are staffed by members of the political and social elites. The two groups not only perform functions to supplement government activity, they actually substitute for it. The Cancer Association, in fact, is responsible for a large network of institutions dealing with the prevention and cure of the disease; it operates clinics for the early detection of cancer and purchases the most advanced technological equipment for its treatment.

Associations for the handicapped are not necessarily comprised of those who were or are inflicted by a physical or mental handicap, although in the case of handicapped children their parents may be the instigators and the activists of the group. The Society for the Education of Deaf Children (Micha) and the Association for the Advancement of Retarded Children (Akim) are typical examples. Each association is responsible for a certain problem and in charge of a particular handicap; however, the lines between the numerous groups are not clearly defined. A retarded individual may also suffer from deafness; a paralyzed child may demonstrate learning difficulties. Some of the associations for the handicapped concentrate on defense-related welfare. Some of these groups are not unique to Israel. An association of veterans providing welfare (and other) services to its members exists in every country that engaged in an armed struggle in the present century. In Israel there are additional associations which were generated by the specific role of security in the Israeli society. These include the Association on Behalf of the Soldiers; one of the largest and best-known promotional interest groups in the country, it enjoys direct access to the ministry of defense and in fact operates under its auspices, albeit with a large degree of autonomy.

Protest associations are also included in this category because their major activity is targeted at improving the general welfare of their sector in society and disseminating egalitarian norms. Protest movement activists enumerated under this section did not organize in order to defend their own interests, but rather to bring about social change and to improve the lot of the underprivileged. Their goal is thus not (only) material but also largely promotional. They demand a change of priorities, a different structure of the political agenda that would lead eventually to a redistribution of national resources.

Authentic social protest activity in Israel is extremely scarce and unorganized. Grassroots associations have been set up in urban neighborhoods to enable their dwellers to contribute to the renewal project instigated by the Likud in 1977. Their impact on the national level was nil. Two groups in this category have, however, made themselves well known: the Black Panthers and Zehavi. The first public appearance of the Black Panthers was on March 3, 1971, in a demonstration staged in Jerusalem by young Israelis of Morrocan origin, most of whom were unemployed and stricken by poverty and distress. The panthers were largely assisted by welfare workers and members of the Social Work Faculty of the Hebrew University. The immediate goal was to establish a countrywide protest movement incorporating all the underprivileged in the urban neighborhoods and in the development towns. Their long-range objectives were to erase inequality and advance Israel toward its vision as an egalitarian society. The panthers accused state authorities of deliberate discrimination against Sephardic Jews and made efforts to heighten self-awareness of the ethnic identity, especially among those who had immigrated from Morocco. The Black Panthers' protest was militant and hostile, like the American group whose name they took. They ripped apart the image of the integrated melting pot that had until then been prevalent in Israel and demanded radical social changes.

Although the panthers did succeed in advancing the issues of the underprivileged to the top of the agenda, and induced important social legislation, their protest activity soon dwindled. The reasons for their demise are grounded in organizational incompetence, in the negative image of their leaders, in internal disputes, and especially in the successful cooptation of the group's militants by the political establishment. Continuous intimidation by recurring fines, arrests, and other legal means also detracted from the group's popularity (Cohen 1972; Peres 1976; Bernstein 1979). The panthers attempted to enter the political arena by submitting lists in several electoral contests, but failed to secure Knesset representation. At present there is no heir to the Black Panthers, since ethnic grievance has been channeled mainly to the partisan arena. A growing number of Sephardic representatives were recruited into the existing party structure. Ethnic protest activity was nipped in its budding.

Zehavi (Hebrew for "My Gold"), the group for assisting large families, presents a more institutionalized aspect of protest. Zehavi did not portray the anomic features that characterize many protest movements. Rather, it featured organizational attributes common among welfare-charity associations.[11] Zehavi, though it also represents part of the panthers' constituency, differs from that group in both social composition and objectives. It does not instigate street demonstrations tainted with violence but employs conventional lobbying techniques. It does not combat discrimination; instead it emphasizes the advantages of large families. Zehavi does protest deprivation, but by different means. It demands public acknowledgment, through legislation, of the national importance of high fertility as a means of encountering the demographic danger. It also fosters Jewish tradition in encouraging multiple-children families. Many Zehavi members have large families of their own and, therefore, have a direct material stake in the activity of their group; but many others became active in this movement because they believe in the idea and deem it necessary for Israel's progress and welfare.

Religious, sports, and cultural associations

The religious associational scene is rife with militancy and violence. The causes of disruptions are numerous: among others, archaeological or construction excavations, (allegedly violating the rest of ancient Jewish bones), public traffic on the Sabbath, and obscene billboard advertisements. In fact almost any public dissension on religious affairs takes a blatant form. One commentator defined the situation like this: "The understatement, the doubt, are unfamiliar to the religious community. The orthodox milieu is featured by exaggerations, by extremities, the intensity of life and its vigorous course are reflected not only in ideological and public affairs, but also in daily life" (Levy 1988: 11).[12]

Religious groups mushroom in the secluded ultra-orthodox community, whose strongholds are some sections of Jerusalem and the town of Bnei Brak. This community is highly fragmented, sundered by deep rifts prompting much associational activity. Some of the religious groups, though, are institutionalized. The Committee for the Integration of the Nation was founded in 1970, during one of the recurrent crises over the problem of "Who is a Jew?" The committee, whose sole purpose is to pressure the Knesset into amending the Law of Return to reflect a strictly orthodox view of Jewish identity, is a genuine lobby. It is linked with Habad, the United States-headquartered Hassidic sect, and enjoys an abundant flow of foreign resources.

Another group, Yad Leachim (A Hand to the Brothers), is active against the allegedly missionary activity of numerous Christian associations that operate freely in Israel. It is the most structured among the Jewish religious associations.[13] Founded in 1950 to protect the religious rights of the immigrants, especially those from Arab-speaking countries, Yad Leachim greatly expanded both in goals and in resources. In the 1980s, one of the targets of its activity was the Mormon university in Jerusalem which was accused of harboring intentions to proselytize Jews. Anti-religious legislation, or what is seen as such (e.g., the liberalization of abortions and the lenient practices of post-mortem operations), has triggered the formation of various, at times ad hoc, religious groups whose aim is to safeguard the Jewish attributes of Israel.

The prosperous activity of the religious associations has not been matched by advocates of the secular way of life. In the past (in the early 1950s), a group was formed—the League Against Religious Coercion—whose goal was to counter religious pressures and curb their influence. The group failed to establish a stable organizational structure. It could not compete with the religious stream's masses of manpower, many of whom were readily mobilized in their institutions of learning, nor could it match the flow of funds from partisan and rabbinical sources. Perhaps most important for its ineffectiveness, it could not have offered a viable solution to the ever-present dilemma of Israel as a Jewish state. In the 1980s a roof organization gathering together representatives of numerous secular and orthodox groups, including the Reform and Conservative Jewish movements, was founded. Termed HEMDAT (acronym of A Public Committee for the Freedom of Science, Religion, and Culture), it is loosely organized and is not publicly acknowledged as the voice of secular Judaism.

Sports associations are crosscut by type of activity (e.g., soccer, basketball, tennis) and organizational affiliations, which are traditionally linked to political parties. The Labor movement has its own sport associations, and so do the religious camp and the right-wing parties. Two roof associations—the Israeli Olympic Committee and the Sports Federation—coordinate the activities of the various sports associations.

Conclusions

This chapter has highlighted the large variety of Israeli interest groups as well as the features they share in common. Elitism is still evident in the group arena. The partisan interest groups are both heterogeneous and centralized. The Histadrut presents a large variety of subunits, crosscutting all occupational and professional domains; it nearly monopolizes the representation of salaried workers in Israel. The agricultural sector is divided on the basis of partisan orientations. It, too, portrays a concentrated organizational structure. The economic group arena presents a picture akin to corporatism. Even in cases where interests conspicuously collide—e.g., between exporters and importers—groups tend to coordinate their activities under roof organizations. The organization of Lahav, the sector for the self-employed, ostensibly refutes the rule of concentration. The fact, however, that the newly established association is excluded from participation in national forums indicates that the associational system is not only a concentrated one, it also tends to be closed, thus providing perfect conditions for corporatism. The professional arena is less concentrated than other occupational sectors. The professional groups' division between unions operating under the umbrella of the Histadrut and associations preoccupied with professional issues hindered concentration. Attempts to establish a roof organization for professional groups (like the Swedish SACO) have repeatedly failed. Yet each association does represent its respective sector. Only one interest group speaks on behalf of the Israeli physicians; only one association represents the social workers.[14] This concentration provides a congenial environment for the development of corporatist practices.

The structure of the promotional associational arena is more proximate to the pluralist paradigm. Issue-oriented groups are highly fragmented and much less concentrated. As a rule, though, Israeli promotional associations do not mirror their Western counterparts. Those domains attracting most attention in industrial democracies are conspicuously lacking in Israel. Here, environmental groups, consumer organizations, protest movements, and feminist associations are only fledgling and have not reached organizational maturity. Some groups are no more than "institutionalized personalities" (Sorauf 1976: 99). Charity associations, however, are more prominent. They fulfill an essential role congruent with Jewish tradition and contemporary welfare needs. Such groups play a vital advocacy role by monitoring social services and unloading some of the burden from the government's shoulders. Finally the groups that are linked to the Arab-Israeli conflict may be said to constitute the heroes of the promotional scene. They express issues of "high politics" (Hoffman 1966); and, in fact, their influence on public opinion and policy has been considerable. The universe of promotional associations thus clearly reflects the priorities set by the national agenda. As predicted by Truman (1951), a political crisis prompts the intensification of group activity. At present in Israel, this is channeled mostly toward a solution of the country's painful foreign struggle, largely turned into a domestic issue by the intensive group activity.

CHAPTER THREE

Interest Groups and Political Parties:
Patrons, Partners, or Rivals?

Classical liberal democratic theory draws a clear distinction between political parties and interest groups (Almond and Powell 1966). Parties aggregate a wide variety of interests; they control the government and through it the state machinery. Interest groups are seen only as promoting narrowly defined causes. They function separately from the state and convey social demands to the parties, which aggregate and integrate the demands into a general program. The process, according to some analysts, puts the two on different planes: "The political party stands between the special 'unaggregated' demands of the interest groups and the authoritative decision-making of the parliament and the bureaucracy" (Ehrmann 1958: 4). This description may be valid to Anglo-American democracies, where the pluralist model is more compelling. It is quite inaccurate, though, for elitist or corporatist configurations. In the first instance, associations are integrated into the party system; in the second, they replace them as a means of securing influence.

Blurring of the lines between political parties and interest groups is more pertinent to party states such as Israel, where parties are credited with being the most important channel of communication in the political system. Here the parties are not only in control of the government, they are also extensively involved in the social life of the country. The highly organized community of prestate Israel was characterized by the existence of many different types of groups (Eisenstadt 1972; Horowitz and Lissak 1977: 167-171), most of them institutionally affiliated with a political

unions exist independently of the party, and maintain an autonomous federation, they have a variety of mechanisms linking them to the party. For its part, the Labor party depends on the unions for membership and, partly, for finance. By virtue of their automatic membership in the party, union members represent the largest bloc of votes—40 percent—at the British Labor party conferences. They thus play a major role in the running of the party, and in the election of the party leader (Jordan and Richardson 1987: 246).

In Israel the situation is much the reverse. It was the trade union that was dependent on the party, which established it. The Histadrut does not constitute an organized faction within the party and is not granted official representation in the party's institutions. It has nevertheless been an integral part of political life. The relationship of the Histadrut with the Labor party were manifest in three domains: internal elections, selection of leadership, and funding.

The Histadrut internal elections serve as an arena for party rivalry. The date for Histadrut elections is determined by party leadership guided by considerations of party benefits (Yanai 1981: 164–250). Members are urged by their respective parties to cast their ballot on the basis of their party affiliation rather than on the basis of union issues. Since its inception the Histadrut has adopted a parliamentary-type electoral system. Delegates to its national convention are elected on party lists in a system of proportional representation which is akin to national elections. The legislative bodies of the Histadrut are composed of party representatives according to the election results. The competition for the control of the Histadrut is thus a microcosm of the national rivaly for control of government. The actual control of the Histadrut executive bodies is based, however, on the principle of "winner takes all." The party that secured a majority in the elections to the national convention controls the central committee as well as the social and economic Histadrut enterprises. Although coalitions have been invariably formed, the opposition had a limited influence on the management of the Histadrut affairs. The Labor party (including Achdut Haavoda and Rafi) and Mapam constituted the historic parties controlling the Histadrut. The practice of majority rule ensured the party governing the Histadrut complete control of its affiliated groups. The foundation of the party's predominance lies in the work places, in the workers committees, and in the local workers councils. To date, there is not one single local workers council in the country in which the Labor party does not enjoy a majority, and with it control of the most important executive positions.[1]

Although parties affiliated with the Labor party have controlled the governing bodies of the Histadrut and its enterprises, factions affiliated with other parties were included in its broader institutions. These included nearly the whole gamut of political organizations in Israel: a General Zionist faction (subsequently the labor sector in the Independent Liberal party), a faction associated with the communist party and a religious faction organized in the Histadrut in the prestate era. The union of the Liberal party joined the Histadrut in 1955; in 1965 a faction affiliated with Herut attempted to enter the Labor Federation. The founding parties sought to prevent its entrance but were overruled by a court decree. In the mid-1960s the Histadrut turned into a multiparty organization. The NRP and Poalei Agudat Israel participate in the trade union department and medical insurance service of the Histadrut. Only ultra (nonlabor) religious parties remained outside the Labor Federation's political framework.

Partisanship of the trade union is clearly demonstrated in the nomination to Histadrut public offices. Selection of leadership was—and still is—controlled by party headquarters. The secretary general, the top Histadrut leader, was selected by his or her party. Although this individual is usually given some say in selecting associates for the Histadrut's executive, the list of nominees is composed by a party caucus. If not exactly rubber stamps, Histadrut leaders usually have been open to direction. In any event, most of their decisions and policies were first deliberated and thoroughly aired in party bodies. The influence of the party was once so deep that any issue, however minor it might have seemed, was discussed in Mapai decision-making bodies. This, however, never implied that the party could dictate to the Histadrut, and two former secretaries general (Pinhas Lavon and Yitzhak Ben Aharon) exercised such assertive leadership as to effectively abrogate the party's authority (Tokatly 1979). The vast majority of Histadrut leaders, however, did not employ the enormous organizational resources at their disposal to challenge the party's authority. In fact there is much evidence to the contrary.

The party not only determined the composition of the Histadrut governing bodies but established a bureaucracy on whose loyalty it could count. The Labor Federation served as a primary source for providing employment to Labor party activists. A study of a local Histadrut leadership (in Haifa) found that close to half of the members of the local party's secretariat were employed by the Histadrut (Weiss and Ben-Dor 1973). The Histadrut also served as a channel of mobility to higher political posts. About a third of the heads of municipalities elected on Mapai lists between 1950 and 1967 had served previously as secretaries of local workers councils (Weiss 1970). The Histadrut local council was responsible in many cases for the municipal activities of the labor parties.

The relations between the Histadrut and its member parties are strengthened by financial links. Membership dues are paid to Histadrut in the form of a tax calculated on a sliding scale according to income. About two-thirds of the fees are allocated to the Sick Fund; the remainder to cover the budget of Histadrut organizational activity. Since 1969 an additional expenditure item has been introduced: financing the Labor Federation's member parties. The background of this arrangement lies in the prestate era. When the Histadrut was founded, the labor affiliated parties suspended their economic ventures and were in need of financial support. The Histadrut filled this need, although intermittently and unofficially. As pointed out by Yanai (1981: 167) the grant-in-aid (to the party) was legitimized by a tacit agreement among the historic parties of the Histadrut. Since 1969 the practice became legalized and fully institutionalized.

The roots of this arrangement lie in the law for the Protection of Remuneration, Amendment No. 5, 1968, ensuring that every worker in Israel receives remuneration for his or her work on time and in full as an elementary right. To safeguard this right the law prohibited deductions from one's work pay, with certain exceptions sanctioned by law. The "party tax" was one of these exceptions, although not the first one. A law enabled deduction of fees for membership in a union from all employees, provided that workers' remuneration were set on the basis of a collective negotiated agreement. However, since affiliation with a workers' organization is not mandatory, an amendment was introduced permitting the employer to deduct the expenses of organizational and trade union protection from a salary even when the worker did not belong to a union. This amendment led to another which permitted an additional deduction for party financing "other than if the worker has informed the employer in writing of his/her objection to the payment" (*Sefer Hachukim* 1968: 256). The law was subject to much criticism. Among other things called into question was the financing of political parties by a voluntary association (the Histadrut), a practice which violated norms of equity. It was nevertheless approved by an overwhelming majority of MKs. The institution of an official appropriation to Histadrut member parties fully legalized the flow of funds from the interest group to political parties.

The triad practices of elections, leadership selection, and funding blurred the boundaries between political parties and the Labor Federation, which was practically identified with the Labor party. With the passage of time, however, the Histadrut began slipping out of the party's control. Three major developments are responsible for the shift that has reformulated the Histadrut–Labor party relationship: the inter-party rivalry within the Histadrut, the declining role of the party in national economic policy making, and the changing party's agenda.

The emergence of a competitive multiparty system in the Histadrut contributed to the weakening relations between the Labor Federation and the Labor party. Mapai has been motivated to exploit its majority position within the Histadrut to tighten control over all affiliated groups, but it always had to share its rule with other parties. Even at the height of the party's power the Histadrut leadership never consisted only of members of this one party. Mapam, the left-wing, Zionist-Socialist party, had broken with Mapai on the national political level but continued to share power in the Histadrut executive. The intra-Histadrut coalition facilitated the eventual resumption of cooperation between the two parties, and the return of Mapam to the ideological and political mainstream of the Israel labor movement. Labor's formation of an electoral alignment with Mapam (between 1969 and 1984) was also instigated by this cooperation, which in return enabled Mapam to increase its power within the Histadrut's executive. The political variety within the Histadrut turned out to be much more problematic when the Herut faction joined its ranks.The Histadrut leadership had to cope with internal opposition which was at times extremely blatant.

The partisan heterogeneity of the Histadrut is clearly reflected in the election results to the Histadrut conventions (see figure 3.1). Although the Labor party still enjoys a comfortable majority and its control has not been seriously jeopardized, erosion in power is manifest. In the early years of statehood the parties identified with the Labor Alignment (i.e., Mapai, Achdut Haavoda, Mapam, Rafi, Haoved Hadati) won overwhelming majorities (over 90 percent of the vote.) The decline in Labor's support was primarily noticed in 1969, after the Likud was granted entrance to the

Histadrut. What had been a steady drop became a fall of more than 15 percent, and the alignment received only 62.1 percent of the vote. Further erosion in the next two elections left socialist parties in 1977 with little more than half of the vote (55.3 percent). In 1981, 1985, and 1989 the parties affiliated with the alignment regained some of their strength.

Fig. 3.1. Election Results to the Histadrut Convention, 1949-1989, by Political Blocs

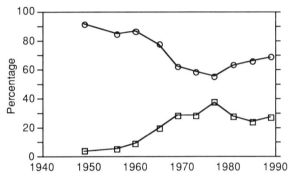

Source: Report submitted to the Histadrut Convention.
*Includes Mapai, Achdut Haavoda, Rafi, Labor party, Mapam
**Includes Igud Ovdim, State List, Liberal Labor Movement, Tchelet Lavan (Herut), Free Center

o   Percentage of Vote for Labor Alignment*   □   Percentage of Vote for Likud**

Although the Likud factions have never attained more than 28 percent of the vote to the Histadrut national convention, they constitute a real threat to the Histadrut leadership. The Likud's major source of power lies especially with the "workers," those holding manual, blue-collar jobs, the majority of whom are traditional Likud supporters in the national elections. The phenomenon of a "right wing proletariat" (Yishai 1982a) is not unique to Israel. Those voters whom Nordlinger (1967) has called "Working Class Tories" can be found in large numbers in several political systems, especially in Great Britain. In Israel, however, the affiliation of the blue-collar workers with the Blue and White political party (i.e., the Likud promoting nationalistic values) has had far-reaching implications for the political system. The possible transformation of Histadrut dominance from the Labor party to the Likud has so far not been structurally manifested within the Labor Federation; however, the fact that the intensification of inter-party rivalry within the Histadrut has been occurring simultaneously with the decline of Labor's appeal on the national ballot has influenced party-group relations. The vested interests of the Histadrut leadership are often incongruent with those of its patron party. Governing the Labor Federation has turned into a goal in itself, not only as a means to increase the power of the party. The internal Histadrut politics are not isolated from party competition in the national arena, but the rules of the game are changing. A split of votes between national elections and Histadrut elections is gradually spreading. The success of the labor faction in the 1989 Histadrut elections (which obtained 55.5 percent of the vote) was attained in spite of its links with the Labor party and not because of them.

Patterns of policy making also reveal the attenuation of group (Histadrut)–party linkage. Wage negotiations serve as an example. In his seminal book on historical Mapai, Peter Medding described the complicated process for determining wages in the early years of statehood. The Histadrut had the potential to bring down the government, and it was able to impose on the employers, and the rest of the country, any wage policy that it desired. The exercise of its power was constrained, however, not only by its national vision but also by its affinity to the ruling party. The tension between the government, as a major employer, and the Histadrut, the representative of the employees, did not develop into a rift precisely because both were controlled by the same party. The power that the Labor party acquired through this dual supremacy was a major incentive for reaching compromises. Medding described the critical role played by the party in the process of decision making:

> Where disagreements occurred between the party's representatives in the government and in the Histadrut, no matter how powerful and prestigious these individuals were, they had to come to the party and its decision making bodies for settlement of the dispute. In short, the party, as such, decided the country's wage policy. In this context it mattered little that the major contenders were the Mapai ministers and the Histadrut leaders, the significant thing was that the forum that decided the matter was a party one . . . a number of recognized party bodies on which were represented all sections of the party. (1972: 206–207)

By the 1980s, the picture had dramatically changed. To begin with, the "party" was no longer the chief arbiter in wage negotiations. These are held directly between the Histadrut and the Coordinating Office, as representatives of the employers. The role of the Histadrut in determining wages has largely increased since the

early days of Mapai's unchallenged control. Until 1977, a joint
party-Histadrut committee determined policy. Since then, as one
of the labor Federation's activists observed, "it is a different party
and a different Histadrut." No such committee operates; policy is
determined by direct negotiations between the representatives of
labor, of business, and of the state.

Another reason for the weakening relations between the
Histadrut and the Labor party is the change in the latter's agenda.
Mapai was established as the party of the Israeli workers. A major
item on its agenda was defending the rights of the working class.
Mapai was obviously a Zionist party, but it also propagated
socialism, the implementation of which was to be carried by the
trade union. In the late 1960s Mapai unified with other parties, but
retained its laborite title. In practice, however, it veered from its
socialist tradition. The Labor party's agenda reflected social
changes: the growing proportion of university-trained workers in
the labor force, the rise in the standard of living, and the shift of
the economy from traditional patterns of production to
sophisticated, technological industry. The Labor party gradually
forfeited its "proletarian" identity and adopted a plank portraying
efficiency, affluence, and economic modernization. These targets
were incompatible with traditional trade unionism. The Labor
party, furthermore, attempted to widen its constituency. To this
end the party blurred its programs and offered an ambiguous
foreign policy; it was also equivocal in regard to socioeconomic
problems. In its attempt to become a catch-all party, the Labor
party in the 1980s has parted from its socialist traditions. In fact, it
has adopted a "statist" orientation which does not necessarily
favor the Histadrut hard-core constituency over other social sectors, but takes into consideration the needs of the economy at
large. The party courted the employers and became identified with
the affluent sectors of society. It is not unusual for the Histadrut to
rally against a policy initiated by a Labor party minister. The
Labor Federation is, in fact, often bitterly pitted against the party
with which it is affiliated. The marriage between the Histadrut and
the Labor party appears to be based more on convenience than on
love. The parentela relations, founded on the affinity of kin, seem
to be replaced by cost-benefit calculations, akin to clientele relations.

A word of caution is in order regarding the implications of the
foregoing picture of events. Although the linkage between the
Histadrut and the Labor party has attenuated, the Labor Federation is still much politicized. The candidates for the post of

secretary general are still determined by the party. Similarly, the candidates for the local workers councils are chosen by party headquarters. Histadrut elections are seen as an arena for partisan competition, with the two major parties (Labor and Likud) devising strategies and investing resources to mobilize public support and to win the vote. Furthermore, the relationship between the Labor party and the Histadrut has survived changes in the makeup of the government. Labor's drop in electoral power produced a dual effect: it increased the Histadrut's autonomy, and it generated a growing dependence by the party on the Labor Federation's political and economic power. Actually the relationship between party and group may be described as mutual, as the economic crisis which racked the Histadrut in the mid-1980s demonstrated. This crisis, which brought the Histadrut enterprises to the verge of bankruptcy, was a major reason for Labor Alignment's giving its consent to join the 1988 coalition government as a minor partner.

Party patronage of trade union activity in Israel is thus not a historical phenomenon; it is part of the current politics of the country. Despite the evident signs of departization it is apparently inconceivable in contemporary Israel to raise issues or advocate stands related to trade union activity apart from partisan politics.

The agricultural sector. Israel's agricultural sector is dominated by political parties of different political shades and ideological strands. The National Religious Party and even the ultra-orthodox Poalei Agudat Israel have a kibbutz movement, and so did the Independent Liberal party. Herut, mostly an urban-centered party, has its own moshav movement. The dominant parties that serve as patrons of settlement organizations, however, are those affiliated with the Labor movement.

Until 1948, much of Mapai's leadership and vision were to be found in the agricultural sectors (the kibbutz and the moshav), which embodied the socialists' most cherished ideals. Although the party membership was mostly urban, farming was the jewel in the crown. The strength of the agricultural sector emanated from its ideological primacy and organizational advantages. The kibbutz movement offered the party the following three major assets:

- Party leaders could readily be drawn from the kibbutz, whose members could more easily devote themselves to a full-time political career on its behalf. The collective system's principle of "mutual responsibility" relieved them from their daily chores as family providers to enable party activism. The kibbutzim could free members for political activity without undermining the collective's economic basis. In 1942, for example, five of the seven members of Mapai's inner secretariat were members of kibbutzim.

- The cooperative style of life in agricultural settlements provided the party with a loyal constituency, whose support in the polls was taken for granted. The lack of tolerance to deviant behavior in these small, closed communities minimized the chances of individual defections, although splits on ideological grounds did occur in the kibbutz movement.

- The cooperative settlement movement could provide the party with organizational resources that were useful during elections. Kibbutz members distributed leaflets, drove cars, made telephone calls, and engaged in all other kinds of campaign activies; they could do so without risking their jobs or, alternatively, without becoming professional party activists. The mass of kibbutz members remained amateurs, whose devotion was unquestioned and whose organizational skills were of much use. When the financial contribution of the kibbutzim to the party's electoral effort was added to the manpower resource, the kibbutz offered the party a considerable advantage.

The relationship of the parties with the moshav movement were founded on a different basis. Having a lesser degree of collective organization and a narrower range of communalism than the kibbutz, the moshav could not dispense manpower or organizational resources for party purposes. Historical connections and large-scale identification with the party, albeit on a more individual basis, was evident, however. In part of the moshav movement affiliated with Mapai, for example, organizational affiliation with parties other than the "patron" was officially banned, not by the individual decisions of the settlers or their communities, but by the general rules of the movement (Medding 1972: 35). The numerical advantage of the moshavim over the kibbutzim turned the political loyalty of the former into a major political asset. In addition, members of moshavim were urged to fulfill national goals at the service of the party. A typical example was Ben-Gurion's call, in the mid-1950s to settle the Negev and assist the new moshavim with the perplexing absorption process.

What benefits accrued to the members of the settlement movement in return for their organizational efforts and political loyalty? Succinctly put, they reaped both economic and political rewards: favorable distributive policies and representation. Until

1977, the settlement movement enjoyed large-scale financial aid in the form of loans and grants, which enabled it to acquire modern agricultural equipment and to develop sophisticated industrial enterprises. Moreover, nationally owned land and natural resources were given to the kibbutzim on a non-profit basis (Brum 1986). No less prominent were their political advantages. The proportion of settlement movements' members in the party's national political institutions has always been higher than their numerical share in the population at large.

Their over-representation in party forums is conspicuous owing to the fact that, with one exception, settlement members do not constitute a major proportion of a party's membership (Sherman 1980: 156).[2] This prominent abundance of "farmers"—most of whom were not engaged in agricultural occupations—dates back to the prestate era. In 1938, for example, settlers constituted 32.3 percent of the members of Mapai, but were represented by 51.7 percent of the delegates to the national convention (Ben-Avram 1976: 150–151). In the last census taken by the Labor party (in 1984), some 27,000 kibbutz residents were registered as party members, amounting to 10 percent of the total party membership; but they accounted for some 18 percent of the party's executive (Yanai 1987: 119). Fearing, nevertheless, that their over-representation advantage may be declining, the kibbutzim offered to impose a high poll tax that would have increased the proportion of their membership in the party and decreased the share of those who had to pay dues on an individual basis. The party rejected this kibbutz ploy and made due with a sum that was presumably more attractive to its urban members.

The shrinking kibbutz representation in the Knesset shows that the apprehension was justified. From 1977 to 1988, the number of MKs from kibbutzim remained stable, with a proportion still far higher than the share of the kibbutzim in total population (see figure 3.2). Nevertheless, the present picture is markedly different from that of the past. Judged by criteria of representation, parentela relations between kibbutzim and political parties have been seriously eroded.

The diminishing role of the agricultural sector is also manifested in the cabinet (see figure 3.3).[3] From the 1960s until Labor's electoral defeat in 1977, the representatives of the agricultural sector regularly constituted a third of the government. A peak was reached in the 13th government (1966–1967) with seven of the eighteen ministers, or 38.8 percent. Among the settlement-member ministers were senior national leaders. One of

Fig. 3.2. Kibbutz Members in Knesset and Population 1949-1988

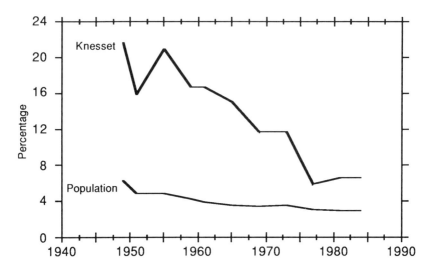

the chief contenders for the premiership, Yigal Allon, was a member of a kibbutz, and so was (in a previous government) Prime Minister Golda Meir's chief political advisor, Yisrael Galili. Moshe Dayan, Israel's most famous general, was a member of a moshav, although he, too, preferred to reside in the city. The rise to power of the Likud left the kibbutzim out of the government, and the moshavim were granted representation through minor coalition parties. With the establishment of the National Unity government in 1984, the settlement movement regained ministerial portfolios. In the government formed after the 1988 elections, Labor was allotted thirteen portfolios; although two of these were handed to members of kibbutzim, they constituted a minority in the cabinet. Thus the size of the government as well as its composition has pushed the agricultural sector to the periphery.

Over-representation of the farming sector in the past resulted from ideological consanguinity and political affinity. But the overarching electoral loyalty of the kibbutz membership proved evanescent in the 1980s, as table 3.1 demonstrates. In 1981, the percentage of Alignment voters in the two labor-affiliated kibbutz movements (Kibbutz Artzi and Takam) was 95 percent and 93 percent, respectively. In 1984 the figure declined to 83 percent each. This declining loyalty was not confined to the labor camp. Herut encountered the same erosion as the proportion of those voting

Fig. 3.3. Government Ministers from the Kibbutz and Moshav

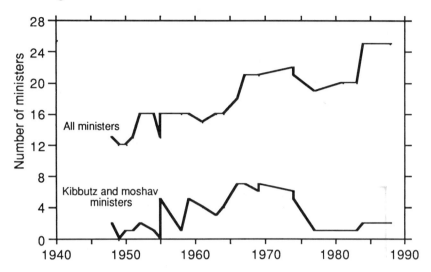

Likud in its moshav movement decreased from 81 percent in the elections to the 10th Knesset (1981) to only 65 percent in the next elections.

Table 3.1
Election Results in Agricultural Settlements, by Period of Establishment and Party Affiliation, 1984

	Population (thousands)	Party Affiliation	Veteran settlements	New settlements	Percent of gap
Moshav movements					
Tnuat Hamoshavim	86.4	Labor	73.5	47.3	−26.2
Hapoel Hamizrachi	27.0	NRP	45.5	41.3	− 4.3
Haoved Hatzioni	5.0	Labor	54.7	47.8	− 6.9
Ichud Hak Lai	13.4	Labor	58.2	44.7	−13.5
Poalei Agudat Israel	2.4	Morasha*	41.0	37.3	− 3.7
Herut	2.6	Likud	81.0	65.7	−15.3
Hitachudut Haikarim	1.5	Likud	26.7	39.4	+12.7
Kibbutz movements					
Takam	67.5	Labor	87.5	78.0	− 9.1
Kibbutz Artzi	38.5	Labor	87.7	79.3	− 8.4
Kibbutz Dati	6.5	NRP	51.7	42.8	− 8.9
Haoved Hatzioni	1.8	Labor	84.3	66.8	−17.5
Poalei Agudat Israel	1.2	Morasha*	90.1	75.8	−14.3

*In the 1981 elections the party was Poalei Agudt Israel.
Source: *Israel Statistical Abstract* 1985: 467; *Results of elections to the 11th Knesset*, 1984, Central Bureau of Statistics. Special Series no. 775, pp. 93–95.

The clearest indication of the parties' loosening grip on the settlement movements is provided by a comparison of election results in the veteran and the "new" settlements. The latter, which consists of those founded after the establishment of the state, are less inclined than their veteran counterparts to manifest electoral allegiance to the party with which their respective group is institutionally linked. This trend has been especially conspicuous in the new moshavim, inhabited mainly by Israelis of Asian-African origin. Although the proportion of those supporting Labor in the veteran moshavim was still rather high (73.5 percent) in 1984, less than half (47.3 percent) of the voters in the new moshavim cast their ballot for their patron party.

Party loyalty in general is less evident in the moshavim than in the kibbutzim (with the exception of the religious kibbutzim). But here, too, the scene is changing, as exemplified by the Kibbutz Artzi movement, affiliated with Mapam. In the past, the movement represented a most vivid example of a "group within a party"; in fact, no real demarcation existed between the two entities. Membership in the kibbutz entailed automatic membership in the party; each kibbutz was constituted as a party branch and conferred with organizational rights and duties. After Mapam withdrew from the alignment in 1984 and once again formed an autonomous political entity, the relationship between the kibbutz movement and the party further tightened. The organizational resources of the kibbutzim in this movement were imperative for the party's electoral prospects. Yet some cracks were undeniable even then in the cement of this structure. Those reflected utilitarian considerations more than patrimonial commitment, and led a widening circle of kibbutz members to begin exerting pressure on their leadership to attenuate, if not sever, their relations with the party. The cause was the gap between the party's egalitarian socialist values and the needs of the kibbutz movement to secure the largest possible share of the dwindling national pie. The words of the general secretary of the Kibbutz Artzi could not have been uttered a decade earlier: "The question is no longer how are we going to carry out our political cooperation [with the party—Mapam] but do we need this cooperation?"[4] This soul searching had been unheard of in the kibbutz movement whose integration with the party had never been called in question. It is possible that kin-based loyalties may persist at a somewhat reduced but still relatively high level among kibbutz and party. There is also a possibility, however, that family relations will be replaced by a more pluralistic pattern, in which rewards are traded for support.

Business associations. A weaker variant of groups within a party is those whose members are marginal to the party's mainstream. As a center of power and as a major channel of communication, a party may be a source of attraction to groups ranging across the ideological and sociological spectrum. For its part, a party may be more than willing to establish a stable relationship with certain groups that are able to deliver the most desired good—i.e., votes. This was the case regarding a few groups in the economic sector. The Association of Artisans and Small Industry is a typical example. The members of this group were neither pioneers nor an integrated part of the mainstream of the national endeavor in Israel. On the contrary, continuing as they did the traditional way of life practiced by Jews in exile, a way of life that was outrightly rejected by the ethos of Zionism, these tailors, shoemakers, shopkeepers, and other owners of small business were business oriented, great believers in free enterprise and economic freedom. Their natural inclination was toward right-wing parties sharing the same values. Yet the centripetal force of the ruling party was in full swing. The Association of Artisans Small Industry forged links with Mapai, which at the time was not based only on give and take. The group was not incorporated into the "family," yet it enjoyed many privileges. The powerful minister of finance, Pinhas Sapir, personally intervened to enhance the relationship by distributing political and economic rewards, albeit sparingly. Within a few years, an Artisans Bank was certified and the treasury increased the artisans' share in the national resources. Residential quarters were established throughout the country that instantly improved the working conditions of the artisans (Avneri 1976). The association's president, Yosef Fisher, was elected to the 4th Knesset (1959). The artisans were given recognition as a "district" within the party entitled for representation, and gained certain organizational benefits inherent in this status. The party went even further, stipulating the separation of membership in the party from membership in the Histadrut. This change in the party's regulations was necessary for accepting the artisans, who were not "salaried workers" but employers, into the ranks of the party.

The love story between the socialist Mapai and the artisans was short lived. In the absence of traditional links, common ideology, and similar background, relations between party and group gradually weakened. To be sure, Labor still courts the artisans and is involved in the nomination of their association's secretary-general, but the spirit of kinship is totally missing. No accurate data are available, but it is widely believed that most ar-

tisans vote Likud rather than Labor. Formally the Labor party
may still be the patron of the artisans, but the mood has changed.
The Association of Artisans & Small Industry has been forging
closer links with other economic groups and drifting away from
the circle of groups within parties. Other business groups, primarily the Manufacturers Association and the Chamber of Commerce,
were once believed to be associated with right-wing parties, but
they certainly were not groups within parties. In the 1980s their
orientation began shifting toward Labor, but the relationship is
not based on a parentela linkage.

Professional associations. The relationship of professional groups
with political parties may be characterized as ambiguous and
dynamic. Some of the professional associations were organized in
the Histadrut's Department for Professional Employees, as distinct
from the Trade Union Department. This device enabled the
smooth integration of professional groups into a partisan structure. Because of the professionals' greater inclination to individual
liberty and freedom, and because of their expectations for a higher
income relative to blue-collar workers, the methods of incorporation that prevailed with other social sectors were inappropriate for
professionals. The measure of independence that was accorded to
them did have a price, as Medding (1972: 62) has pointed out:
"While not necessarily in conflict with party and political commitments, they [the professional groups] competed with the party
for the interest and attention of the professional. Thus professional
ties were far less directly connected with political action than [was]
trade union activity among industrial workers."

In the past the Labor parties displayed interest in strengthening their links with professional associations (many of which
unionized) despite the low potential for electoral support. The major reason was the need to hold down the demands of the professionals, and to adjust them against both the interests of other
groups within the party and the objective reality of the Israeli
economic situation. The capacity to do all this was severely
limited. Mapai, which wanted to enlist the professionals' support,
was unwilling to pay with looking after their interests and fulfilling
their needs. The party regarded with disdain the functioning of independent professional associations of teachers, physicians, and
advocates; but it failed, despite repeated attempts, to incorporate
these groups into the Histadrut and to turn them into groups
within parties.

Some success to this end became visible when the Teachers
Federation became a full-fledged Histadrut union in 1949. In the

Teachers Federation internal elections held in June 1984, the Labor Alignment won 55.3 percent of the members' vote. The association's leaders are declared party activists, policies are coordinated with party headquarters, and party influence on all aspects of the federation is still rife. Attempts by the teachers to gain autonomy of their own internal organizational affairs have met with severe party reaction.[5] The Labor party's ombudsman banned nominations to the federation's institutions without prior consultation with the party. This strong party influence is evinced in all Histadrut-affiliated professional associations. Although the Engineers Federation once threatened to present a "non-partisan" list to the Histadrut elections, their threat was really a deliberate attempt to secure benefits: larger representation and more autonomy.[6] A clear distinction is thus evident between professional associations operating under the aegis of the Histadrut, which are highly politicized, and professional groups dissociated from the Labor Federation in which partization is subtle. In some professional associations individual partisan affiliations have no impact on the group's organizational behavior. The political identity of the Bar Association's leaders, for example, is well known, but is said to be irrelevant to their associational activity.

"Other" sectional groups

Immigrant associations. The fate of the immigrant associations has been similar to that of the artisans' group so far as political affiliation. By virtue of their large mobilization capacity, the *landsmanshaft* were deemed honorable members of the political family. The party had much to offer: jobs, housing, political integration, and social security. In seeking the support of immigrants, the parties (again, particularly Mapai) offered advantages deriving from the bureaucratically administered, centralized, and party-controlled process of immigration absorption (Eisenstadt 1954). In the agencies dealing with the problem of immigrant absorption, immigrants came into contact with officials who were party persons, playing the dual roles of official and party recruiter. Since Mapai had the greatest number of officials it could secure the best results, i.e., attract the most immigrants to its ranks. In order to facilitate the integration of immigrants, Mapai set up organizational structures that consisted of special departments based on country of origin. It also encouraged the establishment of immigrant associations, which were not financed by the group members, but by the party. By the mid-1960s, there were over thirty such associations, representing some 1.5 million newcomers to Israel (those who had arrived after independence). The party's hand was felt not only in matters of financing the associations but also in selecting their leaders. To coordinate the activities of the various immigrant associations, Mapai established a special section at its head-quarters (Medding 1972: 70). Its major function was to advise the different associations on their dealings with public authorities in all matters of immigrant absorption.

Despite these organizational solutions—and in part because of them—the efforts of the parties to integrate the newcomers into their structure were far from successful. A famous comic movie portrayed a new immigrant (Salah Shabati), who, courted by numerous parties, cast his vote for all of them as he was indebted to them all. The considerable decline in immigration from the late 1950s was also responsible for the attenuated party-group links. Many of the associations were no longer preoccupied with pro-viding absorption facilities, since the newcomers of the past had gradually become full-fledged Israelis, many of them preferring to sever their relations with the past and to shy away from any con-nection with their country of origin. At the same time, the party was no longer the effective mediator between the newcomer and the state; immigration absorption was largely monopolized by the bureaucracy.

Notwithstanding the changing patterns in the way immigrants were absorbed, immigrant associations still operate to some extent as groups within parties. Of the eighteen immigrant associations that were active in 1988, two-thirds were (weakly) affiliated with the Labor party. These include the big associations of immigrants from France and North Africa and immigrants from Rumania. The inter-party rivalry for such groups has led to a certain fragmenta-tion among immigrant associations. Thus Herut has its own organization of Russian *olim*, as does the Labor party. There are associations whose links with a party are not openly displayed, but whose leadership is "recommended" by the party's offices. In other cases, in which the relations with a party are overt, changes have taken place. The party no longer supports the association financially, and is not involved in the process of absorption. The provision of housing and employment, the two major deter-minants of absorption, was removed from the hands of the party, whose influence on these matters is now remarkably weak. Although the Labor party did recruit the leader of one immigrant association (Efraim Gur) to its Knesset list, it was not rewarded in the ballot.[7] Immigrant groups are thus to a lesser extent members of the partisan family.

Student unions. A good example of an interest group under the patronage of political parties and enjoying their financial and organizational support is the Student Union. The leadership of both the national and the local student associations is composed of partisan activists, of all shades of the political rainbow. The numerous lists competing for the students vote present a non-partisan platform, focusing on their clients immediate, mostly material, needs rather than on controversial national issues. Yet the student unions in Israel are imbued with partisanship. Party cells, which openly mobilize a student constituency, operate within each of the university student unions. When it comes to elections to the student union, parties place "their" candidates and finance their campaign. This partisan activity, which is very influential behind the scenes, may be crucial in determining the outcomes. Those elected are expected to pay the party back by furthering its interests among the general student body. The beholden student leadership, in turn, is accorded (modest) representation in national and local party organs.[8] In fact, activity in a student union is regarded as a springboard for future political career. Indeed, a "promising future" may be the only reward granted to student activists. Student activists often complain that they are given a "sand box" to play in and are not taken seriously by the party's headquarters. Yet a career in a student union is highly desired by young political aspirants.

Promotional groups

The number of groups within parties in the promotional category is limited. Prominent among those are some women's associations, sports clubs, and religious groups.

Public interests groups. The largest, most important women's association—Naamat—is organized within the broad framework of the Histadrut. Previously known as the Women Workers' Movement, it is a typical within-party group. The elections to its governing bodies are held in conjunction with Histadrut elections. The ruling party (Labor) has generally received over two-thirds of the vote, a proportion well in excess of the party's general Histadrut vote. A major reason for this electoral success can be found in the issues promoted by the women's association. The main focus of Naamat activity is in the less controversial domestic and residential domains. Country-wide branches provide essential services (such as day-care centers), which are valuable in mobilizing the female vote in the Histadrut elections. Noteworthy is the fact that despite the presumed effectiveness of women in socializing females into partisan identification, they have always been under-represented in party institutions (Yishai 1978b).

WIZO has tenuous relations with political parties. On the surface, the group remains non-partisan. Nevertheless, and despite the absence of institutional ties, the WIZO leadership has been identified with the Liberal party (previously the General Zionists). The Shedula (the Women's Lobby), too, has been penetrated by parties. The more visible it became on the national scene the more attractive it became for party infiltration. In the internal elections to the Shedula's executive, party activists have presented their candidacy and competed for leadership positions.

The links between the defense-related interest groups—Peace Now and Gush Emunim—and political parties tend to be ambiguous. Both groups have made deliberate decisions to refrain from becoming parties although a few of their leaders joined political parties and were elected on their behalf to the Knesset. Neither can be said to constitute a "within-party group." Unofficially, however, some subtle penetration does exist. The Kibbutz Artzi, whose interlocking with Mapam was described above, has been a major source of organizational resources for Peace Now. This kibbutz movement was involved in funding, mobilizing manpower, and strategic planning for the peace group. The organizational facilities of the leftist kibbutz movement were made available, since Peace Now deliberately declined, until recently, to set up a formal institutional basis despite its impressive success in rallying large crowds. The lack of permanent headquarters and salaried staff increased the value of the kibbutz movement's support. These ties between the group and the party does not imply, however, that the party's decisions overrule those of the group or that policy making is shared by the two bodies. Still, the interface between Peace Now and Mapam was in the past too strong to be ignored.

The relationship between Gush Emunim and right-wing and religious parties is more complex owing to the fact that the group has sprouted two branches, Yesha and Amana, that are themselves well-organized bodies, and is therefore less dependent on partisan resources. Gush Emunim, however, does recruit Likud MKs (especially from Herut and Hatehiya) to its governing institutions in order to underline the mutual relationship between the group and the party. The incorporation of well-known party figures into its secretariat purportedly demonstrates that Gush Emunim not only attempts externally to affect the party, it tries to establish some form of linkage within it, as well.

The consumer organizations are closely interlocked with political parties. The Consumers Authority was established, and continues to date to operate, under the political aegis of the Histadrut executive. The Consumers Council is ostensibly politically neutral; however, the nomination of its board by the cabinet minister of industry and commerce taints the council with strong partisan overtone. An attempt in 1985 to oust the council's director for having the "wrong" partisan affiliation came to naught owing to vociferous public criticism.

Religious interest groups, particularly those on the extremist pole of the spectrum (i.e., those affiliated with the various splinters of the ultra-orthodox parties), are also intertwined with political parties. In fact, the parties established groups as a means of advancing their causes outside the party repertoire. The Committee for Safeguarding Human Dignity and the Committee for the Protection of Israel's Sanctity illustrate this point. The first group was instigated in 1966 with the purpose of blocking the attempted amendment of the Anatomy and Pathology Law, prescribing more latitude for conducting post-mortem operations. The second group was formed to impede the introduction of an abortion bill (in 1976). The two groups (which, in effect, were the same group under different headings) ostensibly represented non-partisan constituencies and advocated non-partisan objectives; moreover, their phraseology was aimed at delivering a national message not tainted with partisan advocacies. Yet each group's personnel, property, policy, and power all emanated from a patron, Agudat Israel. Thus the two may be counted as "groups within parties."

Groups as Rivals of Parties: The Interest Parties

Once every four years (if not sooner), Israeli citizens are called upon to cast a ballot from amongst a myriad of parties competing for their support. Between 25 and 30 parties launch a vociferous, often acrimonious campaign each election. Some of these parties are merely groups in the disguise of parties, i.e., "interest parties." They qualify as parties because they fulfill the fundamental condition of "nominating candidates for election to an electoral assembly" (Riggs 1970: 580). Yet interest parties are clearly differentiated from regular parties, not only in size, but more important in scope. The interest party is a voluntary association which existed prior to the elections and which decided to present an electoral list. It generally focuses on one identifiable issue; it appeals mainly to a distinct constituency, whether characterized by a specific demographic attribute (e.g., age or gender) or by an ardent concern over a particular public policy.

Interest parties are a recurring phenomenon of the contemporary electoral scene in Western societies. One of their earlier manifestations was the Poujadist party (the Union de Fraternite Francaise), which was originally a taxpayers' defense organization, formed in France in the mid-1950s (Converse and Pierce 1986: 26–27). Interest parties abound on the European elections scene. Some of the Greens, at their inception, certainly fit this category; ecological parties of one sort or another exist in most democratic European countries. Other examples are the anti–nuclear-weapons peace party in Japan, Pensioners' Party in Finland, Women's Alliance in Iceland, and the Swiss Automobile party.

Turning into a party may be costly in terms of an interest group's organizational resources. Support for an issue promoted by an interest group will often cut across party lines and does not entail any violation of traditional allegiances. One may adhere to his or her partisan political organization and still be active in a variety of groups espousing specific issues. Putting itself on the ballot, therefore, may lead to an erosion in the group's cohesion, with members preferring to vote for their own party. It is one thing to go to a rally on behalf of a certain issue; it is something else for voters to be willing to put all their electoral eggs in one limited basket. Furthermore, presenting itself as a party might refute the group's claim of wide support. The election results may clearly expose the group's real standing in the public eye. Finally, entering the political arena may be perceived as a slap to an established party's face, with consequent reluctance within the existing political structure to yield to the group's demands.

Despite the numerous potential disadvantages in such a move, many Israeli associations have crossed the Rubicon that separates in interest group from a political party. Never absent from any of the electoral contests, interest parties in Israel have ranged in number from a minimum of one (in 1961) to a maximum of seven (in 1981) (see table 3.2). The question arises, why did these groups forfeit the relatively comfortable arena of group activity to enter a contest in which the odds were stacked against them? Did they really just wish for exposure in an electoral campaign? Does this phenomenon exhibit corporatist tendencies to skip party mediation, to pass over the preponderance of partisan channels, or does it perhaps simply reflect the divergencies inherent in pluralistic systems? Three explanations have been offered to account for the emergence of interest parties: structural, socioeconomic, and functional.

Table 3.2
Interest Parties in the Knesset Election Campaigns, 1949-1988

	Knesset											
List	1	2	3	4	5	6	7	8	9	10	11	12
Women	1*								1			
Ethnic groups	2*	3	3	4	1	2	1	4	3	2	3	1
Local lists	1											
New immigrants		1		1					1			
Handicapped				1							1	
Young citizens								1	1			
Pensioners										1		1
Economic groups										2	2	1
Foreign and security							2					1*
Political reform												1
Total	4	4	3	6	1	2	3	4	5	7	6	5

*The list passed the blocking percentage and won a Knesset representation.
Source: *Results of election to the the 1st–12th Knessets.* Central Bureau of Statistics.

The structural explanation

The structure of government has been considered a factor encouraging the "transfer to politics." In this regard Israel provides an ideal structural environment for the appearance of interest parties: it has an extreme proportional electoral system, giving a kind of "photographic" representation of the gamut of opinions in the society. This structure offers a temptation too great to resist. The Basic Law: The Knesset requires that a list be represented in the Knesset according to its strength among the electorate, provided that the list achieves at least 1 percent of the vote. Voters choose among national party lists; on each ballot, the candidates for a particular party are listed in the order of priority decided by internal party procedures. To be listed on the slate of a party as eligible for election, a candidate need fulfill only minimal requirements: be an Israeli citizen, aged twenty-one or older; the list (i.e., the party) is required to submit signatures of bona fide supporters (in 1988, 1500 were required) and to deposit a small sum of money, which is not returned in the event the list fails to pass the electoral test, or what is called the "blocking percentage" (attaining a minimum 1 percent).[9]

The structural environment of Israel's electoral system is favorable to new lists in another way: campaign facilities. The state treasury provides an opportunity for each and every list to mobilize votes by giving them at least twenty-five minutes of radio air time and ten minutes of television air time for political advertising. These favorable circumstances provide one explanation for the emergence of a large number of interest parties in Israel. The prominence given to parties, as opposed to individuals, in the Israeli political system thus furnishes a weighty inducement to "partization."

The socioeconomic explanation

A second explanation is derived from the well-known cleavage theory explaining the emergence of parties on the basis of socioeconomic divisions. The classic Lipset-Rokkan model (1967) emphasized the institutionalization and freezing of cleavage alignments, with the structure of the cleavage considered to be relatively fixed. According to the theory the lines have already been drawn and there are few untapped bases of electoral support; however, some marginal facets of social cleavages have induced the formation of interest parties. Most noted among these are ethnic and generational cleavages.

The ethnic cleavage. Israel is crisscrossed by myriad ethnic divisions that not only distinguish between the two major sections, Sephardim and Ashkenazim, but also make distinctions within each community, especially the former. It is hardly surprising, then, that the largest single category among the interest parties is ethnic based; invariably, at least one ethnic party appears in every electoral campaign. Regardless of the political climate, the country's economic condition, or the party in government, ethnic interest groups keep turning to the electorate to seek direct representation in the Knesset. Invariably, though, it is a clique or an individual of an Asian-African origin, that presents such a list. Ethnic lists appeared in the elections to the very first Knesset in 1949. Although they represent a specific ethnic community, they could also be counted as "groups within parties," since it was with the party's blessing that the groups presented their candidates.

The first genuine ethnic interest party appeared in 1973, after the Black Panthers, split between two lists, presented their slates of candidates that year. The Black Panthers challenged the establishment parties, whose patronage they rejected. Individual leaders had been successfully co-opted by those parties, but still other leaders opted for independent channels of political influence. The message of the Black Panthers—as well as that of other ethnic-based interest parties—was not narrow and specific. They demanded the equalization of Israeli society, the provision of more educational facilities and residential opportunities. Their constituency, however, was predominantly Sephradic Jews. Other ethnic group parties promoted the self-awareness of the Sephardim, in appeals usually made in broad terms.[10]

The generational cleavage. The generational cleavage has prompted the establishment of two lists of young people. More prominent were lists representing the interests of pensioners. Israel has been depicted as young, pioneering, and energetic. However the statistical data of the 1980s indicate that at least in terms of biological age, Israel is no longer a youthful society: 8.8 percent of its population are age 65 and over (*Statistical Abstract* 1988: 69). The Jewish tradition prescribes honor of the old (Leviticus 19), but most of the country's elderly do not enjoy the benefits of the affluent society. The young state had to take care of impending problems of immigrant integration and security and, therefore, largely neglected the welfare of the aged. No serious attention has been paid to comprehensive legislation regarding the rights of senior citizens. A regretful outcome of this negligence is that many old-age pensioners live in, or on the verge of, poverty; the financial arrangements for retirement, whether from social security or from a Histadrut pension, are hardly satisfactory.[11] A pensioners list appeared unsuccessfully in the elections to the 10th Knesset (1981). In 1988, it made a second run, with prospects seeming brighter than in the previous attempt. The list appealed not only to individuals but also to organized pensioner groups, those of government ministries, of professionals, and of large public enterprises, amounting to some 400,000 members. The age cleavage, however, was not powerful enough to induce action, and the elderly failed to mold themselves into a party. The overwhelming majority of the pensioners remained loyal to their own parties and failed to cast their vote to the list representing their specific interests.

The gender cleavage. A socioeconomic cleavage conspicuously absent from the interest party scene in Israel is that based on gender. The gap between women and men in terms of occupational opportunity and income is obvious enough, and women's groups do abound. These organizations, however, are reluctant to enter the partisan arena and dare not try to mobilize the female vote. The predominance of Naamat, the Labor-affiliated women's association, in terms of members and national expansion, precludes effective mobilization. In the elections to the first Knesset, WIZO did muster sufficient support to win one mandate. But its representative was linked to a party, the General Zionists.

It was very rare in those days for a political figure to operate totally outside the confines of the all-powerful parties. A second attempt by women (in 1977) was totally abortive. Naamat, the most
powerful female group, cannot possibly sever its ties with its
patron; other groups are either so widely multipartisan (the
Women's Shedula) or so modest in resources (the Feminist Movement) that partization is not a viable option.

The functional explanation

The third explanation for the transfer from the group to the
party arena bases itself on a universal decline in the functional role
of parties over the past two decades (King 1969; Dalton, Beck and
Flanagan 1984). As noted in the Introduction, the growth of
government, the increasing autonomy of the bureaucracy, and the
expanding power of the electronic media have handicapped the
ability of parties to control the policy process. Parties failed to be
adequate means of aggregating interests and have had difficulty in
performing mediating roles. This decline has been especially conspicuous in the post-materialistic era, in which parties have not
been successful in integrating the new values, and therefore have
left the scene to promotional groups, primarily in the ecological
domain.

The environmental revolution has not constituted a source of
emerging politics in Israel. None of the environmental groups have
ever considered the option of partization. The Israelis, preoccupied with demography, security, and the pursuit of the "good
life" (Gottlieb and Yuchtman-Yaar 1983) are not sufficiently aware
of their deteriorating ecology. Environmental groups thus preferred to remain outside the political arena, and their members
have not turned into "gladiators," actively participating in
political life.

The functional explanation, however, is valid with regard to
other issues, particularly those dealing with questions of security.
Foreign and defense issues are prime topics on both formal and
public agendas, yet policy has often been blurred because the alternatives facing decision makers are not specified. The reasons for
the equivocation are grounded both in the external environment
and in internal structures. Official Israel could not always spell out
clearly what it had in mind; often the available options it puts
forth were too provocative and unacceptable for the international
community. At the same time, intra-party divisions also precluded
a clear formulation of policy outlines. This was specifically the

case following the Six Day War, when the two poles of the Israeli attitude toward the occupied territories began to crystallize. One pole represented the yearning for Greater Israel, i.e., outright annexation of the lands taken in 1967. At the other pole stood those who clamored for peace, i.e., the relinquishing of territories in return for peace (Stone 1982). The national coalition adopted neither of these options; rather, it attempted to win time in the belief that there was no rush to formulate a decisive policy.

The gap was filled by two movements that turned into parties—the list for Eretz Israel and the Peace list. Twenty years later another group turned into a party: Moledet (Homeland), headed by a former well-known general. Moledet emerged as a response to the blurring of the demographic issue. Succinctly put, in Greater Israel (including the West Bank and the Gaza Strip) in 1987 there were some 3.6 million Jews and 2.2 million non-Jews, that is 62 percent vs. 38 percent. Demographic forecasts showed that this ratio would drop to 55 to 45 by the year 2000 (Soffer 1988). The left-wing parties adjusted their platforms to this reality and advocated an Israeli withdrawal from densely populated territories. At the other pole, those favoring annexation did not offer any meaningful solution to the problem, for fear that Israel's image (and conscience) might be totally marred. Into this vacuum a group entered that explicitly and unequivocally recommended the transfer of Palestinians from the territories to other Arab countries. Moledet became the only interest party that succeeded in entering the Knesset in 1988.[12]

All interest groups that have presented a slate of candidates for election have sensed a gap between resources and expectations. All had reason to believe that they might enter the arena with confidence: constituencies were large; leadership and other organizational assets were readily available; citizens' frustration with the distribution of resources and/or values was evident. At the polls, however, they have not been able to convert interest into power. Yet, in the end, the phenomenon reveals a political paradox: Groups keep turning into parties because they fail to realize their objectives through the existing party system. At the same time, they still regard parties as an (the?) effective channel for securing influence and making an impact on public policy. Thus, turning into parties does not mark a shift of power from the partisan to the associational arena. It may reveal that parties have failed to represent specific constituencies or to advocate specific issues. It does not mark, however, the replacement of political parties by voluntary associations.

Groups as Partners of Parties: Action from Without

Pluralist theory regarding the relationship between interest groups and political parties is self-contradictory. On the one hand, the inexorable rise in the interest group system has itself contributed to the decline of political parties as key organizations in the political system. Regarding parties as targets for group influence is therefore superfluous in terms of organizational resources. As Lehner and Schubert have observed, parties (and parliaments) often even fail to give a "steering" sense of direction and constraint to the system; "the severely limited role of parties [and parliaments] in policy-making seems to be a fact which can scarcely be disputed in empirical terms" (1984: 134; see also Lawson & Merkl 1988). At the same time, however, parties are regarded as a means of access to policy making.

Comparative data indicate that the links between political parties and interest groups in most liberal democracies are rather weak. This applies not only to the United States but to European countries, as well. Wilson's study of French interest groups, for example, revealed that "the boundary between interest groups and parties is better defined than in most other industrial democracies" (1987: 139). In Norway, interest groups were found to have only limited contacts with the political parties, making the joint state-associations advisory councils a major means of exerting influence (Kvavik 1976). In Britain, the picture is ambivalent. Although most interest groups are detached from political parties, particular associations "do use parties as a means of access and as a means of getting issues onto the political agenda. And in one particular case—the trade unions—party links may be said to be of central importance" (Jordan and Richardson 1987: 238). How do Israeli interest groups cope with this dilemma? Do they ignore the parties, powerful as they might be, and bypass them in favor of other channels of communication to the elite? Or do they regard parties as an effective means to influence decision makers?

The Israeli case also presents an inconclusive picture. Interest groups perceive parties to be the source of power in Israeli politics. This assertion is based on the preponderance of respondents who "fully agree" or "partly agree" with this proposition. Regardless of the category of interest group, only a negligible fraction of associations (less than 3 percent) totally deny the statement. If, indeed, parties constitute a source of power, as was explicated in chapter 1, then groups acting rationally should target their efforts at influencing parties from the outside (if they are not lucky enough to be included in the partisan family and so have access from within). It appears, however, either that interest groups do not behave as rationally as believed or that, despite the evidence in this regard, the power structure is undergoing changes. The groups' reported behavior, emanating from the questionnaire employed for this work (shown in table 3.3) is not compatible with their evaluation of the sources of power in the Israeli polity.

Table 3.3
Relationship between Interest Groups and Political Parties
(Percent Reporting)

	Party-affili-ated	Eco-nomic	Other	Pro-mo-tional	N
Parties as the source of power (fully/partly agree)	97.3	97.5	100.0	94.3	155
Request to include a plank in a party's platform	25.0	30.0	17.8	30.8	156
Party contributes to the group's funding	—	2.3	—	2.0	159
Selection of a party candidate by the group	16.6	12.5	3.4	3.7	159
Internal group elections conducted on partisan basis	35.1	7.1	—	1.9	160
A member of the group's executive is a party activist	64.8	54.7	51.7	42.5	162
Contacts with parties as a strategy (often/occasionally)	30.3	7.8	12.5	8.7	141
Contacts initiated by party	42.8	12.2	29.6	20.4	157

The first question regarding access to parties as a means of influence referred to a group's attempts to influence a party to incorporate a provision in its electoral platform. Although the utility of engineering the inclusion of a favorable plank in the platforms of major parties is dubious, groups often expend great effort trying to win friendly promises from the parties and their leaders. This practice is especially common in Canada (Pross 1986: 161) and the United States (Schlozman and Tierny 1986). In Israel, the practice is limited to a minority, slightly more among the economic and promotional associations than among their counterparts. The Manufacturers Association (MA) phrased its objectives in the form of a written program distributed among the major parties prior to the 1988 elections. The program, phrased in noncontroversial terms, spoke of the importance of industry in the Israeli economy, of the need to achieve economic independence, and of the contribution of industry to economic growth and full employment. Endorsing the MA's provision was in fact voting for motherhood. The association noted with pride that great parts of its program were included in the parties' electoral platforms, regardless of their views on the Arab-Israeli conflict.

The Center of Contractors & Builders has also made efforts to influence party platforms, with less success. One of the chief demands of the contractors has been to denationalize lands owned and operated by the National Lands Administration. Land in Israel is not only a place where one builds a home or grows agricultural products; it has acquired transcendental meaning as a symbol for Jewish national revival. The contractors have criticized the Lands Administration for the rigidity of its procedures and for discriminating against the private sector. They have demanded "the equalization of the private sector building enterprise to the public sector." It is little wonder that the Labor party rejected the contractors' proposal. The Likud, however, fearing public criticism of selling land to profit managers, was also unwilling to give its endorsement.

The Union of Social Workers regularly sends memorandums to all political parties during an election campaign to ask them to incorporate certain welfare provisions in their platforms. Reactions have not been encouraging, according to their secretary general: "Some of the parties ignored us altogether; some gave a polite answer, but none has taken us seriously; none has introduced changes in the platform to make it more responsive to the needs of the poor." Promotional groups are also active in efforts to influence parties' platforms. Peace Now once sent (in 1981) a respected delegation to the headquarters of the Labor party in an attempt to influence the incorporation of an explicitly dovish plank in its platform. The group's expectations loomed large because the party had suffered severe losses in the 1977 elections and because there was a strong intra-party constituency that endorsed territorial concessions in return for peace. Yet the party, not veering from its political program, declined to respond. Apparently the strategy of exploiting a party's campaign activities is not very useful when a group's objectives are controversial or seem to be unpopular among wide sectors of the population.

The links between interest groups and parties were further probed by the questionnaire from the organizational perspective. The data reveal that organizational ties between interest groups and parties are extremely tenuous. For example, less than 3 percent of the economic and the promotional interest groups receive party funds (none of the party-affiliated or "other" associations do). Although there are tacit ways of providing resources, the practice does not exist on the surface. Secondly, an overwhelming majority (over 80 percent) of interest groups have no input in selecting a candidate for partisan lists. Party-affiliated interest groups, however, engage in this practice more than their counterparts.

Trade unions and the agricultural groups stand out also in regard to internal elections. Among the party-affiliated associations more than a third conduct these elections on the basis of party lists; the percentage among other interest groups in considerably smaller.

On one item interest groups did score high on the partisan scale. When asked whether or not one of the members of their executive was a partisan activist, the answer, in many cases, was positive. Over half of the three types of sectional interest groups and nearly half of the promotional interest groups reported that a party activist indeed was numbered among their leadership. Among the party-affiliated organizations nearly two-thirds reported on joint membership. This phenomenon is not unique to Israel. In Norway, for example, over half of the elected leaders in national producer organizations had held office in a political party or represented a political party while in public office (Olsen 1983: 203). Most of the Israeli activists claim, however, that the two hats worn by the same person do not mean that the group is under party influence or that any penetration on the part of the party took place. Business groups, professional associations, and some categoric groups frowned at the idea that they maintain close ties with political parties. On the other hand, individuals who step into leadership positions in interest groups are not expected to throw away their other public activities. Their partisan position may even prove theories regarding the cumulative nature of political participation (Milbrath 1966; Salisbury 1969; Verba and Nie 1972). But, it is argued, the partisan identification of a group's leader is irrelevant to his or her duty as a group member or leader, for this person is expected to act independently of party politics. This nonpartisan behavior may be true in some cases. In the IMA, the political identities of the members of the central committee are indeed irrelevant to their activity in the medical association (although noted partisan members are often requested, during a crisis, to secure a favorable hearing in their respective party). This is not the case regarding the party-affiliated groups, where party penetration on the personal level is still deep. Hardly any trade union admits being associated with a political party although all of them are, for all practical purposes, intertwined with the Labor party. Although trade union activity does not grant automatic membership in the (Labor) party's central committee, the party incorporates members of all respective interest groups into its representative institutions through the branches.

The study also referred to contacting political parties as part of a group's repertoire of strategies. The percentage of those choosing parties as their target (often and occasionally) is not impressive. As will be shown below, it is far lower than that contacting either the Knesset or the government bureaucracy. Here, again, the proportion of appeals among party-affiliated interest groups is far higher than among their counterparts.[13] A leader of a trade union or a settlement movement is thus more likely to approach the party, not because it is an effective channel of influence in a pluralist distribution of power, but because of the parentela links between the two entities. If associations do not regard parties as worthy of interaction, it may happen that parties will initiate contacts with certain interest groups and appeal to them with specific requests/demands. Interaction between political parties and party-affiliated interest groups is based on reciprocity: in over 40 percent of the cases party-initiated contacts were reported by these groups. In all other categories, however, the initiation of such a contact was a rare occasion: between 12.2 percent (economic groups) and 29.6 percent ("other" sectional associations). The contents of these contacts, as reported by the groups, did not purport to limit the autonomy of action available to the group.

The last question (the results of which are presented in figure 3.4) investigated the tendency over time of contacts between interest groups and parties.The groups were asked whether their relationship with political parties has weakened, strengthened, or remained the same in the past decade. To begin with, the proportion of groups that claim to have "no relationship with parties"—neither as a means of access to decision makers nor as partners or patrons—is high among all categories of interest groups except those affiliated with parties. Data regarding tendencies over time are mixed; some conclusions, however, may be drawn. Among the party-affiliated groups, no significant changes have taken place. The percentage of reporting either weakening or strengthening of ties is meager. Yet, when compared to the other categories of interest groups, party-affiliated groups display the highest tendency of weakening contacts with political parties. Unexpectedly, the proportion of those reporting on strengthening contacts with parties is highest among promotional associations. Also worth noting is the fact that a sizable majority of these groups (72.2 percent) are virtually dissociated from political parties. The answers given by the groups' activists thus do not reflect a dramatic change in their contacts with political parties, although they cast doubt on parties' initial role in the life of Israeli interest groups, at least in the past decade.

Fig. 3.4. Trends of Contacts between Interest Groups and Political Parties (Percent Reporting)

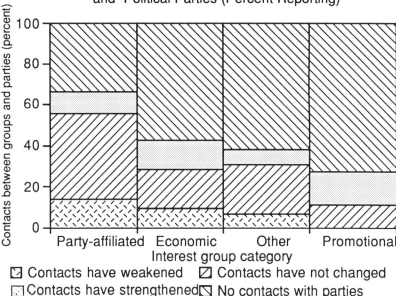

☑ Contacts have weakened   ☑ Contacts have not changed
☐ Contacts have strengthened☒ No contacts with parties

Conclusions

The pattern of interest group–political party relationships that emerges in Israel is essentially an uneven one. The first question discussed in this chapter pertained to the familiar traditional phenomenon of "groups within parties." In the focus of this discussion were interest groups that traditionally integrated with political parties and enabled them to form an elitist pattern of politics: trade unions and agricultural groups. In these domains, parties still capture interest groups and still penetrate their organizational structures, although counter forces are clearly visible. The Histadrut has turned into a multiparty organization, whose internal party strifes do not always mirror political divisions of power on the national arena. The Histadrut, in other words, has its own power game. The Labor Federation may still serve as an agent for mobilizing party constituency and providing jobs to party activists, but the interests of the two bodies are increasingly bifurcated. The Histadrut is gradually turning into an interest association, representing the interests of the workers in Israel. The Labor party, on its part, increasingly represents the upper middle class, the affluent, and the professionals. This bifurcation is bound to further attenuate the links between the Labor party and the Labor Federation.

As regards settlement movements, on the surface no dramatic changes have taken place. They still constitute legitimate factions within their respective parties; they still (although to a lesser degree) portray loyalty and obtain in return representation. Much of the halo of the agricultural movements has, however, been eroded. By virtue of traditional, parentela-type loyalties the Labor party is still seeking ways and means to benefit the settlements, but the rules of the marketplace are gradually being adopted.[14] Politicians can no longer, for the most part, abruptly intervene in the internal organization of farm associations. Even the leaders of Kibbutz Artzi, a most avowed party-affiliated interest group, enunciate rejection of party dominance. Elitist practices were found to be scarce in associations not defined as "party-affiliated."

The second question focused on the possibility of interest groups replacing parties. Even a cursory glance at the Israeli "interest parties" demonstrates that this is not the case. Those groups attempting to obtain parliamentary representation were not the economic organizations wishing to substitute party rule, but the frustrated and marginal—in terms of power rather than numbers—constituencies whose needs have not been satisfactorily articulated by the established parties. The mushrooming of interest parties indicates, however, that partization is still considered and effective channel to obtaining power. This observation is corroborated by the views of the groups surveyed for this work. Although political parties still loom large in the groups' perceptions, only among the "politicized" groups (trade unions, farmers organizations) is this perception congruent with relevant action.

One of the major findings of this chapter is that interest groups do not interact with political parties in the frequency and intensity expected to derive from their presumed importance in the political process. Traces of integration with political parties are still evident, especially on the leadership level. Activists in interest groups tend to occupy central positions also in a political party, regardless of the type of association. When all indicators of relationship between interest groups and political parties are considered, promotional associations do score lower than their counterpart groups: internal elections are considerably less based on party lists, there is a wider differentiation between party and group activism, parties are chosen in a lower frequency as a target of influence, groups are less often approached by political parties.

Judged by the criteria of actual contacts with political parties, issue-oriented groups do appear to confirm their association with the pluralist model of interest politics. This conclusion may be qualified by the relatively high proportion of promotional groups that reported on "strengthening contacts with political parties" in the past decade. This does not necessarily imply a shift toward elitism. Instead, it may indicate that promotional associations are not very choosy in seeking allies. Empirical data may distort reality by leaving out undercurrents in the political process. The data nevertheless suggest that there is much smoke and less fire in the relations between political parties and interest groups in contemporary Israel. In fact, these relations are far less intimate than expected.

CHAPTER FOUR

State and Groups: Defending
The Public Interest

The attitude of the state toward interest groups has been influenced in Israel both by the political culture, derived from past heritage and experience, and by the political dilemmas of contemporary democracy. The complexity of circumstances has produced a combination of extreme tolerance of associational freedom with deep suspicion of grassroots political behavior. The promotion of the freedom of association had its roots in the diversity of the Zionist movement. It was politically expedient to muster all fractions of support and harness the wide diversity of the Jewish people to the effort of nation building. The arch pluralism of the prestate *yishuv* inculcated political tolerance of subdivisions, the major manifestation of which attitude was an extreme partisan fractionalization. The blurring of the line between political party and voluntary associations contributed to enhancing the legitimacy of the latter. It was easy for the ruling elite to accept, both psychologically and politically, the development of associational life because of the open or tacit partisan control of the objectives and activities of the interest groups. Being agents of mobilization, the groups had no difficulty in acquiring a legitimate status in the political community.

The fusion of groups and parties had enabled the institutionalization of tolerance, manifested in the incorporation into the state's fledgling legal structure of an early (1909) Ottoman law prescribing far-reaching freedom of association. As the state matured, however, and as groups released themselves from the grip of partisan control, and as the partisan arena itself began posing some elements of a threat to the political establishment, the

137

state reconsidered this freedom of association. It placed more limitations on group activity. This chapter will analyze the bifurcated attitudes of the state toward interest groups. The analysis will deal with the formal legal bases provided by the state for group activity and the attitudes of senior state officials toward groups and their role in public policy making.

The Formal Legal Bases

One of the first steps taken by the newly established state of Israel was the incorporation of British Mandate legislation into its legal code. One of the laws inherited was the 1909 Ottoman rule stating that "Ottomans possess the right of association." A voluntary "association" was broadly defined: "An association is a group consisting of a few people who integrate their knowledge and energy for a continuous period of time in order to achieve a non-profit-making goal." Establishing an association did not entail administrative difficulties, nor did it require applying for a license or certificate. It was sufficient to notify an authorized official (at the time—the Turkish governor; subsequently—the Israeli district commissioner). The act of notification constituted the legalization of the association. Tolerance of freedom of association was imbued in the ethos of the Young Turks, but it was also based on the realization that the wide diversification then prevailing under Ottoman rule was expedient in terms of political stability. The Turks, though, also took into account the dangers to the survival of their empire that were inherent in unlimited freedom to organize; they qualified the law by inserting a clause prohibiting "any formation of associations that violate the territorial integrity of the Ottoman state, that operate to change the [constitutional] regime and government, and that are contrary to civility and order."

This somewhat vague qualification enabling the prohibition of voluntary associations was not put to the test in Israel's formative years. The state did not abridge the freedom of association and did not interfere with the mushrooming of groups known as Ottoman associations. Yet the attitudes of the state, which feared that subversive activities might evolve under the umbrella of the permissive Ottoman law, remained ambiguous with regard to unlimited freedom to organize politically. The government set about replacing the existing law with an Israeli version in December 1954. The catalyst for reform was the inability on the part of the state to prohibit the formation of politically "undesired" public associations or even to keep track of their activities. But the minister of justice, who presented the bill in the Knesset, specified a different motive: financial corruption. He stated it in these terms:

> There are many voluntary associations ostensibly carrying honorable titles and established for honorable purposes. But in reality they are no more than flourishing family business enterprises, providing their members with a considerable income. The government's legal approval of the association legitimized its existence and induced many people to accept its founders' credibility. More often than not, despite the enormous funds collected by its founders, no attempt was made to advance the cause which gave rise to the association's formation.[1]

The law sought to curb the unlimited freedom of association, which allegedly served as a cover for corruption. Regulation of the registration of voluntary associations was one of its major goals. The proposed bill included the following provisions:

1. Seven people or more (aged eighteen or older) who wished to associate for a nonprofit purpose may establish an association.

2. The establishment of an association would come into force by registering it with the registrar, this official appointed by the minister of interior.

3. The registrar would be granted far-reaching authority. In principle he could exercise no discretion as to which requests for registration should be rejected, as approval was mandatory. But this provision was qualified by vague, sweeping conditions. Registration could be denied if the objectives of the association were contrary to law or public morale, if they endangered the security of the state or public order, of if one of its founders had committed a criminal offense within three years prior to presentation of the request for association.

4. Once the association was registered, it would enjoy all vested rights, e.g., the right to hold property and the right to appear in court. It would be autonomous with regard to its internal organization, strategies of action, and the mutual relationship of its membership. It would nevertheless be obliged to convene general meetings, to elect a central committee, and an audit committee. An association would be free to issue its own regulations, but in case no such regulations were issued, the "general regula-

tions" (i.e., sample regulations attached to the law) would be in force, providing detailed rulings for the daily operation of the association's life.

5. The dismantling of associations could take place under three circumstances: first, if the association itself decided to disband; second, if the membership was below the size required by law; third, if the registrar (after due warning) took measures against the association on account of its violation of the Associations' Law. The association had a right to appeal to the district court in Jerusalem whose decision was final.

6. The Associations' Law was not intended to interfere in the affairs of political parties; this was explicitly excluded from the law. The Supreme Court was the arbiter of whether a particular association was to be considered a party or not.

This first attempt at legislating the right of association was particularly careful to provide for broad limitations on associational freedom. The law demonstrated the state's growing involvement in civil society. The minister of interior, under whose auspices the registrar exercised authority, could deny registration to groups that, according to the extremely vague definition, "violated public morale." Under this provision, a religious registrar could ban the establishment of an association that aimed to protect the interests of producers of pork, whose eating is prohibited by the Jewish faith; a pacifist registrar could reject the appeal of a group advocating the idea of Greater Israel. As one of the MKs who opposed the proposed law said: "I have already learned how in our daily reality one can turn everything upside down and claim that this or the other undermines state security or public morale. Only later on it becomes clear that the allegation was false and groundless."[2] With such broad authority the registrar was in effect determining which objectives contributed to the "public morale" and which were detrimental. Applicants denied registration were not granted a right to appeal to a higher level if the decision of a (Jerusalem) district court went against them. Among the ardent opponents of the law was a member of the religious coalition party, who denounced the totalitarian aspect of the pending bill:

> I would like to know who is the minister that would determine by himself these critical issues. Who will decide what constitutes a breach of state security and violation of public morale.

You have no right of appeal. You cannot prove this is not the case, because it won't help you. The minister has already determined your fate.They first shoot you and later you have to prove that you are not the bear.[3]

Despite substantial objection to the proposed law, the Knesset approved it on the first reading (on December 13, 1954) and passed it on to the Committee on Constitution, Law, and Justice for preparation for the two other readings. The opposition had effect, however, for there it was buried for a full decade and did not reappear on the Knesset's agenda until the mid-1960s.

The government's declared reason for introducing the legislation—its concern with the public welfare—had not been baseless. Associations did take advantage of their legal status and did engage in soliciting funds for "nonprofit uses" that proved to be extremely profitable. Increasingly instances were uncovered in which the title "association" was a legal cover for financial manipulations. Nevertheless, the actual reasons were grounded in the broader environment. Israel was undergoing a rapid process of centralization, and the attempt to keep an eye on voluntary associations may have been part of this process. In the mid-1950s "statism" was at its peak. The state was called on to act as chief regulator curtailing, even substituting for, the free play of semi-autonomous social and political bodies. This prominent emphasis on the powers of the state, however, incorporated a paradox that has characterized many other post-revolutionary situations. On the one hand, few of the factors that contributed to the reestablishment of the Jewish homeland in Palestine were more effective than the autonomous Jewish social and economic institutions. These counter-agencies formed the instrument by which the Zionist settlers achieved a fair degree of independent home rule long before the formal establishment of Israeli sovereignty in 1948. On the other hand, the cult of the state worked to supplant the influence of the voluntary associations. Implementing David Ben-Gurion's dictum, to turn the Israeli melting pot into one nation, led, in this context, to perceiving state organs as being the most fit to perform the enormous functions confronting the developing society. Thus in 1953, the State Education Law was enacted, enabling partial nationalization and centralization of the party-affiliated school system. The previous separate, so-called "general," trends in education were combined into one option; henceforth curricula would be determined by the ministry of education. Only orthodox trends and the agricultural settlements' educational system were granted some autonomy. The same year, the Knesset enacted the Social Security Law, which committed the state to providing social benefits under fixed criteria to all Israeli residents. This act also "requisitioned" the provision of welfare services from voluntary agencies and transferred it to the state.

The centralization trend continued through the decade. One major step toward state control of important social functions involved the nationalization, in 1959, of the Employment Bureau, which had previously been operated by the Histadrut. The Employment Bureau, operating under the auspices of the minister of labor, was granted a monopoly. It was explicitly forbidden to accept a worker or to request employment outside the bureau. A written approval was required to approve affiliation with the official organ. The extension of state control over voluntary associations thus was part of a more comprehensive process of centralization.

In 1964, the Associations' Law was once again put on the Knesset's agenda. The circumstances under which the bill was being reconsidered were different. In that year, there was an identifiable cause of anxiety triggering the authorities to curb, by legislative measures, the unlimited freedom of association in Israeli society. This was Al-Ard, the legally constituted Ottoman association of Arab nationalists. The Communist party for a long time claimed to be the sole protector of the Arabs in Israel, although all Zionist parties courted the Arab vote (Lustick 1980).[4] Attempts to establish an independent Arab party failed, Israeli Arabs making little progress in this field because of their lack of political experience, their traditional way of life, and the stern measures taken by the authorities against autonomous Arab political activity. Thus Israeli Arabs who wanted to engage in this activity had two outlets: to join the Communist party or to establish voluntary associations of their own.

Cooperation with the Communist party became very popular with the raising of the banner of Arab nationalism, especially after the 1952 revolution in Egypt and the Suez Affair in 1956. In 1958, however, an open split occurred between Arab nationalists and Communist parties around the world that led to a cooling of relations between Arab nationalists in Israel and the Israeli Communist party (Jiryis 1969: 131). A group of dissidents subsequently withdrew from the party, founded an organization known as Al-Ard (the Land), and applied for registration as an Ottoman society. Since the Ottoman law was incorporated into the Israeli legal system, it was sufficient ostensibly to "notify" the district commissioner of the establishment of the association. The official, utilizing the provisions in the law, refused approval on security grounds. A case was brought against the commissioner in the Supreme Court, which upheld his ruling. After an appeal, however, Al-Ard was finally registered.

The formal act of registration did not lead to the legitimation of this group. When Al-Ard attempted to form a political party and presented a list to the 1965 elections, it was denied legitimacy by the Central Elections Committee. The group reappealed to the Supreme Court, which this time rejected the Al-Ard request. The judicial ruling held that the group had been established with the aim of prejudicing the security, indeed the very existence, of the state, therefore it could not base its claims on the freedom of association. Although Al-Ard supported improved conditions for Arab workers, improved Arab education and health services, its constitution, however, also openly advocated the Arab national cause:

> . . . The founders of the Al-Ard Movement regard all matters connected with relations between the Arabs and Israel, such as the Arab refugee problem, the frontiers, property left behind by Arabs when they left Israel, the Jordan waters, etc., as a single whole which requires a final and comprehensive solution. . . . Al-Ard proposes a solution which would restore political entity to the Palestinian people and which would enable them to decide their own future, without any outside interference whatsoever. . . . As regards the highest aspirations of the Arab people, the founders of the Al-Ard Movement consider that the Palestinian people are an indivisible part of the Arab nation. It is therefore natural that these people, when deciding their own future, should accord their due weight to Arab interests and aspirations. (Article 3)

This statement of objectives was totally unacceptable in Israel. On November 11, 1964 the Supreme Court of Justice ruled against the association. Supreme Court Judge Alfred Vitcon ruled that Article 3 of the Al-Ard constitution was tantamount to seeking the destruction of the existence of the State of Israel in general and of its sovereignty within its present borders in particular. As phrased, the article raised the Palestinian problem and demanded that its solution accord with the wishes of the Palestinian people, as they alone were entitled to decide their own future. Since, moreover, this self-determination was to be carried out within the framework of the highest aspirations of the Arab nation, the judge held "those who advocate such objectives ignore the existence of the State of Israel and the rights of the Jewish people who live in it." The judge went on to say that the founders of Al-Ard had not seen fit to mention their recognition of Israel as a sovereign state or the principles on which it was established. Their constitution also failed to accept the principle that the area of the State of Israel was connected with acceptance by the Jews of the principle of the existence of Arabs within this political unit. The judge concluded with what became the hallmark of the freedom of association in Israel:

> It has never happened in history that in countries where there is a sound democratic regime, monopolistic fascist movements have been allowed to operate against the state, using the rights of freedom of speech, freedom of the press, and freedom of association to organize destructive activities under cover of those freedoms. Never in all history have such associations been permitted without calamitous results following. No one who witnessed the events that took place in the Weimar Republic will ever forget the lesson they taught. With this in mind, we shall not be long in reaching the final conclusion that it would be blind error to grant a license to the Al-Ard Movement.[5]

Judge Moshe Landau, who joined in this ruling, added the following: "The most elementary rights of any state call for the protection of its independence and existence, against its enemies both at home and abroad, and it is too much to ask of any government that it should help to establish a fifth column within its frontiers in the name of maintaining freedom of association."[6]

Al-Ard thus provided the catalyst for reopening the Knesset debate on the freedom of association. The new legislative proposal, presented in March 1964, still reflected contradictory tendencies. All the clauses pertaining to the internal structure of voluntary associations were reiterated, but establishment of an association, including political parties, required state confirmation. The Al-Ard case had taught the government a lesson: any new party—and for that matter any party that already had representatives in the Knesset—was obliged to register while specifying its objectives and exposing its internal affairs to state control. One concession was made to political parties: the exclusion of their financial affairs from state auditing. It was expected that this provision would greatly reduce opposition to the new bill.[7] Trade unions were exempt from the law because Israel was prohibited, under international commitment, from passing legislation that included the option of disbanding a trade union by court ruling.

Despite the Al-Ard trigger, the declared motivation for enacting the law was once again financial: the inordinate activity of voluntary associations, some of which were a mere disguise for fraud. The political implications of tightening control over public political activity were self-evident. However, at the same time, the 1964 proposal was actually more lenient than the previous one. The conditions whereby a group applying for registration could be denied were limited to two circumstances: First, when one of its founders had committed a security offense—rather than any crime—up to ten years before the request was submitted; second, when the objectives of the group were counter to the sovereignty of the state. The right to appeal a denied status in a Jerusalem district court was retained. Associations were also granted a measure of self-regulation to settle conflicts between members in internal judicial bodies.

By 1964, the ruling party's control of the polity was not as firm as in the past. Internal frictions in Mapai had already surfaced, this strife reaching a peak when Ben-Gurion threatened to resign on account of the "affair" (see chapter 1). Although these political undercurrents were not reflected in the deliberations on the Associations' Law in the Knesset, criticism of the proposal did reflect suspicion of the government's intentions. It was feared that the law would serve as a means of curbing civic freedom of association; that it would be an instrument of control by an already over-centralized state; that the government would use the law in order to intimidate those whose views were incongruent with mainstream ideology. Not only was the content of the legislation subject to criticism, so was its form; over ninety provisions of detailed regulations. As one MK noted: "People sat for days and hours and composed over ninety provisions. . . . Why did they take this trouble? In order to enhance control? They could have taken the Ottoman Law of Association of 1909, peel it, leave the grain, and give it a new Hebrew garment."[8] Those opposing the bill were perturbed precisely by the calming statement of the minister of justice, who said: "It is the state's duty to ensure that the associations will not lead astray their members, will present annual reports . . . that they will not deceive nor deceit the public."[9] It was for many a typical patronizing statement that also reflected the state's tendency to widen the scope of its functions. It did not explicitly reveal any growing need to limit possible subversive activity by legal means.

The Knesset approved, on April 6, 1965, the first reading of this new Associations' Law and passed it to one of its committees for final processing. Once more, however, the committee proved to be a (temporary) graveyard for the bill, which was removed from the Knesset agenda for more than a full decade. The issue was raised again in the Knesset plenum in December 1979.

This third attempt at an Associations' Law was submitted by the Likud-led government. The Labor Alignment, which on the two previous occasions had led the campaign to approve such a law, now opposed it. Opposition was in fact more vociferous than ever. A Mapam (Alignment) MK said in the debate: "If we continue the path we are being driven into, we shall reach a state whereby any individual wishing to leave his or her home will have to request permission from an authorized body, that is from a government official." He elaborated the faults of the law in the following words:

> A person has a right to walk freely without permission; a person has a right to speak out his opinion with full liberty; a person has an ordained right to act jointly with his fellowmen for a common purpose which is not profit making . . . without previous approval. The proposed law is aimed at locking individual freedom within bureaucratic walls and submitting it to state control. We thereby seriously and needlessly violate the liberty to associate.[10]

Lumping together voluntary associations acting on behalf of handicapped individuals and future political parties propagating solutions to world miseries was a special cause of parliamentary concern. The possible implications of the provisions limiting the registration of new associations also bothered many representatives. The definition of "anti-democratic activities" was too broad to be applied to concrete situations, opponents of the bill argued. Since "democracy" is in the eyes of the beholder, the clause could be used as a means of silencing opposition. And, in the words of one MK, was not "one of democracy's manifestations . . . [the] democratization of expression?" Similarly the term "Israel's security" was ambiguous: "A group may advocate the return of the West Bank for the sake of peace. The Registrar may recall he read in the daily press that the Chief of Staff of the IDF, General Eitan, the highest military authority, said that Israel cannot survive without Judea and Samaria. The implication is that the platform of an association subscribing to withdrawal from the

West Bank contradicts security imperatives." The same qualification applied to orthodox groups that espoused the rule of *Halacha*, which may be benevolent but is incongruent with liberal democracy.

The Knesset debate reflected the ambivalence of Israeli democracy. On the one hand, MKs of all political streams—communists, religious, laborite, and right-wing nationalist—feared that the institutionalization of the registration process would not be compatible with democratic norms and would breach the fragile equilibrium between state and society that had been forged during three decades of independence. The proposed law could serve as an instrument for limiting civil rights, and it could also enhance the already immense authority accumulated by the government. The possibility of even greater state involvement in associational life was undesirable and threatening. On the other hand, the Knesset members acknowledged the particular circumstances under which Israeli democracy operated. An Alignment MK articulated the problem:

> I would happily join those advocating free association without limitations. Why curb liberty? But we have not reached the days where the Wolf liveth with the Lamb, and not only because we are surrounded by enemies, but because we are a society that forges itself out of exiles, a society that crystallizes itself, absorbs itself, a society that unlike other nations, has not yet chosen its own path. Can we afford letting each individual live as he or she desires, without any restriction, without regulation that would determine a person's behavior within the boundaries of the broadest democratic definition? I support the freedom of association. But there is no escape from determining the rules that will serve as traffic lights for each of us, rules of behavior that would enable every citizen in this country to live a free life without being exposed to deprivation or limitation of any behavior.[11]

The security theme was also interjected into numerous parliamentary speeches, sometimes bluntly:

> We are not playing children games here, we are dealing with matters of existence, matters of life, determining our survival or our extinction. Can we afford, circumstances being as they are, to register an association that even implicitly negates the existence of the state of Israel? Can we afford to legitimize Moslem saboteurs whose goal is to destroy us? Let us not bury

our heads in the sand . . . for us security and existence are one
and the same. . . . If we have no security, one day they will rise
up and not only abrogate our independence but slaughter us
outrightly. Not one citizen alludes that our case is akin to any
other state whose independence is denied. How can we afford to
play games and allow the development of these circumstances?[12]

These excerpts clearly expose the democratic dilemma of interest groups in Israeli democracy. On the one hand, the political
leadership is committed to the guiding principles of liberal
democracy, namely, the right of individuals to enjoy the largest
possible freedom, as long as it does not impinge on the freedom of
others. On the other hand, a deep sense of insecurity, based on bitter historical experiences and on contemporary real or imaginary
threats, prescribes cautious restrictions on freedom and intensive
state involvement in the internal affairs of associations.

This third time around the law was enacted (on August 12,
1980); and its final version, though emphatic in endorsing the principle of associational freedom, also includes specific statements
recognizing the need to limit that freedom. Paragraph 1 maintains:

> Two persons or more who wish to associate for a legal pur-
> pose that is not aimed at distributing profits among its members
> are entitled to form an association. The association's establish-
> ment will be completed upon its registration in the Associations'
> Register. Excluded from registration are associations whose ob-
> jectives negate the existence of the State of Israel or its
> democratic features, or if there is sufficient grounds to conclude
> that the association will serve as a cover for unlawful activities.

A clause found in the former proposals, "violation of the
country's integrity" as one of the reasons for disqualifying an application for registration, was omitted from the law. Nevertheless
the legitimation of associational life was embedded in restrictions
phrased in somewhat vague language.

The most novel aspect of the 1980 legislation was not the
jeopardy in which it placed freedom of association; it was the
overt intention to subject associational activity to executive control. The law enables the state to pry into almost every aspect of
an association's life. It obliges an association to register with the
registrar, who is nominated by the minister of justice but who is
officially linked to the minister of interior. It gives the government
the right of continuous surveillance over and an inspection of
association's internal organization and operations. The statute

specifies in great detail the kinds of internal committees that each association must establish, the responsibilities of every committee, the methods and timing for convening them, the procedures for conducting the meetings, and the rules for electing officers. For example, if a general meeting is not assembled, the registrar is authorized to convene one. The association is obliged to notify the registrar of the election of a committee member or of an auditing committee member within two weeks of that election. The financial affairs of the association are also under strict supervision. The registrar is authorized to appoint an audit if the need arises.[13] The law also enables an association to pry, to an extent, into its members' activities. A membership registry, containing the member's identity, address, and dates of membership in the association, was made mandatory. This provision may be problematic in a party-state such as Israel owing to the linkage between polity and the economy. Workers employed by a Histadrut institution, for instance, might be reluctant to declare membership in an association affiliated with the Likud.

The most draconian provision of the Associations' Law comes in regard to the circumstances for the dismantling of such groups. The state can, without much difficulty, resort to dismantling an association under one of five options specified in the law: (a) if the association's activities are exercised contrary to the law, to its objectives, or to its regulations; (b) if the association aims at undermining the existence of the State of Israel or its democratic nature; (c) an authorized investigator can examine an association's financial affairs and recommend its dismantling; (d) if an association cannot repay its debts; (e) if a court finds it justified to disband the association. The state thus took two precautions to cope with potential associational subversive activity: registration and continuous inspection by the registrar. All these provisions, it must be said, did necessitate court approval so as to protect the association against arbitrary decision. In order to extend supervision over existing associations, the law mandated all Ottoman associations to register according to the new procedure within a year. Failure to do so would mean erasure from the list of legal associations.

The 1980 Associations' Law, designed to generate manipulable associations, produced what was termed by Bianchi (1984: 114) "debilitating pluralism," restricting the freedom to associate. A review of the changes that took place since the first legislative attempt, in 1954, at enacting this law indicates a decrease in these restrictions. First, the number of people eligible to form an association was reduced from seven to two, thereby enhancing opportunities to practice freedom of association. Second, a proclamation of the state in the 1950s was nearly final; only one court was authorized to rule out administrative decisions. By 1980, judicial authority was much expanded, the right of appeal broadened from the capital, Jerusalem, to the country at large. The fact that the courts were granted final authority to establish or dissolve associations had a moderating effect on "debilitating pluralism." Finally, the law did not apply to political parties already represented in the Kneset, but only to those that would be formed two years after the law came into effect. The reason for the exclusion of existing parties is simple enough. The parties safeguarded their own interests, rejecting any move made by the "state" (a possibly non-favorable administration) to meddle with their affairs. Israeli legislators failed to enact a law regulating the internal processes of political parties. (A proposal to this effect has been submitted by a Likud MK in 1976, when that party was still in opposition. In 1979, the same MK, now as a minister of justice, reintroduced the proposal. A private Member's Bill of the issue was also submitted by Labor MKs. None of the proposals materialized into a law, for the reason that the representatives of the parties, acting as Knesset members, did not wish to approve a bill that abrogated the interests of their sponsors and gave the administration an opportunity to control partisan affairs. The legislators sufficed with enacting a law that established state control of interest groups.) Finally, in 1980 changes in registration qualifications were introduced. In the early years of statehood the emphasis was on security, public morale, and individual civility; by the 1980s, more than security was at stake, as Israel's democratic features had to be guarded against enemies from within. Concern with "democracy" was a double-edged sword: it could have been used as a weapon against associations whose goals were incongruent with mainstream ideology; it could have acted against interest groups, such as Kahana's Kach, whose objectives were indeed detrimental to liberal democracy.

The administrative restrictions of the Associations' Law regarding the groups' internal affairs tend to be so complex and limiting that their violation is inevitable. Ostensibly they provide the state with a means to curb any associational activity. With the passage of time, it has become evident that the provisions of the Associations' Law were a declaration of intent more than a blueprint for action. To begin with, the provision obliging interest groups registered as Ottoman associations to resubmit applications for registration has not been carried out. The state comptroller

(1989: 505) reported in 1989 that of the 16,592 Ottoman associations registered in 1980, 11,835 (that is, 71 percent!) had not complied with the regulation to reregister. To date, they continue to operate without any state interference. Second, the financial records of the registered voluntary associations largely escape state supervision. Keeping track of thousands of annual financial reports has been beyond the capabilities of the registrar, whose department is very poorly staffed (only six workers, operating with a token budget, in 1987, of some $160,000). The state comptroller (1989: 504) has indicated that many associations do not present annual reports and the registrar does not insist they do so. This may be due to administrative slackness. It can also demonstrate that delving into an association's affairs does not take priority in the Israeli administrative elite. Yet an attempt by the Treasury to transfer jurisdiction over the voluntary associations from the ministry of interior to the ministry of finance met with strong opposition. The reason was that the interior minister, traditionally a member of a religious coalition party, did not want to relinquish authority over the associations, many of which are religious learning institutions.[14]

The registrar has not once implemented the authority to disband an association and has denied registration in only a handful of cases. Even in the latter cases, the rejection became the subject of negotiation and an out-of-court settlement. Nor have new groups apparently been deterred by the rigid procedures of the Associations' Law. In fact, the number of registered associations jumped from 3,186 in 1983 to some 15,000 in 1989. The proliferating number of voluntary associations that seem to operate in every social and political domain may be regarded as evidence of a tendency toward liberal pluralism. Theoretically associations may be vulnerable to state colonization; but in practice, they do not labor under administrative scrutiny.

The Associations' Law thus exposes the paradox of Israeli democracy: the state acts as custodian both of liberty and of national interests. It guarantees every individual adult the right to join a voluntary association. It prohibits the ousting of a member without due notice. In the same breath, however, it imposes so many limitations that the lines between the state and interest groups tend to blur. The legal space within which groups operate was narrowed by the provisions of the Associations' Law. The political space, however, remained intact, not only because of administrative inefficiency but also because the freedom of association was grounded in traditions. The law gave the state a means to control associational life, should it see fit to do so. As of now the restrictive clauses of the law have largely remained a dead letter, yet one that may be revived.

The Bureaucracy and Interest Groups

The importance of the bureaucracy in decision making is almost a truism. Bureaucrats have been regarded as "the core of modern government" (Friedrich 1963: 464), and the rule of officials is considered to be a major feature of modern politics (Putnam 1975: 81). The growth of de facto rule-making power in the administration, the emergence of delegated legislation, and the burgeoning of welfare-state activity have turned bureaucracy into a major target for group activity, especially in parliamentary systems of government. Extensive consultation between group leaders and civil servants has long been viewed as a fundamental democratization of the administrative process. A prerequisite for the emergence of such a process is the elite's favorable attitude toward interest groups and their representatives. This "democratization," however, does not provide the key to understanding the type of relationship that arises: Does it demonstrate patronage, partnership, or bargaining?

The Israeli bureaucracy, as elaborated in detail in chapter 1, has unusual powers deriving from the centralization and scope of government, and from the primacy of the executive. Senior officials tend to be personifications of the state, and their influence on policy making is probably greater than that of any other branch of government. In order to distinguish between "party" and "state" it is important to reveal the extent to which the state's administration is embedded with party politics. As already noted, the recruitment of senior officials is to a certain extent politicized. Israeli government officials are not recruited through special schools or screened by a rigid examination system. Some, especially the directors-general, entered their positions and were promoted through a spoils system. Loyalty to a political figure and partisan activity, in addition to personal competence, in the past were important in gaining entry and crucial for advancing to higher positions. Though top administrators provided continuity to the business of the state, they are also highly attuned to political voices.

The reasons for the politization of the civil service have been elaborated in the literature. Hans Daalder (1966: 60) argued that the degree of party permeation of state bureaucracies is a function of the relative timing of the emergence of these institutions in different national settings. The permeation is more pervasive in those situations in which political parties preceded the development of administrative bodies. Valenzuela (1984: 272) agreed that the major condition for a politicized bureaucracy is the timing of its emergence; for him, however, what counts is the formation of a strong legislative body rather than the parties. Had a parliament developed before the institutionalization of a large-scale state bureaucracy, it would be in a better position to create bodies responsive to party control. Israel fits neatly into these two categories. The parties preceded the state and its machinery; furthermore, semi-legislative organs also existed in the prestate era and, therefore, preceded the development of the bureaucracy. Yet, the change of government, as well as the professionalization of the civil service, may have freed the bureaucracy from party influence. The attitudes of senior officials toward interest groups may serve as one indicator of this change. Bearing in mind the economic advancement of Israel and its shift toward a technological society, bureaucrats would be expected to view interest groups as legitimate actors in the policy process, if not as full-fledged partners. Adversely, if elitist norms are still in force, the top administrative elite would be expected to deny the legitimacy of associational contribution to making policy, and to patronize interest groups; that is, to demonstrate an "elitist" attitude toward voluntary associations.

The administrative attitude toward interest groups in Israel was investigated for this work in an empirical study of forty-one senior officials in seventeen government ministries. In order to further an understanding of the position of these officials toward interest groups, a distinction was drawn between ministries responsible for dispensing and producing resources, and ministries whose major responsibility was to provide services. The first category consists of the ministries of finance, industry and commerce, economic affairs, tourism, transportation, communication, energy, and construction. The second category is comprised of the ministries of education, welfare, health, interior, justice, environment, absorption, and defense. The ministry of defense is also a major producer of resources by virtue of its control over Israel's large defense-related industry, but it was defined as a service ministry because the functions relevant to this study were basically of the service category (e.g., benefits to war victims and handicapped associations; security services to borderline settlements and

localities). Of the forty-one officials studied, twenty-two belonged
to economic ministries and nineteen to the service section.
LaPalombara (1964: 347) postulated that a bureaucracy's susceptibility to a parentela relationship is less visible in highly technical
agencies, which in the present study would be akin to the
economic ministries. Agencies providing services, on the other
hand, are expected to be more politicized, that is, to be more prone
to patronizing of interest groups. The pluralist orientation was expected to cut across types of ministries. The answers to the questions presented to state officials were expected to reveal whether
they approve of interest group influence (pluralism), cooperate
with interest groups (corporatism), or patronize them (elitism).

The first question presented to the officials regarded the
general pattern of policy making. The bureaucrats interviewed in
the course of this study were asked about the principal source of
influence on policy formulation. All of them concentrated on
intra-agency actors. Some stressed the role of the minister, others
of the director-general, still others of senior officials. Their
answers appear to have reflected differences in personalities rather
than in structural patterns of policy making. From their answers it
appears that the governmental bureaucracy in Israel, as in any
complex society, offers a major source of power. Insofar as the executive and the legislature become dependent on the information
that the bureaucracy collects, organizes, and communicates, the
top officials become an intimate, important, and sometimes dominant factor in the policy-making process. This is less true of the
ministries excluded from this research, the foreign ministry and the
bulk of the ministry of defense, whose activities relate to highly
controversial issues. Regarding these issues, bureaucrats may or
may not play an important role.

Given the paramount role the bureaucracy plays in the
strategies of interest groups (discussed later in detail), the second
question addressed to the administrators attempted to confirm this
picture from their own perspective. Interaction between senior officials and interest groups representatives is indeed intensive. Not
all the officials communicated with groups to the same extent. The
directors-general of the ministries were less liable to interact with
association leaders than were officials on a lower administrative
level, whose contacts, in most instances, were on a weekly basis.
Although most officials could not recall precisely who was the first
to initiate such contacts, the meetings were conducted on a continuous basis. Only two bureaucrats said they interacted with interest groups only "rarely"; and in both cases, the administrators

occupied positions in service ministries. The respective interest groups represented public issues.

The officials were asked to report on the purpose of their interaction with interest groups. In order to juxtapose their answers with those of association leaders, they had to choose one of three possible answers (or to add a "different" response), as follows: (a) to acquire views or opinions on a proposed policy; (b) to attempt to reach concurrence; (c) to bring notification of a decision that had already been adopted. The majority of interest groups, subscribing to the first answer, assert that they are consulted mainly to reveal their opinion about a specific issue. The officials confirmed this assertion. The most common answer to this question, given by over half of the administrators, was that the purpose of interaction was to secure the group's opinion. In twelve of the seventeen ministries included in the research, interaction was found to be geared *mainly* toward acquiring information of a group's attitude toward the issue at stake. As one official explained this need, "I do not monopolize wisdom; I need to know what they think. My own information regarding the issue would be totally distorted if I remained seated in my heated office and exercised my authority without knowing what is the opinion of the people involved." The administrators thus turned to the groups in order to obtain specialized information from those social sections mostly affected by the issue at hand; they also wished to be aware of the associations' views regarding the focus of the debated policy.

Regarding interest groups as a source of information is a widespread phenomenon, especially among ministries whose responsibility entails modern technology know-how. Ehrmann has pointed out the consequence: "Where the sources of official information, statistical and othewise, are as notoriously insufficient as in France and Italy, many bureaus must rely on the data provided by trade associations, trade-unions or other groups. But also in other countries the administration is compelled to utilize the groups as technicians and experts rather than as partisan advocates even though their advice may be that of an expert *engage*" (1968: 259). In Israel, however, most interest groups are less equipped than is the state to gather and utilize data. The big economic organizations of both labor and business provide exceptions to this pattern, but the information they provide is said to be biased in favor of their advocacies. The Chamber of Commerce presents data revealing the detrimental effects of custom barriers on Israel's economy; the Manufacturers Association emphasizes, in the figures it presents, the contribution of local industry to the country's welfare and underscores the need to protect it from undue competition. Data provided by the associations is dispensed more for media use than for official use. The administrators of the ministry of industry and commerce claim they have their own sources of information because "private" data are unreliable. This type of autonomy constitutes a major source of state power (Atkinson and Coleman 1989). Data provided by the MA and the chamber are considered a useful supplement but certainly not a sole (or even principal) source of information. They are suspiciously regarded as a means for promoting the group's cause. Nevertheless administrators in both types of ministries deem it necessary to seek the views of groups.

Interaction is also prompted by the need to secure consent. In Sweden, the avoidance of confrontation between the bureaucracy and interest groups is not only a practice entrenched in political arrangements, it is also part and parcel of the political culture that rewards social skills of "getting along with others" (Heclo and Madsen 1987: 21). Swedish officials are distinguished for not pushing advantages too far, encouraging the cooperation of others, avoiding outright confrontation, and not casting anyone in the role of permanent loser (Anton 1980). In Israel, the need to obtain consent, as distinct from the wish to obtain an "opinion," as reported by the groups and confirmed by the administrators, is not very pervasive. A major difference, however, was visible between the economic and the service ministries, with twice as many bureaucrats in the former than the latter responding that the major purpose of contacts with interest groups was to secure agreement. The pure elitist attitude (i.e., retroactive notification of a promulgated policy) was rarely the case (see table 4.1).

Table 4.1
Reported Reason for Interacting with Interest Groups (Percent)

	Ministry category		
	Economic (22)	Service (19)	Total (41)
Seeking information and opinion	50.0	57.7	53.7
Securing consent	45.4	26.2	36.6
Notifying of decision	4.6	5.2	4.8
Other	—	10.5	4.8

In order to examine further the bureaucracy's attitudes toward interest groups, the officials were asked about the perceived contribution of groups to their ministry's daily activities. Here again the respondents were faced with three possible answers (and a "different" category), as follows: (a) interest groups play a major role in setting the agenda of the ministry's programs; (b) interest groups aid the ministry to deliver its programs and implement its policy; (c) interest groups mobilize their members to support government policy. Table 4.2 reveals that administrators in the economic ministries view interest groups as playing a minor role in the process of agenda setting. Rather, the perception is that groups often seek to preserve prerogatives they already enjoy or to block initiatives they believe would reduce these benefits. They hardly ever raise issues that can be processed into policy outputs, according to the administrators. They often cajole and exert pressure, but their attitude is reactive rather than proactive. In short, associations are not thought of as a source of productive policy guidelines. This Israeli attitude contrasts with that in the United States, for example, where "interest group pressure does have positive impact on the government's agenda, and does so with considerable frequency" (Kingdon 1984: 52). The officials in the service ministries portray a different picture: a third report that welfare associations occasionally succeed in drawing attention to a certain need or problem that officials were not aware of themselves. The advocacy role of voluntary associations is thus more pronounced in ministries dealing with human welfare.

Interest groups are regarded by nearly a third of the respondents as aiding a ministry in administering its programs. The fact that administrators place heavy stress on policy implementation is not unique to Israel (Suleiman 1974: 327). The most popular answer among senior officials in the economic ministries was to describe the function of interest groups in terms of mobilization. Groups were regarded as agents of policy administration, as transmitting ideas, values, and programs from the administrative elite to the rank-and-file membership. Two-thirds of those interviewed in these ministries were of the opinion that interest groups contribute to a ministry's work by presenting an effective buffer between the officials and the group's members and by shielding the bureaucrats from excessive grassroots pressures. An official remembered, "We can close the issue with them. Not having to deal with pests who keep pressuring us for all kinds of benefits is a great advantage for us."[15] The proportion of those adhering to the elitist version was far lower among the officials of the service ministries.

Table 4.2
Function of Interest Groups, as Perceived by Senior Officials (Percent)

| | Ministry category | | |
	Economic (22)	Service (19)	Total (41)
Agenda setting	—	31.6	14.3
Delivering programs	31.8	31.6	31.7
Mobilizing support	63.6	26.3	46.3
Other	4.6	10.5	7.3

The research questions turned to the officials' subjective views regarding the major disadvantage or advantage of group activity from a given list (or they could add to the list). The disadvantages listed were as follows: (a) contacts with interest groups encourage too much pressure on the bureaucracy; (b) contacts with interest groups lead to favoring certain groups over others; (c) contacts with interest groups prevent the bureaucracy from advancing the national interest. There was also an option to indicate that contacts with interest groups entail no disadvantage. Only about a fifth of the respondents saw "no disadvantage" in interacting with voluntary associations (table 4.3), three times more among the service ministries than among the economic ministries.

Responses reveal a further difference between the two types of ministries. In the service ministries contacts with interest groups, to the extent that they are regarded as disadvantageous and dysfunctional, are so deemed mainly because they tend to blur the national interest. Not one single official was perturbed by excessive pressure that groups may exert, but rather by their particulate bias. The officials' answers to this question thus reflect images that are more congruent with elitist norms. One respondent said that a major disadvantage of group activity was that it determines facts which the government perforce has to accommodate. The official, who was responsible for the delivery of welfare services, castigated the over-activity of interest groups in his field in the following words:

> Interest group activities are admired by the public and the media, but in effect they put a heavy burden on the state's shoulders. They initiate projects and they put them on my lap. They enjoy the gratitude of the clients, and I have to pay the bill. They actually force upon me activities that are not congruent with the state's order of priorities. They have a blurred, incoherent vision of what should be done to ameliorate the public welfare and they force this distorted vision on state agencies.

Another administrator stated that the major disadvantage of group activity lay in diverting attention from the real issues. Interest groups, according to this official, are "invariably searching for media attention; they will do anything to capture it. The noise they make while trying to influence policy-making is detrimental to national objectives." Top bureaucrats in both types of ministries apparently were not concerned with violating egalitarian norms by seeing any disadvantage in favoring certain groups over the others.

Table 4.3
Disadvantages of Contact between Senior Officials and Interest Groups
(Percent)

	Ministry category		
	Economic (22)	Service (19)	Total (41)
Contacts encourage pressure	54.5	—	29.2
Contacts favor strong groups	13.7	5.3	9.7
Contacts blur national interest	22.7	63.1	41.5
There are no disadvantages	9.0	31.5	19.5

Adversely, administrators in the economic ministries were concerned mainly about the pressures exerted by interest groups. Being susceptible to such pressures, the officials often shunned what were described as undue attempts to influence their decisions. These administrators were aware of the power of interest groups to disrupt the process of national resources production. A strike staged by a trade union, such as the Electricity Company workers, has an extremely high damage potential. Officials were also cognizant of the capability of groups to interfere in the process of decision making by mobilizing the support of politicians. "Pressure," regardless of origin (an MK, a minister, a fellow official, but primarily interest groups), was perceived as the root of much evil. The fact that officials in the service ministries were more concerned with violation of the national interest does not mean that pressures were not exerted, nor does it imply that they were welcomed. Owing, however, to the centrality of the economic ministries, especially the Treasury, in the process of decision making, they are probably more susceptible to interest group prodding than are their service counterparts.

When asked about the advantages of contacts with interest groups, state officials in both types of ministries demonstrated positive attitudes (table 4.4). In fact, their initial reaction was to regard such contacts as advantageous. (Only four respondents saw no advantage in interacting with groups.)[16] To survey attitudes, the administrators were presented with three possible answers (and the option of "no disadvantage") to the question of contacts: (a) consultation is indispensable in a democratic form of government; (b) contacts lead to a more rational policy; and (c) contacts with interest groups enable effective socialization. Over two-thirds of the respondents in the economic ministries noted the contribution of interest groups to the rationalization of the decision-making process. As expected, among the service ministries the proportion of those emphasizing the rational aspect of the groups' contribution was far lower. In this sector adherence to democratic (i.e., pluralistic) norms was much more visible. The top administrators responsible for providing services are likely to denounce interest groups for their narrow perceptions and goals. At the same time, these officials realize that ongoing interaction allows them to be in touch with reality.

Table 4.4
Advantages of Contacts between Senior Officials and Interest Groups (Percent)

	Ministry category		
	Economic (22)	Service (19)	Total (41)
Contacts are indispensable in a democratic society	9.0	42.1	24.4
Contacts lead to a more rational policy	68.2	26.3	48.8
Contacts enable effective socialization	13.7	21.0	14.7
There are no advantages	9.0	10.5	12.1

In order further to comprehend the role ascribed by holders of important positions in governmental ministries to interest groups, the officials were addressed with a straightforward question: whether, in their opinion, interest groups should or should not be regularly consulted in the process of decision making. Their answers (presented in table 4.5) reveal that a sizable proportion display positive attitudes toward interest groups by regarding them as important actors in the political arena. Respondents supporting regular consultations with interest groups had warm words of praise for the groups' positive contribution to the performance of the bureaucracy. Respondents who believed in the necessity of this relationship were divided, however, between those who appreciated the groups' contribution and those who were haunted by their pressures. Thus, a senior official in the ministry of health stated that a policy on medical manpower and expertise could not have been implemented without the active cooperation of the IMA. The absorption ministry administrator responsible for the social aspects of integration claimed that the immigrant associations provided him with essential input regarding their clients' needs and desires. There were also officials who based their positive attitude on considerations of utility. They were aware of the limitations of their own authority and were convinced that joining the groups was preferable to fighting them. As a senior official in the ministry of finance pointed out: "They [referring to the Histadrut] can declare a strike and paralyze the whole economy. I worked too hard to advance our sick economy to where it is now. I would not risk it for anything. I must interact with them and accommodate their needs. I know that they, too, have a stake in the economy. For them any retreat would not be less harmful, so why not reach an agreement?"

Yet the picture depicting amicable relations between Israeli top administrators and interest groups is misleading. In fact, the proportion of those opposing regular consultation with voluntary associations or who conditioned it on the fulfillment of specified conditions was higher than the proportion of officials who unequivocally affirmed such a practice.[17] Almost a third of the officials in the economic ministries and over half in the service ministries equivocated. They stated that consultation with interest groups was desirable only when the following conditions were fulfilled by a group:

- adherence to a "policy," i.e., to target other than material benefits for their membership;

- cooperation with the ministry instead of putting sticks in the wheels of the administrative process;

- sticking to the "rules of the game" and not playing dirty tricks on the administrator, such as pulling strings and contacting politicians behind the official's back;

- being under the ministry's surveillance, that is, acting on behalf of the ministry, not just against it;

- coordinating activities with the administrators, especially in regard to pressures on other branches of government;

- finally, and most emphatically, promoting the national interest and eschewing a parochial outlook, meaning to stop acting selfishly and to begin adopting a general view; to cease pursuing material objectives and to espouse some values; in short, to discontinue promoting "interest" and stop being "group."

Some fifth of the officials were unconditionally against consultation with interest groups on policy decisions. As one of them remarked: "I always prefer to play with hidden cards. Once you reveal them, the associations mess everything up." But the views expressed by those who conditioned interaction on the fulfillment of specified conditions indicated a large pool of resentment toward voluntary associations. Some officials castigated interest groups in harsh words. They were accused of promoting selfish interests and of totally disregarding the welfare of the society. "They can see as far as their pockets" was how one official summed up the objections. The literature regards interest groups as representing the more dynamic aspect of political life owing to their proximity to grassroots participation. Israeli officials held a different view. Powerful economic associations were accused of blocking all reforms aimed at making the system work more efficiently. They regarded interest groups as rigid and more bureaucratic than bureaucracy itself: "They could hardly be convinced to agree to any move geared to change the status quo that serves them well. They plead short-term causes and block any long-term proposals. Status quo is so important to them because they fear any modification may rock the boat and diminish their power." The obstructionism of groups was also a cause of complaint: "They nag you from morning to night. You cannot perform your job when you are incessantly put under such a heavy pressure. It is a sheer waste of time to contact them. They quarrel among themselves so much that any agreement between you and them is bound to be breached. The next morning they would reopen the case for further discussion and nothing would be accomplished."

Senior officials regarded themselves, on the other hand, as custodians of the national interest in the face of obtrusive, selfish groups. They saw themselves as professionals whose function is to manage the process of policy making in accordance with political guidelines. Groups, in this view, are nothing but a nuisance. Ehrmann (1968: 269) observed that contacts between bureaucrats and interest groups are determined by the age and seniority of the former: younger officials tend to show a more technocratic attitude and are likely to demonstrate more autonomy vis-a-vis interest groups. In Israel, relations with associations do not appear to hinge on any demographic factor. The "technocratic attitude" was prevalent among all types of administrators, regardless of age, seniority, or ministry. There were even senior officials in the ministry of agriculture who showed a negative attitude toward their sectoral partners, who ostensibly are considered allies of the ministry's political leadership. Similarly, some officials in the Labor party–controlled ministry of finance were very critical of the Histadrut and its affiliated organizations.

Table 4.5
Opinions of Officials on the Desirability of
Consulting Interest Groups (Percent)

	Ministry category		
	Economic (22)	Service (19)	Total (41)
Yes	45.4	31.5	39.0
No	22.7	15.7	19.5
It depends on . . .	31.8	52.6	41.4

In view of this critical disposition, it was quite unexpected to find that almost two-thirds of the respondents stated that the relationship between the bureaucracy (that is, the senior officials) and interest groups have become closer during the last decade than in the past. This trend was more pronounced among the service ministries (table 4.6). The questionable legitimacy of interest groups apparently precluded the development of an amicable relationship between them and state officials. Yet administrators and groups communicate more often than in the past. Officials also tend to consult interest groups more frequently than in the past. The gist of this finding is that a certain gap exists between perception and reality, between views and behavior. While senior officials in the Israeli government bureaucracy continue to espouse typical elitist orientations and use pejorative terms to describe what they see as self-seeking groups that feather their own nests, they include them, perhaps willy-nilly, in the policy process.

When asked to explain this apparent contradiction, officials blamed, as it were, the intensification of relations between the bureaucracy and interest groups on the "weakening" of the state and its inability to withstand pressure. A senior administrator in the ministry of health cited cases in which officials could not put an end to a project initiated by a voluntary association (regarding

Table 4.6
Trend of Relationship between Administrators and
Interest Groups (Percent)

	Ministry category		
	Economic (22)	Service (19)	Total (41)
Relationship has weakened	4.6	5.3	4.8
Relationship has remained stable	41.0	15.7	29.2
Relationship has become closer	54.5	79.0	65.8

the detection of cardiovascular ailment) despite a deep conviction that it was incompatible with the best interests of the public at large. The state was in effect viewed as vulnerable, susceptible to pressures from outside parties. Although its appetite for activity in the social domain is almost limitless, its capacity to implement lags much behind. The ensuing reliance on voluntary associations to perform a host of functions generates dependence on interest groups, which, on their part, acquire a tremendous amount of influence. (Suleiman [1984] has described a similar situation in France). Powerful interest groups, such as Kupat Holim or Magen David Adom (the Israeli equivalent of the Red Cross), that provide essential health services to wide constituencies have turned into the proverbial tail that wags the dog. The state that helped to create them, to consolidate their authority, and that furnished them with a continuous flow of resources is no longer in a position to determine the shape or the extent of their activities.

The increase in interest group power vis-à-vis the state is more evident in ministries providing services than in those producing them. In the economic ministries, the power of officials has remained intact, if not increased in their dealings with representatives of interest groups. Administrators still have broad discretionary power to determine who will get rich or who will be impoverished; whose enterprise will fluorish or who is doomed to economic extinction. An official can determine the fate of a request for an investment subsidy, for funding of exports, or for an import license. Despite this conspicuous might, many officials expressed a sense of insecurity in handling their overarching powers. The dilemma was posed in this reaction:

> True, I make decisions and they [the activists of interest groups] rely on me and watch me closely as I make up my mind; but they can easily overrule me. They can make use of their good political contacts and appeal directly to the minister or to some influential member of the party center who is indebted to

them. I will be on the dock and the group will make the day. That's the reason for my caution. I have to be careful and not to antagonize interest groups having an important political patron. That's why I try to accommodate them. By doing this I do not act in the best interests of the state, but I have very little choice. You can never tell whose support they obtained in each particular case.

Not less effective is the pressure exerted on the administrator by a Knesset member, who, unlike the minister, has no formal authority over the branches of government. Nevertheless, the MK may be influential with regard to promotion or (in the case of a director-general) job stability. A senior official in one of the economic ministries concluded the interview by emphasizing the enduring role of the parties: "The party still dominates although in different means. This is our democracy. It is a nuisance, but you cannot avoid parties. There are economic and political interests at stake. It may be a sore evil but it is part of our life. We, in government ministries, cannot insulate ourselves from the general environment, which is still permeated by partisanship." Evidently political contacts are employed and much prodding goes on behind the scenes. This kind of pressure, exercised in the dark corridors of the political maze, appears to be most difficult to resist.

This does not imply that alliances between state officials and interest groups are forged exclusively on a partisan basis. A senior official in the ministry of housing who does not hide his dovish opinions on the future fate of the occupied territories did not hesitate to cooperate with the hawkish Gush Emunim group. It remains dubious, though, whether this answer reflects a typical attitude. With but one official, no official was willing to discuss openly the role of parties in their decisions; their excuse was that as "civil servants" they could not do so. The impact of partisanship on administrative behavior did, however, emerge implicitly in the interviews.

Officials are thus often caught between the political Scylla and the interest group Charybdis. On the one hand, the "politicians," including their own ministers, encourage them to take a certain position and to adopt a stand favorable to their clients. On the other hand, groups also exert pressures, which are not always compatible with ministerial preferences and are not always avoidable. This dilemma may be resolved by an alliance between the interest group and officials, both lining up against a tough, stringent ministry of finance. In this capacity, the organs of state tend to become interest groups themselves, rather than regulators of group conflict. The bureaucrats of the Treasury, in the unanimous opinion of the officials interviewed, formed "a state within a state." The Treasury is where the real power resides and where national policy is forged. It is a common practice for officials in other ministries to coalesce with interest groups in order to enhance their share of the national pie. "A common front of the ministry and interest groups is less resistible than are intergovernmental negotiations," one official explained. Such an alliance has enabled, for example, the electronic and high-tech industry to obtain a larger slice of the research and development budget. The combined effort of the department in charge of this section in the ministry of industry and its counterpart in the Manufacturers Association proved extremely effective, according to the testimony of various officials.[18] The alliance between state officials and representatives of interest groups does not lead to a formation of a "policy network," characterized by interdependence between members (Wilks and Wright 1987). Rather, bureaucrats and associations form ad hoc alliances for the purpose of advancing a specific issue at a particular time. The interaction is, more often than not, so intermittent and unstructured that it could not even be regarded as taking place within a "policy community" consisting of those with a vital interest in the policy field, who are constantly engaged in a host of undertakings that demand cooperation between the state and organized specialists (Pross 1986: 113). Yet interest groups do play a role in the bureaucratic maze of power.

One of the peculiarities of the Israeli system of government is that pressures on government officials are exerted from within the state as much as they are exerted by extra-state associations. A commentator noted that the "government consists of representatives of clients that are government opponents."[19] Thus the ministry of agriculture pressures to raise the price of farm products ("There is no disagreement between the ministry of agriculture and the farmers. . . .; our dispute is with the government ministries that do not regard agriculture as a prime national and economic asset," the ministry's deputy director-general asserted); and the ministry of health puts pressure on the Treasury to raise the salaries of the hospital workers. Knesset members, too, join the bandwagon of those exerting pressures. On July 10, 1988, twelve MKs staged a hunger strike to protest the government's (i.e. the ministry of finance's) indifference toward the disarray in the health system. The Israeli policy-making arena thus appears to be crisscrossed by many divisions, as well as by many forms of cooperation. Bureaucrats and interest groups may be pitted against each other, but they also may become allies against a common adversary: the agency responsible for the national cashier.

Interest Groups and the Bureaucracy: Patterns of Relationships

From all the foregoing, three types of relationships between interest groups and bureaucrats seem to prevail.

First, interest groups are regarded as equal players in the political game. They are legitimate actors whose attempts to influence public policy are seriously considered, even acknowledged. A senior official in the justice ministry summed up the situation as follows: "You cannot tell in advance who will be the winner. Everyone is entitled to his or her own view. Their [the interest groups'] particular interest is no less legitimate than that of the state. We are responsible for the general welfare so we take the lead, but we try to do so only after differences between us and them have been straightened out."

Such pluralistic views are in the minority. Contrary to expectations, they are more common among officials in ministries providing services mainly because they usually share the occupational backgrounds of the interest group membership. Thus "the social origin of the top-bureaucrats facilitates feelings of kinship with groups outside the administration" (Ehrmann 1968: 269). Under these circumstances, interest group activists have close ties with their colleagues occupying top administrative posts, enabling the former to negotiate on safer grounds. The relationship between the state and interest groups tends to be horizontal more than vertical (Suleiman 1974: 342). Each party retains its autonomy, but interaction tends to be reciprocal. As a result, under these particular circumstances contacts between the administrators and interest groups are conducted within the framework of a policy network. Face-to-face communication is facilitated by the similar background, and a framework for policy discourse is thus provided. Since cooperation remains mainly unstructured, however, the discourse has not evolved into corporatist practices.

The second type of relationship between administrators and interest groups is more in line with liberal corporatism. This type tends to develop when associations fulfill a functional role in the policy process. The functional contribution of interest groups to a ministry is manifested in two ways. First, the group must have

competent experts who can help the administrators solve problems
involved in the issues at stake. A few government ministries are
really "dependent" on groups in terms of functional performance.
One of these is the ministry of agriculture, depending on settlement movements, whose know-how and experience contribute to
settlement policies. As one of the administrators has put it: "I can
count on them to help me with the delivery of programs. They
give me professional help, they know what settlement is about.
Without settlers I could not have done my job. Those clerks
around me, they have hardly seen a green tree or a live chicken in
their entire lives. I cannot take settlers out of my pocket. I
desperately need these people in the settlement movements in
order to scatter Jewish farms all over the country." Even in cases in
which functional dependence is visible, no love story between civil
servants and the representatives of the group is necessarily implied.

The second manifestation of groups' functional contribution
is the aid given by interest groups when lobbying other state agencies, especially the ministry of finance or the Knesset. It is perhaps
inaccurate to describe this aid as given to the administrators, since
the main benefactors are the group's members themselves rather
than the state agency. In effect, though, both actors stand to gain,
since the goal of one becomes confused with that of the other. This
type of mutual relationship often develops; but it may also happen
that an interest group—or powerful individuals within it—will
bypass the ministry and interact directly with the major source of
power, the Treasury. Bypassing is, in fact, a two-way street.
Senior administrators in the ministry of industry and commerce
reported that they were often approached by individual entrepreneurs rather than by an association. In one case, an official
noted that 80 percent of the appeals to the ministry were made by
individual firms rather than by the MA. These contacts often
substitute for the institutional link between officials and the interest group headquarters. The owner of a big textile enterprise,
for example, may negotiate with the administrators on the terms
of state aid without resorting to the mediation of his or her
association. The case is the reverse in regard to service ministries,
whose officials may overlook organized interests. The physicians
have been integrated into the policy process to the point where the
bureaucracy actually ignores the association. It is very common
for Israeli authorities to set up a committee of experts nominated
on an individual basis rather than on the basis of interest group affiliation. A manager of a central hospital is much more likely to

represent the profession in a state-sponsored committee, his or her membership in the IMA being a mere formality and a secondary consideration. The study thus reveals that organized associations' functional contribution to state affairs is not regarded by the bureaucracy as crucial in the process of policy making.

A third type of attitude, one associated with elitism, is exclusion. This view is grounded in the disdain that administrators evince toward groups. Israeli top administrators seem to be heavily guided by the notion of the "general interest." Although officials expressed an outright hostility to interest groups only rarely, their behavior did demonstrate exclusion. Thus although some officials paid lip service to the need to incorporate interest groups into the decision-making process, they did very little to implement this position. Admittedly, their interaction with interest groups may have been intense; but in some cases, the intensity had about it a ritualistic rather than a substantive air. They may seek a group's consent but it is all pro forma. "The consent of the interest group,"one official said, "is sought only after the policy has been determined. It can make no difference in the final outcome. I let them shout and cry, since the final word is ours."[20]

Such an explicit rebuttal of public associations was rare. In fact, a substantial proportion of the officials interviewed did not perceive interest groups as a necessary evil, and the groups's expediency in the political process was often acknowledged. Yet the need to cooperate with "outsiders" or the dependence of administrators, at least to some extent, on interest groups operating outside the confines of the bureaucracy, was conspicuously missing. Not one official was willing to establish permanent, institutionalized links with interest groups which would have the effect of diminishing some of the powers of the bureaucracy. "Even an incompetent junior official functions better than a joint committee," an administrator remarked. Liberal corporatism was thus ruled out as a model for emulation or adaptation by Israeli state officials.

As the answers to the questionnaire reveal, there was much derogation of the motives of interest groups. There were also doubts regarding the groups' contribution to the general welfare. Many officials used stereotyped and unsympathetic terms to describe the objectives of interest groups. In this respect, hardly any difference in attitude was displayed toward the different types of interest groups. Even the Society for the Protection of Nature, known for its dedication to the national cause, was charged with "promoting issues that happen to concern some of its leadership [such as archaeological excavations] rather than caring for acute problems, such as pure water and clean environment."

The difference between attitudes and behavior, alluded to above, was noticeable. A widespread deligitimation of particular interests coexisted with intensive (and growing) interaction with the promoters of these interests. This inconsistency may be explained by a time lag: behavior is more susceptible to change than is attitude. Interest groups are, in point of fact, integrated in the policy process. They have become an important thread in the political fabric and cannot be ignored. Nonetheless, administrators are more comfortable with espousing "national" objectives which are not marred by benefiting particular individuals. Although rewards are continually and generously bestowed, the administrators have yet to adopt an attitudinal stance that would legitimize pluralistic responses to external pressures.

The policy issue was also listed among the factors determining the attitudes of bureaucrats toward interest groups (Lowi 1964). This research deviated from the conventional classification of policy issues by making a distinction between two types of ministries: those providing services and those responsible for generating them. Some degree of variation did manifest itself. Bureaucrats in the economic ministries attempted to secure more consent, to appreciate the interest groups' role in mobilizing support, although they denounced the pressure they exert. In their view, interest groups nevertheless contribute to rationalization of policy making. More than half of the administrators in the economic ministries conceded that contacts have consolidated with time. One can cautiously conclude that the officials responsible for the conduct of the Israeli economy are more prone to acknowledge the impact of interest groups than their counterparts in the service ministries. On the other hand, the administrators in the latter ministries tended more to seek the opinion of interest groups and to be aware of their contribution to formulating the policy agenda. Although they deemed contacts indispensable in a democratic society, they were also more likely to charge associations with overlooking the "national interest." This seeming contradiction may be explained by the "conditions," described above, inserted by the officials to justify their interaction with group representatives.The fulfillment of these conditions offered a key for legitimizing the pressures of "outsiders" in a society still imbued with many elitist values. On the other hand, the gap between "conditions" and reality provide a clue for understanding the incongruity between perceptions and behavior.

Knesset Members and Interest Groups

The findings presented in this section are based on research conducted in 1978, probing the relations between MKs and interest groups, and therefore may be only tentative when applied to contemporary Israel. As will be further elaborated (in chapter 6), the major conclusion that emerged from that study (Yishai 1978a) was that Knesset members highly value their interaction with interest group representatives, or at least they assume that such contacts are expedient in terms of their public image. To begin with, MKs tend to exaggerate reports of contacts with interest groups. In 1978, 65 percent of the MKs responding to a mail questionnaire (n=83, which constituted 69 percent of the total members of the Knesset) replied they had initiated contacts with associations. This information, however, was not confirmed by the groups, only a quarter of which (n=81) claimed they were frequently approached by Knesset members.[21]

In the 1978 survey Israeli MKs were also asked whether their interaction with interest groups was aimed at (a) obtaining information; (b) securing support for their party among "out" groups; or (c) strengthening links between the Knesset and the public at large. It was expected that, as partisan-oriented politicians, the MKs would place prime emphasis on their respective parties' needs. The answers refuted this assumption, as an overwhelming majority (87 percent) of the legislators ranked first their ties to the general public as the major objective of contacts with interest groups. The low preference for partisan-oriented goals may have reflected three trends: first, disbelief in the ability of interest groups to secure votes and mobilize electoral constituencies; second, a belief that partisan channels of socialization are sufficiently effective to render group's election efforts superfluous; third, changing public preferences. Declaring that a linkage with interest groups is geared to benefit the party was already incongruent with the public mood by the late 1970s. The MKs' propensity to woo interest groups has emerged as a widespread practice; although their power may emanate from their partisan institutions, their popularity could be enhanced by keeping a cozy relationship with voluntary associations. The attitudes of Knesset members toward interest groups thus seems more favorable than those demonstrated by senior government officials. Even if interest groups do interfere with legislation, and occasionally succeed in blocking policy intentions, it appears that the benefits derived from the interaction with these groups outweigh the losses.

CHAPTER FIVE

The Organization of Interest Groups: The Institutional Framework

Interest groups are organizations, and the way in which each an organization formulates its structure and mobilizes its resources affects the way its interests are represented before the government—and hence the manner in which its influence is secured. One widely held school of thought believes that organization is power and that it is a key to political clout (Michels 1958). Understanding the organizational characteristics of interest groups is thus essential for delineating their relations with the authorities. As elaborated in the Introduction, organizational distinctions are discernible between the three interest group configuration models. These differences are evident on four planes: the degree of monopolization of an interest domain, inter-relations in the group arena, the degree of dependence on state/party organizational resources, and internal centralization. The underlying question is whether the structural characteristics of Israeli interest groups reflect their close affinity to political parties, or alternatively, do they demonstrate autonomy and independence. A second important question focuses on the associations' likelihood to deliver the goods required in a corporatist relationship, that is, the leadership's ability to impose discipline and to secure cohesion.

This chapter will analyze the complex attributes of the Israeli interest group universe, which operates under heavy monopolistic constraints. Centralization on the national level, however, is mitigated by intra-group centrifugal forces, that is, by the right to raise a "voice." The chapter will also demonstrate that dependence on state/party sources for the solicitation of resources is both limited and equivocal.

Basic Organizational Features

Date of establishment

The growth and proliferation of contemporary interest groups have not advanced at an even pace. In order to place the founding of Israeli interest groups on a time continuum, three periods were distinguished: the first, up to the establishment of the state (1948), when party influence was preponderant; the second, from independence to the Six Day War (1967), when economic development was in full swing; the third, from 1968 to 1989, when the values of post-materialism have presumably spread. Systematic data (presented in figure 5.1) reveal that issue-oriented interest groups in Israel indeed, as postulated in the Introduction, emerged only after the sectional interest group arena was already well established. In fact, some four-fifths of the material-oriented organizations were in business before 1967; but only about a half of the promotional interest groups predated the Six Day War. Among the promotional sector the cultural and sports groups came first. If, as postulated by Truman (1951) group activity reflects concerns of individuals, the early Jewish settlers were not only preoccupied with solving their material problems, but also catered to their cultural needs. The fact of the matter is, however, that these organizations, the sport clubs being a good example, were not founded by individuals, but rather by political parties, regarding them as an effective means of mobilization. Among the early birds on the sectional group scene are the farmers, whose settlement effort paved the way for Jewish national revival. Proliferation in the agricultural sector spurred associational formation after 1948. Farmer suborganization, such as the Union of Fruit Growers, were not established until Israel's economic upsurge. Physicians, attorneys, teachers, and dentists expressed their unique problems by forming associations. Some of the groups were extremely small at their inception. The Israel (then Hebrew) Medical Association was established in 1912 by seven of the few dozen physicians practicing in the country. Welfare organizations and public interest groups are late arrivals on the associational arena. Israelis became aware of their nonmaterial needs some two decades after the establishment of the state. There are noted exceptions to this rule. Major women, environmental, and consumer groups predated 1968 and were, in fact, tightly linked to values and norms prevailing in the early days of statehood. Most of the non-material associations emerged, however, only in the late 1960s.

Chronological sequence thus confirms the movement of Israel toward a new style of interest politics.

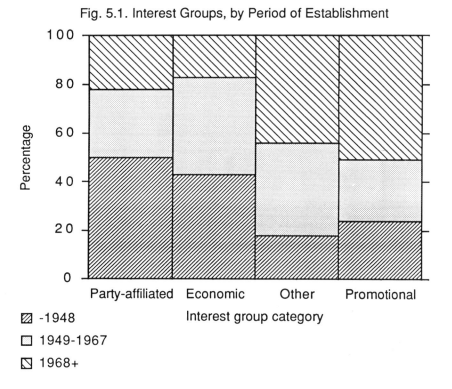

Fig. 5.1. Interest Groups, by Period of Establishment

Size, budget, and managerial staff

Israeli interest groups exhibit a bifurcated picture in regard to their size. Over half are large in terms of membership since they have passed the threshold of 1,000 registered, dues-paying members (see figure 5.2). In some cases the figures are striking. The Histadrut encompasses an overwhelming majority of Israel's adult citizens and so do some of its affiliated organizations, such as Naamat. Among the giant associations (membership over 10,000) are the large professional associations such as the Teachers Federation (with 65,000 members in 1988) and the Engineers Federation (with 35,000 members in 1988). The Union of State Workers, representing the interests of white collar state employees, comprised (in 1988) of 120,000 members. The size of these big associations has not resulted from successful mobilization efforts, but from their monopolization of representation, to be discussed below. Nearly half of all interest groups may be considered small; that is, with a membership of less than 1,000. These small groups cut across the associational arena, but they are prominent mostly among the business sector, where proliferation on the basis of subsectors has taken place. The fact that the economic groups, like their labor counterparts, are organized under roof-organizations is not reflected in the figures pertaining to the size of their membership. The data are misleading in regard to public interest groups too; some half of which lay claim to having no membership at all.

Fig. 5.2. Interest Groups, by Size of Membership

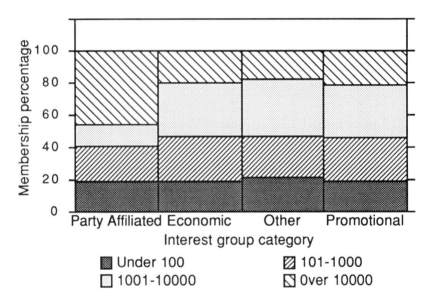

Membership provides financial resources. In 1988 more than one-third of the sectional associations had an annual budget over half a million shekels. Promotional groups, despite the large number of non-membership organizations, also portray a picture of relative affluence: nearly half report such a budget (see figure 5.3). Israeli sport and welfare associations are very well funded. For example, the annual budget of Ilan, the Association for the Physically Handicapped, totaled in 1988 30 million shekels. In the financial respect, the variation between the different types of interest groups is not significant, although none of the "other" sectional associations is numbered among those having an annual budget of over 10 million shekels.

Fig. 5.3. Interest Groups, by Size of Budget

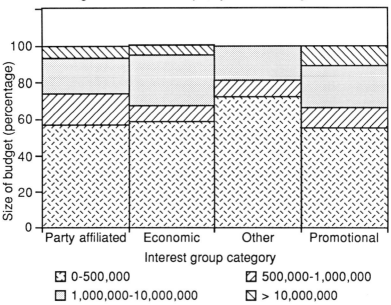

The organizational weakness of promotional associations lies in their bureaucratic structure. Most of these organizations are not well staffed. Among the promotional interest groups, a large percentage either have no staff or just a few employees (up to ten). Surprisingly, the employment of an administrative staff is modest, too, among the sectional category: some three-quarters report staffs of fewer than ten persons. The paucity of administrative manpower notwithstanding, the organizational viability of interest groups is not hindered, as this emanates mainly from their monopolization of a domain of interest.

Sectional Monopolization

The diversity and number of interest groups described in chapter 2 present a misleading picture when judged from a pluralistic perspective, for the associational arena is characterized by a high degree of monopolization. The density of membership (i.e., the proportion of members of those eligible to join) in all Israeli interest groups is impressive by any international standard. In the sectional category as a whole, more than half the organizations reported a density of 85 percent and more; in the party-affiliated organizations density was even higher. Some examples will illustrate the degree of monopolization. The Histadrut announced in 1988 that it had a total of some 1.6 million members, which would constitute approximately 90 percent of Israel's working population. Trade union membership figures for European countries are pale by comparison: France, 20 percent; West Germany, 41 percent; and the United Kingdom, 50 percent. Only Sweden displayed a density of unionization reaching 80 percent (quoted in Wilson 1987: 142). As shown in figure 5.4, the Histadrut's membership has grown in a higher proportion than the rise in population. The argument has been advanced that the major incentive for joining the Labor Federation is not grounded in class consciousness but in the services of the Histadrut-sponsored Sick Fund, Kupat Holim (Arian 1985: 210). Despite the affiliation of the Histadrut with the Labor party, the socialists' electoral failure in 1977 did not induce a loss of trade union membership. On the contrary, figures indicate that the percentage of growth in 1978—a year after the election—was slightly higher (a 2.13 percent change from the previous year) than in 1977 (which had recorded a 2.09 percent change from 1976).

High membership levels are evident, also, on the employers' front. The density of members in the Manufacturers Association is around 90 percent even though the group is quite selective in recruitment. Furthermore, dues are extremely high. Still, the number of those wishing to formally (as distinct from practically) bypass the MA and establish direct links with the authorities as an alternative (rather than a supplement) to its services is scant. It should be recalled, however, that the Histadrut-owned giant industrial enterprise, Koor, is not part of the MA, but it exerts its influence through the channels of its parent association. Other business and industry groups also display a high level of density: the Union of Hotel Owners reports 100 percent membership; the Union of Insurance Companies, 90 percent. Only the Association of Artisans and Small Industry presents an exceptional low density, of 20 percent. The reason for this low density may be grounded in the partisan affiliation of this organization, which was not compatible with the members' political preferences. The establishment of the Coordinating Office further increased the centripetal

Fig. 5.4: Histadrut Membership as Percentage of Israel's Population, 1950-1987

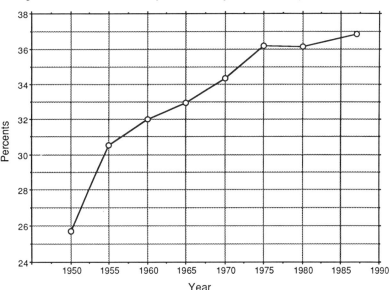

Year

Source: Bartal, 1989, Statistical Abstract 1988:31

tendencies of large businesses. With that umbrella organization's rejection of the independent sector, the Coordinating Office indicated that the sectional arena is closed to new contenders and that monopolization, a kind featuring corporatist arrangements, has nearly been achieved. Concentration in the private sector of the Israeli economy is also confirmed by economic data: some one-quarter of the hotel rooms were owned (in 1987) by less than ten percent of the hoteliers (*Statistical Abstract* 1988: 492); 63.8 percent of all industrial workers were concentrated in 7.7 percent of the industrial establishments (*Statistical Abstract* 1988: 430); and about 15 percent of the contractors built 36.7 percent of all dwellings (*Statistical Abstract* 1988: 476). Much of Israel's economic activity, then, appears to gravitate to the center.

The degree of density in the farm associations is also without precedent in the developed industrialized world, owing to the specific characteristics of the agricultural sector in Israel. The cooperative way of life leaves little choice to the "farmers," many of whom may actually be engaged in non-agricultural occupations. Interest group membership for the respective associations is thus comprehensive, in fact nearly total. Data on the output of the Agricultural Center indicate the extent to which agricultural production in Israel is centralized. The center is responsible for 86 percent of all investments in farming, for 82 percent of its production, for 76 percent of its exports, and for 70 percent of its employees (Bartal 1989: 123). Although the Farmers Union is not incorporated in the center, a coordinating body was established in January 1989 to enable joint activity when it comes to pressuring the authorities.[1]

Membership in professional associations also runs extremely high, for the simple reason that most professionals in Israel are salaried workers whose membership dues are deducted by the special arrangement described in chapter 3. For example, a university professor may not be a Histadrut member, but dues are nevertheless automatically transferred to the local faculty union. There are other organizational devices helping to all but exclude non-membership in a professional association. For example, a physician's automobile decal can be obtained only through the IMA. More importantly the Medical Association also controls tender committees and may block the promotion of a non-member physician. As already noted, membership in the Bar Association has been made compulsory for lawyers by law. One cannot practice law in Israel unless registered with, and licensed by, the Bureau of Advocates (the Bar Association). A professional may, in some cases, belong to two associations, one representing his or her professional interests (such as the Bureau of Engineers) and the other promoting union rights (such as the Engineers Federation). In most cases, however, representation of a specific profession is concentrated in one association. The Union of Social Workers, the Federation of Psychologists, and Israel Dentists Association are examples of groups that encompass all those practicing the respective profession. Only in the teaching sector is there organizational division, accompanied by deep rivalry, between the bigger Teachers Federation, affiliated to the Histadrut, and an independent Union of Post-Elementary School Teachers. Both of these organizations claim a high membership density. As noted earlier, Israel lacks a roof organization like the Swedish SACO (Elvander 1974) to coordinate the activities of the professional-academic associations.

Not all sectors enjoy the benefit of a high density. The immigrant associations have a low membership rate. Even the powerful association of American & Canadian immigrants reports a density of only 60 percent. The high degree of fragmentation among Soviet and the Ethiopian Jews further diminishes membership density in each of their respective associations. Absorption authorities have attempted to mitigate fractionalization of the immigrant associations by using the power of the purse: the ministry of absorption thus grants funds only to the one national association deemed most representative. The rationale is that the need to agree on the internal distribution of these funds would spur unified action. It appears, though, that the tactic is ineffective.

Over half of the promotional groups in Israel do not have a registered membership even though some may have a host of sympathizers. On the national level these associations do not tend to monoplize their domain. The high fractionalization of this sector is evident in two arenas, ecology and defense. The groups protesting the Lebanon war, the handling of the Palestinian *intifada*, and the continuing occupation of the territories seemed to mushroom daily. Moves initiated by one of the small left-wing parties, Ratz, to forge an alliance and coordinate the multiple groups advocating peace policies have not proved successful. Internal diversity, coupled with personal rivalries, have brought the attempt to naught.[2]

A marked variation is thus visible between different types of interest groups, with the sectional category (including its three subtypes) demonstrating tendencies for monopolization higher than the promotional category. The reasons for the monopolization process are grounded in Israel's political environment: a collectivist political culture, a preponderant unifying national objective, and central control of resources. There is also an organizational device, in the form of state recognition, that further spurs monopolization. The government in Israel is rarely involved in the establishment of interest groups, but it holds power to grant official recognition to groups that qualify as "representative." The status of "representative group" confers special privileges, perhaps the most important being that the group is eligible to represent its members in wage negotiations and in other formal dealings. More than 60 percent of all interest groups enjoy this status. Among the sectional associations the percentage is two-thirds.

The origins of this status date back to the Labor Agreements Law of 1957, dealing with employer-employee contracts. A group is recognized as "representative" when its membership is comprised of the plurality of workers to whom a work agreement applies, on condition that this number is not less than one-third of the total employed in the work place. Since 1970, employers' associations have also enjoyed the privileges of representative groups. By means of an "extension order," the Manufacturers Association was designated the only group eligible to represent the interests of the industrialists. Professional associations have a similar privilege. For example, the Medical Association, and it alone, may negotiate with the authorities on the matter of physicians' incomes. The IMA is also granted monopolistic status in regard to professional matters. It is the only body involved in issuing licenses to practice medicine. Its advice is legally sought in some matters pertaining to medical services and practices, such as medical experiments subject to the Helsinki Agreements. It is also the one and only body responsible for the training of doctors for medical specialization positions. Under these circumstances, it is hardly surprising that even though the IMA is plagued by deep divisions (to be discussed below), it is the only association representing the 12,000 medical doctors in the country. Entry to the arena by additional groups of physicians is all but prohibited, not by law, but by the fact that the existing association enjoys the status of representative organization.

A few promotional groups have also been privileged with this position, as representative of a respective handicap or sports domain. Three consumer associations were granted representative status, which, in their case, implies the right to represent clients in court on three legal grounds: the Law of Consumer Protection, the Law of Unified Contracts, and Small Claims Litigation. The acknowledgment by state authorities of multiple representatives in the consumers' sector stems from both political and historical circumstances. The Consumers Council is, for all practical purposes, an extension of the ministry of industry and commerce, and therefore was the first in line to acquire the recognized status. The Consumers Authority, as mentioned above, is a subunit within the Histadrut, whose powerful political clout led to the inclusion in the privileged club. The third group—the Independent Consumers Organization—was the first to arouse interest in consumers affairs. By virtue of historical right (and also because of strong political backing of WIZO and its latent patron, the Liberal party), it was also eligible to be representative. Other groups that entered the scene after the big three were already well established have been denied state recognition.

The granting of representative status tends, as has been seen, to freeze the division of power and prevent the entrance of new actors. The government has the authority to decide whether or not a group meets certain qualifications, which are not legally set. A clear definition of eligibility is pertinent only to trade unions, otherwise criteria are sufficiently vague to allow diverse interpretations of what constitutes representativeness. The ambiguous prerequisites regarding the acquisition of this status allow the state to reject requests for recognition. In fact, the state seems not at all anxious to grant such recognition to aspiring groups: there have been several cases in which associations have been denied the status, despite evidence of their having a significant following.[3]

One of the famous rejections, widely discussed in the media, pertained to the widows of war casualties who demanded the right to exit from the parent organization, Yad Labanim, which serves all war-related bereaved. The status of representative group was necessary for the widows to be able to conduct negotiations on behalf of their members. The ministry of defense, with which Yad Labanim is associated, refused to make a distinction between bereaved parents and the widows, although the interests and objectives of the two are said by the widows to diverge. In another case, a group of widows of civilians was denied recognition by state authorities for the reason of safeguarding freedom of association. It was claimed that granting the representative status may impede "other groups of widows wishing to organize outside the confines of this particular one."[4] State recognition has been denied not only in cases in which the group was small and/or marginal, but also in regard to prestigious, influential associations, such as the Civil Rights Association. The CRA, despite its effectiveness and popularity, did (and does) not belong to the inner core of power. It acts on behalf of the Palestinians, on behalf of people who may be hurt by religious legislation, and on behalf of others whose rights are violated by the legal or political system. In rejecting official status for the CRA the state was ostensibly protecting the right of association by saying it was safeguarding the rights of future contenders for representation. In effect, however, it was defending the status quo and the rights of those already enjoying a privileged position.

Interest groups not linked to the political establishment confront difficulties in their attempt to acquire representative status. Yet they continue to seek this recognition.[5] Material benefits are not at stake, because representative status does not necessarily entail eligibility for government funds, subsidies, or positions on a formal government advisory board. The sense of legitimacy conferred upon the group and the official confirmation that this group possesses sufficient weight that must be taken into consideration afford it important assets. More important, from the group's perspective, is the monopolistic status it acquires. Although monopoly is not an iron-clad law or result (e.g., the three "official" consumers' organizations), the state's recognition generally solidifies the status quo.

Granting an interest group the right of self-regulation constitutes another form of state recognition. Indeed self-regulation, mainly in regard to professions/vocations, is regarded as a stateconferred privilege. A crucial element in the very definition of a profession may be considered the extent to which aspiring occupational groups "have gained the organized power to control themselves, the terms, conditions, and content of their work in the settings where they perform their work" (Freidson 1970: 22). The next step is statutory power to set and enforce rules of behavior which constitutes the apogee of professional status (Gilb 1966: 136). Self-regulation may be sought for ideological reasons (i.e., only members of a profession should, and can, govern themselves properly), but tangible benefits are also entailed through control of the availability of manpower into the profession. Professional monopoly can also lead to employment security and to a clear definition of the standard of service. A self-regulated profession can successfully define itself as the key group in the delivery of a particular service (Wilding 1982: 54–57).

To the consternation of a number of professional organizations, the practice of self-regulation in Israel is all but nonexistent. Only the Bar Association has been fully acknowledged by the state as responsible for a profession: it dispenses licenses, it legally exercises disciplinary powers, it controls professional relationships between members, and it sets minimum fees for legal services. No other organization has been granted these privileges although many seek them. The Medical Association presented its request to be recognized as a bureau (a statutory representative organization with mandatory powers over its membership) in 1949; to date this recognition has been denied. The engineers, the accountants, the psychologists, and the social workers all wish to be granted statutory recognition, which would legalize their monopoly over their respective profession. In August 1989, the Association of Pharmacists was added to the list of those applying to the authorities with the argument that granting it self-regulation would benefit the public at large.[6] The reason for the reluctance of the authorities to give this right emanates more from their fear of loosing power than from their rejection of monopolistic arrangements. The latter, as already noted, are partly an entrenched product of the Israeli system of government, and result from the state officials' attitudes toward voluntary associations.

Inter-Group Relations

Competition between groups is one of the characteristics of the pluralist form of society; it is antithetical to both the corporatist and the elitist styles, in which rivalry is anathema and harmony is both an ideal and a practice. Data (presented in table 5.1) reveal that Israeli interest groups, according to their own testimony, do not operate in a free, competitive market. A "low" degree of competition is reported by a majority of all the associations. Among the public interest groups, not even one reported a high level of competition. The spirit of unity is thus reflected in the associational leaders' attitudes, even though it may not necessarily be backed by forms of behavior. A similar picture emerges when the extent of integration with other groups is examined. A sizable majority from all groups (between 77.7 percent among the promotional associations and 89.1 percent among the party-affiliated groups) reported having frequent, and harmonious interaction with other interest groups. Bearing in mind the uncompetitive nature of this interaction it appears that the promotional arena, characterized by a relative degree of fragmentation, is not plagued by the rivalry evident in pluralist politics. The spirit of accord does not include the defense-oriented interest groups (mainly Gush Emunim and Peace Now), whose differences are sharp and bitter.

Table 5.1
Inter-Group Relationships, by Associational Sector
(Percent Reporting)

	Party-affiliated	Economic	Other	Promotional	N
Harmonious interaction with other groups (high and medium)	89.1	78.5	78.6	77.7	180
Competition with other groups (low)	68.6	70.0	79.3	62.3	157

When identifying their adversaries, neither labor nor business sees itself pitted against the other as competitor or adversary. Neither the Labor Federation nor the Manufacturers Association view their counterpart as an opponent. Rather, ways and means are sought to increase cooperation and to foster joint action. Some rivalry did show itself, however, within the Histadrut; thus the Union of Diamond Workers appeared to be threatened by Metal Workers, who in turn named the Union of Technicians as their adversaries. To a lesser extent, internal rivalry also exists in the business sector. The national union of Commerce regarded the Federation of Merchants (owners of retail shops) as their competitors, and the Union of Travel Agents charged that the Hotel Owners reap the benefits and leave them with a meager share of the income from tourism. Competition is even more evident in the welfare domain, in which associations race for a larger slice in the highly competitive market of donations and contributions. Although the ministry of education allocates "days for contributions" solicited by school children, the game is still zero sum, with each organization striving to obtain one of the more popular dates. Despite these rivalries only a few pairs of associations maintain outright opposition to each other. The two teachers organizations fall into this category, although in more recent years they seem to find themselves increasingly in the same boat. On the other hand, the Organization of Tenants and the Association of Landlords still remain adamant, uncompromising opponents. As a rule, however, Israel presents a case that differs greatly from the findings of Salisbury et al. (1987: 1224). Interest groups relations in the United States were found to be rancorous, in contrast to the generally cooperative trend characterizing voluntary associations in Israel.

Mobilization of Resources

One of the crucial questions regarding the relations between interest groups and political authorities has to do with the former's degree of autonomy in securing organizational resources. The source of resources determines their strategies of action and the effectiveness of the means chosen to present demands and to secure influence. The bottom line of "organizational resources," as it were, is the funding available for group activity, for disseminating its message, for recruiting new members, and for influencing public authorities.

The data gathered for this book (presented in table 5.2) reveal the extent to which interest groups are funded by the government and by political parties. Generally speaking, parties are not an openly reported source of funding. Israeli parties themselves are generously funded by the state, although they always seem to be suffering from an acute shortage of resources. Their funding of various interest groups is not, though, the reason for their financial stringency. Parties do not fund even their affiliated associations. As noted above, the Histadrut funds political parties, rather than the reverse. Agricultural settlements also contribute to the parties' resources by diverting manpower to their needs, especially during electoral campaigns. Public interest groups endorsing controversial issues may be granted indirect aid through affiliated organizations by a political party having a stake in the issue under concern. Even the provision of vehicles to drive group members to the site of a central demonstration constitutes a form of subsidy.

As to state funds, the four categories of interest groups show a striking difference. The proportion of those receiving state financial aid is the lowest among the economic interest groups. Business groups and professional associations do not, as a rule, receive direct government funding. Instead, being nonprofit associations (in Hebrew, *amutot*), they are exempt from paying income tax. Tax deductions involve sophisticated accountancy, since some of the business groups (e.g., the Chamber of Commerce, the Manufacturers Association) have turned effectively into economic conglomerates with large financial assets, the profits of which are not tax deductible. Party-affiliated interest groups are not frequent recipients of state funding. The highest proportion of organizations that derive resources from the government is found among the "other" category of sectional groups. These include immigrant associations funded by the ministry of immigration and welfare. The data reveal that promotional interest groups are also benefactors of state funding, with over 40 percent reporting that to be the case.

Table 5.2
Sources of Interest Group Funding (Percent Reporting)

| | Interest group category | | | | |
	Party-affili-ted	Eco-nomic	Other	Pro-mo-tional	N
Party funding	—	2.3	—	2.3	159
State funding	13.8	7.2	57.7	43.4	157

Promotional associations do not own economic assets and, therefore, they do rely, more than their sectional counterparts, on state aid. Some associations solicit funds by selling services. For example, the Society for the Protection of Nature adds substantial funds to its budget by selling tours and information. One important source of finances specific to Israeli promotional interest groups is World Jewry. Many associations have established "friendship societies," especially in the United States (Ben-Meir 1988). Yet reliance on the state is widespread: the proportion of issue-oriented groups receiving government funding is nearly twice that of the sectional sector as a whole. The activists interviewed insist, however, that their group's autonomy is not infringed by the government. The state incorporates interest group funding in the budget books of the different ministries[7] and does not inquire into the purpose or forms of expenditure. Funding is not employed as a means to limit a group's independence or to pry into its affairs. Although the state is due an annual financial report from all those receiving financial aid, it employs the budget carrot stick approach only in rare instances.

If the state does not follow the pay with a decisive "say," the question arises as to the purpose of government funding. State funding of interest groups is prompted by two major aims: as a means of influence and for functional purposes.

Funding as a means of influence on budgetary allocations

Authorities do not, as a rule, ask questions about how the money they allocate is spent. Occasionally, though, they use funding as a means of influence on the organization. Perhaps the best examples of this point are the associations enjoying the financial support of the ministry of defense. As was discussed earlier, the intention of the widows of war casualties to withdraw from the roof organization of Yad Labanim was rebutted by the ministry, which threatened to terminate the budget allocation to the recalcitrant group. The use of funding as a means of influence also came into play with the Organization of the IDF Handicapped, and the Association for Soldiers. Ostensibly the two associations are autonomous, making their own decisions regarding patterns of expenditure. The ministry, however, may make its preferences known and may tacitly be involved in the process of allocation. It is worth noting that a sizable portion of the ministry's administrative staff are members in one or more of the ministry-funded associations. This personal interlock increases the state's ability to exert influence through funding. The ministry of defense, however, appears to be the only one that accompanies allocation of money with explicit or implicit influence on the manner in which the money ought to be spent.

Funding for functional purposes

About a third of the public interest groups are recipients of state funds, the ecological groups being among the chief benefactors. The purpose of their funding may be found in the nature of their activities. The Society for the Protection of Nature derives a quarter of its budget from government sources. Malraz, the Council for a Beautiful Israel, and other small environmental associations are also funded by the state, though to a lesser extent. Some public interest groups—the Council for Consumer Affairs, the Society for Better Housing, and the Council for Prevention of Traffic Accidents—obtain their entire budget from government sources. The rationale for this funding in each case is grounded in the objectives fulfilled by the recipient, which presumably, propagate goals congruent with the collective good.

Public subsidy of public interest groups is not unique to Israel (Vogel 1981: 614). The justification for funding in this country is that such groups defray state expenses in fulfilling functions of socialization (e.g., inculcating the love of the land, educating the people to cherish and safeguard national sites and landscapes, making drivers more aware of their behavior behind the wheel). State funding of public interest groups is not tied up with party politics. By virtue of their public orientation, public interest groups are eligible to receive official aid regardless of their political color. The chairman of Malraz, for example, has been a Likud activist and is former member of its Knesset faction. His affiliation with the right-wing camp did not impede funding of Malraz by the ministry of health, which at the time was controlled by ardent members of the Labor party.

Immigrant associations are also eligible for public funding on account of their functional role in absorbing the newcomers in their case, allocation of funds is based on some objective criteria: the overall population of newcomers who arrived during the past three years, the number of Jews still remaining in the country of origin, and an annual report on last year's activities and next year's plans. Yet the accurate amount of money is negotiable. A group's initatives and pressures may be important in determining the amount of funding it receives from public authorities. As a result of this bargaining, immigrant associations representing Third World or distressed countries tend to be poorer and weaker than those representing the affluent democratic states. Attempts on the part of the ministry of immigration to induce the adoption of weaker associations by stronger ones have not met with success (Korazim 1988: 176).

Welfare interest groups and sports associations also enjoy government aid, owing to their functional social role. Welfare groups have filled in many gaps in governmental service programs. Although a high proportion (42.1 percent) of these groups receives state funds, the amounts involved are relatively small. The policies and the conditions under which funds are made available and distributed are inconsistent. Kramer (1981: 150) suggests that the purpose of funding is to cover up a deficit more than it is to raise standards. The ability of the welfare associations to "create facts" and then to request government support has given them significant influence over the distribution of funds. Once a welfare association demonstrates a service, Kramer noted, it can usually expect to obtain some government support or, at least, to be bailed out if it flounders. The proportion of cultural and sports organizations reporting on receiving government financial aid is the highest among all categories of interest groups (60 percent). Their functional role in socializing the citizenry and in providing entertainment have qualified them for government funding.

Internal Cohesion

There are two faces to the coin of cohesion: one pertains to the degree of unity and discipline, which is not common in pluralist regimes, is absolutely necessary in corporatist configurations, and is common also in elitist politics; the other aspect is that of internal democracy, which implies the opportunity and right to dissent. This section will examine the organizational properties that demonstrate the degree of unity vs. the right to dissent. The internal cohesion of Israeli interest groups was examined through a series of questions referring to their organizational structure and behavior. Group activists were requested to report on the rules of their organization. Is the periodic convention held on its designated date? Is leadership incumbency limited? Is there a turnover in leadership regardless of the written provision? In short, are the tenets of organizational democracy followed and obeyed? The group activists were also asked to assess the degree of internal cohesion by describing membership participation, internal dissensions, challenges to leadership, the opportunities available to an opposition (in case one exists) to express its views, and finally the degree of organizational centralization.

These questions presented some methodological difficulties, since they lack operational definition. For example, "high membership participation" could mean different things to different people. Nevertheless, interviews with dozens of group activists filled in the gaps and enabled a deeper understanding of each of the categories used to probe a group's cohesion. The extent of the internal organizational cohesion of Israeli interest groups and their internal patterns of democracy were tabulated (table 5.3). Discussion of these aspects follows.

Leadership turnover

Turnover in leadership is one of the classical symptoms of democracy. If this indicator is used as a major criterion, then interest groups in Israel have passed the test of democracy. A vast

Table 5.3
Internal Democracy of Interest Groups (Percent Reporting)

| | Interest group category | | | |
	Party-affili-ted	Eco-nomic	Other	Pro-mo-tional	N
Convention held on designated date	62.1	73.1	75.0	70.3	160
Limits on leadership incumbency	37.8	40.4	46.4	22.6	160
Chairperson in office less than eight years	83.3	83.3	78.5	73.6	159
High membership participation in group life	43.2	26.1	35.7	42.3	159
Major internal dissensions (some, many)	78.3	60.9	51.6	53.7	161
No serious challenge to leadership (almost never)	54.0	57.5	65.5	55.8	158
Opposition is given a voice (often and occasionally)	58.0	45.8	22.0	28.0*	137
Decentralized organizational structure	27.7	50.0	34.5	60.8	153

*Only one-third of the promotional associations issue some type of internal publication.

majority of all four types of interest groups report an incumbency for their elected chairpersons shorter than eight years (that is, the equivalent of not more than two terms in the Knesset). More than four in ten economic interest groups (and "other" sectional associations) formally limit incumbency in the top position. The proportion in the party-affiliated groups is somewhat lower. In the issue-oriented associations, in contrast, the percentage is a little more than two in ten. The formal limitation on incumbency may be on paper only. As one interviewee said: "our chairman steps down from his chair for two years. During this period he serves as a senior board member. His reelection for a subsequent term is reassured."

The election of an interest group's leadership is regulated by law (discussed in chapter 4). In most cases, conventions are duly held, not only because the regulations so require, but also because this forum provides an opportunity for media publicity. Conventions are attended by senior politicians; grievances are vented by dissident minorities without seriously harming the group's cohesion. Only a quarter of the economic interest groups do not hold their conventions on the designated date. Party-affiliated groups adhere less than their economic counterparts to the formal rules of democracy. In this respect, the findings of Lipset et al. (1956), who highlighted the oligarchic tendencies among United States trade unions, may be applicable to the Israeli scene. The strong partisan affiliation of most unions, and their dependence on Histadrut ruling make the convention superfluous; decisions are arrived at in forums other than the union's elected institutions. Deals between the various partisan factions comprising the trade union leadership often make the election process obsolete. Outcomes are determin-

ed before the ballot is cast. Promotional associations show more
adherence to the formal rules, and a large majority do hold conventions on time. In the absence of selective benefits, "democracy"
in these groups, even in its formal sense, is more prevalent than it
is in the sectional groups. The practice of holding a formalized national meeting is more common among the more institutionalized
issue-oriented associations. Conventions are not held by the
associations lacking a firm organizational basis (such as Peace
Now).

Patterns of leadership

The authority structure of the universe of Israeli interest
groups provides a framework for decision making on the allocation of resources, the selection of issues, and the devising of
strategies for action. Within the variety of interest groups, several
principal types of leadership styles may be identified: leaders
associated with political parties, leaders subject to outside constraints, autonomous leaders, and leaders constrained by their
own rank and file.

Outside constraints: Partisan leaders. Trade union members in
Israel elect their leaders according to their partisan political affiliation. The same principle is applied to all associations operating
under the auspices of the Histadrut, including sports groups and
professional organizations. The leadership of the Teachers Federation, the Union of Hotel Workers, and the Federation of Nurses
owes its nomination to the Labor party, a fact that in the past
limited its autonomy. Freedom of action, however, has greatly expanded in recent years. Although the road to the job still passes
through party corridors, the union is, in most cases, free to formulate its own policy. Even though the members of associational
elites owe their position to a party, they are not bound by its directives. It is often the case that the interest group leader is courted by
the party and gets his or her way because of the solid backing he or
she enjoys within the association.

Interviews with group activists also reveal an opposite trend,
whereby the party strengthens its hold on partisan group leaders.
This is especially true with regard to sports organizations. "Spectator sports" has become one of the major entertainments of
Israelis, who spend a great deal of time watching especially televised sporting events. The heroes of the games, the basketball and
the soccer players, may not be chosen on the basis of their party
loyalty or world view, but the executive boards of sport societies

are elected strictly on the basis of service to the party. The position of "sport activist" (*askan sport*), entailing prestige, influence, and perhaps a side income and/or trips abroad, is usually reserved for people active in other walks of political life. Within Hapoel (in Hebrew, the Worker—the sport association affiliated with the Labor movement) for example, leadership is divided among the numerous sections of the Histadrut: settlement movements, trade unions, etc. A recent Histadrut reform had the purpose of severing the financial relations between the workers' councils and the sport clubs; nevertheless, political infiltration remained intact. Although sports in Israel are becoming more professionalized and the economic performance of a club is a major criterion for success the politicization of this domain is still considerable. The leaders of the sports associations are by and large people benefiting from the spoils system of the partisan regime.

No constraints: Elected leadership. In business interest groups, professional associations, and charity organizations, leadership is freely selected/elected by rank-and-file members. The leaders thus enjoy full autonomy to lead their group in the desired direction, provided they mobilize the necessary resources and secure sufficient support. The test of leadership, as suggested by Salisbury (1969), is in its ability to exchange rewards for support. The relationship between leaders and followers in Israel, however, cannot be explained simply in terms of such a trade-off. In many cases, the leadership tends to demonstrate a response to a calling. In the early days of statehood, the practice was not to seek positions of authority, but rather to "yield to the movement's order." Some of this ethos has persisted to date. Activists presenting their candidacy for executive positions in economic interest groups ostensibly stand for election in order to fulfill a public duty. Admittedly, being a leader in a strong national association does not entail only sacrifices. An executive position in a powerful interest group may serve as an avenue for personal, social, and economic mobility. The contacts established with authorities, the national fame, the media exposure, and the opportunity to become part of the power establishment cannot be overlooked. Yet the line of contenders for leadership positions is reportedly much shorter in economic associations than in, say, the trade unions. For instance, in the Manufacturers Association, there seems to be a genuine fight, but not of the usual type, over chairs; as one commentator described it, "everyone wants the other person to occupy the respected leadership chair."[8] The chairpersons of professional associations, such as the Bar Association or the IMA, are bound to devote time and energy to public work instead of advancing their own career, thus detracting from the desirability of the position. For some of them, a leadership position is a "public mission," rather than a career pattern. Charity organizations also seek a leadership responding to a calling. These are usually headed by celebrities active in politics, in business, or in professional life. Also prominent are women, especially wives of political figures, whose name adds prestige to the group and increases its attraction for prospective contributors.

The job of managing an association belongs not to the elected leadership but to the professional managers. Generally speaking, the managerial staffs of the sectional interest groups in Israel do not display the signs of organizational decay prevalent in other Western countries (Pross 1986: 302). They do not subordinate members' goals to those of their own; they do not demonstrate a lack of courtesy. There is in general no evidence of tensions in the office as a result of an incompetent or arrogant managerial staff. On the contrary, the Israeli professional staff, although generally not large in size, is in many ways the backbone of the group. It takes the lead in organizing the association's internal life and external strategy. The task of the manager is to organize the economic side of the group's activity (i.e., to provide selective benefits to the membership and to furnish the necessary resources). The managerial staff is also responsible for formulating the group's agenda to meet the ever-changing issues facing it.

The staff of the Israel Medical Association provides a good example of effective management. The secretary general of the IMA has served in his position since 1956. He was the initiator of an organizational reform enabling the association to form a federative structure and to maintain its unity in the face of disintegrative forces (Yishai 1987: 97–99). A lawyer by training, he has also been the chief spokesman of his association in wage negotiations. Despite all this, he prefers to remain behind the scene and not distract attention—essentially that of the media—from the elected chairperson. Obviously there are officials in other groups who play a technical role in the management of their association. For example, the staff of the Union of Post-Elementary School Teachers has very little say in conducting the group's internal and external affairs. It may also happen that a skilled managerial staff operates simultaneously with charismatic and ambitious leaders, in which case control of the association is divided between the professional and the volunteers. The Union of Hotel Owners and the

Association of American and Canadian Immigrants are good cases in point.

Internal constraints: Rank-and-file expectations. The third type of constraint is evident mainly in the public interest domain. Groups promoting public values have various types of leaders. The Society for the Protection of Nature elects its leaders through a regular democratic procedure. This is also the case with women's groups and the Civil Rights Association. Public interest groups, Like Malraz or A Good Eretz Israel, that lack a membership basis, are merely self-nominated elite organizations. Interest groups devoting their efforts to promoting issues of war and peace portray a third pattern: the leadership is not elected by a formal procedure but "emerges" as the activists take on leadership roles.

The leadership of public interest groups in Israel have shown a low extent of turnover. The founders of Gush Emunim in 1974 are still active and still identified as its top elite. Obviously younger recruits have joined the group, but those determining the agenda are the old guard (now in their late forties). The same principle applies to Peace Now, although to a lesser extent. In both groups the leadership is not institutionalized, in the sense that no formal elections ever took place. Understanding the constraints on this type of leadership necessitates probing the leaders' motives for activism in a public interest group.

The prospects of economic gains hold no inducements for those manning positions of power in associations that promote values, although a close relationship with decision makers may yield future material benefit. They are usually attracted to their jobs by purposive incentives (Clarck and Wilson 1961) that offer no direct, material benefit to the leaders. For example, interest groups associated with defense policy offer their adherents one major incentive: the satisfaction that they have done their part to make Israel a better, safer, and more equitable place in which to live. People who care enough about problems of war and peace to donate a fair share of their time and energy to the cause want to have a say in determining the policy of their association. Although many of them are "sporadic interventionists" in politics (Dowse and Hughes 1977) and enter the political arena only intermittently, they would like to see their ideological preferences considered and implemented. At the same time, organizational cohesion is an absolute must for a promotional interest group, lacking, as it usually does, material resources enabling the distribution of selective benefits. The result of this ambiguity is a leadership constrained by the members' anticipated reactions. It is not a formal constraint, and it will not be tested by taking a vote. Nonetheless, the anticipated opinions of the more active strata of members are taken into consideration. The rule of anticipated reactions may also be valid in sectional associations even when elite positions are determined by elections. In the final analysis, however, the ability of those occupying positions of power to manipulate election results, and therefore the policy of the organization, is far higher among those controlling the distribution of selective benefits than among those whose only reward to membership is identification with a cause.

Membership participation

One cannot expect an outright violation of the "Iron Law of Oligarchy" in Israeli associations in terms of comprehensive membership participation. In fact the data are surprising. Among all types of the interest groups, approximately one-third report "high membership participation in the group's activities"; the proportion among the promotional groups is, as would be expected, even higher. The party-affiliated groups also demonstrate a high rate of membership participation (see table 5.3). From the organizational perspective, membership presents a mixed blessing. On the one hand, the larger the association the greater are its prospects for influencing decision makers and having its priorities considered and receiving a favorable response. On the other hand, more extensive membership may provide a source of challenge to the authority of the leadership. The membership dilemma is particularly evident in associations in which an increase in size threatens the interests of a powerful minority. This is the case in the Organization of the IDF Handicapped, in which the seriously injured make up the leadership. The vast majority of the handicapped veterans (over 80 percent), however, suffered mild injuries, which nevertheless entitled them to membership in the organization and to a concomitant share of its benefits. The specific interests of the seriously injured are neglected even though they constitute the organization's leadership. The proposal to limit membership only to those heavily handicapped was outrightly rejected. One activist summed up the majority's self-righteous position like this: "We should present a membership representative of all strands in the Israeli population. This is the source of our power. We cannot afford to be an exclusive elite association, despite the glory of heroism."

A similar dilemma confronts economic associations. The Histadrut boasts of its large size, but as noted in chapter 3, the incorporation of a Likud faction into its ranks (enforced by a court decree) had produced serious centrifugal tendencies. The leading industrialists in the textile sector traditionally head the Manufacturers Association. The large-scale recruitment of members from the small computer companies may lead to a redistribution of power within the association.

Despite the possible threat to cohesion, the limitations on membership in the Israeli interest groups are only formal. Even the technical requirements, though formidable on paper, are in the end formalities. For example each applicant to the IMA has to pass a "candidacy period"; acceptance is completed only after the name of the applicant is printed in the IMA's monthly bulletin and does not raise any objections. The Chamber of Commerce requires two recommendations and a candidacy period. The fact is that interest groups are anxious to have as many members as possible. The paucity of membership participation may pose a problem to the leaders of professional and business associations. The physicians, for example, are never quite sure whether their militant professional policy is widely accepted; the contractors complain they can hardly activate their members to exhibit at least a little interest in their organization's program. Larger membership, which would of itself increase participation, is thus considered an asset. The major question, however, is to what extent is membership a reflection of social variety and therefore an organizational resource? Alternatively, is membership subservient to the leadership for either corporatist or elitist purposes? The extent to which internal opposition is tolerated provides some of the answers to these questions.

Internal opposition

Over half of all the Israeli interest groups report that serious challenges to leadership are rare. Adversarial participation is infrequent especially in categoric groups and immigrant associations, but it is uncommon in all categories of voluntary groups. The picture that emerges is not very bright in terms of democratic practices. In one respect promotional associations are less "democratic" than their sectional counterparts: of those groups having a publication, less than a third give the opposition a voice (often or even occasionally) to express its opinions. In contrast, among the party-affiliated groups the proportion of those acknowledging giving the opposition a "right of voice" is as high as 58 percent. Granting a voice, however, does not necessarily imply tolerance of disobedience. When breaches of discipline are evident, group leaders tend to take disciplinary measures against the recalcitrant members. During the three-month-long medical strike staged by the doctors in 1983, there were twenty-eight cases of violation of IMA directives (out of some ten thousand who participated in the strike). All violators were penalized by the IMA. The Union of Post-Elementary School Teachers has also employed disciplinary measures against "deviant" behavior. Four members were reprimanded for publicly criticizing a one-day strike (staged on September 1, 1988).[9] The disobedient teachers argued that it was inconceivable that all members agree with every decision taken by the leadership, particularly when the rank and file is not even consulted. The reaction of the executive was termed by the opponents "a Bolshevik practice." The incident illustrates that the freedom of expression available to opposition factions in some interest groups on the Israeli scene is rather limited.

Division of power

Is the power in an association concentrated in the center or is it diffused among subunits or branches? This is a critical question for determining internal democracy. The study of interest groups in Israel revealed that branches have little say in the decision-making process, that the people at the center devise the organizational strategies, collect membership dues, communicate with the authorities, distribute resources, and make the decisions that shape the group's life. Only 38.2 percent of all the sectional groups claim to be decentralized. Within this category, division of authority between center and periphery is highest among the economic groups. In others the role played by the center is decisive. Members in several branches even refused to be interviewed with regard to their group's activities, and referred the researcher to the "center." Centralization is much less visible in promotional associations: 60.8 percent reported having a decentralized structure.

Centralization as a feature of the sectional interest groups as a whole is not surprising in a country whose periphery suffers from inherent weakness. The parliamentary system of government and the over-centralization of the state have probably left their imprint on associations, too. Jerusalem is the capital of the state, but political power and economic resources are concentrated in Tel

Aviv, a fact which also encourages centralization. Branch members are represented in the central group institution, but contacts with decision makers on a national level are forged overwhelmingly by people from the center.

Israeli interest groups, then, particularly in the sectional arena, are centralized organizations, in the sense of being ruled by those occupying positions in the "center." Within this center, however, there are rivalries, clashes, and discords over organizational and ideological issues. From an operational perspective, cohesion indicates the extent to which the internal components of the organization are in accord, whether or not the same interests are shared by the association's membership, which then unites around common objectives. The presence of a centralized organizational structure does not necessarily imply this cohesion. To determine whether, or the degree to which, it exists also requires a close examination of the division of power within an association and a probe of rank-and-file reactions to leadership initiatives. Although the scope of the research for this book did not cover the membership level, indications of associational elite control over the grassroots are readily available. As already noted disintegrative tendencies may be evident but they are tamed by the elite. Splits and withdrawals are scarce. There are, nevertheless, several powerful factors within the sectional arena that act to reduce internal cohesion considerably and to militate against centralization. The factors accounting for internal divisiveness may be economic, political-ideological, and professional.

Intra-group divisions: The economic basis. Owing to their high degree of centralization, some interest groups include units that are economically markedly distinct from each other. The Manufacturers Association includes both Israeli tycoons, whose fortunes are high even by international standards, and also those who are constantly on the verge of bankruptcy. Clear economic distinctions are evident, too, in professional associations: Some lawyers/physician/accountants have a national reputation, and incomes high above the average; others are striving to cut corners and survive in the competitive market. Even among the agricultural groups an economic variety is evident. Affluent settlements with profitable industry coexist with settlements living hand to mouth. The leadership is under constant pressure to cater to the needs of all sectors. Economic differentiation is not confined to sectional interest groups, but may even be more pronounced in promotional associations. The parents of retarded children from

affluent suburbs have interests different from their counterparts
from poverty-stricken areas. In most cases, this differentiation
does not have structural manifestations and is not sustained by
organizational arrangements. In one case, however, economic differentiation has led to organizational tension and generated centrifugal forces. This is in the Histadrut, which provides a striking
example of intra-group friction based on members' varied
economic status.

The Labor Federation serves as the organizational home for a
host of trade unions, covering almost the whole spectrum of occupational activity in Israel. Lawyers, pilots, clerks, and metal
workers, journalists, farmers, and the "wives of policemen" are all
organized under the auspices of the Histadrut. The major division
is based on education: manual workers vs. academic and professional workers. In the early days of statehood, the egalitarian
norm precluded any preferential treatment of workers possessing
higher educational qualifications. Industrial or professional,
workers were remunerated on the basis of the same principle. Occupational status was thought to be of no consequence. In time
professional groups within the Histadrut came to demand greater
recognition, which step was incompatible with the central ethos of
the Labor Federation. It was against this background, that the
first—and only—withdrawal from the Histadrut took place. The
Union of Post-Elementary School Teachers strived for higher
wages and the right of an independent existence outside the confines of the general Teachers Federation, which was composed
mostly of elementary school teachers without academic qualifications. They demanded adequate social recognition of this separate
status. The Histadrut, which backed the larger, more powerful
Teachers Federation, denied the secondary school teachers such
recognition and threatened to oust their members from the
Histadrut. This happened in 1958, when such a threat could be
translated into a severe sanction because ouster meant a denial of
membership in Kupat Holim, which was practically the sole provider of ambulatory health services in the country. Despite the
unpleasant prospects, the Union of Post-Elementary School
Teachers withdrew from the Histadrut and established an independent association. The refusal of the Histadrut to grant it recognition was grounded in a fear of setting a precedent. It was feared that
other unions with unfulfilled professional or economic demands
would follow suit. The autonomy of the secondary school
teachers, moreover, challenged the right of the central bodies of
the Labor Federation to decide the section to which a union

belonged. More importantly, it called into question the Histadrut's wage policy, in particular its policy on differentials (Medding 1972: 211). After a series of strikes staged by the dissident union, an agreement was worked out between the secondary school teachers and state authorities. Still, the Histadrut could not be swayed from its position and did not agree to acknowledge the union's right to negotiate its own wage terms. The conflict between the secondary school teachers and the Histadrut presents a paradigm of internal associational tension based on socioeconomic differentials. The struggle for recognition was linked not only to material benefits in this case, but also to professional status. The demands of these academics—as most were—could not have been assuaged only by one or the other type of material reward.[10]

A similar pattern of tension emerged in the early 1980s, when the academic unions within the Histadrut waged a militant campaign to free themselves from the Histadrut-negotiated all-encompassing "Framework Agreement," which had the effect of limiting their right to separate wage negotiations. Since the successful challenge by the secondary teachers to the Histadrut's authority, there has been a dramatic rise in the number of workers with higher-education training. In 1949, the total number of graduates from the two universities that then existed was 193. By 1987, the number of universities had more than tripled, and the number of graduates that year alone had reached 15,000. The fact that the academic unions formed an inseparable part of the Histadrut led to intra-group tensions. The growing number of academics joining the work force aggravated a situation that already had led to severe organizational consequences in the past. The Histadrut attempted to quell dissatisfaction by establishing a special Committee for Academic Affairs, which was to serve as an umbrella body for the six academic unions operating under its auspices. Having been spurred on, some of these unions continue to the present to be a thorn in the side of the Histadrut.

The major proponents of differentials in income are the engineers (more precisely, the engineers in the public service), who took the lead in the academics' struggle in the 1980s for recognition and higher income. The engineers' grudge was based mainly on the salary scale of their counterparts, the technicians, who were being remunerated at the same rate although they had little of the academic training of the engineers. The aim of the Federation of Engineers was to secure a salary based on "education, function, learning, expertise and individual achievement"; in other words, on values incompatible with the egalitarian norms of the early pioneers. That a transformation of values has swept Israeli society is widely acknowledged (e.g., Eisenstadt 1985), but institutions seem to lag behind these changes. For organizational purposes, the engineers and the technicians (who by far outnumber their academic counterparts) were treated on an equal basis. The engineers' claims and frustrations are brightly exposed in the following words written by their secretary general:

> It is no wonder that separatist inclinations are mounting. The better educated feel that the Framework Agreement protects the interests of the "commoners" and grants them benefits. It does not quell the demands of those who invested between four and seven years of their life in intensive university training, those who do not receive the expected compensation for their investment. Obviously, a person who had any type of university education will under no circumstances be prepared to receive a poverty allowance from the General Federation of Labor, which is general only for the poor sectors.[11]

This style, in a Histadrut-funded publication, showed the tip of a huge iceberg of discontent. The engineers increased their pressure by threatening to quit the Histadrut and join their counterparts in the independent Bureau of Engineers which focused on professional issues. The threat of disintegration induced the Histadrut to yield to some of the demands of the engineers' union. At the same time, however, fierce measures were taken to safeguard cohesion. At its thirty-sixth convention, in 1985, the Histadrut adopted a provision enabling the sanctioning of a union "whose decision and/or activities are incongruent with the Histadrut's constitution, or [a union] which ceased to fulfill its functions inscribed in this constitution, including, inter alia, a decision or recommendation to withdraw from the Histadrut."

A withdraw decision has never been implemented. Independence, recognition, and freedom to negotiate are valuable assets, but their price is excessively high, for defection from the Histadrut carries with it the denial of essential organizational resources, of a comfortable nest, and of the protection of the all-powerful labor movement. Still, the disruption of organizational cohesion engendered by the engineers seems to have had a snowball effect. In the winter of 1988–1989 internal opposition (this time by the engineers of the Aviation industry) challenged the leadership and threatened to break up the Engineers Federation itself.[12] Since trade union leadership in Israel is determined by political affiliation, there were also some political assets at stake.

In the end, the benefits of corporatism, coupled with the exigencies of elitism, thwarted the disintegrative forces, both within the Histadrut and within the Engineers Federation. Nonetheless, cohesion had a price: the Histadrut leadership allowed the engineers a measure of autonomy in conducting wage negotiations in the public service. Concessions, moreover, were applicable to other academic unions.

The case of the Engineers Federation clearly illustrates the dual—one should rather say the triad—nature of the Israeli interest group arena. Internal divisions within the Histadrut are blatant and deep; however, they prove to be much ado about nothing. Party strings are pulled, and benefits dispensed to leadership and constituencies; the extant structure of labor relations and, above all, the comfortable organizational nest provided by the roof organization, the Histadrut, prevent a rift. A purported attempt to cut across the professional sector and to form an alliance of academic associations, of those both within and those outside the Histadrut did not materialize. The differences between the various professional groups and the mutual suspicions doomed these efforts, perhaps from the start. The engineers continue their struggle in a different framework. Instead of fighting the technicians, they joined forces with them.[13] Professional-academic stakes were subordinated to economic interests, which could best be served by an alliance of those responsible for the technological aspects of Israel's economy. Most academically trained professionals within the Histadrut shy away from identification with the "working class"; but they suffice with exerting pressure at home, since in the outside arena, they are part and parcel of the General Labor Federation, which remains the centralized, core organization of workers in Israel.

Intra-group divisions: The political-ideological basis. Political-ideological disagreements are evident in almost every single interest group in Israel for the simple reason that groups unite individuals on the basis of an interest or value and not on the basis of a comprehensive outlook or ideology. Even interest groups focusing strictly on the promotion of certain values (such as Gush Emunim and Peace Now) encompass members with differing political colors and shades, albeit within a smaller circle than, say, in an economic interest group. Political divisions are paramount among the manufacturers, the physicians, the taxi drivers, and the merchants. Holding different opinions on the future borders of the state or on which economic regime should prevail constitutes no threat to a group's cohesion and integrity. Only rarely do members of an interest group form a separate unit on the basis of ideological dissension. Left-wing lawyers who once staged a demonstration to protest the alleged silence of the bar in the face of what they termed "a denial of basic norms of justice across the Green Line"[14] provide an example. Arab and Israeli physicians also protested the alleged deterioration of health services in the occupied territories. These associations, however, were ephemeral, lacking any substantial organizational basis. There are not many other examples of this type of intra-group dissident organized activity. Group members holding opinions diverging from mainstream values do not, as a rule, form a separate association; they suffice with acting as individuals within the confines of their respective political parties.

A political basis for internal divisions exists within associations in which the political parties form the organizational units, especially within the Histadrut. The deepest internal rift within the Labor Federation is between the factions associated with the Labor Movement and those associated with the Likud. The cleavage is less manifest in the apex, which is dominated by the Labor, than at the shop level. The plant committees are often controlled by Likud activists, a fact which contributes to the mounting tensions between rank-and-file Histadrut members (many of whom are Likud voters) and the Histadrut leaders, all of whom are Labor supporters.

Intra-group divisions: The occupational basis. Large, heterogeneous interest groups face organizational problems because of their size, which results in diverging interests among the membership. The IMA provides a good example of internal tensions based on occupational considerations. The medical association is the organizational home of both primary-care physicians and hospital doctors. Many of the former are older and said to be less qualified professionally. The luster and glory lie in the hospitals, where modern technology is available and dramatic medical events take place. The two sectors of doctors have different working conditions and concomitant wage demands. The division between the clinic doctors and the hospital doctors, however, is not ensconced in organizational subunits. Rather, it is crisscrossed by another division based on occupational employment. The Israel Medical Association is a federation (though centrally controlled) of two major units: state doctors, who comprise over one-third of the membership, and Kupat Holim doctors, who make up some 45 percent of the total membership. The latter are internally divided between a minority of hospital physicians (40 percent) and a majority of clinic doctors (60 percent). The IMA subdivisions of state doctors and Kupat Holim doctors are constantly at odds, each attempting to outstrip its counterpart of any particular benefit it may have secured for itself that the other does not share. The privileged status of the IMA as a representative group, professional identity, and the advantages of unity have so far thwarted any secession.

Rifts on an occupational basis are evident also within the Histadrut, with trade unions, especially the stronger and larger ones, wishing to release themselves from the grip of the Trade Union Department. In mid-1981, the Thirteen Committees, consisting of workers in essential services, such as the Electricity Company, the Aviation Industry, and the Postal Authority, joined forces and challenged the Histadrut's authority to represent them in wage negotiations. Their militancy, acrimony, and blatant activity threatened the unity of the Histadrut, but the centripetal forces have thus far been too forcible to resist. The Histadrut employed a carrot and stick strategy: it co-opted recalcitrant union leaders into top institutional positions and it reprimanded others. These divide and rule tactics proved effective. The committees realized that their power was also a source of weakness. The highly paid Electricity Company workers found it difficult to cooperate with the much-less-privileged x-ray technicians, for example, even on an ad hoc basis. The stronger groups were reluctant to commit themselves to long-term reciprocal relations with the weaker unions. The Histadrut was much better equipped to handle general policy questions. The committees soon declared that they were not against the Histadrut and would prefer to act from "within."

One of the belated results of this mini-revolt was the introduction in 1988 of an organizational reform granting trade unions a larger measure of autonomy. Since 1977, the local committees have demanded a greater say in negotiations over work agreements. Plant committees are theoretically subservient to both the local workers council and to the national trade union, which in turn is coordinated by the Trade Union Department of the Histadrut. Although wages are determined on a national basis, first between the Histadrut and representatives of the employers and then between the national trade unions and the corresponding employers, there have been many breaches of these agreements. The number and volume of unauthorized strikes has grown considerably in recent years, over two-thirds of all strikes reportedly

not having the approval of Histadrut officials (Shirom 1983: 241).
Trade unions may at present negotiate their own work
agreements. So far as the Framework Agreement, a distinction was
made between the "fixed salary, determined on a national basis,
and "changing" part of the salary, subject to free negotiations. Furthermore, the Histadrut legitimized wildcat strikes on condition
that they be approved, in a secret ballot, by the majority of plant
workers. The Histadrut did retain an important sanction: without
its approval, strikers are not eligible to receive Histadrut financial
aid.

The Histadrut thus attempted to hold onto the rope from both
ends: to widen the leeway available to its occupational subunits,
while at the same time to retain its overall central structure. This
practice is valid for other economic groups, as well. The rapid
development of the Israeli economy has generated pressures for
differentiation. The centralized structure of the interest group
arena has impeded adequate adjustments to the changing environment. Still, interest groups have successfully adapted to these
changes by granting more freedom to subunits, including the right
of presenting separate demands. Giving a voice, limited as it may
be, has, in most cases, impeded any exodus.

Intra-group cleavages, by and large, have not generated fatal
organizational outcomes. There are very few instances in which
subunits splintered from a wider interest group. The arthitects, not
finding a common language with their fellow professionals in the
Bureau of Engineers, once attempted to form their own organization. Qualified (i.e., with full university training) dentists
withdrew from thier association after charging it with representing
the interests of the unqualified practitioners, most of whom were
immigrants from East European countries. In both cases, unity
was resumed after the defectors realized that their interests were
better served by a larger, more encompassing interest group; and
that their specific needs and demands were better presented and
handled within the association rather than by splitting into a
smaller group.

Conclusions

Recapitulation of the organizational attributes of Israeli interest groups shows a picture that is remote from pluralism. In
most instances political parties are not involved in the organizational affairs of interest groups. They may be invisible actors, or

they may influence interest groups through their activists occupying leadership positions; but the integration expected in elitist configurations is largely lacking even in the associations technically affiliated with political parties. In almost all organizational indicators, Israel fits neatly into the corporatist pattern of interest politics. Monopolization is high among many sectors: business groups are organized in concentrated associations; professionals are represented by one union; agricultural groups and trade unions operate under roof organizations. Many groups have been granted official recognition by the state, thus passing another corporatist test. The principles of corporatism apply much less to the arena of promotional associations, where atomization is much more evident.

Relationships between interest groups and across sectors seem to be harmonious and accommodative. Only a minority of the groups admit to rivalry. Public policy in Israel makes such rivalry superfluous because the distribution of income (i.e., wage policy) is guided by the principles of non–zero-sum game. Thus the Union of Nurses does not become concerned of a wage raise granted to the physicians, because its members are bound to enjoy similar privileges owing to the "linking" dictum. On the other hand, Israel is not a strictly egalitarian society: some contenders are left out of the game and others play unfairly, receiving covert benefits in return for no less covert services. But the rules guiding the game discourage competition.

Leadership turnover is rather high. The question is, does this turnover enable responsiveness to rising needs or does it reflect personal changes at the apex? The answers appear to be ambiguous. Leaders change, but the style of leadership remains stable. A certain amount of oligarchy is expected in organized interest groups; however, it seems that the power disposed by the associational elite is more influenced by past, elitist practices than by possible future winds of participatory democracy.

Membership participation is not very effective. Serious challenges to leadership are rare. The limitations on the concentration of power are not productive. The exit option, in some cases, acts as an important brake on oligarchical tendencies within interest group organizations. It should be remembered, though, that this option is largely controlled by the state, which has the ability to grant and to remove recognition. The power of the state to give and to take away sets up a major hurdle to internal opposition, while at the same time serving as a major incentive to enforced cohesion.

Israeli interest groups appear to be highly disciplined. This does not mean that breaches of organizational authority are a rare exception. The scope of such breaches and their results, however, justify a high grade on the scale of internal cohesion. Concentration and monopolization, as predicated by the corporatist theory, demand their toll. Interest groups wish to be "respectable" and "responsible" bodies with whom agreements can be forged; qualifying as such, many interest groups have paid with increased organizational rigidity. Internal tensions thus seem to be inevitable. Surprisingly, in most categories of analysis, promotional groups do not significantly vary from sectional associations. As expected, the degree of membership participation is higher and so is decentralization. But, as with the sectional sector, challenges to leadership have not been a common practice, nor is the opposition granted formal expression.

To sum up, when judged by structural criteria, interest groups in Israel are largely molded by the image of the Israeli political system, rather than by their counterpart associations in the West. Associations are centralized, encompassing, and intrusive. From the organizational perspective, it seems that more than providing citizens with a channel for expressing demands, they offer the authorities a counterpart with which partnerships can be forged.

CHAPTER SIX

Interest Groups and State:
Opportunities for Influence

If parties are no longer targets for group action, or even if they are, but to a much lesser extent than in the past, then groups will necessarily seek other avenues to decision makers. They will, in fact, concentrate directly on the "state," which consists of three levels: at the base is the bureaucracy, the officials whose influence on decision making was said to be unsurpassed; in the middle are the legislators, who in Israel owe little to the public and may care little about its immediate concerns; and lastly the cabinet ministers, situated at the top of the political pyramid. Three questions are pertinent to group-state relations regarding the access of interest groups to forums of policy making, their participation in the policy process, and their integration with decision makers.

The first question is: Do interest groups have *access* to the state and its organs? Access does not necessarily connote and is not equivalent to influence. It only implies that one has an opportunity to express his or her desires. The Association of Garage Owners can testify before a Knesset committee and alert it to the anticipated dangers to traffic safety should the price of spare car parts be raised. Needless to say, this useful information may not necessarily yield the results desired by the group, which has been listened to but not heard. Yet access is a prerequisite for transmitting political demands. Its absence indicates that channels linking organized citizens to political authorities are clogged and that demands cannot be forwarded by the conventional means. Access is particularly important in pluralistic regimes, in which a clear demarcation between interest groups and the state is evident. Access is available when groups are not denied the opportunity to make their views known and to present their demands in forums where decisions critical to their membership and objectives are made.

Secondly, do groups *participate* in the policy process? Participation encompasses a variety of ways in which the demand to "join the club" can be satisfied. The range for individual participation extends from passive acquiescence at one end to a town meeting form of participation at the other (LaPalombara 1974: 53; Milbrath 1966). With regard to interest groups, participation implies actual inclusion in the policy process. An individual's participation is induced by a sense of efficacy (Almond and Verba 1963); that is, a belief that access can be translated into political action and influence. A group's participation, on the other hand, is also—and perhaps primarily so—a function of state choice. In democracies espousing free enterprise, groups are consulted, whether to a lesser or to a greater degree. In fact consultation has been listed as a major form of comunication in liberal democracies such as Great Britain (Jordan and Richardson 1987; Hogwood 1987). A still higher level of participation is reached when elaborate formal structures of cooperation or coordination are designed, in line with corporatist practices.

Thirdly, are the interest groups *integrated* into the policy process? Integration is the final step in the process of attaining influence. Access provides groups with the opportunity to fulfill their mediating function, i.e., to articulate demands and transmit them to decision makers. Participation enables the groups to exert influence from within and thereby increase the chances of changing policy priorities in accordance with their own choices. Integration implies that interest groups are involved directly in shaping policy, not as outsiders, not even as partners, but as extensions of the ruling elite. The operational significance of this integration is the membership of group representatives in state institutions, i.e., in the legislature and the administration. Direct representation of group members is common in many Western democracies; this is especially true for trade unions. The British trade union movement, for example, has had members stand for and be elected to the House of Commons. "Integration" is not a pejorative term; it indicates that a group is amalgamated with the state. In this capacity, the group loses much of its unique attributes as a body operating outside the formal system of government. A separate question—beyond the scope of this book—is how this amalgamation affects the internal organization of groups, their strategies, and the outcomes of their activities.

This chapter is devoted to an analysis of the extent to which interest groups in Israel have acquired access to state institutions, have been granted the privilege of participation in decision making forums, and have been integrated into the state machinery. Data (presented in a series of figures and tables) will demonstrate the differences between the four categories of interest groups under discussion.

Access

Interest groups in Israel enjoy a rich tradition of access to decision makers. As pointed out by Galnoor (1982: 311), "The many voluntary, highly motivated, and well-organized groups and associations of the *yishuv* enabled their members to have access and to participate in the social and political life of the community." Although party constraints were visible, interest groups had no difficulty in securing access to authoritative institutions. The reason was simple enough: the vast majority of the groups were connected with a political network or center (Horowitz and Lissak 1977). The key word opening the door for influence was affiliation with a political party. Organizational affiliation and integration thus provided groups with wide access, not by virtue of their resources or public support, but rather on account of their ideological identifications and, just as important, their political loyalties.

The passage from *yishuv* to state was a turning point in the pattern of associational activity (Eisenstadt 1972). In the early years of statehood, the groups that were not linked to the political establishment found it difficult to gain the desired access. Some of these groups, such as *Shurat Hamitnadvim* (the Row of Volunteers), had a head-to-head collision with the authorities. The group, which operated in the early 1950s, when Israel was at its peak of elitism, charged the political establishment with corruption and discrimination. Not being sufficiently resourceful to stand up to the authorities, the group dissipated after a short while. Other groups, such as *Haolam Hazeh* (This World, organized around a weekly of that name), chose to become parties. Haolam Hazeh entered the Knesset in 1965. So did the Movement for Civil Rights, three of whose members were elected to the legislature in 1973. By the 1980s, most groups and associations, including those that had lasted from the prestate period and those that formed later, had obtained wide access to both state organs, the Knesset and the executive, whether they were or were not affiliated with political parties.

Access to government

The doors of Israeli administrators are left wide open to absorb the claims of various groups. The susceptibility of the Israeli government elite to the demands of groups may be gleaned from the data presented in table 6.1. The table first registers the percentage of interest groups that had ever been denied the right to meet with a government official. As will be shown in chapter 8, meeting with officials is a common practice in the arsenal of groups' strategies. It may be, however, that although junior officials are willing to meet with representatives of associations, the ministers themselves do not welcome groups in their offices. How often does a minister reject a requested meeting is the second question. A third question looks into the actual patterns of contact between interest groups and the executive branch of government. Do interest groups actually ask to meet with ministers or, alternatively, do they communicate mostly with the lower echelons of the civil service?

No substantial differences may be found between the four main interest group categories in regard to rejection; in all cases, moreover, is the minister slightly less likely to reject a meeting than is an official. Since contact with government officials was reported by the groups to be a major (and frequent) strategy, the implication of the data on the question of access is fairly clear. Within this generally low proportion of rejections, however, there may be found variations, some of which are rather unexpected.

To begin with, a high percentage of groups actually requested a meeting with the minister. The proportion was the highest among the party-affiliated associations. Every farmer group that responded to the questionnaire had asked to meet with the minister of agriculture in the past three years. Issues on the agenda were numerous. Their excruciating debts constituted perhaps the major problem plaguing the settlement organizations in recent years, but other issues, too, were the subject of deliberations between the minister and representatives of agricultural interest groups: exports of agricultural products, the price of water, the imports of raw materials and of agricultural machinery, the relationship with the Common Market, and contingency plans for the critical year, 1992, to name a few. Requests for a meeting with a member of the government were also forwarded by immigrant associations (90 percent of these requested such a meeting). Like the farmers, the immigrants were anxious to meet the highest executive, but probably for the opposite reasons. The farm groups regarded the minister, traditionally a member of a settlement movement, as one of their own. The agricultural groups believed that a common background and purportedly shared goals entitled them to close interaction with the top decision maker in their area of interest. The immigrant associations, on the other hand, requested meetings because they felt the strong pressure of the unresolved problems of absorption. The shortage of adequate housing, the hardships of adjustment, and, primarily, the difficulties facing the newcomer in the job market necessitated relationships with the top echelons of the administration. Promotional interest groups were the least interested in meeting with ministers (76.9 percent), although they were not above requesting ministerial attention.

An examination of the "denials," the cases in which a minister or public official refused to meet with representatives of an interest group, is revealing. The category of "other" sectional groups, including the categoric groups and the immigrant associations, was the category most frequently denied access to ministers. Categoric groups comprise respected members of the associational community, such as the Students Union and the Union of Veterans; but they also number many marginal groups such as the Association for Individual Rights (the homosexuals), the Association of Widows, and the like, that enjoy much less legitimacy and power. The activists of immigrant associations often complained, in the interviews, on the minister's refusal to grant them access. Relations between the *landsmanshaften* and government authorities are far from amicable. Officials charge immigrant associations with being "selfish" and pursuing their own interests without regard to the problems of society at large. For their part, these associations blame authorities for failing to deal competently and adequately with the enormous problems of absorption. Personal aversions and individual preferences may have been responsible for the high proportion of ministerial rejections. In the late 1980s the minister of absorption was a kibbutz member whose interests in foreign policy exceeded his concerns with immigration; he was replaced by the leader of the ultra-orthodox Shas, with whom the representatives of immigrant associations found it difficult to communicate. This difficulty did not deter them from requesting meetings, but it may have inhibited a positive response to their requests.

Public interest groups (one category among promotional associations) also scored high on the scale of rejections. Although ministers were not interviewed in the course of the research for this book, and therefore any explanation regarding their behavior is only hypothetical, it is not surprising they shy away from meetings with representatives of public associations. Defense-oriented interest groups may take issue with the minister in charge of the nation's security on ideological grounds. Civil rights associations (including women's groups), on the other hand, are considered pests. Ecological movements are also a nuisance, particularly if they attempt to influence policy, which they do only rarely. They do not enjoy the legitimacy, nor the clout, of their counterparts in Western European countries.

A glance at the list of refusals reportedly given by high state officials leads to a few surprises. The category of "other" interest groups still is the most denied (more than a quarter of their requests are turned down). The great surprise is the proportion of refusals received by party-affiliated associations: one-fifth (a figure, though, that was not verified by the officials interviewed in the course of the study). Among the agricultural groups the proportion was even higher. The reasons for this may have been technical, since the flood of requests to arrange meetings could not possibly have all been positively responded to by the bureaucracy. The inability to cater to all (or even to a large part) of the farmers' demands may also have been a cause of their rejection. It appears that belonging to the same political family does not fully open the administrative door to these groups, despite the high prestige attached to settlement movements in Israel.

At the other side of the spectrum, one finds the professional associations, which have been granted unlimited access to ministers; in fact, they reported never having been refused a meeting. Their command of knowledge, expertise, and functional contribution to society have earned them a large measure of access to members of the Israeli government. The proportion of refusals from administrators is also exceedingly low.

Interest group access is not limited to ordinary ministers; it extends, too, to prime ministers, although such meetings are not a daily occurrence. They are, in fact, the exception rather than the rule. Four major circumstances in which interest groups gain access to the prime minister have been identified (Yishai 1987a: 147). First, a meeting may be held when the issue promoted by the group has stirred public commotion, regardless of the prime minister's own views on the subject. The example of Peace Now is il-

Table 6.1
Interest Group Access to Government and Knesset
in the Past Three Years (Percent)

	Type of group				
	Party-affili-ted	Eco-nomic	Other	Pro-mo-tional	N
Denied a meeting by an official	21.7	9.5	26.0	21.1	158
Denied a meeting by a minister	13.9	7.1	23.1	17.3	156
Requested a meeting with a minister	94.4	83.3	80.7	76.9	156
Requested access to a Knesset committee	74.3	78.6	48.1	65.2	153
Denied access by a Knesset committee	8.6	11.9	7.4	8.1	153
Appeared at least once in a Knesset committee	62.1	71.4	53.6	52.9	158

lustrative. Although this group advocates the relinquishing of territories in return for peace, it was granted a meeting with Menachem Begin on April 21, 1978, despite the fundamental ideological differences between the prime minister and the group. The presumed reason for the meeting, which obviously furnished Peace Now with access but not influence, was the successful and rapid expansion of the group's advocacies. Peace Now had made its first public appearance on March 8th that year, and within a few weeks mobilized large crowds to demonstrate in support of peace. The momentum generated by Peace Now and the wide attention it had captured gained it quick access to the apex of the political structure. In comparison, Prime Minister Yitzhak Shamir refused to meet with members of Parents against Silence,[1] with which his philosophy differed, because the movement showed much less success in expanding its cause (Gilat 1988). another example of access following expansion was provided by Golda Meir's meeting with the Black Panthers. The prime minister had a totally unfavorable opinion of the Panthers and their demands, believing as she did that Israel had been successful in integrating the exiles and was essentially an egalitarian society. After twice rejecting the Panthers' request for a meeting, she yielded on the third time around because the Panthers had proved too successful in mobilizing public opinion and in capturing the media's attention.

Meetings with a prime minister also occur when the controversy between a group and the authorities reaches a dead end and compromise is not imminent. The Ethiopian Jews who were granted a meeting with Premier Shimon Peres in September 1985 provide a case in point. The major bone of contention was the religious status of these black-skinned Jews. The orthodox establishment refused to accord them full acknowledgment as

Jews. The Ethiopians, who followed their ancestors' version of the Jewish faith, believed they were full-fledged Jews and rejected the chief rabbinate's demands to undergo certain rituals. To emphasize their rejection, they convened a mass rally in Jerusalem and threatened a hunger strike. The controversy lingered for weeks, to the dismay of those who were publicizing Israel's success in liberating and integrating the black immigrants. The prime minister's granting access to the representatives of the Ethiopian Jews contributed to diffusing some of the tensions and enabled the forging of a compromise that ended the protest.

A meeting with a prime minister may also constitute a tactic devised by the authorities in the framework of what is known as "The Symbolic Uses of Politics" (Edelman 1985). Such an encounter confers prestige upon its participants, and, consequently, it may be used as a substitute for power. One famous example of this ploy relates to the country's teachers. The educational system in Israel suffers from a shortage of qualified teachers owing, among other things, to the profession's low pay. A judicial committee (the Etzioni Committee) recommended in 1985 that teachers' salaries be raised. The government endorsed the recommendations but, fearing a subsequent avalanche of wage demands, failed to implement them. In order to compensate for the government's backing down from its commitment, a meeting with the prime minister (Peres) was granted. During this session, the reasons for what was said to be a delay in implementation were explicated. A teachers' strike was reportedly averted owing to this direct access to the nation's highest politician in the administrative branch of government.

Israel may be an open society, but limitations do exist. Not every interest group registered in the phone directory is eligible to meet with the prime minister. As in other democracies, the privileged groups or those having ideological proximity are usually the ones given access to the top of the political ladder. The industrialists, the big businessmen, members of the Histadrut executive committee, meet with a prime minister much more frequently than do less-endowed groups. Two examples will illustrate this point. In the summer of 1988, a group of leading industrialists decided to seek Prime Minister Shamir's intervention in support of immediate measures to aid what they claimed was industry's rapidly deteriorating conditions. Shamir reportedly said he would definitely intervene on their behalf.[2] Shamir also met with Yesha representatives, who were staging a hunger strike to protest the deteriorating security for motorists in the occupied territories and to demand harsher measures against Arab vigilantes. Since the prime minister basically shared the settlers' views, it is not surprising that he summoned them to a meeting and assured Yesha of his intention to accede to its demands.[3] The door of the government, as the foregoing shows, is left open on a selective basis, depending on susceptibility to a group's demands, by administrators occupying high positions in the bureaucracy, by ministers, and even the prime minister, whose meetings with group representatives are often recorded by the press.

Access to the Knesset

The major indicator of successful access to the Knesset is the appearance of the interest group in a Knesset committee. The figures presented in Table 6.1 demonstrate, once again, that the access opportunities provided by the state are readily available. Well over half of the party-affiliated and the economic groups, and some half of the "other" and the issue-oriented interest groups, have testified at one time or another in legislative committees. A substantial proportion of these groups, moreover, did so "several" times during the past three years. One particular interest group regularly participates in committee meetings: the Bar Association is always present at sessions of the Committee on Constitution, Law, and Justice, to make its views known to the committee members, most of whom are also members of the bar.

Contacts between interest groups and Knesset committees is a two-way street. Associations may request to appear before a committee after being informed—usually by one of the MKs—that the discussion will relate to an issue pertinent to the group's interests. It may also happen that a group asks to testify without reference to a specific piece of legislation. For example, the Committee on Immigration hosts representatives of the *landsmanshaften* to hear their views on the prospects of *alia* (immigration). This practice, while not very common, reveals the hidden rivalry between the two branches of state authority. The division of power in a parliamentary system of government circumscribes the influence of the legislators, whose authority is limited compared to the overpowering executive. Israel is no exception, its Knesset forever attempting to exercise whatever power it can capture. The Knesset Finance Committee is the most powerful of state legislative agencies, and hence a popular target of influence among interest groups. Other committees, too, take every opportunity to demonstrate their initiative and contribution to shaping public policy. If an imaginative, energetic person chairs a Knesset committee, its impact may be palpable. Inviting an interest group to appear before a committee may be used as an instrument to attack a ministry. The ambitious chairperson of the Welfare Committee, a well-known female Labor MK, has regularly clashed with ministers of welfare services and sided with interest groups to demonstrate her power vis-à-vis the administration. One example was her support of the minimum wage allowance, endorsed by the Knesset despite the objection of all the ministers concerned (August 1987).

Groups may thus well serve the purpose of a Knesset committee's chairperson, who can mobilize support by granting an invitation to testify only to those associations whose views are known to be congruent with the chair's. This does not mean that Knesset committees serve as an arena for exerting power and discriminating between friends and foes. In fact the proportion of interest groups denied access to the Knesset is exceedingly small, even if in some cases the rejection was caused not by an overcrowded agenda but by political dissension. An instance of this took place in 1976, in the IMA's dispute with the chairperson of the Public Servies Committee.

The government that year had proposed a national health insurance bill, a key provision of which gave the Histadrut's Sick Fund special privileges in the country's health system. The IMA adamantly opposed the bill on grounds of possible damage to the physicians' interests and their freedom to practice private medicine. The medical association initially appeared before the committee, but asked to testify again in order to elaborate on subsequent developments. The request was rejected by the chairperson, a member of the left-wing Mapam and an avowed advocate of Kupat Holim's services, who explained: "The continuous inclusion of a voluntary association in the legislative process contradicts the foundation of democracy" (quoted in Yishai 1990). The denial of access did not deter the IMA from recourse to other strategies of influence, which eventually proved to be highly effective. But the doors of this Knesset committee were shut. It appears, however, this event represented past history by 1989; in contemporary politics, it is the exception rather than the rule. The proportion of refusals of MKs to grant access to representatives of interest groups is far lower in most cases than that among either ministers or state officials. Surprisingly, the economic associations have been rejected most, compared to other categories of groups. The detachment of these groups from party politics may be the reason.

That the appearance before a Knesset committee is an integral part of most interest groups' repertoire is evident from the proportion of those that requested to testify in this forum—some three-quarters of the party-affiliated and economic associations and two-thirds of the promotional groups. Only the "other" sectional interest groups largely refrained from requesting access to the Knesset, with less than a half attempting to do so. The data clearly demonstrate the relative marginality of the interest groups included in this category, which have been subject to more refusals and initiated less requests for access than their counterparts.

Forms of Participation

Cooperation

In European welfare states, interest groups and national associations are generally regarded as necessary building blocks for national policy making. In Sweden, for example, "each organization carries its own legacy of past involvement in making particular policies, a busy schedule of current consultations, and a well-justified expectation that the organization's views will be sought and listened to in the future" (Heclo and Madsen 1987: 16). Consequently, at any one time, over 100 official commissions may be at work investigating various problems and drafting proposals for new legislation and regulations. Israel is also a welfare society and, to a certain extent, has adopted its own particular version of the famous Scandinavian practice of rule by commissions. The data (presented in figure 6.1) show the representation of Israeli interest groups in a committee or council established by a state agency. As might be expected, the rate of participation among the party-affiliated and economic associations is considerably higher than among the promotional groups. There are also internal variations within these categories. Farmers' groups demonstrate the highest rate of membership in government-formed bodies, the network of agricultural councils providing them with many opportunities to cooperate. Business associations also excell in such participation. Professional associations participate in the policy process mainly through the licensing procedure. The certification of accountants, engineers, psychologists, and dentists is carried out by joint state-association committees whose members are appointed by the relevant minister. One of the most important forums for cooperation between state authorities and interest groups is the Social-Economic Council (to be discussed in detail below).

The immigrant associations, as well as the categoric groups, show the least amount of cooperation with state authorities. Since their access to decision makers is relatively restricted, it is hardly surprising they have also, relatively, been denied participation. They are simply not considered partners. The state has made no effort to incorporate the representatives of the newcomers or of the handicapped or of any other public interest group to defend their special interests in the policy process.[4] Although these groups score considerably lower on the scale of participation than do the important economic associations, some 40 percent do take part in a government-sponsored committee. Thus Naamat is a member of the National Council of Women, which operates under the aegis of the prime minister's office; the Society for Better Housing is represented in a relevant committee in the ministry of housing; the Society for the Protection of Nature participates in committees sponsored by the ministry of education.

Fig. 6.1. Membership of Interest Groups in State-Sponsored Committees (Percent)

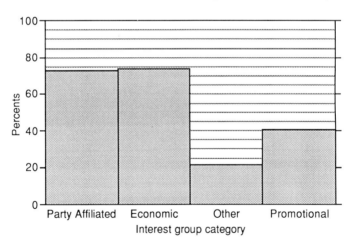

That interest groups are represented on national councils, committees, or commissions does not necessarily mean that they dominate these bodies. More often than not, theirs is but a single representation among a host of other members. Even when the membership is divided equally between an association and the ministry, the chairperson is a senior state official, and it is that person who usually determines the agenda, steers the discussion, and implicitly determines the vote. "You cannot overrule the state. They can always have the final say," one group leader claimed.

It may happen that the committee serves as an arena in which different interest groups compete for power. The Standards Institute provides one such case. The institute operates as a government company, and is staffed with representatives of both the government and interest groups, including the Engineers Federation, the Manufacturers Association, the Chamber of Commerce, and consumer associations. When the institute engaged in determining standards on the basis of professional consideration, it attracted little public attention. When, however, power struggles erupted between the representatives of various sectors, the activities of the institute were exposed to the limelight of the media. The major adversaries were the industrialists, who wished to use the institute's rulings as a means to curb imports and protect local products, and the representatives of the Chamber of Commerce, who bitterly complained that their interests were being neglected in favor of the manufacturers'. In between were the members of the consumers associations, who were denied adequate representation. The executive committee of the institute numbers more than twenty members, only two of whom represent the consumers. The alleged reason for their exclusion from power positions was their being "incapable of dealing competently with the technical intricacies deliberated with in the special committees staffed by professionals . . . there [was] no point in granting them representation while outsing the engineers and other experts."[5] The real reason for the under-representation of consumers was their relative weakness compared to the economic organizations.

What functions do the various committees/councils/commissions perform with regard to policy making? Three major functions though not mutually exclusive, may be identified. First is a problem-solving function, in which the joint bodies provide solutions to technical questions. In this respect, interest groups play the traditional pluralist role of mediating between their members and the governing authorities. Second is a coordinating function, in which the state bodies aim at reaching agreement on the principles of long-term cooperation, in line with corporatist patterns. The third function is implementation, in which the joint bodies serve not as mediators between citizens and state, but as aides to the state in performing its functions (Hayward 1984). Although performing an output function was numbered among corporatist attributes, in a party-democracy it connotes integration with the elite. In practice the distinctions between the three types of functions may be less clear-cut than in theory. The groups were nevertheless requested to choose among the three as the dominant function.

The function of problem solving: Interest groups as mediators. The number of committees dealing with day-to-day affairs is quite large. Although one cannot speak of an explosion of these bodies, as is the case in France (Wilson 1987: 154) and Sweden (Heclo and Madsen 1987: 13), almost every Israeli ministry maintains numerous committees that deal with technical problems arising during the course of governing. The Bureau of Engineers is represented in a committee that decides on standards for air-raid shelters; the Teachers Federation participates in a committee that discusses the system of supervision in the elementary school system; the Israel Medical Association is represented in a host of committees dealing with "technical" issues, such as the inspection of pharmaceutical products. These committees, which are prevalent in pluralist societies, have little significance in terms of power and influence. They do not play any role in shaping major policies or in forging solutions to problems that surface on the national agenda. Technical-type committees seem to have mushroomed, although there is no central registration of committees operating under the aegis of government ministries to enable a compilation of systematic data to verify this impression. The absence of registration may serve as one of the indicators for their dubious effectiveness in shaping national priorities.

The function of accommodation: Interest groups as partners. Reaching agreement is a major dictum in the Israeli polity. The "Guidelines" of the coalition agreement forged between the Likud and the Alignment on December 22, 1988, include a special paragraph committing the government to "reach a socio-economic agreement with the Histadrut, the employers, and other factors in the economy."[6] Reaching agreement between contenders is the essence of corporatism. It enables the state to forge policies on a consensual basis. Accommodation is essential when redistributive policies are at stake. By allocating authority to interested actors who have veto power over decisions, objections can be tamed and hurdles removed.The best example of this type of arrangement is the Social-Economic Council (SEC).

One of the major forums in which the representatives of interest groups sit alongside government officials is the SEC. The council brings together representatives of the major interest groups to discuss the agenda of the country's social and economic policies. The council has had a long history in the Israeli polity. It was first established in the late 1950s, when industrialization became the primary concern of policy makers. The SEC operated under the auspices of a minister of finance, Pinhas Sapir, whose contribution to the industrialized productivity of the country remains unsurpassed. The council did not have mandatory powers, but its recommendations were seriously considered by decision makers.[7] Unfortunately it did not provide solutions to Israel's critical economic problems; nor was it active during the economic slowdown in the mid-1960s, which was perceived as a major national crisis. The Six Day War terminated the activity of this first SEC.

Another version of the Social-Economic Council was established in 1977, following Israel's affiliation with the European Economic Community. The council included, in addition to senior officials in the major economic ministries, the representatives of the Histadrut, the Coordinating Office, the Bar Association, and the Medical Association. The function of the European Council was to provide the institutions of the Common Market with information regarding the structure and activity of the major local interest groups. This information was geared to enable EEC authorities to become acquainted with regional economic sectors. In turn, the interest groups involved were to profit by obtaining access to the fledgling European government apparatus, thereby acquiring an opportunity to express their views and demands. Regulations issued by the EEC commit the Council of Ministers, representing the various countries, to consult with the Economic Council in matters pertaining to economic legislation. The Economic Council has thus been legally incorporated into the process of decision making. In Israel, no such commitment exists, and the council was largely moribund, with only paper existence.

A third version of the Social-Economic Council was established under the auspices of the ministry of finance, following the elections to the 12th Knesset (1988). The intention to establish such a forum had been a plank in the Labor-Alignment's electoral platform. The proposal was implemented when Peres became the minister of finance in 1988. The declared goals of the council were "to jointly deliberate and analyze major issues of the Israeli economy, with the purpose of designing adequate solutions, while maintaining full coordination among its members." The blueprint for the council's work includes a specific reference to "the achievement of maximal coordination among the major forces in the economy, while acknowledging their respective desires and demands." The structure and function of the SEC present an illuminating example of the participation of economic and party-affiliated interest groups in the policy process. It highlights a particular variation of what may be considered the epitome of corporatist practice.

The composition of the SEC demonstrates the spirit of accommodation. The council initially included only twelve members: four representatives each of government, labor, and business. The small size was aimed at making its deliberation straightforward and more effective. The government's representatives consisted of the chief economic ministers: the minister of finance (who serves as chairperson of the SEC), the minister of industry and commerce, the minister of communication, and the minister of economy and planning. As in other contemporary state bodies, the principle of parity between ministers of the two major political blocs was safely guarded. The remaining members were equally divided between the Histadrut (including one representative of the women's movement, Naamat) and the employers, represented by the four major members of the Coordinating Office. Within a very short time, however, pressures for inclusion were irresistible and the number of council members increased to over twenty. The minister of interior was added because of his functional role in physical planning, and also because of the fact that the minister (a member of Shas, an ultra-orthodox party) was considered a future prospective partner in a coalition led by the Labor party. The secretary of the Histadrut insisted on including some of his personal allies, which opened the door for the chairperson of the Consumers Authority. This addition led to a larger representation from the business sector. The chairman of the Zionist Federation pleaded for membership with the argument that it was inconceivable that the "Jewish people" would remain outside the council. Directors-general of government ministries were added because of their functional role in the policy system. In short, what was meant to be a small, effective forum turned into a sizable body, highly susceptible to bureaucratic malaise. It was precisely the high degree of exposure of SEC deliberations that diminished its effectiveness.

The SEC had been established "in order to provide business and the Histadrut with a greater role in the management of the economic affairs," as Peres remarked in one of the council's sessions. He also warned that "letting a few planners situated in one of the government's offices do the job simply won't work."[8] The council was designated to play an active role in coordinating and planning socioeconomic policies. Among its announced purposes was "forging operational recommendations for the member-bodies and for the state's executive branches." It soon became evident, though, that the SEC served seven separate functions, not all of which are compatible with the principles of "integrated participation."

The council's first function, as stated by the minister of finance, was to serve as a forum for long-term planning and coordination. To this end, a subcommittee was established to deal with Israel's impending integration with the Common Market in 1992. Such a committee was already operating in the ministry of industry and commerce, but allegedly it lacked the ability to oversee all aspects of the Israeli economy. The council provided the finance minister with the opportunity to extend his authority to this important issue. The second function was to provide a means to settle ad hoc disagreements without resorting to cumbersome negotiations. The slogan "a war against bureaucracy" became the presiding rubric in Israel in the late 1980s. The council enabled direct interaction among the representatives of the major economic sectors, who could settle controversial issues simply by putting them on the agenda and discussing the matter. Thirdly, the SEC provided a means of airing grievances. The Histadrut, which often found itself in a minority in the council, complained that several commitments formulated in previous agreements were not implemented. For example, the secretary-general's concern was with the unfulfilled promise to aid weak industrial enterprises, most of which were owned by the Histadrut. Raising the issue on the SEC agenda publicly exposed this concern over the faltering enterprises.

The fourth function of the council was to devise changes regarding technical aspects of economic policy. The proposal to change the conditions under which house mortgages would be provided illustrates one such change; this particular proposal was subsequently elaborated into a bill. The fifth function was to solve problems that could not have been settled outside the confines of the council. The shift to a five-day work week, adamantly opposed by the manufactuers, and not less adamantly pushed by the Histadrut, offers one of these problems. A subcommittee found ways and means to settle the differences, and mutual concessions enabled accommodative arrangements to the satisfaction of all those involved. The sixth function was to provide the finance minister with a forum for expressing opinions and backing his moves. The war on unemployment was discussed at length in council meetings, although no operational measures were offered. The seventh, and perhaps most important function, was for the council to serve as a socializing agency. In this context, it set about launching a public campaign "to encourage production and export." The campaign was not geared to offering economic incentives for export industries; rather it was purported to disseminate values: pride in Israel's production and esprit de corps among its workers.

From the foregoing description some of the SEC's functions appear to be typically corporatist. Forging agreements, enabling representatives of interest groups to take part in the process of planning, establishing a forum in which accommodation and coordination can be developed to their utmost—these are basic characteristics of "integrated participation." Other features, however, are more in line with elitist patterns. Manipulation of councils for political uses is part of Israel's political repertoire. In 1986, the minister of health established such a council (for Medical and Social Affairs). The IMA was granted a token representation of one member among dozens of others, and was not consulted, despite its demand, in regard to determining the agenda of this body. The council was instrumental in mobilizing support more than in policy making. Coordination among those who were already in agreement was forged before the forum was ever convened. The professional association was thus not a genuine partner. Turning councils into feudal estates dominated by partisan ministerial overlords is not compatible with the West European characteristics of this type of mechanism, which is intended to provide interest groups with the opportunity to be partners with the state rather than subjects.

The life of this third SEC up to the time of this writing is too short, and precludes any serious evaluation of its operation and achievements. Some tentative conclusions, however, are possible. These tend to confirm an elitist pattern. Participants in the council's meeting have conceded that neither the government nor the Knesset has paid much heed to its deliberations. Since all the associations represented in the council had direct access to the government, especially to the minister of finance, who is the key figure in forging Israeli economic policy, the council was described as providing an "outlet for steam" more than serving as a policy-making body. Inter-ministerial rivalry also impeded the council's effectiveness. The subcommittee responsible for Israel's preparing itself for 1992 was virtually paralyzed because the ministry of industry and commerce obstructed its activities. Coordination was thus not achieved among the various government agencies involved. The importance of the SEC in providing an opportunity to smooth out differences between rival groups was also questioned. In fact, a forum for this specific purpose had been in operation before the establishment of the SEC, carrying the cumbersome title of the Forum for Strategic Thinking on the Future of Industry and the Economy in Israel. It had been formed by the MA for the purpose of reaching agreement with the Histadrut on controversial issues and for injecting some systematic thinking, allegedly lacking, into the policy-making process.

The SEC did not replace the forum but provided another channel of communication in what became the economic triad of state-employers-unions. Primarily, the council enabled the state to air ideas, to mobilize support for new schemes, and to attract media attention. The council discussed issues relating to economic growth and to the rising rates of unemployment. It confined most of its deliberations to issues that were not seriously disputed before they were put on the SEC agenda. Unity at all costs was the guiding theme of council resolutions. Organizational weakness has also impeded effectiveness. The SEC is not institutionalized; it has no office space or paid staff. Its secretary-general is a lawyer who volunteered to do the job and, therefore devotes only a small part of his time to council affairs. The SEC is also narrowly based in terms of socioeconomic interests. Although it encompasses the major associations in the economic sector, many others were left out. A request by the self-employed to join the council was rejected, a veto being cast by the Coordinating Office. A letter written by the chairman of the Israel Center for Economic Security and Social Justice (a marginal, unstructured group) urged the finance minister to erase the word "social" from the council's title, since none of its members supposedly was concerned over Israel's social problems. The structure and operation of the council, however, reflected the policy agenda of the finance minister who set it up: Shimon Peres, who had a special penchant for coordinating bodies and whose style of leadership was more consensual than conflictual. It remains to be seen whether this council will encounter the same fate as its predecessors, or whether it will outlive changes in leadership and turn into a stable forum for cooperation between the state and interest groups.

Despite the limitations of coordinating bodies in the Israeli polity, the practice is apparently gaining momentum. Such councils, whose function is to forge consensus, to smooth differences, and to enable representatives of interest groups to air their views, are being established in other government ministries. The minister of communication, Gad Yaacobi, established a council aimed at being "a strategic forum with binding forces."[9] Ariel Sharon, the minister of industry and commerce, did not lag behind his Labor counterparts and notified the press of the establishment of a Council for Commerce and Industry.[10] This initiative was a partial response to the Merchant Federation's investigation into their exclusion from the Peres-dominated SEC. Yitzhak Modai, the minister of economy, set up his own Planning Council and promised that it would be instrumental in forging long-term economic policies.[11] The visible success of the SEC, at least in attracting wide media attention, has kindled the fire of "cooperative" mood among Israeli ministers. Whether this cooperation will be translated into corporatist partnership remains a dubious question.

The function of implementation: Interest groups as agents of policy output. The role played by farmers in corporatist structures is equivocal. Lehmbruch (1979) saw organized agriculture as being less frequently included in corporatist arrangements and, when granted participation, as having no decisive voice. Schmitter (1982: 265), on the other hand, found agriculture to show a marked propensity for corporatism. Keeler (1987: 258) supports Schmitter's view. He postulated that the "states of all democratic capitalist regimes have intervened in an attempt at least to 'iron out' wide and erratic fluctuations in agricultural production, price and income." He added that the "peculiarly vulnerable" nature of agriculture, the strategic importance of food production, and the policital power of the farm vote have been additional factors inducing state intervention. The result of this intervention was the establishment of corporate bodies. In other democratic societies the decentralized structure of agricultural production, and the generally lower levels of education and income of farmers compared to other social sectors, placed obstacles in the way of corporatization. As Keeler argued, however, the organizational structure of the farmers association compensated for these difficulties.

In this regard Israel presents a deviant case. For one thing, its agricultural sector is highly concentrated, with production and marketing all but monopolized by the Agricultural Center, to which the overwhelming majority of Israeli farmers belong. For another, the educational level of Jewish farmers is far higher than the national average. Then, too, farmers enjoy the high esteem traditionally attached to toiling the land. Israel's agricultural sector, being among the most "politicized" sectors in the country, is most prone to elitist relationships with the authorities, that is, to integration with decision makers. Indeed, the agricultural councils provide an illuminating example of government-led organs whose purpose is to assist the state in carrying out its policies. The first of these, a marketing council, was established in the prestate era, in 1940 (Aharoni 1979: 24). As minister of agriculture between 1959 and 1964, Moshe Dayan expanded the councils to all branches of agriculture. They are empowered to oversee production, to assure regular supply of products, to facilitate marketing, and to deal with surplus. There are fourteen such councils—statutory authorities that can enter into contracts. By law the government does not constitute more than 25 percent of the membership. The producers' representation amounts to 50 percent, the marketers–15 percent; the rest, the retailers and consumers. In exercising their formal authority, the councils can set quotas, minimum prices and surplus policy, hand out subsidies and incentive bonuses, provide funds to encourage export; they even deal with packaging and categorization (Arian 1985: 216). In fact they are responsible for the implementation of agricultural policy forged by the authorities. The councils enable direct contacts between interest groups and decision makers; they ostensibly make policy a joint product.

Theoretically the agricultural associations thus play a major role in the policy process in matters pertinent to their interests. They are formally granted the right of integrated participation and can exert influence through this mechanism. The government, apparently, has relinquished much of its authority, handing it over to those having a direct stake in the policy in order to enhance agricultural production, prevent crises, and promote stability. In effect, the inclusion of the agricultural sector in the policy-making system resulted from a parentela linkage with the elite. This very inclusion, however, may also have paradoxically signified the decline of its political integration.

The agricultural councils, formed during the period of technological-industrial development, were aimed at providing long-term solutions to problems plaguing not only the Israeli farmers but also their counterparts in other democratic societies. The aid, consent, and cooperation of farmers were needed in order to introduce new techniques, new products, and new devices aimed at making farming compatible with modern economic developments. They were also designed to inject an element of

planning into Israeli agricultural production. The political coordinating bodies, operating under the auspices of political parties
and their affiliated organizations, were no longer suitable for
achieving these purposes. The establishment of the councils thus
marked a new era in Israeli politics in which agricultural production was regarded not just as a Zionist endeavor, in which
economic calculations could be set aside in favor of ideological
considerations (Kimmerling 1982), but also as a modern form of
production subject to rational planning. The agricultural councils
were supposed to abide by this rationality.

There is, however, another side to the operation of the councils, an aspect that is more in line with the political features of the
Israeli system of government. Council membership is composed,
on a proportional basis, of representatives of all settlement streams
and movements, according to political affiliation. But the councils
do not have any adjustment mechanism to handle changing circumstances both in the political division of power and in
agricultural production. The composition of the councils may
have enabled each farming sector to receive its share of the spoils,
but the over-politicized and highly bureaucratic management of
the councils gave rise to much frustration. There are increasing attempts to break the rigid framework and to introduce more
liberalization into the agricultural sector. One of the most notable
examples involves the flower growers, about one hundred of
whom have bypassed the state-run marketing council and signed
contracts of their own with European companies. The Citrus
Marketing Board has also been under attack, drawing heavy fire
for mismanagement and inefficiency that forced citrus growers to
pay allegedly unjustifiably high commissions for its services.
Although government authorities have taken pains to settle the
disputes and to retrieve for the agricultural councils full control
over farm production and marketing, the cracks appear to be too
deep to prevent permanent fissures. The councils are viewed by
their members (representatives of the farm movements), not as
"their" forum, but as a platform available to authoritative
manipulation. A senior member of one agricultural council put it
thus:

> It is the director general [heading the council] who deter-
> mines decisions. We talk for hours, but he can easily manipulate
> us, he can and does use strategies of divide and rule. He is the
> spokesman of his minister. Even though he is one person and we
> constitute the majority, he encounters no problem in achieving

his goals. In fact he determines the agenda, so he can remove from the floor issues that are not compatible with the ministry's interests, or have no chances of being approved by the budget authorities.

The integration of the farmers into the policy process has not obtained the councils' designated goals. The councils failed to forecast and prevent the severe agricultural crisis of the late 1980s. Israel's agricultural sector became racked by financial hardship, and only massive state aid (not provided through the councils) prevented total bankruptcy. The moshavim movement, as of this writing, still faces the danger of disintegration as a result of its failure to cope with sky-rocketing debts. The failure of the agricultural councils to confront the crisis indicates that this kind of corporatism, cloaked in elitism, may indeed be a "fair weather product" (Schmitter 1982: 275), not a mechanism to promote stability. Cooperation was thus largely spurious. The representatives of agricultural movements guard their interests both against rival movements and against the state. At the same time, one cannot ignore the tremendous achievements of Israeli agriculture, part of which may be attributed to the integration between farmers and the state. The councils, which began operating in the early days of statehood, played a historical role by distributing the means of production to prospective farmers, by inhibiting intra-sector competition, and by providing a shelter against natural disasters. Eventually, however, the economic crisis of the 1980s, the failure of the councils to curb surplus agricultural production, and the winds of liberalization had the effect of emptying the councils of much of their powers. Vulnerable, the councils began losing their ability to impose their will on individual farmers and settlements. The opportunities available to individuals for profit making, coupled with economic stringencies, make it extremely difficult for the councils to enforce their decisions. Although they do possess a series of possible sanctions against recalcitrant farmers, the councils have been reluctant to use them. The story of the agricultural council thus presents an equivocal picture regarding the utility of this corporatist arrangement, and its implication regarding state-group relations. They exhibit cooperation, but they are also germane to elitist themes.

Numerous other councils deal with a variety of other issues and operate under different auspices. The National Insurance Institution has its own council, and so does the national lottery. There is a sports council, an anti-drug council, a council for the

protection of children's rights, and a council for combating traffic
accidents. A council has been recently established for the country's
senior citizens. Most councils are state agencies under a different
guise. The voice of interest groups is usually ignored. They certainly do not play a significant role in shaping policies.

The three functions of joint bodies—namely solving technical
problems, attaining agreement, and implementing policies—are
not equally divided between the four major categories of interest
groups. The data indicate that party-affiliated organizations
perceive their participation in state committees as targeted mainly
at "attaining agreement over policy issues." This was also the view
most prevalent among promotional associations. On the basis of
the responses to this question, both party-affiliated and issue-
oriented associations tend to adopt a corporatist interpretation of
their membership in joint group-state bodies; the other two remaining categories showing inconclusive patterns (see table 6.2).
The ambiguity of the answers does not provide a clear clue to the
understanding of the group's perceptions regarding their participation in the policy process. The question was further probed in
regard to patterns of consultation.

Table 6.2
Most Important Committee Function (Percent Reporting)

| | Type of group | | | |
	Party-affiliated	Eco-nomic	Other	Promo-tional
Solving technical problems	16.8	38.2	40.0	9.7
Attaining agreement over policy issues	46.6	38.3	26.7	58.0
Implementing policies	36.6	23.5	33.3	32.3
N	30	34	15	31

Consultation

Consultation in pluralist societies abounds. The term,
however, may be misleading if it is taken simply to mean that
groups are invited along to the department to air their views
(Hogwood 1987: 61). In that case, they then go away and the
government makes up its own mind. It would be better to regard
the process as one of negotiation or bargaining, in which compromise is sought on both sides. Consultation is the major policy
style in Britain (Jordan and Richardson 1982; 1987). It takes on the
form of "horse trading" between government and interest groups.
Consultation imparts a pluralist flavor to the relationship between

groups and state organs. Is consultation a basic characteristic of interest politics in Israel? Figure 6.2 provides the answer. Among those which, according to their own testimony, are "always" or "occasionally" consulted, are the party-affiliated interest groups and even more so the economic organizations. Low on this list are the "other" groups, including immigrant associations and categoric groups. These latter obviously are not partners with government in any form of "participation." Neither are public interest groups, which the government only rarely consults.

Fig. 6.2 Consultation by State Officials
with Interest Groups (Percent Reporting)

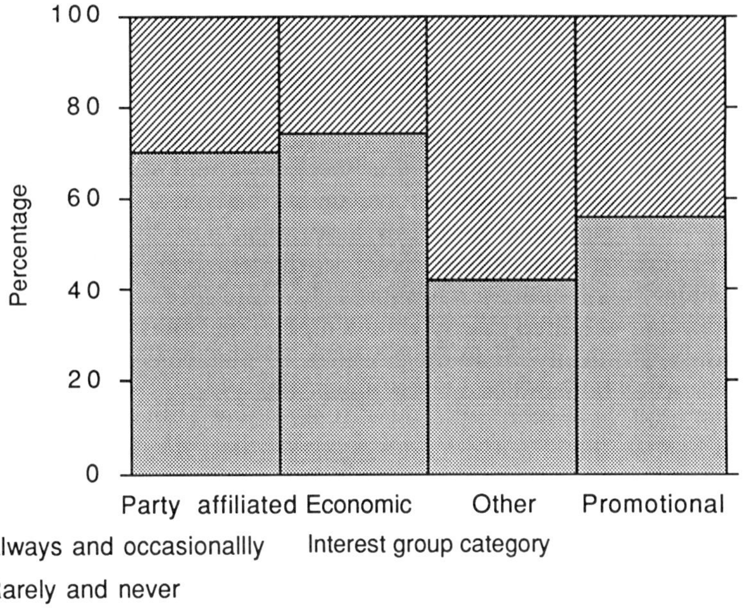

☐ Always and occasionallly   Interest group category
☑ Rarely and never

Consultation allows for distinguishing among three types of political styles: the first is based on information, the second on accommodation, the third on retroactive confirmation. Probing the opinions of the affected group is the first step in the bargaining process. As reported by the state officials interviewed in the course of this study, the attitudes of interest groups are widely sought; the opinion of those involved is always appreciated. Acquiring information on the association's views may also forestall possible opposition. The search for accommodation highlights the state's need to consult groups in order to forge consensus prior to policy mak-

proportional electoral system and by the high salience of politics, which induced economic and social groups to seek influence over the allocation of resources. A subsequent study conducted by the author (Yishai 1978a) found that nearly half of the MKs identified themselves as representatives of groups or social movements out-side their parties. This information, however, was not cor-roborated by the groups themselves; only a third of those named by the MKs confirmed that representation indeed took place.

Who are the direct representatives? The secretary-general of the Histadrut is traditionally a (Labor party) member of Knesset, and so is the head of the Histadrut Likud faction. Trade union delegations within the Histadrut are not recruited to the Knesset. The agricultural representation in the Knesset, as previously men-tioned, is impressive. It was once estimated that roughly 15 per-cent of the top political positions in the country were held by members of the settlement movements. Former members of the kibbutz movement alone held some 30 percent of all seats in the Knesset (Elon 1971: 314). The Knesset representation of the business community included, in the past, the chairman of the Center of Contractors & Builders and a member of the Chamber of Commerce board. The MA had no direct parliamentary represen-tation, nor did any major professional association. Naamat, the women's organization, has successfully delegated one of its leaders to the Knesset. Gush Emunim has also been represented in the legislature. Other promotional interest groups failed to do so.[14] Direct representation appears to decline over time. Some Knesset positions are safely secured for group members, but the vast ma-jority of interest groups, including the major associations of the business sector, do not enjoy the advantages of direct representa-tion. Less than 10 percent of the economic interest groups reported having an MK among their formal leadership; promotional groups had over twice that percentage. Members of Knesset identifying with ideological causes do tend to take part in the organizational life of the groups with which they associate.

Knesset lobby

The Israeli public is not very familiar with the "commercial lobby" prevalent in Western societies. When an Israeli mentions "lobby" in Hebrew, it is usually in reference to MKs organized in a Knesset subunit and acting within the parliament on behalf of an extra-parliamentary interest group. A Knesset lobby features the following characteristics:

1. The lobby has at least a minimum measure of organization in the form of an identifiable leadership and communication network. Some lobbies show more organizational vigor, others have only a rudimentary organizational structure, but the lobby is no ad hoc meeting in the corridor of MKs united around an issue.

2. The lobby demonstrates more than ephemeral coordination between members of Knesset. Although it is self-perpetuating, its boundaries are not rigidly fixed. Members go in and out of a lobby as their interests shift.

3. A Knesset lobby does not focus on specific legislation. Rather, it concentrates on an issue that has broader implications. The intensity with which the lobby operates, however, is influenced by the urgency with which the issue at hand is treated. A pending piece of legislation does invigorate a lobby's activity.

4. The lobby is a cross-party organization. It is not tantamount to an intra-party faction based on demographic attributes or ideological propensities. Its MK membership comes from different political parties, but represents the interests of a particular group, whose constituency also represents a variety of party affiliations. The lobby may be chaired by an MK representing a minority of its members. Party considerations are subordinate to the issue at stake.

5. Finally, a lobby is generally not associated with a single particular interest group. Rather, it advances issues having a broader perspective. A women's lobby may thus overlook the political and sociological distinctions between the various female organizations focusing on gender equality.

A lobby in the Israeli sense is not only a form of representation. It actually enables the integration of interest groups into the legislative process. Their voice is heard from within, not intermittently, but continuously. The legislative lobby does not allow only influence on policy making, but also actual participation in the process through the legislative machinery. Access of interest groups is secured from within. Although parliamentary lobbies often cut across political parties, their activity also indicates the blurring of the lines between associations and state. The lobbies may increase the effectiveness of interest groups, but they may also diminish their autonomy.

Lobbies representing special interests have mushroomed in the Knesset in the last decade. Just to cite a few examples, there

have been lobbies for the city of Jerusalem, for the Oriental communities, for development towns, and for women affairs. The
following review of the more visible lobbies in contemporary
Knesset politics reveals their expansion in the Israeli polity.

The welfare lobby. The heterogeneous structure of Israeli political
parties in terms of social composition enabled the establishment of
an effective lobby concentrating on welfare issues. The lobby thus
reflects a wide variety of partisan affiliations. It includes members
of the social democratic Labor party, Socialist Mapam, and right-
wing Herut. Members of the Communist party, Hadash, and of
Ratz (originally the Civil Rights Movement) are also active in the
lobby, whose constituency is the underprivileged in the Israeli
society. As explicated in chapter 2, the extent of protest politics
focusing on poverty in Israel is extremely limited, with most such
activity channeled through the parties. Groups representing the interests of the poor are active mainly on the local scene, in urban
neighborhoods and sites undergoing rehabilitation. The Knesset
lobby is not a mirror of, but actually a substitute for the extra-
parliamentary activity. The poverty constituency in Israel neatly
fits the definition of a nonassociational interest group (Almond
and Powell 1966: 76–77). This lobby articulates the interests of the
underprivileged and enables them to exert influence, as limited as
it may be, on the policy process. The Union of Social Workers, in
addition to being a professional association, regards itself as a
spokesman for the poor, but this self-image is rejected outrightly
by government authorities.

Membership in the welfare lobby is heterogeneous from the
social perspective, too. Although the Sephardim constitute the
majority of Israel's underprivileged, the Knesset lobby for the poor
is not based on ethnic origin. In the 12th Knesset, seventeen MKs
from various Knesset parties were associated with the welfare lobby, the declared goal of which is "to veto anti-social legislation."[15]
One of the recent successes of the welfare lobby has been to block
the Treasury's attempt to impose registration fees in the secondary
school system. Within this broad range of goals of the welfare lobby, there are also narrower advocacies.[16]

The farming lobby. The welfare lobby may be a substitute for
weak organized activity outside the Knesset; the agricultural lobby
supplements such activity. The farm lobby is the most organized,
and perhaps has been the most effective, in the history of Israel's
parliamentary life. Several references have been made to the fact
that the representation of the agricultural associations in the

Knesset far exceeds their members' numerical proportion in the population. In the past the MKs representing the various farming movements were deeply divided by ideological inclinations. The historical rift between the Western (U.S.)-Oriented Mapai and the Eastern (USSR)-oriented Mapam was a major barrier to cooperation between the MKs of the former's kibbutz and moshav movements and the latter's kibbutz movement. Ideological dissension was bitter, to the extent that it triggered a split within the kibbutz movement. The Farmers Federation was branded an outcast because of its identification with capitalism and free enterprise, which were anathema in the early days of statehood.

The maturation of Israeli society, the decline of ideology, economic developments, changes on the political map (in particular, the establishment of a National Unity government in 1984), and primarily the economic crises in the agricultural sector blurred differences between the representatives of the various farm groups, which then found ways to collaborate in a Knesset lobby. The unifying tendencies in the agricultural sector are not confined to the halls of the Knesset building. The centralization process, in the form of the forum that was established, and that encompassed all settlement movements in the country, facilitated and encouraged intensive intra-Knesset activity. In the late 1980s, the farm lobby was headed by a representative of the Farmers Union, whose membership constituted a minority among farm groups. A major arena for the agriculture lobby is the Water Committee, a joint subunit of the Finance and Economy committees, on which representatives of the farmers exert strong pressures to influence the allocation and pricing of water. The farm lobby is also active in the Finance Committee, whose decisions determine the extent of state financial aid to the agricultural sector.

The farm lobby has evinced a few impressive successes, the most important of which was the Compensation for Natural Disasters Law. The bill was approved despite the government's reluctance to assist social enterprises and to dispense public funds for sectional purposes. Apparently the organizational cohesion of the agricultural lobby and its past ideological glory has enabled the farm community to be integrated into the political establishment, not only through the parties' institutions but also through the legislature.

The religious lobby. In 1988 the religious Knesset representation was divided among no fewer than four parties, formed on the basis of ethnic cleavages, degree of orthodoxy, and personal rivalry. Yet there is also a strong lobby in the legislature promoting religious issues. The religious parties do not all belong to the same ideological camp. Some are willing to withdraw from the occupied territories for the sake of securing peace; others, clinging to the ideal of Greater Israel, endorse the annexation of these lands. When the issue at stake concerns religious affairs, however, the majority of orthodox MKs join forces and act to influence legislation.

"Religious affairs" include material as well as nonmaterial issues. First and foremost among the latter is the lingering issue of "Who is a Jew?," proposals regarding which have repeatedly been placed on the Knesset agenda for deliberation and legislation. The religious constituency, on the whole, may be characterized as non associational, but there are also organized interest groups promoting religious affairs. Shleimut (Integrity) is one such extra-parliamentary group, whose major objective is to secure a change in the Law of Return and to modify the legal definition of Jewish identity. The interest group is engaged in a host of activities, but its thrust is the Knesset, where the real action takes place. The group is less interested in the mobilization of public opinion at large than in soliciting the support of MKs, whose vote will determine the fate of their demand. This Knesset lobby thus plays a major role in advancing the religious cause. The same applies to other groups that were active in the past but ceased to operate, mainly because their goal had been achieved. The Committee for the Sacredness of Israel obtained, through its Knesset lobby, cancellation of the "social paragraph" in the abortion law; the Committee for the Defense of Human Dignity secured, through intensive parliamentary activity, amendment of the Anatomy and Pathology Law (requiring explicit family approval for post-mortem operations).

The effectiveness of the religious lobby results not only from its organizational resources, its degree of unity, and the sophistication of its strategies. Outcomes are also, and perhaps primarily, a function of the role played by religious parties in the government coalition. The more critical the role, the more successful in the lobby. Regardless of these circumstances, the lobby has attracted wide media attention and excelled in organizational coherence. On a material level, the desire of religious institutions and associations to increase their share of government allocations is not subject to the efforts of the religious lobby. Rivalry between the various religious parties inhibits concerted action in this regard. Since it is a zero-sum game, the reward given to one contender means a loss for the others. No lobby could possibly mitigate the competition for government (or Knesset) spoils. Unlike the farming sector, where benefits are allocated according to fixed criteria, religious contenders never agreed on the rules of allocation.

Development towns lobby. In March 1988, the Knesset unanimously approved the Development Towns Law, committing the state to grant huge financial aid to the residents of Israel's periphery. The press termed the law a "Seasonal Sale."[17] It reported that the bill was opposed by many MKs and the ministers of the economic offices. Yet not one Knesset member dared raise his or her hand against the law. This legislation gave recent proof of the effectiveness of the lobby for development towns in the Israeli Knesset. As noted above, the socioeconomic attributes of development towns' residents are below the national average, whether in terms of education, occupation, or density of housing. Their numbers, however, make them a critical electoral force, which in recent elections has been a target for intensive party courting. Owing to the intense rivalry of the two major camps of the Israeli Polity, it is widely believed that the development town vote will determine the election results. Therefore, both parties, Labor and Likud, have made special efforts to recruit the mayors of development towns to their Knesset lists. Development town representation in the Knesset grew considerably in the 1980s.

Development towns have also established a formal organization outside the parliament, the Forum of Development Towns, which operates under the auspices of the Center for Local Government. Its members cut across party lines as well as geographical zones.[18] Normally, though, the development towns lobby in the Knesset attempts to influence only those issues pertaining to the periphery as a whole. The lip service paid by the Israeli elite to integration, on the one hand, and to population dispersal on the other hand, paved the way for effective influence.[19] The outcomes of this influence, however, remain only on paper. The Development Towns Law was approved without difficulty, but it was never implemented. The power of the lobby was sufficiently strong to induce legislation, but not so great as to bridge the gap between promise and performance.

A separate though somewhat related lobby consists of MKs representing municipal authorities. The association behind this lobby is the Center for Local Government, which in effect is an institutional interest group, owing to its statutory authority in the local arena. It consists of officials of municipalities, including mayors, across the country. It is said to be one of the most organized lobbies in the Knesset (Weiss 1988: 103), although so far it has attracted only limited public attention.[20]

The women's lobby. The scarcity of women in the Israeli parliament might have been expected to prompt intensive lobbying activity on behalf of this constituency. The fact of the matter is, however, that Israeli women are deeply divided over ideological issues. It is difficult for Geula Cohen (Hatehiya), for example, who is an arch-hawk, to collaborate with Shulamit Aloni (Ratz), who is not less ardent a dove. Furthermore, as a study of women politicians' opinions and identity revealed, (Yishai 1978b), the two aforementioned MKs, who constitute between a quarter and a third of female representation in the Knesset, do not regard themselves as representatives of Israeli women. They were elected on the basis of their views on general policy issues. The women's lobby is thus not highly organized and its activities are not often coordinated. Yet Knesset women members do collaborate when specific issues arise. One example is the legislation regarding women's right for retirement, which in 1988 were equalized with those of men.

In conclusion, an Israeli lobby not only provides access for interest groups and enables them to exert influence on the process of legislation. The lobby actually represents organized associations or would-be associations in the parliament. This type of integration does not limit a groups' capability to pressure from without. The question is whether this form of internal access limits their autonomy and restrains their freedom of action, or, alternatively, whether it is another strategy among many, which facilitates penetration into the locus of power. In the past, there were cases in which the lobby preceded the associational activity. The environmental lobby, for instance, initiated the establishment of the Council for a Beautiful Israel. Most of the lobbies, however are products of extra-parliamentary activity and not its instigators. Intra-Knesset organized activity on behalf of outside associations does not seem about to threaten a group's autonomy with domination by the state.

Conclusions

Interest groups in Israel appear to have broad access to the two branches of the state, the government and the Knesset. The overwhelming majority of voluntary associations requested and were granted meetings with state officials, with ministers, and occasionally with the prime minister. They also made their claims heard by Knesset committees. Their ability to address the state through the means of "participation," is, however, more limited than in European democracies. Although there exists a myriad of joint state-group bodies, partnership emerges only rarely. Councils in various economic policy domains also abound, but are largely caricatures of their European counterparts, with short life span and little effectiveness. The Social-Economic Council is a typical example: it has no statutory powers and very few responsibilities. It does serve the function of mitigating tensions, but does not delve into profound economic issues. The road to corporatist state-group relation appears to be paved by political parties. Output functions are fulfilled by the party-affiliated farm groups. The agricultural councils have shown continuity and past utility, but there are signs that they, too, are becoming suffocating organizations, from which the farmers are trying to release themselves. Consultation as a form of state-group interaction was found to be widespread in regard to party-affiliated and economic organizations, but it was not aimed at establishing corporatist relationship with voluntary associations. Instead, consultation is focused on problems having little policy relevancy.

Integration with state authorities has been more conspicuous in the past in the form of direct representation. The number of MKs nominated by interest groups, or selected by the parties as the groups' representatives, appears to be declining. The Knesset lobby, whose activity is expanding, offers an adequate, though limited, substitute. With the exception of the farming groups, MKs do not voice claims of the economic sector but of the less-privileged or less-organized constituencies. The evidence regarding the pattern of group-state relations remains inconclusive. Corporatist tendencies, although identifiable, do not appear to predominate. Features congruent with the elitist model are also partial. Pluralistic characteristics are in evidence, but they are marred by the elite's attitudes, as perceived by group activists and as expressed by state officials themselves. The relationship between interest groups and state in Israeli politics were further probed in the associations' strategies, which form the subject of the next chapter.

CHAPTER SEVEN

Strategies of Influence: Bargaining, Coordination, or Integration

In November 1988, a huge rally was held in Tel Aviv to demand that the government make election reform its top priority. The organizers, members of the Public Committee for a Constitution, declared that if the demonstration did not bear immediate fruit, public pressure would be increased.[1] The election reform movement was not the only one that took to the streets that year. Tens of thousands of Israelis urged the government to impose military service on the ultra-orthodox who receive deferment so long as they study in a *yeshiva* (an institution of higher religious studies). They were confronted by observant reservists, who protested this stereotype of "draft dodgers."[2] Demonstrations were staged by citizens hailing from varied social sectors. Even the families of the drug addicts conducted a public rally to urge the government to stop ignoring the problem and to take immediate action to prevent the spread of dangerous narcotics.[3]

A cursory glance at the Israeli press reveals that the scope of "direct action" is wide. This impression is substantiated by the findings of pioneer studies of Israel's political culture (Wolfsfeld 1988). The question, however, is whether or not the institutionalized interest groups have also resorted to this type of strategy of influence. Direct action is presumably prompted by blocked gates to the corridors of power. Do interest groups experience difficulties in their attempts to influence decision makers through the more conventional channels? Put differently, is a demonstration another tactic employed by associations, or is it the only strategy available to them? This chapter will delve into the tactics and strategies groups employ in order to advance their causes.

Many lists of interest group strategies have been compiled (e.g., Ziegler and Peak 1972; Schlozman and Tierney 1986). The conceptual framework of this book, however, provides a tentative yardstick for gauging the distinctions among three forms of strategies, in accordance with the three models of interest group politics. The arsenal of strategies under pluralist regimes is extremely varied. Groups resort to (nonviolent) demonstrations, stage strikes, appeal to the courts, address the media, and lobby state authorities. They may also forge personal relations with decision makers. Admittedly, this last strategy is hard to classify, since it may evolve under all types of state-group interactions. Although in Israel the implication of such relationships may tilt the scale toward the elitist model, because they manifest a lack of differentiation between groups, parties, and political elites, personal links to decision makers are nevertheless universally regarded as a "pluralist" attribute. In the two other configurations, strategies are narrower in scope. Under corporatist circumstances, the groups' input into the policy process is exercised through joint committees. Under elitist circumstances the party is chosen as a major channel of influence.

It is very rare for an interest group to choose only one tactic or strategy. It is much more common for an association to employ a combination of strategies, and to use whatever means of influence are available. The number and scope of channels are both an outcome and a cause for the group's clout. The combination of several approaches is needed, therefore, for it to succeed in shaping policy. Despite this theoretical difficulty, an attempt will be made to identify the major means of influence (by the frequency of their use) and to place Israeli interest groups on the triangle of the three models of interaction with political authorities.

The Pluralist Nexus

Direct action: demonstrations and strikes

Both demonstrations and strikes comprise only one form of direct action. Other forms frequently resorted to in Western societies are conspicuously absent in Israel. Mailing letters or calling legislative representatives is not a standard practice. The electoral system insulates Israeli parliamentary delegates from the people. The tight party discipline renders this method of direct appeal ineffective, and therefore superfluous. Knesset members do not vote in response to the public mood and do not abide by the wishes of a defined constituency; rather, they follow for the most part—with a few prominent exceptions—the directives of their respective party's organizations. The literature presents ambiguous explanations of the reasons for staging direct action. According to one version (Verba and Nie 1972), it is an expression of efficacy, the demonstration of a belief that one can influence government policies through the mechanism of individual participation. Another version, suggested by Kornhauser (1954), among others, regards direct action as anathema to democracy. It is not a manifestation of a viable polity, in this view, but an indication of clogged channels of communication between the elite and the citizens. Institutional decay hinders the flow of demands through the mediating organizations and necessitates the entrance of individuals into the political arena.

In Israel, prospects for the choice of direct action as a frequent strategy employed by institutionalized interest groups, as distinct from unorganized individuals, is rather low among all categories of interest groups (see table 7.1). Even public interest groups, which in Europe and the United States capture public attention by summoning their members to demonstrate, show a low record of direct action. The reason for the absence of this strategy from the Israeli arsenal is probably not grounded in the "deterioration" of the polity. In a country where consensus and unity are key elements in the political culture, one cannot expect a wide diffusion of demonstrations and strikes. Although Wolfsfeld (1988: 22) reported that the percentage of Israelis ready to demonstrate against a law considered to be very unjust or harmful is far higher than in other democracies, leaders of interest groups apparently hold a different view.

The data indicate that the percentage of groups that "often" resort to demonstrations or strikes is not impressive: between 16 and 30.5 percent. At the same time, the proportion of those that reported that they never exercised direct action as a means to achieve group ends is considerable. Relative to other categories of interest groups, salaried workers—i.e., trade unions and professionals—engage in a higher frequency of direct action. When the category of "occasional" direct action is added, the data appear even more striking. The similarity between the two types of groups is another indicator of the unionization of professionals in Israel. The academics not only carry the banner of human welfare and progress (Wilding 1982), but they also employ techniques involving bitter struggle over scarce resources. Medical staffs, for example, stage strikes with far higher frequency than in other Western countries.[4] The number of doctors' work days lost in

Israel on account of strikes during the 1980s exceeded 200 (Yishai 1990). Work stoppage causes the cancellation of operations, reduces the quality of health care, and brings misery to many people; but perhaps for these very reasons, the effectiveness of this means appears to be extremely high, at least for the short term.

Table 7.1
Reported Frequency of Recourse to Strategies of Influence
(Often and Occasionally)

| | Interest group category | | | | |
	Party-affiliated	Economic	Other	Promo-tional	N
Demonstrations	30.5	17.5	16.0	19.5	147
Litigation	21.2	23.1	12.5	20.0	141
Knesset lobby	57.6	56.5	46.0	50.0	142
Contacts with administration	79.4	82.1	76.0	67.4	147
Media	60.6	68.6	44.0	74.0	146
Personal contacts	81.9	86.9	65.5	65.9	141
Membership in joint bodies	72.7	83.9	30.0	43.8	143
Contacts with political parties	33.6	23.7	33.4	21.7	141

Whatever the reasons for staging a demonstration, this particular act has some obvious advantages in a group's struggle for influence (Etzioni 1970). To begin with, a demonstration contributes to the group's organizational cohesion, spurs its integrity, and enhances internal solidarity. It provides the members with an opportunity to identify with the group's objectives and strengthens their affiliation with its cause. Demonstrations also have manifest media advantages. Since they capture attention, they are used as a major means of disseminating information about an issue (Kingdon 1984: 61). In short, a demonstration is an effective strategy if it is employed with caution and prudence; that is to say, if it is not too repetitious and does not expose a group's vulnerability insofar as its mobilization capacity. A demonstration, though, can prove counterproductive if rank-and-file membership prefers not to join in. In that case, the threat that is incorporated in every direct public action to delegitimize the authorities vanishes.

The demonstrations held by Israeli interest groups are not, as a rule, spontaneous protests, acts of despair in consequence of severe grievances. Rather, the organizers of a demonstration face a legal obligation, as it were, to anticipate such activity. Every public outdoor assembly of fifty people or more requires police authorization. Permission is denied only in rare cases (unfortunately no systematic data are available), but the procedure does require that a demonstration should be planned ahead of time. Despite this obstacle, which is more technical than substantial, the number of demonstrations staged since 1960 has grown considerably (Lehman-Wilzig 1981: 180; also Etzioni Halevi 1975). A major part of the expansion of protest in Israel, however, was carried on by unstructured groups or nonassociational groups that had acquired a loose organizational structure, such as the Black Panthers. During the Lebanon war (1982–1984) demonstrations mushroomed: during this three-year period, ninety-five were held whose major cause was the war; of these seventy-eight were anti-war protests (Yishai 1985b). A more detailed chronological analysis shows that about half of the demonstrations took place during the first half year of the war; that is between June and December 1982. Most of these demonstrations were "small", i.e., attended by fewer than fifty people. The demonstrators represented the variety of groups formed to protest the war. Only two of these groups—not including Peace Now, which was not established with the specific purpose of opposing the Lebanon war—succeeded in mobilizing sufficient resources to maintain themselves until the end of the belligerency. One of the two—Parents against Silence—dissolved with Israel's withdrawal of forces; the other group—There Is a Limit (Yesh Gvul)—focused its activities on the territorial issue.[5] The anti-war protest was not a calculated strategy but a means of direct participation in the political process. It was not the typical pattern characterizing organized interest groups on the Israeli scene.

Every demonstration focuses on a "dilemma" that provides the catalyst for people to confront the authorities by taking to the street (Eshcen et al. 1969). In Israel six such major issues can be identified (Sella and Yishai 1986): foreign affairs, social injustice, economic inequality, religious affairs, the quality of the environment, and the structure of government.

Foreign policy. This issue predominated even without including an anti-nuclear movement or any other public group demanding the demilitarization of the region. Yet the Arab-Israeli conflict provided the major cause of some of the largest demonstrations Israel has ever experienced.[6] Blatant demonstrations focusing on foreign policy issues did not start with the Lebanon war. Israel became a deeply divided society over questions of security immediately after the 1967 Six Day War, although it took a full decade until the issue of foreign policy triggered massive street demonstrations. The rallies that were held in the wake of the 1973 October war were not critical of Israel's external policy but of its internal political structure. These demonstrations, which were also staged by short-lived anomic, unorganized groups, were also sporadic. More systematic taking to the streets by associational groups on account of foreign policy issues started in 1975, following Henry Kissinger's plan for interim agreements that would entail Israel's retreat from occupied lands. Anti-Kissinger demonstrations turned violent. Blatant demonstrations to protest Israel's agreement to withdraw from lands were staged during the IDF's eviction of settlers from Yamit in the Gaza Strip. Peace Now also called for demonstrations as a major strategy and held thirty-six of them from 1978 to 1984 (Bar-On 1985)—that is, an average of one demonstration every two months. For a country as small as Israel, this frequency indicates a high mobilization capacity. Demonstrations have also been conducted to prove that the desire for peace was not confined to a bunch of leftists (who are derogated as having a "beautiful soul," the equivalent of a "bleeding heart"); rather it has become widespread among the Israeli populace. With a relatively large constituency supporting retreat from territories in exchange for peace, the stalling of the peace process provided a major catalyst for street action. There was a feeling that only dramatic manifestations of grassroots adherence to peace would arouse those members of the elite who were willing to pay the price of withdrawal and would convince them of their strong, stable public support.

Social Protest. This is the second cause of direct action. During the 1950s there were sporadic demonstrations of new immigrants facing the hardships of absorption. The newcomers left their tents and camps and marched to the big city (Tel Aviv) to bring their grievances directly to the top politicians. They demanded food, housing, and particularly employment. Access to policy makers was denied by the Knesset speaker, who commented that he would not communicate with those "who destroy fences" (Segev 1984: 136), and violence was condoned to disperse demonstrators. Direct action was unacceptable and not granted legitimacy in those days. The exclusive dominance of the parties, including their monopolization of the absorption process, had left frustrated immigrants with few choices insofar as "strategies." A decade later, another wave of mass protest erupted in the Haifa neighborhood of Wadi Salib. Demonstration became riot (in May 1959), and was unprecedented in violence: shops were looted, the local Mapai club was attacked, and a number of policemen and demonstrators were wounded. The government, taken aback by the severity of the protest, took measures to improve living conditions in the neighborhoods where the trouble started and attempted to co-opt some of the leaders into its ranks (Galnoor 1982: 357). Although the protest subsided, under the surface of ostensible integration there was much discontent and alienation.

In 1971, the Black Panthers made their first public appearance, on March 3. The founders of the movement, like the Wadi Salib activists, were Israelis of Moroccan origin, whose protest against social inequity shattered one of the fundamental conventions of Israeli society: that it was an egalitarian society. The Panthers, whose fight was aided by social workers and academics from the Hebrew University of Jerusalem, captured wide media, public, and elite attention. The expansion of the protest this time was broader and more rapid than of the Haifa agitation twelve years earlier. Exposure on television and a relatively high degree of organization, both lacking in the earlier protest, provided the movement with a means of attracting large crowds. The major issue for the social protest this time, in the early 1970s, was a sense of relative deprivation. Jews from Morocco largely did not share in the affluence that had swept the country in the aftermath of the Six Day War. Their deprivation was most accentuated when contrasted with the generous benefits conferred upon immigrants from Western societies, who arrived in greater number than ever before in the early 1970s, The Black Panthers' demonstrations subsided gradually, but their impact was significant. A government-appointed committee was established to look into the problems of children growing up in large families in distress. The recommendations of this committee (headed by Dr. Israel Katz, later minister for welfare during Begin's first government) led to major changes in compensating, through the national insurance system, large families. These results have not drastically changed the overall plight of the Sephardim, but protest activity grounded in social inequity was stilled.

Economic grievances. These have been staged by a variety of interest groups, first and foremost by the country's salaried workers of all types: the blue-collar metal workers, the white-collar employees of the public service—even the professionals, especially the teachers, have taken to the streets. One possible trigger of demonstrations to press for economic demands is that of forthcoming elections. Although no direct linkage between voting behavior and economic affluence has been established, the "election economy"—i.e., distributing benefits to large constituencies—has offered a temptation to increase pressure on decision makers. Lehman-Wilzig found (1981: 186), however, that *post-election* years are marked by large numbers of demonstrations. The disillusionment of the citizens and the gap between the high rate of political involvement, expressed in the high voter turnout, and the low sense of political efficacy, constitute catalysts for protest. This type of protest, however, does not include demonstrations staged by salaried workers, who clearly seek to increase their share of the national pie. Groups other than trade unions also demonstrate, although infrequently, on account of economic grievances: farmers have broken baskets of eggs to protest the low price they receive for this commodity; the handicapped have blocked traffic with their wheelchairs; students have disrupted the higher education system in strikes against tuition hikes. Activities of this type, widely televised, receive immediate public attention. Their frequency, however, is rather low.

Religious issues. These are part and parcel of the Israeli repertoire of direct action. There are seasonal confrontations between the ultra-orthodox and the secularists, most of which are extremely emotional and heated. Stone throwing, verbal abuse, and mutual acrimonies are common features of these demonstrations. Pitted against each other are the extremists among both the religiously observant and the confirmed secular Jews, both camps claiming the right to maintain their particular way of life. In the overwhelming majority of the cases the religious constituencies are those staging the protest. They demonstrate to demand that traffic be halted on Sabbath, that public entertainment not take place on holy days, that archaeological excavations be ended if found to interfere with an ancient Jewish gravesite, that "distasteful" and what they view as obscene public advertisements be removed from bus stops and billboards. These demonstrations are reputedly not organized by groups associated with the religious parties but by extremists, for whom such street activity constitutes a major form of confrontation with the secular world (Levy 1988: 214–216). Since demonstrations by the religious are prompted by the desecration of religious practices, they are reactive rather than proactive. Their purpose is also to make show of power within the religious community to support contending leaders, and to stimulate fund raising abroad. Public violation of religious codes thus provides an essential, though not a sufficient, condition for staging a demonstration. In fact the organizers of religious demonstrations may target their efforts at objectives other than religious ones. The religious-secular cleavage has triggered bitter confrontations that have ended at times in violent clashes. Most of the demonstrators, however, may be described as "sporadic interventionists" in politics, rather than members of associational groups.

Ecological problems. Unlike other Western countries, in Israel these induce relatively little direct action. The Society for the protection of Nature once in awhile—i.e., less than "occasionally"—calls upon its members to demonstrate against a plan deemed to bear harmful environmental effects. Such protests are usually staged outside the urban centers and they attract small crowds. Demonstrations on behalf of the environment have been held in Haifa, a city with a grave air pollution problem, but they have been relatively small, incidental, and not sponsored by nationally organized ecological associations.

The structure of government. The number of interest groups organized to promulgate this issue is extremely small, and few demonstrations have taken place to advance causes pertaining to the characteristics of the political regime. Several notable exceptions to this rule do exist. The Movement for a Constitution has resorted to demonstrations as a major strategy, but the frequency of such acts indicate that the issue, as important as it might be, is not sufficiently exciting to enable the frequent summoning of large crowds. The post-1988 election period provided the impetus for pro-constitution demonstrations. The process of forming the government coalition that year was fraught with many difficulties owing to the near equal influence of the two major political blocs, Labor and Likud, both of which increased their dependence on the support of the small religious parties. The latter used extortionist practices to increase their benefits. Since to many a constitution seemed to offer an instant cure to Israel's political malaise, the stage was set for a large demonstration on behalf of a written constitution.

The vast majority of demonstrations that are held in Israel are both peaceful and lawful. Between 1968 and 1979, the percentage of violent protests was merely 18.3 percent (Sella and Yishai 1986: 120). Lehman-Wilzig (1981: 207), in concluding a comprehensive study of demonstrations in Israel, asserted that this type of activity did not constitute a threat to the political system. Perhaps a major reason is that most of the protest groups are co-opted into the establishment. In contemporary Israel social protest activity has been greatly absorbed by the political parties. Furthermore, direct action geared to advancing economic causes has also dwindled. The lingering economic crisis of the 1980s, manifested in the lack of economic growth and in the increasing rate of unemployment, has reduced the propensity to demonstrate—or, for that matter, to strike—for a salary raise. The religious issue awaits its seasonal eruption. Thus only foreign policy continues to ignite direct action. Should Israel veer from the status quo on arrangements for the occupied territories, mass protest, on either or both sides of the ideological fence, is expected to explode. Demonstrations offer a strategy for rationally calculated behavior of interest groups rather than an outlet for accumulated frustration or a means to destroy the system. The likelihood of future direct action aimed at undermining the regime's legitimacy is quite remote, although not excluded. Profiles of these public protests are presented in table 7.2.

Table 7.2
Selected Demonstrations Held by Interest Groups, by Issue, Trigger, and Period

Issue	Major group	Trigger	Period
Foreign policy	Gush Emunim	Interim Agreements (Egypt-Israel)	1975
	The Movement for Withdrawal	Camp David Accords	1982
	Peace Now	Sadat's initiative	1978–82
Social equity	Black Panthers	the post-1967 affluence	1971
Economic inequality	trade unions	approaching wage agreements	intermittently
Religious affairs	the orthodox community	descretion of religious practices	intermittently
Environmental affairs	Society for the Protection of Nature	anticipated or present ecological damage	intermittently
Structure of the regime	The Movement for a Constitution	the electoral deadlock	1988

Strikes present another strategy. Their function is to "withhold supply" (Wootton 1985: 230) from the market in order to influence public policy. The railroad workers who stopped the running of the country's trains, the Electric Company employees who paralyzed Israel's economy, and airport technicians who disrupted the country's air links with the outside world have all withheld important supplies. Although Israeli citizens may wake up in the morning to hear that an essential service is not being provided on account of a strike, the rate of strikes in Israel, judged by the index of lost days of work per 1000 employees, is lower than in many other countries, including Italy, Great Britain, Belgium, Denmark, and France (Michael and Bar-El 1977). Until 1977 the long-standing political alliance between the government and the Labor Federation, both of which were under the leadership of the Labor party, provided a prime explanation for the low frequency of labor strikes. During the years of Likud government, there was a considerable increase in the number of days of work lost on account of strikes (Shirom 1983: 243). It thus appears that the strike weapon not only falls within the pluralistic framework of behavior, it also offers a means of fighting a political battle on an unconventional front.

Litigation

Litigation is a strategy widely used by North American interest groups. Minority groups, church organizations, the disadvantaged, and civic associations often turn to the courts to find redress for grievances (Wootton 1985). A United States Common Cause, for example, maintains a special litigation division that specializes in lawsuits involving the regulation of political campaigns (McFarland 1984: 142). In Israel the strategy of litigation is far less common (see table 7.1), although a few interest groups do employ this measure quite extensively.

The strategy of litigation is undertaken mainly by trade unions and professional associations, which appeal to the labor court when disagreements persist with employers. It is also resorted to by public interest groups, primarily by the Civil Rights Association, which includes among its members many in the legal profession. Environmental groups also make use of the litigation strategy. Malraz, for example, has sued violators of the ecological laws. The shortage of resources, however, prevents an extensive use of litigation as a means of action.

An appeal to the court appears to be especially useful in cases in which there is an urgent need to prevent the government from taking an undesired action. The instant remedy provided by the court is specifically helpful in these instances. The government's oil reform plan illustrates the circumstances under which interest groups resort to litigation as a strategy of action. On July 11, 1988, the cabinet took a decision, described by the minister of finance as "an unusual event in the history of the Israeli economy,"[7] that was aimed at some of the country's most deeply entrenched monopolistic interests. A chief target of the proposed reform was the "cost plus" system, under which a fixed profit above costs was guaranteed to the providers of goods or services, without any inquiry into the reasonableness of the reported costs in a competitive

context. Israeli oil companies were practicing such an arrangement. It took two and a half years of often acrimonious negotiations for the government to push through a reform in the oil
market, which could have the effect of breaking the monopoly of
Israel's three big oil companies, which were organized in a semi-
cartel. The case for reform was compelling. In 1987, a year of
relatively low prices in the world energy market, Israel paid $1.15
billion for imported crude oil. It stood to reason that the break up
of the cartel would force the three companies, which were the
country's sole importers and distributors of oil, to search harder
for cheaper sources of oil and to start engaging in competitive
practices. The reform permitted the six big institutional oil consumers, including the Electric Company, Israel Chemicals, and the
refineries to import oil independently. This move was intended to
open up, for a start, only one-third of the domestic oil market, but
the oil companies were unwilling to settle for such a compromise.
Their argument was that by consolidating the power of the
monopolistic refineries, the reform would result in the opposite of
what it was intended to do. They took the case to court, which
ordered amending the reform and issuing criteria to guarantee fair
competition between new companies and existing ones that could
now enter the fray.[8] The court decree did not terminate the confrontation between the energy minister and the oil companies, but
it enabled an interregnum.

The case of the oil companies underlines the merits as well as the
disadvantages of using litigation as an interest group strategy.
Turning to the court may result in immediate relief and also provide an opportunity to capture public attention. Appeals, especially to the Supreme Court of Justice, are extensively reported in the
media when the matter concerns the public at large. If successful,
the appeal constitutes an effective device in blocking the
undesired action of the authorities. At the same time, litigation
may prove costly both in financial terms (which indeed it is) and in
having a narrow scope. The targets of interest groups are less comprehensive than those of political parties, but still usually are comprised of more than a single narrow issue. Unless a group is staffed
by professional jurists, as is the Civil Rights Association, the investment in a court case may not be worth the effort. Furthermore,
the judicial process itself exposes the "private" aspects of a group's
activity. Even public interest groups appear in court to defend the
rights of individuals rather than to promulgate the good of society
at large. In a collective-oriented society such as Israel, highly

dubious benefits accrue from upgrading the private interest and protecting it in the Supreme Court of Justice.

The private bias of litigation is, perhaps, the major factor inhibiting widespread resort to this strategy. In legal phrasing, the barrier is a lack of *locus standi*, that is, "an interest in the subject matter of the legal proceedings that is greater than and different from that of the general public" (Pross 1986: 172). Put differently, the court has to be convinced that the individual or group requesting the hearing is directly and substantially affected by the action of another, with which it is being asked to interfere. In the past the Supreme Court of Justice has strictly held by its demand for a personal stake, a fact that greatly diminished groups' resort to litigation. For example, the court rejected a plea by a citizen who claimed he had to serve a longer period of military reserve service because religious students were exempt from the draft. The voice of the secularists was thus silenced by the court on grounds of the absence of *locus standi.*

A partial remedy to the problem of standing was found in the ploy of having individuals issue a petition for a group as a whole. Thus, for example, three immigrant physicians from the Soviet Union complained that the IMA's Scientific Council had treated them harshly and unfairly in regard to recognition of their expertise titles. The Court rejected their argument, not on grounds of standing, but because the discretionary authority of the Medical Association with respect to professional qualifications was acknowledged (Yishai 1990). In recent years, the court has shown much more latitude, and appears to be more favorable to groups' demands. The Bar Association, for example, appealed to the Supreme Court in an attempt to frustrate the nomination of two specific individuals to the rabbinical court.[9] Laor, a public interest group advocating far-reaching reforms of the political system, went to court against all political parties represented in the 12th Knesset for having retroactively increased their annual financial allowances.[10]

In the absence of a written constitution, and with the freezing of the proposal to enact a Civil Rights Law, the Supreme Court serves as a major vehicle for guarding the civil liberties and rights of Israelis, including the less-privileged sections of the population represented by interest groups. It should be remembered, however, that the remedies provided by court are only temporary. The sovereignty of the legislature in a parliamentry system of government precludes policy making by the judicial branch. The

court cannot overrule the legislature, to whom a coalition government can always resort if it is determined to carry through its
course of action.

To sum up, the recourse to litigation by interest groups (see
table 7.1), at least in terms of quantity, is not very impressive.
Unlike in the United States, Israeli courts are not crucial policy-
making institutions empowered to make authoritative decisions.
They mainly settle particular disputes and shy away from making
sweeping policies. Although they redress grievances of individuals, their sensitivity to public mood is rather low. They are
not attuned to the articulation of political interests, but rather to
the spirit and language of the law.

Lobbying

In parliamentary systems, the legislature does not appear to
be an attractive target for interest group activity. In Great Britain,
for example, Parliament plays a minor role in policy making, compared to the role played by the government. British policy has
been described as "a package arrangement agreed between civil
servants and the representatives of the outside groups" (Finer
1970: 157). In Israel, as in Britain, party discipline inhibits
parliamentary back-benchers from challenging party leadership.
In view of these circumstances it is quite surprising that the
Knesset does serve as a target for group strategies (see table 7.1).
About half of the respondents in all categories of interest groups
reported frequent or occasional recourse to lobbying the Knesset,
with the party-oriented and the economic groups slightly more attracted to the legislature than "others" and promotional associations. What kinds of interaction exist between group representatives and Knesset members?

As already pointed out, lobbying in the American sense is not
practiced in Israel. All books dealing with interest groups politics
in the United States devote chapters to this subject, lobbying being
considered a major mechanism for exerting influence. "Lobbyists
representing organized interests are a seemingly ubiquitous force
on Capitol Hill, forging mutually beneficial relationships with
legislators and their staffs, and finding ways to make the structure
and operation of Congress work for them" (Schlozman and
Tierney 1986: 289). In essence, American-style lobbying represents
the institutionalization of the influence process. It is manifested
through the establishment of an office, located in Washington,
D.C., staffed by professionals, who weave the fabric of pressure.

They provide services, assistance, and support to legislators; they furnish them with information and a wide assortment of other services.

Israeli professional lobbyists, in contrast, are not extensively involved in "working" the Knesset. There is no need for lobbyists to register, to declare their intentions, or to reveal their financial records and means of influence. There is also no need for any parliamentary representative to disclose his or her relationship with interest organizations outside the legislature. The lack of legislation in this regard was generated by practical politics. The fact is that interest group activists seeking to influence decisions do roam the halls of the Knesset, although not as professional lobbyists but as amateurs. Only a tiny number of interest groups, primarily in the economic sector, keep (intermittently) professional, paid lobbyists, whose main job is to keep their eyes open and their ears alert to any move relevant to the groups represented. The reason for the lack of structured lobbying activity is twofold: first, for some associations there is no need to lobby because some Knesset members already consider themselves representatives of groups; secondly, and paradoxically, lobbying does go on, but it is cloaked with a heavy curtain of secrecy.

As elaborated in chapter 6, representation of groups by Knesset members covers important aspects of associational life: religious organizations, development towns, and urban neighborhoods are amply represented, but this situation pertains to only a minority of groups. Thus such large groups as the physicians, the teachers, and the university professors cannot rely on intra-parliamentary advocacy in their search for influence. In fact, less than a quarter of all respondents claimed to have a "lobby" in the Knesset to represent their particular interests. These include interest groups perceiving an MK to sympathize with their goals. There are ardent spokesmen in the Knesset for both the cause of Gush Emunim and Peace Now. Neither, however, has hired a professional staff to look after its interests in the parliament. Only a few economic organizations (prominent among them are the Manufacturers Association and the Center of Contractors and Builders) influence the Knesset through paid service.

If interest groups are not represented by professional lobbyists, and if just a small proportion of them are represented by professional politicians, the only avenue available for interest groups to approach Knesset members by is that of direct access. This takes the form of "accessing" a committee, since the Knesset as a whole is not perceived as a major arena in which important decisions on a group's affairs are determined. And usually the target is one specific committee—the Knesset Finance Committee. This body is a focus of interest group pilgrimage, most of which does not occur in the limelight but takes place in the shadows of the political corridors. The Finance Committee is among the few legislative institutions whose decisions really make a difference. The public is well aware of this status:

> It's a pleasure being a member of the Finance Committee. Just ask any one of the members and he will tell you. Recent weeks provide an example of its condensed schedule, which is part and parcel of its routine work. During this period, the committee deliberated the state's budget and financial allowances for various sectors. There are not many other opportunities available to an MK to be involved in an activity bearing prompt results. The Treasury is obliged to present for the Committee's approval every decision, every intended step, every budget transaction. The professionals in the ministry of finance take all necessary measures to shape decisions to the best of their knowledge, while resisting the pressures of ministers and organized interests alike. In the final stage of deliberations, however, they resign their authority, which is then transferred to the political representatives [in the Knesset Committee]. Only a few Knesset Members are acquainted with the facts that led to the decision, several more will work hard to study the economic arguments. Voting is not determined by the validity and persuasion of these arguments. Rather, MKs are exposed to endless entreaties by bodies and organizations aiming to enlist their support.[11]

The obvious conclusion is drawn by interest groups: "Find yourself an MK. Use all forms of persuasion available to you. If you tackled the right person your chances for success are formidable."[12]

Admittedly, the Knesset Finance Committee is not a source of parliamentary initiative. Its major power lies in being able to block the Treasury's proposals. But its veto potential is a powerful tool. Like other Knesset committees, the composition of this highly politicized body reflects the partisan structure of the legislature. If, however, the committee were guided only by partisan considerations, its appeal to interest groups would provide an indication not of pluralist politics, but of elitist patterns, associated with party dominance. The Finance Committee, though, is also highly aware of constituencies outside the party structure, even those lacking clear ideological or political affiliation. For example, attempts to reintroduce a registration fee in high schools have met with stubborn refusal by the committee. The fees would, in practice (though not in theory), have abolished Israel's Free Secondary Education Law, which came into force in the early 1980s. The opposition to registration fees for public schools was not triggered by a powerful parents association; it developed because the committee members cast a squinting glance at the large, unorganized (or to use Almond and Powell's term, nonassociational), extremely broad constituency of Israeli parents.

Contacts between interest groups and Knesset members are not conducted in a formal manner. There are many social occasions in which relationships may be established and influence exerted. This is true mainly for "first world" interest groups (Benewick 1973), whose resources qualify their leaders or even rank-and-file members to associate with political notables. Well-established business people, famous media personalities, and noted physicians (especially surgeons) are always welcome in the "right places" frequented by Knesset members. The leaders and activists of groups need not use formal channels. The cohesiveness of Israeli society enables the use of the more effective informal venues. Owing to the broad social spectrum represented in the Knesset, access is not confined to the "haves." It may emanate from a common-ground basis: a shared ideology, residency in a development town or urban neighborhood, vegetarianism, love of animals, parenting retarded children. Almost all interest groups will somehow and at some time find their way to "their" MK and seek his or her support. Whether or not support is indeed forthcoming and results in a favorable policy will be discussed in the next chapter, which is devoted to the role of interest groups in the policy process.

Formal contacts between interest groups and government officials

Formal contacts are believed to be an extremely important form of political action. This course was mentioned by three-quarters of all groups as a frequent or at least an occasional strategy. The party-affiliated group showed a somewhat lower tendency than their economic counterparts to make formal contact (see table 7.1). Indeed, leaders of economic interest groups reported that formal contacts with bureaucrats occur almost everyday. Thus the staff of the Manufacturers Association was said to maintain a close (formal) relationship with those officials in the ministry of industry and commerce who were responsible for the MA's respective branches. The promotional associations, however, resort less than the sectional groups to "contacting the administration." They target their activity more to the public than to state officials.

The institutionalized contacts with government administrators take various forms: letters are written, phone calls are made, and meetings are arranged. The volume of contacts reported by the respondents corresponds with the evidence presented in chapter 4, which is based on interviews with senior state officials. The ties with these officials cut across sectional differences. Members of the settlement organizations meet regularly with government officials in order to advance settlement plans, to reduce tariffs and customs on agricultural machinery, to obtain compensation for a lost crop, to secure professional advice on agricultural production problems. The Bureau of Accountants contacts government officials to demand clarifications of the tax laws and regulations; the Teachers Federation maintains almost daily contact with the ministry of education in regard to the operation of the school system. In short, the big hand of the state, which in Israel is far from being invisible, necessitates frequent contact between interest groups and government officials. These contacts are initiated not only by representatives of associations or their administrative staffs, but also by individual group members.[13]

Since formal contacts between interest groups and the bureaucracy do not result from party affiliation but from the functional needs of those involved, they do not decrease or increase with every change in the division of political power. No matter who is the incumbent minister of housing, "contacts" are still part of the Center of Contractors' repertoire of activities. These meetings are imperative for associations and administrators alike. For the former, they enable the access that is essential for influence; for the latter, they provide some form of feedback, as rudimentry as it may be. Group leaders interviewed emphasized that the extent, scope, and content of formal contacts are directly linked to the personalities occupying the official's chair. Some senior officials were identified as congenial and receptive, "a pleasure to work with"; others as being less favorably disposed to interest groups' communications. The same rule applied to the ministers.[14] In this study, "contact with the government and its officials" is an indicator of pluralistic politics. It should be remembered, though, that in cases in which the administration is highly politicized, these contacts may substitute for appeals to party centers. Furthermore, contacts with bureaucrats stand the chances of being one sided, extremely formalized, and lacking the reciprocity available in pluralist systems. By writing a letter, one may establish contact and therefore justify a positive answer in the right column of the questionnaire. The outcome of such a contact in terms of group politics, may remain questionable, however.

The media as an interest group strategy

One of the characteristics of Israeli interest group strategies is the reported secrecy in which interaction with decision makers is cloaked (Arian 1985; 194). Since "lobbying" is a pejorative term in Israel, a group is unlikely to publicize its recourse to this means of pressure/influence on a member of Knesset. The curtain of secrecy is lifted, however, by the extensive use of media strategies. This takes place not to win the vote, but to win the expansion needed to persuade those decision makers whose vote determines the group's benefits, be they material or ideological. The use of the media enables a wider, more immediate dissemination of a group's interests and is considered by a large majority to constitute a useful, effective strategy.

The proportion of interest groups that resort "often" or "occasionally" to media techniques is high, especially among the promotional associations (see table 7.1). Newspapers, radio, and television serve expansion purposes equally. This access to media is influenced, however, by the cost. A distinction should therefore be made between media attention available free of charge and the media space or time available for purchase. What rules and practices govern the use of each type of strategies?

Access to free media. The Israelis are avowed consumers of media. More than four-fifths of the country's Jewish population over the age of fourteen read a newspaper at least one day a week. About three-quarters read a newspaper daily (*Statistical Abstract* 1988: 694). The rates of listening to radio news, which is broadcast every half hour, is also very high. Most of the Hebrew newspapers are independently owned and present a wide range of opinions. In the past, there were many newspapers affiliated with political parties; however, at present even the partisan-oriented papers (such as *Davar*, the Histadrut's daily) try to appeal to a growing market, and therefore downplay political and ideological matters. It is a truism that "newspapers depend on good reporting, and reporters are only as good as their sources" (Arian 1985: 255). Israeli reporters find it extremely important not just to secure information, but to extract from their sources what may be sensational and provocative. Many reporters are said to have developed symbiotic relations with interest groups, especially when the journalists specialize in an issue domain. Each of the country's five major dailies maintains a special correspondent for health issues, for legal issues, and for environmental affairs. There are also reporters with expertise in economic affairs, tourism, and agriculture. If information released to friendly reporters catches a good headline (such as "Hoteliers show Tel Aviv to be 31st, not 5th most expensive city"[15]), the group is able to reap the fruits of its cooperation by having its case presented in a most convincing manner, and often with the added benefit of having the vulnerability of its adversary exposed. The reporter, of course, has been satisfied with having presented the story.

Television air time is much more difficult to achieve than is a report in the press. Only the big economic associations and/or those whose objectives attract broad public attention are privileged enough to appear on TV. The president of the Manufacturers Association is a regular guest on the screen; his opinion and comments are sought with regard to current affairs and planned economic policy. His Histadrut counterpart is no less frequently interviewed on the air. Television also presents pictures of the mass demonstrations held by both Peace Now and (in the past) Gush Emunim. In fact, all groups whose strategies have any newsmaking value receive media coverage, regardless of their political affiliation or social origin. Because of Israel's free press and fairly independent broadcasting system groups are able to reveal their activities to a wider, media-consuming public than might otherwise be the case, at least so long as professional media considerations regard the particular "news" as meriting publicity.

Despite the obvious advantages of media exposure, there is an inculcated norm in the Israeli political culture that denounces the search for personal publicity. The modern campaign techniques of the Western world, especially the United States, are gradually gaining ground in Israel. Public relations experts are attached to most politicians and to those seeking to gain public support. Israeli style publicity, however, still retains some of the old-time flavor that derogates emphasis on personal attributes and objectives. Even in the late 1980s, an Israeli politician does not boast of his or her individual qualities but enumerates ways in which devotion was shown to the national cause. A Peace Now activist once described the group's reservations with regard to media exposure: "When the editorial board of *Alie Koteret* [a popular television program] invited one of the signatories [of the letter that marked the inception of the movement], there was a general flight of young activists from the room. They were all startled by the public exposure they had to encounter" (Bar-On 1985: 16). Their apprehension was caused not only by their lack of experience in public life, but also by the norm forbidding personal exposure. It is the goal that counts, not the people that carry it out. Nevertheless, much of the reservation with regard to the use of the media as a group technique is short lived. Even Peace Now's reluctance to be seen on television is a matter of the past. Like other public interest groups, it, too, makes extensive use of the media and devotes efforts to attract reporters' attention.

Purchasing media attention. Many political battles are fought and won with the aid of purchased media space or time. Because the Israeli press is decreasingly dependent on partisan sources, advertisements bring in a considerable share of a newspaper's income. Presumably the paid-for, self-publicity of interest groups does not provide the lion's share of this advertising revenue, but it is still highly welcomed. All categories of interest groups attempt to mobilize public opinion and to establish communication with their membership through bought media space, but the frequency among promotional groups is higher than among their associational sectional counterparts. Public movements rally their adherents to demonstrations; other groups make their views known by printing them in the newspaper. The advertising may also be used to convene a meeting or to disseminate information regarding the group's internal life.

In addition to these functions, purchased media space also purports to represent "public opinion." The fact that the message was paid for by an interested association matters little so long as the press campaign is extensive. A good example of this point may be seen in the IMA's struggle against the government's attempt to enact the National Health Insurance Law (see also chapter 6). The bill, originally proposed by the Alignment in 1976, was meant to consolidate the monopolization of the Histadrut's General Sick Fund over other providers of health services. The physicians, having a stake in the free market system, or at least in maintaining some form of competition, limited as it may have been, opposed the bill. The medical profession refused to be limited to Kupat Holim and advocated a variety of health provision arrangements, including private medicine. Despite the objection of the professionals, the coalition steam roller gathered sufficient momentum

to enable the bill to pass its first reading. Thereupon, the IMA
launched an aggressive press campaign through one of the largest
advertising agencies in the country, and its effect on the final vote
was dramatic. Admittedly IMA pressure was not exerted on all
MKs, but mainly on the representatives of a small, marginal coalition party, the Independent Liberals, which happened to play a
crucial role in the coalition make-up. The party had little to lose
by withholding its vote, thereby defeating the proposed National
Health Insurance Law. On the contrary, it could with this act
demonstrate adherence to its liberal ideological principles, a
recognized virtue in Israeli politics. The bill's third reading was
prevented owing to the declared opposition of the Independent
Liberals, and further Knesset action was delayed until after the
elections. The subsequent Likud administration, however, meant a
death blow for the proposal, as this party adamantly opposed
granting any special privileges to Labor-backed organizations,
such as the General Sick Fund, especially if such privileges were to
be inscribed in national legislation.

The effects of the purchased media space on legislation cannot
be gauged precisely. According to the IMA's own evaluation, the
media played a crucial factor in its success. Huge daily ads, which
were very expensive, presented the public with the "facts," as seen
by the medical profession. These ads presumably helped shape
public opinion. Editorials looked unfavorably on the law. Again,
there is no way of telling whether these editorials would have been
written had the IMA not used the media as a major means of
mobilizing public opinion. In any case the outcome was rather
unusual in that it is rare for a proposed law to be defeated in the
Knesset, or even to be removed from the agenda. The IMA prides
itself on being one of the few interest groups that has overcome the
political hurdles and prevented the enactment of an undesired bill
after it had already been approved by the coalition majority and
presented for the first reading. A large portion of the credit, it
claimed, was due the press.

Resorting to the media is not reserved to the affluent groups
of the sectional category. It is in fact the less-established associations that need the media for communicating to members, for
soliciting support, and for recruiting new joiners. A review of interest group ads that appeared in the press one summer weekend
(September 8, 1989) showed the variety of associations taking
recourse to a media strategy. The Association of Interior
Decorators (small and weakly organized) informed its members of
a scheduled Study Day. The ad, as well as the event, were spon-

sored by a marble enterprise, which of course had a commercial stake in maintaining contact with the association. The Histadrut—to be more precise, the various political factions within the Histadrut—swept the newspapers with ads urging Histadrut members to vote for their respective lists in the approaching elections. The majority of political ads that appeared that specific day were published by promotional interest groups. Pregnant women were offered free consultation by a pro-life association, Efrat (the ad apparently being funded by the Demographic Center, which is affiliated with the minister of labor and welfare).[16] WIZO declared the opening of a recruitment campaign. Yad Labanim, the association of relatives of war victims, publicly denounced the widows, who wanted to go their separate way and who in turn castigated the association in a series of (free) news articles in another newspaper. Finally, the Association for Deprived Men,[17] a marginal group with a very tenuous organizational structure, urged prospective members ("those who feel discriminated owing to the circumstances of their divorce and parenthood") to join the struggle and attend a designated meeting ("participated by the media and members of the elite," the ad promised). This variety of advertisements illustrates the need of Israeli interest groups to resort to media techniques.

Advertising on television is another purchased media technique. The Israeli television network—actually one channel—was established in the aftermath of the Six Day War. A state-financed agency, it purported to penetrate the bloody curtain separating Israel from its neighboring countries and to enable the state to disseminate its own message to the Arab population across the border, including that residing in the occupied territories beyond the Green Line (the pre-1967 state boundaries). Israeli television operates under the auspices of the Broadcast Authority Law, which grants it a large measure of independence, albeit restricted by some forms of public (i.e., partisan) supervision. Being a public station, the channel officially does not sell air time to private companies. In the 1980s a way was found to bypass this regulation. Air time is still not "sold"; however, private companies are allowed to grant their "aegis" to a variety of programs for large sums of money. On the other hand, public enterprises, including voluntary nonprofit organizations, are entitled to present "public service announcements" whose declared goal is to disseminate useful information or to solicit support for a national-oriented cause. In effect, however, these "public service" ads are little more than commercial advertisements. Supervision over the service ads is extremely lax. For example, the Dairy Council, facing at the time marketing difficulties and decreasing consumption of dairy products, resorted to "public service" messages as a means of commercial publicity. It had no difficulty in obtaining approval from the authorized body to publicize its high-fat products, such as yellow cheese and ice cream, as "providing calcium from nature." Likewise the Beef Council, encountering similar difficulties, urged the public through a service message to consume calf meat, asserting that it was "stimulating and invigorating." No mention was made of its high cholesterol rate.

Among those purchasing TV time are public interest groups, not only private enterprises disguising their private interests in public clothing. The Society for Prevention of Smoking has used TV as a major strategy for persuading Israelis of the damage caused by cigarettes. The Cancer Society has urged women not to neglect breast checking. Naamat launched an extensive campaign aimed at increasing gender equality. Other "service" ads have urged Isrealis to join pension funds (despite the fact that the vast majority of employees are already insured in old-age schemes), to participate in the weekly national lottery, and to engage in a host of other activities recommended and deemed appropriate by public authorities.

Television time is extremely expensive, restricting access. The giant economic organizations have a substantial advertising budget (in 1989 the Histadrut, for instance, allocated 380,000 shekels to advertising). The nonprofit associations simply cannot afford this luxury. Nevertheless, associations on behalf of the handicapped do make extensive use of television "service" advertising, and regularly urge the public to contribute on the specific day allotted to the organization for soliciting funds. No accurate data are available on the effectiveness of television in mobilizing resources, but according to the testimony of one activist, "Without television we would have been completely at a loss. This is our only means of opening the people's eyes, and subsequently their pockets. Most of them are not familiar with our misery. We have to remind them that behind their doorstep, there are people with dire needs, who need help. This is our chance to mobilize resources and to help all those who so desperately need our assistance."

Personal contacts with decision makers

Organized interest group administrators and tenured state officials tend to develop amicable relationships between them even in the most pluralistic societies (Kingdon 1984). Table 7.1 shows that intimacy between interest groups and senior politicians is a recurrent phenomenon, particularly among the economic interest groups. Even the party-affiliated associations score lower in this regard. Personal contacts are far less evident among "other" sectional groups and issue-oriented associations. Asher Arian (1985: 194) made this observation about the special relationship between association activists and the political elite in Israel: "Keeping in mind the pyramidal structure of Israeli political life and the relatively small numbers of people at the apex of the pyramid reminds us that the probability of elite members meeting often—formally and informally, in official capacities and socially—is very high." The tribal aspects of society are apparently still evident despite the fact that Israel counts a population of over four and a half million. The pronounced social cohesion (as distinct from political diversity) which enables the establishment of intimate relations beteen subsections of the population, especially within the elite, is a mixed blessing. It enables cutting through the red tape. Discussing an issue over a cup of coffee—or, increasingly more in Israel, over a drink—may be very convenient to all those involved. The relationship and its benefits may also lead to unfavorable consequences: inequality and deprivation for those that remain outside the intimate club, and, worse, grave disappointment if expectations are unfulfilled.

A striking instance of the futility of intimate relations was provided by a bitter controversy in the late 1980s between the minister of tourism and the president of the Union of Hotel Owners. The close relations between the two did not deter the minister from confronting the association on the disputed issue of hotel prices. The conflict was bitter precisely because the issue was expected to be resolved by conventional means, i.e. within the framework of the cozy relationship between the authorities and the affected group. Having failed to achieve results from this intimacy, the controversy erupted in full force. It thus appears that a close relationship is difficult to manage when a particularly contentious issue is involved.

Apart from the foregoing reservation, the high frequency of "personal contacts with the political elite" indicates that not many institutionalized interest groups are excluded from the cozy club of intimacy.[18] Thus it appears that in Israel, personal ties are often very important in obtaining access and in receiving a hearing. They represent, however, but one among several channels of influence. The closeness between interest groups and the elite does not necessarily translate into intensive interaction with what is perceived to be the source of power, i.e., political parties. It may very well be that the intimacy is an outcome of an old boy network, characteristic of a nation under (psychological) siege, whose male population spends a substantial portion of its adult life in military service, in which the spirit of comradeship is highly appreciated and nurtured.

To conclude the discussion on the pluralist nexus, it is evident that there are no substantial (statistically significant) differences between the categories of associations. All Israeli interest groups make extensive use of "outside" tatics to influence decision makers. The variety of means employed, moreover, accentuate their access to many forms of persuasion or pressure. Succinctly put, groups act as if they were operating in a pluralist society. Yet a comparison of the various types of interest groups does reveal some variation. The strategy most popular among both the party-affiliated groups and the economic associations is that of personal contacts with decision makers; formal appeal to the administration is also a popular means of activity. Issue-oriented groups, in contrast, choose the media as their favorite mode of action. This is hardly surprising. The promotional groups rely on mobilization of wide publics. Their inferior resources make the media a prime channel of influence. The problem, however, is that unless direct action is taken, the media are unlikely to pay much heed to associations and their activity. Since approximately two-thirds of the promotional interest groups "never" hold a demonstration or stage a strike, their effectiveness may be hindered.

Cooperation between Groups and State: The Corporatist Configuration

The essence of the corporatist strategy is institutionalized participation in decision making forums: committees, councils, and the like. As a rule, the more established sectional interest groups are far more linked to the government than are promotional associations, whose major concern is with social values, rather than with economic benefits. Israel is no exception. The two types of institutionalized sectional interest groups (party-affiliated associations and economic groups) show a considerably higher frequency of discussing policy issues with the authorities "in joint bodies" than do promotional associations (see table 7.1). It should be remembered that the structure of the issue-oriented group arena is highly infiltrated by the state. It appears, however, that this does not lead to joint forums of decisions. Both the Consumers Council and the Association for Better Housing report no such strategy as participating in a joint committee or any other similar body. Officials in the respective ministries (industry and commerce, and housing) also abhor the idea of joint committees. As may be recalled, senior officials in these ministries have charged the public groups with pursuing interests that are not public at all.

The single category of groups that scored highest on the corporatist scale was that representing the farmers: over 90 percent of their interest groups have been members in joint bodies either "often" or occasionally." The councils for production and marketing of farm products constitute one forum of participation; but the bureaucracy and the associations are intertwined in a host of bodies in the ministry of agriculture. Despite the fact that the agricultural sector is already saturated with committees, councils, subcommittees, and forums carrying other titles, one of the first steps reportedly taken by the minister of agriculture in the newly formed National Unity government in 1988 was to set up several additional committees. These committees were formed, among other reasons, to examine the mediation gap in the agricultural sector, to investigate agricultural export, and to look into the tax rates imposed on farmers. All these committees included representatives of the farming associations.[19] Despite the fact that agricultural associations were defined by virtue of their historical ties and internal organizational structure as "party-affiliated" groups, when judged on the merit of their strategies they appear to lean heavily toward corporatist patterns.

Trade unions also indicate that cooperation is resorted to often, but to a much lesser degree than the farmer groups. The low figure for the unions' participation in state-group committees is a result of the structure of trade unionism in Israel. The Labor Federation may or may not be a full-fledged partner of decision makers, and in some cases, pertaining particularly to wage policy, it in fact is. But its subunits, the sectoral trade unions, are actually cut off from the policy process. They are represented, for better or for worse, by the roof organization of the Histadrut.

The business community scored the highest in cooperation. The list of committees on which representatives of the Manufacturers Association and other members of the Coordinating Office serve is impressive. For example, the Chamber of Commerce is represented in thirty-eight committees operating under the auspices of thirteen ministries. As already noted, however, the vast majority of these committees deal with issues placed low on the association's agenda. There are some exceptions to this rule. For example, the Chamber of Commerce participates in two committees focusing on issues of utmost import to the association—the Advisory Committee on Import Policy and the Advisory Committee on the Anti-Dumping Law (1977). The delegation of one representative among several (or even dozens of) committee members, however, is insufficient to secure genuine influence.

What is important in this regard is that interest groups relate to "cooperation" as a regular strategy employed. They do not believe that the administration is always applauding this cooperation. In fact, as noted in chapter 6, the purpose of joint bodies, in the overwhelming majority of cases, is not to secure cooperation but rather to keep the associations informed, secure their opinions, or "notify" them of a pending decision. Insofar as shaping policy is concerned, Israeli interest groups are much less "partners" than would be expected even in the mildest version of corporatist politics. Yet, the pursuit of coordinating channels is a legitimate strategy and a widely practiced tactic, regardless of its influence on the final outcome.

A more genuine cooperation has been obtained on the professional arena. The professional associations are, in fact, prominent on the scale of cooperation. A preponderant majority among them reported that cooperation with the authorities in joint bodies is a frequent or occasional strategy. The Bar Association and the IMA are among the groups most integrated in the process of decision making—the first, by virtue of its statutory role; the second, owing to the essential functional role it plays in health policy. The number of committees on which the Bar Association is represented is too numerous to be listed (according to its chairman). Two recent examples are the Committee to Examine the Administration of the Courts, and the Advisory Committee on improving the Efficiency of the Civil Courts. A host of subcommittees operating under the auspices of the ministry of justice can point to Bar Association representation, usually, however, one delegate among a host of officials. In a letter addressed to the director-general of the justice ministry, the chairman of the Bar Association reiterated the agreement committing the ministry's legislative department to coordinate all legislative proposals with the respective bar committees. That agreement also called for no testimony to be presented in the Knesset Committee on Constitution, Law, and Justice without prior joint state-bar deliberations.[20]

The participation of the Israel Medical Association in joint state-group organs is perhaps not as extensive in volume, but it is extremely effective when exercised. The "joint committees" are responsible for licensing doctors, for acknowledging qualifications for the title of "expert physician," for determining (on the basis of qualifying examinations) the eligibility of a physician who studied and practiced medicine abroad. In the case of the medical profession, the so-called "joint discussions" imply that the IMA has the major, if not the final, say, the proficiency and expertise of the professionals having qualified them to play the determinant role in regulating the profession. Participation in joint bodies indeed constitutes a key strategy for the IMA.

Among the promotional groups, the lowest rate of cooperation is found for the welfare associations. Although over 40 percent of the groups in this category reported cooperation, this percentage is lower by far than that reported by other interest groups (except for the categoric groups). The lack of cooperation in this policy domain may be explained by the nature of the activity of welfare groups and their relationship with the state. Owing to its redistributive features, welfare policy is monopolized by the state and its administrative agencies. On the other hand, welfare associations play an important role in implementing policies. They deal with grassroots problems and effectively carry on their own shoulders the burden of providing essential services to the handicapped or offering help to the needy. The two ends of planning, as much as it exists, and implementing do not seem to meet. Hence "cooperation" is not defined as a major strategy of action.

The least integrated into the policy process are the interest groups classified as "others." Immigrant associations are not members of group-state bodies; neither are categoric groups of students, tenants, homosexuals, or the deaf. Less than a third among the groups in this category reported membership in joint group-state committees is frequently or even occasionally practiced. The exclusion of immigrant associations from the policy process will be dealt with in chapter 9.

Integration with the Authorities: The Elitist Configuration

Elitist-oriented strategies in a democratic society are a function of integration, that is, the lack of differentiation between interest groups and political parties or their respective agents in the bureaucracy. The strategy distinctly suitable for achieving integration is the affiliation with political parties.

"Contacts with political parties" is thus the last item in the repertoire of strategies. Communication with political parties has been seen to be extremely tenuous. Group leaders were asked whether, and how frequently, they contacted political parties as a group strategy. The proportion who gave a positive answer (shown in table 7.1) was rather low. Only one out of five promotional groups contacted political parties; within other categories of associations the figure was somewhat higher, but still rather low. Even among the party-affiliated associations no more than a third reported frequent or occasional interaction with political parties. Contacts include appeals to all parties during the electoral campaign to include in their platform a plank that is favorable to the group's priorities (see chapter 3). This type of interaction may be enumerated among the pluralist strategies, but it does not necessarily imply elitist characteristics of interest group politics. As will be further elaborated, political parties are not seen as bodies making decisions important to the groups' activities. Their influence may be perceived as preponderant, but not as directly relating to the associations' demands.

The Choice of Strategies: A Detailed Look

The choice of strategy is influenced by many factors: the availability of access, the extent of resources at the group's disposal, the issue at stake. A detailed comparison of the strategies often and occasionally resorted to by different types of interest groups (presented in table 7.3) yields some interesting conclusions. An analysis by category of groups reveals that each type "specializes" in one (or more) types of strategy. Trade unions tend to personal meetings, their traditional proximity to the centers of power making it possible for unions to command this strategy. Their low recourse to political parties is surprising in view of their organizational link to the Histadrut. Farmers, more than other groups, excel in cooperating with the government in joint bodies. They also rank extremely high in their intimacy with decision makers, as well as official appeals to the administration. The closed network of the agricultural sector in Israel is still manifest, although agricultural policy making does not necessarily reflect any extensive accommodation. The business associations also prefer "personal meetings." in fact, over 90 percent of the associations in this category reported such proximity. None of the groups listed under the business category was engaged (in the three previous years) in a demonstration or a strike, a strategy that seems reserved for the less-privileged sectors of the Israeli population. The professionals choose "personal meetings" and participation in joint bodies as their major strategies. Members of this category also do resort, more than any other type of group, to litigation.

Their proficiency and their abundant resources supply ample opportunities to turn to the courts. The matters they espouse, mainly regarding the material benefits of their members, necessitate appeals to the judicial branch of the labor court. Compared with other sectional interest groups, both categoric groups and immigrant associations are remote from politics. Both these types turn extensively to decision makers, but they enjoy less of the intimacy that characterizes the latters' relationship with other interest groups.

Table 7.3
Reported Frequency of Recourse to Strategies of Influence,
by Group Category (Often and Occasionally)

Group	N	Demonstrations & strikes	Litigation	Media	Knesset lobby	Formal contacts	Joint bodies	Personal contacts	Parties
Unions	22	31.8	33.8	51.4	47.6	71.4	61.9	76.2*	19.0
Farmers	15	28.5	—	75.0	75.0	92.3*	91.7	91.6	58.3
Business	23	—	4.8	63.1	63.6	86.3	85.0	90.4*	23.8
Professionals	19	36.9	44.5	73.6	47.0	76.5	82.5*	82.4	23.6
Immigrants	12	20.0	11.1	50.0	50.0	90.0*	50.0	72.8	33.3
Categoric	17	13.4	13.3	40.0	42.8	66.7*	33.3	61.0	33.3
Public Interest groups	22	30.0	26.4	86.4*	59.1	63.6	40.9	63.2	28.5
Welfare	19	6.7	20.0	66.6	35.7	81.3*	33.3	71.5	13.3
Sports and culture	17	19.2	27.3	60.0	50.0	54.6	63.6	63.7*	20.0

*The strategy most frequently used by the interest group.

Public interest groups differ from the other associations with regard to the choice of strategies. Their major preference is for media strategies. As revealed by the data, the ecological groups, consumers organizations, civil rights organizations, and the like adopt a plethora of means to influence the authorities. Their accentuation of the media may be attributed to two possible causes. The first is linked to the opportunity structure. Channels for influence may not be as open as they are for the sectional groups. The second reason has to do with the objectives of the groups themselves. For them mobilizing public support and/or raising public consciousness is more important than securing a governmental decision or influencing legislation. When asked what their next step was following the authorities rejection of their demands, half of the public interest groups reported that they would appeal to public opinion. The respective proportion among the business groups was less than 10 percent; their first choice was to contact decision makers. The media provide the most effective means of capturing the public's attention and of mobilizing broad constituencies. Welfare interest groups focus mainly on calling on the formal authorities to redress their problems. Sports and cultural organizations, on the other hand, interact with the authorities on an informal basis. This is truer for those sports groups belonging to the partisan family. Cultural groups are more likely to use the more conventional channels in the pursuance of their objectives.

Conclusions

Judged by the strategies taken by associations, the features of the Israeli group arena remain indistinct. The variety and preponderance of pluralistic means of activity are striking, but some of the classical means employed by associations in other Western democracies appear to be lacking on the Israeli scene. The number of demonstrations staged by organized interest groups is rather small. A critical event does induce citizens to take part in a street demonstration; but even in the heated climate of Israeli politics the temperature of critical issues tends to decrease over time. The deepest controversies have triggered demonstrations of only short duration. With few exceptions (such as in the medical sector), the frequency of strikes is also lower compared to other industrialized countries. The absence of wide-scale litigation also stands out, and cannot be explained only by the structure of the regime or the absence of a constitution. In most cases, interest groups have simply not acquired the habit of redressing their problems through the court system. The use of media is extensive. Although Israel has entered the era of computerization, lists of potential members or adherents are not yet readily available. The media provide the most effective channel for reaching the public at large and for disseminating groups' objectives. Lobbying, in its Western sense, is only a fledgling activity. As elaborated in chapter 6, a substitute for associational prodding was found in group representatives' acting from within the Knesset. The idea of group representatives stalking the corridors of the legislature in an attempt to influence Knesset members from the outside was almost unknown until recent years; now the practice is slowly and gradually spreading. Formal appeals to the bureaucracy abound. The advantages of this course are widely described in the literature: It enables groups to bring issues to the attention of decision makers, to gain access, and to avail themselves of influence. Formal contacts with decision makers offer interest groups the opportunity to negotiate their terms, although, as was seen in a previous chapter, there is much to be desired regarding the attitude of the partners to the negotiations toward interest groups and their activity. Informal contacts with decision makers remain the most popular strategy among the majority of interest groups, and professional associations, regardless of the group, its objectives, constituency, type, or size. The Israeli political elite appears to be more reluctant to forge close ties with leaders of promotional associations or the more marginal groups within the sectional category.

Consultative patterns carried on within the joint state-group bodies is also common, though the adoption of this strategy varies, depending on the type of group. Agricultural groups, the business community, and the professional associations are highly integrated into the system of cooperation. The other types of associations lag far behind. On the basis of these data, it might be cautiously concluded that Israel is disposed to some elements of cooperation between interest groups and the authorities. The formal configurations of this corporatism, however, are not akin to those found in other democracies.

Finally, elitism remains the most dubious characteristic of the interest group arena. Judged by their recourse to political parties, Israeli associations are much removed from any traces of elitism. The farmers exhibit a relatively wide measure of appealing to partisan-oriented strategies; so do "other" sectional associations, removed from the centers of power. One ought to remember, though, that the major test of elitism is in the integration of the voluntary associations with a partisan-affiliated political elite. By maintaining close contacts with the country's political leadership, Israeli interest groups do, indeed, recourse to this strategy in a strikingly high frequency. Pluralism, Israeli style, is thus tainted with strong elements of elitism. Whether or not this pattern impinges on a group's influence on the policy-making process is the subject of the next chapter.

CHAPTER EIGHT

Interest Groups in the Policy Process

Interest groups not only attempt to influence public policy; the targets of their activity may also aid in identifying sources of power. Guided by the principle of efficiency and availability, interest groups will tend to choose those targets likely to yield the highest results. The first part of this chapter will thus focus on the choices made by Israeli interest groups. Where, according to their views, are important policy decisions made? Do groups follow the logic of efficiency and target their efforts at the source of power?

The second part of the chapter will probe, in line with interest politics configurations, the stage of policy making open to group intervention. As elaborated in the Introduction, in pluralist regimes associations are mostly involved in the stage of initiation. In its purest (though perhaps unrealistic) form, public policy in a polyarchy may be perceived as the sum total of grievances expressed by its members. In contrast, in the corporatist model of interest politics, groups play an output role; they implement policies decided upon by joint state-group bodies. In the elitist model the role of groups in shaping policies is modest. They are most likely to rely on the elite for determining national priorities.

The third and final aspect dealt with in this chapter pertains to the response of the elite to the groups' inputs. The hallmark of pluralism is a responsive elite, unwilling and unable to have its own way in the face of a group's relentless opposition. Under corporatism, at least theoretically, the need to veto is superfluous, because of the harmonious relations between groups and state. In elitism such a harmony is also visible. Should an association breach the harmony, however, the national interest embodied in the norms applied by the ruling elite is expected to take precedence over recalcitrance.

In Israel the range of public policy is extremely wide owing to the extensive involvement of government in socioeconomic affairs. With so much at stake in every sphere of life, be it the economy, education, security, health, natural resources, or personal well-being, the groups' involvement in shaping public policy may be critical to the fate of their objectives. Although the overwhelming majority of Israeli group activists regard political parties as a major "source of power," this assertion need not necessarily be translated into operative patterns of associational behavior. What, then, is the "power map" available for group activity?

Whither groups, government, Knesset, or party?

When faced with the choice of authoritative decision makers, Israeli interest groups may be influenced, first and foremost, by the fact that Israel is a parliamentary democracy which inherited many characteristics of its regime from the British model, evident during the British Mandate over Palestine (1922–1948). Samuel Beer (1958), on the basis of comparative research, concluded that interest groups in parliamentary systems of government incline more toward the administration than toward the legislature. How ready groups are to intervene in the legislative process and how assiduously they seek to influence individual lawmakers will vary with such factors as party discipline, the power of individuals to introduce legislation, and the involvement of the bureaucracy in actual policy making. The high cohesion of parties in a parliamentary system, the ensuing lack of autonomy regarding privately initiated legislation, and the excessive bureaucratic involvement in policy making tip the scale toward the administration. Samuel Finer (1970: 157) further elaborated the issue by explaining why a parliament is an unpromising arena for interest group activity. Israeli interest groups are thus expected to concentrate on the administration, rather than on the legislature. Since the parliament is more associated with partisan politics than the civil service, this tendency is expected to be more accentuated with time, as Israel moves away from its elitist posture and adopts features of a liberal democratic state.

Based on the views of Israeli interest groups, the data to a large degree confirm this hypothesis. To begin with, the priority given to the executive branch of government was indicated by an answer to a question requesting interest groups to identify the forum in which decisions most important to their interests were adopted (see table 8.1). A sizable majority of all groups investigated in the course of this study regarded the "administration" (as distinct from the "government") as the source of decisions most important to their affairs. The proportion was highest among the economic groups, whose dependence on the state's bureaucracy is perhaps the largest. The comparable figure among the promotional groups was slightly lower, but still a majority. The lowest proportion of interest groups assessing the administration as a major source of important decisions was among the party-affiliated groups. The structure of both the trade union and the agricultural sectors in Israel explains this unexpected finding. As the data show, the proportion of those perceiving an "interest group" as the core of power is highest among trade unions and farm groups, their activists believing that the Histadrut or the Agricultural Center have the leverage over their activities. Ranking far behind the administration, the Knesset was described as being the main source by no more than two in ten promotional groups and even fewer sectional groups. Only among the "other" sectional groups did the Knesset rank higher on the scale of power, perhaps because immigrant associations and categoric groups are far removed from the administrative centers of power compared with their sectional counterparts. The preponderance of the government administration in the group's labyrinth of power was thus largely confirmed.

Table 8.1
Source of Most Important Decisions (Percent Reporting)

	Interest group category			
	Party-affiliated	Economic	Other	Promotional
Government	13.6	7.7	4.2	12.0
Knesset	5.4	12.9	29.2	19.1
Administration	43.2	69.2	54.2	45.1
Political parties	—	—	4.1	—
Another interest group	37.9	10.2	8.3	23.8
N	37	39	24	42

The question of priorities regarding groups' interactions was further investigated by tracing their contacts with authorities, namely, with a government agency, with the Knesset and with political parties. Judging by the data gathered for this study, government agencies hold the lead in being targets for group appeals. Only a fraction reported on having no contacts with the state bureaucracy. The survey also indicates that Israeli interest groups do not place legislation high on their order of priorities, or perhaps, disregard the Knesset's role in making laws. Except for the economic groups, some third of the respondents reported that they have "no contacts with the Knesset." Operating in a party-state, interest groups were expected to lean heavily toward political parties and interact with them in a high frequency. Here the distinction between the party-affiliated groups and the other categories is striking (and statistically significant). Among the former only a third have declined to maintain any contact with their partons. Trade unions and agricultural settlements still regard political parties as their saviors and staunch friends. Among all other types of associations some two thirds have reported on "no contacts with political parties." Among the pro-motional groups the proportion was over 70 percent. Not all public interest groups keep away from party forums. As already noted, both Gush Emunim and Peace Now solicit party support and regard partisanship as an important avenue for influence. This holds true for the politicized groups among the promotional sec-tor, such as Naamat. But the majority of associations, focussing their activity on post-materialist objectives keep away from political parties, the reputed heroes of the Israeli polity.

The examination of tendencies over time is revealing. First, many interest groups operate in a stable environment and cannot trace any significant changes in the past decade, despite the turn-over in government and despite other discernible changes on the domestic and foreign scenes. This finding should not be surprising in view of the contrasting features of the Israeli polity: stable and volatile, immutable and dynamic at one and the same time. It is "stable" according to the conventional indicators of stability (Hur-witz 1971). There are no frequent resignations of government, elections are conducted in due time. The dominant party of the past was replaced by its opponent, but a pattern of unity was re-established. The country, too, has undergone dramatic changes in the past ten years: peace with an Arab country was concluded; a bloody, and highly controversial, war was fought; inflation precipitated; a new economic program launched; a Palestinian uprising in the territories has threatened to shatter the status quo, to name just a few unusual events. These transformations have had little impact on state-group relations, which for a large pro-portion of groups "remained the same." Secondly, very few in-terest groups reported that their contacts with the authorities have weakened. Evidently associations are not drifting away from the core of political power, but instead intensifying their contacts with formal decision makers.

Finally, where do the groups gravitate? The answers (presented in table 8.2) reaffirm, at least to some extent, the classic explanation of interest group behavior in a parliamentary system of government. The percentage of groups whose relationship with the government has strengthened during the past decade is impressive: one-half of the economic groups and barely a third of the other group categories. As in other parliamentary democracies, the ruling government in Israel captures the lion's share of the attention of groups. The Knesset, however, also seems to offer incentives for advocacy. The percentage of interest groups reporting that relations with the Knesset have also strengthened is high, compared to those reporting they have weakened, among all categories of associations. Political parties lag behind the Knesset and the government with a low percentage reporting on strengthened contacts. The highest proportion is found among the promotional associations, the perceived proponents of pluralist politics.

One of the major conclusions emanating from the data is that the government maintains its primacy as a target of group influence, but the Knesset is also gaining grounds. This phenomenon may be attributed to the dynamics of the macro-political arena. To date, all attempts at changing Israel's electoral system have been aborted, but pressures mount to the extent that some modification appears to be inevitable. Although the purported changes, from a rigid proportional system to some mixture of plural and proportional systems, is not bound to affect directly or immediately the relationship between legislators and country-wide interest group constituencies, the efforts of MKs to secure the support of associations has grown considerably. Commentators report that MKs invite representatives of interest groups to be present whenever the Knesset is discussing their case (Weiss 1988). This practice led one MK to charge that legislators' "intellectual capacities to make decisions are diminished" because of the constant pressures they themselves help to generate. The legislators summon the representatives of associations, many of whom are also members of party central committees, to the Knesset, and act under the whip of the spectators. In consequence, in no other parliament in the world is the "production of demonstrations targeted at parliamentary attention . . . so common and so sophisticated."[1] To sum up, the key word for understanding the interaction of interest groups with public authorities is "more." Within a time span of a decade associations have intensified their contacts with all forums of decision makers, focusing particularly on the administrative branch.

Table 8.2
Trends Over Time in Contacts of Groups with Public Authorities
(Percent reporting)

	Interest group category							
	Party-affiliated		Economic		Other		Promotional	
	+	−	+	−	+	−	+	−
Knesset	25.0	11.1	31.7	2.4	18.5	3.7	28.8	1.9
Government	30.6	8.3	50.0	4.8	32.1	28.5	32.7	7.7
Political parties	11.2	13.9	14.2	9.5	7.0	7.0	16.7	—

+ Contacts have strengthened
− Contacts have weakened

The Groups' Role in the Policy Process

Students of public policy have noted the "overcrowding" of the policy environment (Heclo 1975; Richardson et al. 1982). Many policy sectors are subject to participation by increasing numbers of interest groups and other actors, and this participation created the "crowded policy environment" which often clogs the decision-making process. In addition to the multiplication of actors, there is also a growing number of potential public issues which far exceed the capabilities of decision-making institutions to process them. The density generates competition between issues or their proponents over the political agenda. "Agenda" has been defined as "a general set of political controversies that will be viewed at any point in time as falling within the range of legitimate concerns meriting the attention of the polity" (Cobb and Elder 1972: 14). The analysis of political agendas highlighted the role interest groups play in the policy process. Interest groups have been perceived as initiators of a policy process, as partners to an initiating state, or as being excluded from participation (Cobb, Ross, and Ross, 1976).

Following these distinctions, the interest groups surveyed for this research were asked three questions about their role in the policy process. Their answers reflected the distribution among the three alternative models, as well as inter-group variations. The general picture that emerges (presented in figure 8.1) shows a mixed picture. The proportion reporting that policy was forged without any reference to their wishes was rather high among all categories reflecting a deep sense of alienation among Israeli associations. At the same time, however, interest groups are part and parcel of the policy process. They attract attention to public issues (especially promotional groups) and they cooperate with authorities, sharing power to shape policies. The following will illustrate the forms of groups' involvement in the three stages of policy making.

Fig. 8.1. Role of Interest Groups in the Policy Process (Percent Reporting)

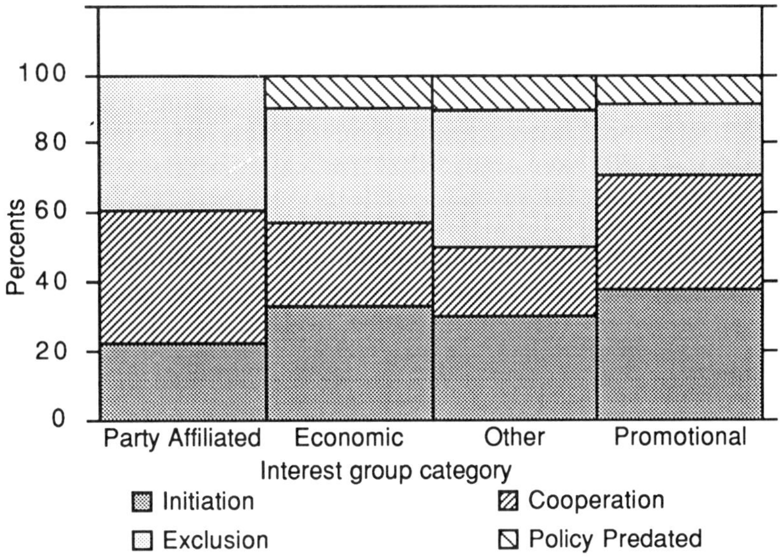

Interest groups as initiators

Although less than one-third of the groups investigated have played a role in initiating the policy process, some of the most prominent public policy issues trace their origins to groups' grievances, subsequently articulated into policy options. The initiating role came mainly from two specific sectors: professional associations and public interest groups. The issue of nostrification (qualifying examinations), fought for by the Israel Medical Association, provides a good example of initiating policy to achieve a group's objectives.

put up by the European Economic Community, the farmers demanded prompt government aid, not on an ad hoc basis but in the form of legislation. Their demand was warmly supported by the minister of agriculture. It took only a fortnight before the issue was placed on the formal (government) agenda and processed into legislation. On March 15, 1989, the Knesset approved the Natural Disasters Law, which made provisions for generous compensation. As might be expected, the Histadrut has proved a major actor in raising labor issues to the formal agenda, although its prominent role was not fully reflected in the answers given by the trade unions surveyed. Generally speaking, these unions are not engaged in legislative initiatives.

The highest percentage of legislative initiatives is found among the public interest groups, half of which claim they have brought an issue to the policy surface. The Women's Lobby, for instance, initiated legislation prescribing gender equality in conditions for retirement. The Society for the Protection of Animals perceives itself as the first (and only) instigator of legislation covering its domain of interest. The ecological groups make the claim of having played a major role in prompting environmental legislation (the claim is denied by policy makers). The Society for the Protection of Children has also successfully initiated bills. Most prominent, perhaps, among the public interest groups in this regard is Gush Emunim, whose efforts neatly fit the pluralist model described by Cobb and his associates.

Gush Emunim was not the first group to present decision makers with the alternative of a Greater Israel. It was preceded by the Land of Israel Movement, which emerged in the wake of the Six Day War. The translation of the idea into policy guidelines, however, and attracting public and elite attention to the problem of Samaria and other densely populated Arab areas, were outcomes of this group's initiative. Gush Emunim not only inculcated the idea of settling the land over the Green Line, but also provided the means for implementing this policy. The manpower, the material resources, and the strategic planning were all a product of successful group mobilization. At the outset, the government coalition (headed by the Labor Alignment) rejected settlement in densely populated Arab zones. But Gush Emunim, for reasons that will be elaborated below, was successful in placing the issue on the national agenda and in carrying it out.

Initiation of a policy does not lead, however, to the automatic inclusion of the initiator in the policy process. For example, the Association of Housing Agents (Maldan) initiated a law requiring licensing in order to prevent malpractice in their field. Their proposal triggered the establishment of an inter-ministerial study committee, in which they were not granted membership. The representatives of Maldan were invited (as were representatives of other interest groups) to present their views in regard to the issue which they themselves raised, but not to take an active part in the policy formulation.[3] Another striking example, this one of a hidden initiation, was the decision to cut the corporate tax rate from 45 percent to 43 percent. The cut was initiated by the manufacturers, who were nevertheless not partners to turning their initiative into a binding law.[4]

Interest groups as partners in the policy process

According to the data gathered in the course of this research, some forms of partnership can be traced in the process of policy making, especially between authorities and the institutionalized types of sectional groups, i.e., farmers associations, trade unions, and business groups. The representatives of the welfare sector also reported on a fairly high degree of "partnership," emanating, at least in their own view, from their pioneering role in the provision of walfare services. Every association in the welfare domain promoting the interests of the ailing, the handicapped, the underprivileged, had in fact cooperated with a government agency to serve their respective clients. Partnership, of course, has passive as well as active aspects. "Passive" cooperation implies that a policy was initiated by the elite, but received the endorsement of the group. Welfare groups give their blessing to all forms of legislation advancing the interests of their clients and, therefore, do not foster an adversary self-image. Their only wish is that more such legislation be enacted to confer state benefits upon the needy.

The most vivid example of "active partnership" is provided, however, by the farming sector. Take water policy: Water resources in Israel are a national asset. Their supply and preservation thus constitute a state responsibility. The scarcity of water results from the climatic conditions of the country, where rain falls only four or five months of the year. Water quality has deteriorated considerably in the past decade, because, inter alia, of the overuse of water resources. The problem of allocation has been subject to fierce political debate involving myriad groups and administrative bodies. The minister of agriculture is legally responsible for the country's water resources. The ministry is aided by three organizations: Tahal, a government corporation engaged in

water-resource planning; Mekorot, also a government corporation, which is responsible for transmitting producing, and
distributing the available water; and perhaps the most important
body, the Water Commission, headed by a commissioner who has
broad authority with regard to the allocation of water and its consumption. In addition there are regional water associations,
regional offices of the ministry of agriculture, the Agricultural
Planning Authority, and many other such bodies (Galnoor 1978).

Despite this variety of groups, the water policy presents an example of an integrated system controlled by agricultural interests.
The agricultural sector consumes 67 percent of the water in Israel;
not surprisingly it comprises more than half of the Water Commission. The Knesset Water Committee is headed by a representative
of the settlement movement, as is the water department in the
ministry of agriculture. The water commissioner has always been a
member of an agricultural settlement. The major contentious issue
in the policy arena has to do with the price of water. Those in
charge of water policy believe that the needs of agriculture far
outweigh those of urban consumers (including industry); consequently, the latter have to pay a higher share of the cost. The price
of water has been constantly rising for this sector, while remaining
frozen for the agricultural sector. The success of the farmers in
curbing increases was not only the result of powerful lobbying activity, but also of the fact that water had turned into a political
resource, its allocation determined jointly by state agencies and interest association. When efforts were made in the early 1980s to
raise the price of water, the resulting controversy led to an open
clash between the minister of agriculture and the Water Commission. The ministry's attempt to counter the farming sector was
overridden by Prime Minister Begin, who like his Labor
predecessors acknowledged the farmers' legitimate role in determining water policy.

Cooperation is also the hallmark of Israeli economic policy.
In this area, though, smaller organizations in the business community or subunits within the Histadrut do not necessarily regard
themselves as "partners." The formulation of new economic programs illustrates the type of partnership prevailing in the Israeli
policy system, which is marked both by adversary relations and
mutual benefits.

Economic policy was a restricted elite domain during the three
first decades of Israeli statehood. The public was notified, once in
awhile, of a devaluation of the currency or of other measures
aimed at combating economic difficulties. The Histadrut was in-

tegrated into the process by virtue of its partisan affiliation but the industrialists were largely excluded. Overall economic policy making was dominated by the country's political leadership. Even Simha Ehrlich, the first Likud minister of finance (member of the Liberal party), whose economic plan was meant to revolutionize the Israeli economy and redirect it in line with the liberal tradition, did not consult with representatives of interest groups. By ignoring economic organizations in his own country and seeking the advice of foreign experts (such as the well-known economist Professor Milton Friedman), he was less suceptible to interest group pressure. Policy making was solely in the hands of the party in power and its affiliated groups. This practice largely changed in the 1980s, when a pattern of regular cooperation between state and economic interests began to develop, though much of it was less than comprehensive. Among the major reasons for this turn to cooperation were the bifurcation of political power, on the one hand, and, paradoxically, the blurring of lines between political camps, on the other. The emergence of the Likud as a major political power created a new situation in Israeli politics. For the first time in its history, the Histadrut was pitted against the government. The size and central role of the Labor Federation, however, excluded the option of ignoring its opinions. At the same time the need of each finance minister to secure agreement within a heterogeneous government, and to mobilize support among his own ministerial colleagues, necessitated forging alliances with outside groups. Within both the Likud and the Alignment there were proponents and opponents of economic reform, whether such measures were purported to further state involvement in economic affairs or to curtail it; whether they were aimed at alleviating the plight of the underprivileged or at providing incentives to the already well-to-do for the purpose of invigorating economic growth.

The economic reform launched by the Likud proved to be detrimental to Israel's economy. The liberalization of the economy may have opened a new chapter in the country's financial market, but it also (in combination with other factors) was the cause of a precipitating inflation that reached its peak in the mid-1980s. A new economic program was presented a few months after the inauguration of the first National Unity government (September 1984). It was initiated by Yitzhak Modai, the finance minister, in cooperation with Prime Minister Shimon Peres. The program's major goal was to cope with the spiraling inflation, which in 1984 reached an unprecedented 399.3 percent, and to stabilize the economy. The three-digit inflation had plagued Israel since 1980. The country stood (and to some extent still stands) unique in this regard compared to other Western democracies. Inflation in Israel has numerous causes. Some analysts claim that the chronic deficit in the government budget is the major culprit (Bruno and Fischer 1984). Others assert that it is due to the low economic growth that Israel has experienced since 1973. The sizable government investments in industrial research and development and its subsidies for export activities also directly make for state overspending (Meishar 1984). The subsidization of major commodities and services has been pointed to as another cause of inflation. Finally, the continuous pressure of the trade unions for higher wages and increasing outlays for social services fanned the inflationary flames. Although the effect of inflation on the economy has been equivocal (Sharkansky 1987), inflation has always been placed high on the economic agenda owing to its alleged destructive social consequences. Throughout Israel's history there have been several package deals on wage and price controls, formulated after protracted negotiations among the finance minister, the Histadrut, and the Manufacturers Association. They were, however, limited in time and scope. The crucial pact arrived at in late 1984, took the form of a New Economic Policy (NEP).

Modai, a member of the Liberal party who served as a finance minister from September 1984 to April 1986, had to cope with opposition to his policies from his own party, from the Likud (to which the Liberal party was aligned), as well as from the Labor party. He was supported by a policy community consisting of the Bank of Israel, Treasury officials, and other economic ministers. Initially, the participation of the economic interest groups was only symbolic. Upon assuming office, Prime Minister Peres established a mini Social-Economic Council, made up of the Histadrut, the MA, and the economic ministers. Modai, however, accused the council of serving as an outlet for "venting steam" and not as a forum for real partnership. In actual fact, it enabled the government to pursue its own plans, regardless of sectoral interests (Modai 1988: 141). His charge was confirmed by the leaders of the MA, who complained that council deliberations were essentially ritualistic, providing a facade for cooperation rather than genuine partnership. One MA executive described the group's role in this forum as follows: "Evidently when we enter the scene, they have already reached a decision. We could raise hell, but that's all. They have already passed the resolution. We could not have turned the wheel, so we can only dispute the details. Did anybody ask us?

Did anybody consult us? They just 'landed' it on us, to generate an atmosphere of agreement."[5] The real locus of decision making was within the administrative policy community, in which academics were included as sporadic participants. The prime minister and the finance minister were personally involved in most stages of the deliberations. Senior government administrators from these ministries had an immense impact both on the composition of the agenda and on the way controversial issues were resolved. According to various testimonies, they virtually controlled the economic arena, their power aggrandized by intra-cabinet rifts.

That the Histadrut and the MA were not genuine partners is evident also from the reaction of these two groups to the public proclamation of the New Economic Policy on June 30, 1985. Two days later, the Hisatdrut declared a general strike in protest against the major provisions of this program. The manufacturers also expressed dissatisfaction: "They [the government] do what they want. They agree with you on every single item. But when it comes to implementation, they repudiate what they said a day earlier, they simply do not stick to their commitments."[6] Cooperation, it seems, was thus more spurious than real.

A year later, the second stage of the NEP was placed on the agenda. Its initiator was once again the finance minister, this time Moshe Nissim, who replaced Modai after the latter had been forced to leave office for sharply criticizing the prime minister. In the early stages of drafting the plan, the extensive scrapping of tax exemptions and the taxing of various welfare, social, and cultural allowances were proposed. One essential condition for the success of the plan was the Histadrut's agreement to these harsh measures, as well as its agreement to a restrictive wage policy that would limit all salary increases. Firms were also requested not to pay their workers cost-of-living allowances or to grant wage hikes if these were beyond their means. Frequent meetings were held among the Histadrut, the employers, and members of the economic inner cabinet.[7] The incorporation of the Histadrut and the MA into the policy process was forced upon the government, which willy-nilly opened the gates of policy making to outside intruders. Initially the government adopted a strategy of divide and rule when it invited the employers to join and left the Histadrut outside the consultative process.[8] The Histadrut, however, soon rallied its forces in objection to the plan and had to be reckoned with. At the initial stage of deliberations both the Histadrut and the employers were very much opposed to the program. The Labor Federation could not accept a plan to cancel tax exemptions, regarding this as an exercise designed to redistribute income from the poor to the rich. The MA also harshly criticized the plan for not providing answers to the plight of the industrialists. Concurrence was forthcoming from both groups, however, at a subsequent stage.

Agreement to wage restraint was not a novel Histadrut tactic. Acting determinedly in the "national interest," the Histadrut embraced the view that labor discipline, avoidance of strikes, and increased productivity formed the essential basis of a healthy economy. In the past, it had often acceded to government demands to freeze wages and to limit wage linkage to the cost-of-living index. Now it also supported the principle of linking pay to productivity, both at the individual level (through incentive schemes) and at the macro-level in the overall wage policy (Shalev 1984: 371). The 1986 to 1987 period, though, proved a difficult time for the Histadrut to grant its consent to economic restrictions. Dwindling backing from the Labor party and growing internal oppostion that verged on a revolt by the rank and file, stimulated a harsh insistence on "workers' rights" on the part of the Histadrut. A leading journalist described the process of forging the new economic policy as the "crumbling of government." This was happening, he averred, because the government gave in and let groups (i.e., the Histadrut and the MA) participate in the policy process. Instead of making authoritative policy, the state chose to cooperate.[9] The government was urged "Not to Ask, to Decide!"[10]

The public mood was thus against incorporating interest groups as partners in deliberating economic reforms. The reluctance of the government to make the vested interests full partners in the decision making was also triggered by other circumstances. First, the chief economic officer, the minister of finance, had a personal dislike for "partnership." He was a loner in politics and did not share the cooperative mood of some of his cabinet colleagues (especially Peres). Secondly, during the year that had passed since the inauguration of the NEP, the alarming economic crisis of Histadrut enterprises was publicly exposed. The vulnerability of the major partner did not exclude it from the decision making process, but it did make its cooperation more equivocal. Eventually each of the partners received a share of the spoils. The Treasury gave up its plan to abolish tax exemptions but secured consent for holding down wage increases; the Histadrut increased the employees'share in the pension funds, and obtained sizable financial aid for Kupat Holim. The employers were also content, since the devaluation that was part and parcel of the new plan enabled them to decrease the price of production inputs and increase industry's profits. The corporatist rule of "everyone a winner" was therefore partially validated. Yet, cooperation between the government and major economic interest groups never fully materialized.

Another step toward the inclusion of economic groups in the policy process was taken in 1988. Once again, however, "inclusion" did not imply genuine partnership. In 1988 the problem was not inflation, which had been kept under control since 1985, but the devastating interest rates, the dwindling foreign currency reserves, and primarily the economic stagnation. The Bank of Israel, in an unprecedented display of open intervention in public policy, pressed for another "new economic plan."[11]

The new National Unity government of 1988, saw Peres installed as minister of finance. One of his first acts in this capacity was to announce plans to re-establish the Social-Economic Council, which had gone into limbo during Nissim's tenure. At stake now were major economic issues that could determine the fate of the Histadrut, i.e., the political future of Peres' camp. The gravity of the situation was one of the major triggers for reducing the Histadrut's opposition to the policy proposals. The NEP of 1988 was designed to lead Israel into a new economic era. It called for stable exchange rates, tighter control over monopolies, reform of both the labor market and the banking system. Primarily, it espoused deregulation of the money and capital markets. The major economic sectors responded to the program with a mixture of enthusiasm and caution, but essentially agreed to be "partners," i.e., to comply. The industrialists were assuaged by the long-demanded devaluation; the Histadrut was granted generous aid for its faltering institutions.

Was this partnership a reflection of an alliance between the state and the big economic forces? Or did it demonstrate "more of the same," i.e., the partisan-state network and its extension to interest groups? The answer, though equivocal, tends to support the corporatist interpretation. Some qualifications, however, are in order. Cooperation did not entail the formulation of a grand design; instead, it focused on the deliberation of details. It was not a form of social architecture, but a stage for bargaining, dispensing rewards, and warding off pressures. "Partnership," Israeli style, greatly differs from the Swedish variation of this practice, whereby a professional class of politicians, administrators, and interest group functionaries must constantly expect to keep dealing with one another. In Sweden, the spirit of "getting along with each other" predominated (Heclo and Madsen 1987: 21). Cooperation in Israel is characterized by adversary proceedings, by a mutual attempt to push advantages as far as possible. Partnership does not exclude outright confrontation, which is often acrimonious. Judged by the immediate results, however, any losses, if they occur, are only temporary. In the end, all actors seem to be (temporarily) content with the outcomes.

The long-term results of cooperation, however, are less promising than might be assumed. The minister of finance was reportedly (in 1989) not fulfilling his role in agreements arrived at through cooperation;[12] the Histadrut, for its part, called for a general strike, in effect protesting the very economic policy to which it was an ostensible partner.[13] In fact, a demonstration against the economic plan was staged by the Histadrut a short time after it was signed. The manufacturers also equivocated, criticizing the program for being too late and too little, despite its obvious advantages for their membership. Lasting cooperation, based on a fundamental agreement in the Israeli economic sector, apparently seems difficult to achieve.

Interest groups as subservient actors

The proportion of groups whose role in the policy process was, according to their own testimony, overlooked, ignored, and shunned was higher than expected. The famous theory predicting a deep sense of frustration as a result of unfulfilled expectations (Gurr 1970) appears to have materialized in the Israeli interest group arena. Among the party affiliated groups, which are mostly associated with the centers of power, almost 40 percent have reported on "exclusion"; that is, they have not been considered in the policy process. Even members of the economic groups, who appear to be tightly linked to the administrative centers of power, demonstrated a sense of exclusion. Overlooked in the policy process, too, is input from the associations of the handicapped. One has to remember that "the trend of entitlement" (in Hebrew *magia li*), that is, "the stress on the right to obtain various goods or services without any relation to achievement or performance" (Eisenstadt 1985: 417–418) also invokes a sense of deprivation when what has been achieved is compared to what was expected and, even more so, desired. A high sense of frustration is evident also among immigrant associations which found it difficult to comprehend the gap between Israel's yearning for *aliya* and its treatment of *olim*.

Surprisingly, public interest groups demonstrate the least sense of alienation. This does not mean that environmental groups or consumer associations make Israel a better place to live in. Likewise, it does not imply that Peace Now has convinced authorities to relinquish land in favor of peace or that Gush Emunim has persuaded the government to annex territories. The implication of this finding is that public interest groups are, perhaps, less frustrated either because their expectations are lower, or because they are, in fact, integrated in one way or another into the policy process. The high proportion of group activists reporting on "Exclusion" is incommensurate with the general spirit expressed in other findings (such as the intensification of interaction with public authorities). It nevertheless reflects prevailing attitudes regarding, perhaps, the core of policy making, rather than its fringes.

Government's Response to Group Demands

The strength of the state and its involvement in the socioeconomic life of its citizenry, the presence of disciplined and powerful political parties, and the persistence of nationally oriented values cast doubt on the willingness of authorities to respond positively to the demands of interest groups. Asked what was the most common response of political authorities to their demands, group representatives were presented with four alternatives, extending at the extremes from comprehensive acceptance to outright rejection. The middle two options were "a willingnes to reach a compromise," which may be considered a form of mildly positive response, and "a favorable attitude that is not followed by action," considered a mild form of nonresponsiveness. The dichotomized model produced by this four-point scale largely ignores the difference between pluralist regimes, in which the elite is said to be highly responsive to its citizens' demands, and the corporatist configuration, in which the elite cooperates with organized associations. It does differentiate between elites whose ears are attuned to groups' demands and those who manipulate the public mood and monopolize politics. Respondents' answers (tabluated in table 8.3) reveal a bifurcated polity. Only a tiny minority are of the opinion that Israeli authorities have been utterly unresponsive to their demands, the proportion of discontent being similar in the four categories of groups. When this answer is combined with the more moderate version of rejection, the percentage of the disenchanted rises considerably—to some third of the respondents in the sectional sector and over a half in the promotional category. Many group activists believe that state officials, ministers, and Knesset members do not reject their pleas but, at the same time, do not deem it necessary to issue a response. Their mildly responsive attitude is merely a smoke screen for inaction. In describing the situtaion, some group activists quoted the saying "the dogs bark but the caravan moves on." Political leaders do not wish to have direct confrontations with the representatives of organized interests; on the other hand, they will do very little to comply with their request for influence. "They make do, but they continue with their business." "You can speak out, shout, cry, and yell. They will nod their head and demonstrate understanding. But I know that the minute I turn my back and shut the door, they will forget I ever existed." "It's like talking to the wall. They won't listen to me. Why bother with my problems? We are a small group, we cannot harm them. They are secluded in their shielded offices, out of reach and not susceptible to influence." These were typical reactions from those who complained of not having achieved adequate response from agencies or individuals who supposedly were subject to their influence.

Table 8.3
Elite Responsiveness to Interest Group Demands (Percent Reporting)

| | Interest group category | | | |
	Party-affiliated	Economic	Other	Promo-tional
Favorable response	13.5	18.0	11.1	18.0
A willingness to reach a compromise	51.3	43.6	33.3	30.0
Favorable response, not followed by action	27.0	33.3	51.9	46.0
Unfavorable response	8.1	5.1	3.7	6.0
N	37	39	27	50

The identity of the groups that do not encounter responsiveness from the authorities casts light on the spots in society where the shoe pinches but does not, in these groups' judgment, receive the remedy that would relieve the pressure. The groups that have experienced positive response are integrated into the policy process through institutional links and partisan affiliations. The farmers, professionals, business groups, and trade unions are less likely than other group categories to regard the political system as unresponsive. Still, over 10 percent of the workers' associations did select the extreme version of "unresponsiveness." One has to remember, though, that some of the trade unions included in this study hold a grudge against their own roof organization. They are always ready to compare their own attainments with those of their counterparts situated next door or on the same corridor. The microbiologists, for instance, cannot help wondering why the engineers' share is better than their own and why the pharmacists secured higher benefits than their own members, who are also employed in the health sector. A sense of relative deprivation may be a major trigger for describing the elite as being unresponsive to a group's demands.

The category of promotional groups, contrary to expectations, reveals a lower sense of dissatisfaction with regard to the responses of the authorities than do the party-affiliated and economic organizations. Two policy areas, immigrant absorption and environmental protection, are, however, particularly subject to unresponsiveness.

Immigrant absorption

Jewish immigration has been the raison d'être of the Zionist endeavor. The role of Israel as a refuge for Jewish people is one of the fundamental collective values, if not the most important one. The state assumes responsibility for all Jews, regardless of their country of origin or political affiliation. Jews supporting the apartheid regime in South Africa are welcomed as much as Jews identifying with the left-wing guerrilla forces in the countries of Latin America. The black Jews of Ethiopia are taken in no less than their fair-skinned kin from Soviet Russia. The right of every Jew to regard Israel as his or her home and haven has been put to the test when extradition requests were issued for persons who had committed a crime outside the borders of Israel. One famous case in the mid-1980s was that of William Nakash, who had committed a murder in France. For months the Israeli government was reluctant to extradite him, although this inaction deliberately violated international law. The state's high regard for Jewish immigration is also manifested in laws and administrative decrees. Israel admits Jewish immigrants and gives them citizenship upon their arrival in accordance with the provisions of the Law of Return, acknowledging the right of every Jew to immigrate to the country. Newcomers also enjoy a host of economic benefits, such as exemptions from customs duties for durable goods and electrical appliances, state aid in housing, and miscellaneous tax deductions. Despite the central role of immigration in the national ideology and ethos, reports on the effectiveness of absorption have not been very encouraging.

The functions of absorption are divided between the immigration and absorption ministry and the Jewish Agency; each of these bodies is keen to safeguard its domain of activities. In addition, several other ministries are responsible for certain aspects of absorption. The housing ministry, the ministry of education and culture, and the ministry of labor and welfare contribute their share to the process of absorption. Several attempts were made in the past to define the boundaries of the division of labor among those involved (Gitelman and Naveh 1976), but all were of no avail. An effort in the 1980s to amalgamate absorption functions and to transfer major spheres of responsibility to the ministry of absorption also failed. The separation of functions remains a bone of contention between the two major bodies responsible for absorption—the absorption ministry and the Jewish Agency.

Meanwhile the immigrant is left confused, stranded in a complex, blurred bureaucratic maze. Investigation of the state comptroller revealed that one of the immigrants' major frustrations is having to run from one to another of the numerous agencies dealing with absorption. Not knowing who is responsible for what and being unfamiliar with the whereabouts of the Israeli bureaucratic system, immigrants face enormous difficulties in their efforts to integrate into the new society. This is true for immigrants of all countries, but especially for those whose language is not widely spoken by Israelis. Here is where the immigrant associations could be extremely useful. Unfortunately, their sense of frustration is the highest among the interest groups in Israel.

The major complaint of the immigrant associations concerns their access to the decision making structure. The access granted to new immigrants and their representatives is the lowest among all organized interest groups. During the interviews, the leaders of immigrant associations kept complaining that "they won't listen to us. They are doing only what they wish to do." The groups' representatives insist they are treated as unwanted clients who have to buy the merchandise they are offered, regardless of its quality. "We are perceived as pests, not as respectable representatives of important sections of Israeli society." Natan Sharansky, who heads one of the numerous organizations of Soviet immigrants, once declared in frustration, "No one wants absorption." The trigger for his assertion was the difficulty in finding a political figure of note willing to head the ministry of immigration and absorption after the formation of the 1988 National Unity government. He added that "the parties fought over all the portfolios except absorption. No one really wanted it."[14]

One of the conspicuous examples of a failure to achieve any response has to do with the financial support of housing. The ministry of immigration and absorption devised a rule whereby a mortgage was provided only for small apartments (up to 85 square meters). This apartment size limitation hurts the interests of immigrants from the United States, whose standard of living in their country of origin enabled them to enjoy better housing facilities than those offered by the public authorities in Israel. Despite the fact that different immigrant associations presented the ministry with rational arguments based on hard data against this particular aid eligibility restriction, a "response" could not be secured. The newcomers' representatives quoted the officials as follows: "We will study the issue; we will take care of it in due course." The closing of absorption centers (where immigrants acquire some knowledge of Hebrew and get acquainted with their new country) in Israel's major cities was also subject to much (ineffective) associational pressure. Lack of responsiveness was alleged not only by the immigrant associations representing constituencies from the affluent countries, who were socialized into pluralistic and responsive norms of the political culture; the Association of Ethiopian Jews has also expressed a sense of frustration. In the 1988 *Annual Report*, the state comptroller enumerated the hardships encountered by Ethiopian immigrants and the inefficiency with which their absorption was handled. Their problem was even more basic: an inability to obtain a venue to decision makers in order to have their complaints and suggestions heard in the first place.

Unresponsiveness to immigrants' demands may be due to the vulnerability of the newcomers, and the decision making structure. The immigrants' pressure appears to amount to occasional (in fact, rare) press headlines. Their associations were never accorded legitimacy as genuine representatives of newcomers. The immigrant associations, for their part, are interested not in moral support but in housing and employment opportunities. These are hard to obtain, especially under conditions of bureaucratic diversity, in which each agency blames the other for incompetence and malfunctioning. It has been often suggested that the Israelis cherish immigration as a value but do little in regard to placing it high on the political agenda. The wide gap between expectations, nurtured by national mores, and economic reality has produced the image of an elite that is by and large unresponsive.

Environmental policy

In the 1980s environmental groups of Europe linked together as a political entity to form various Green parties, which have been extremely successful in raising environmental awareness and in instigating political action. Even Great Britain, which lagged behind much of Western Europe, has become environmental conscious. "Green" concerns were legitimized by such national figures as Prince Charles, who warned that the world was "sleepwalking into disaster."[15] The spectacular rise of the British Green party, from 1.4 percent in the 1987 national vote to 15 percent nationwide in the elections to the 1989 European Parliament, evidences the growing importance of the ecological issue in Western societies. New Green forces are emerging all over Europe; but in addition, the major parties are themselves turning greener, not only to capture the vote of possible defectors but also because of increased concern for the environment.[16]

Although vital statistics indicate that Israel is not a Third World country, its standards of public sanitation, quality of air and water, and infrastructure are far from satisfactory. Yet in Israel environmental concern is extremely rudimentary. Despite the country's accelerated industrial development and rapid growth of population density, environmentalism has ranked low on the national agenda. The problem, however, looms large. The considerable growth in the number of vehicles moving within densely populated urban areas, the installation of power and coal stations consuming immense amounts of oil, and the establishment of industrial enterprises producing chemicals and raw materials with high pollutant potential present major sources of environmental problems. Private and public companies alike have seriously damaged the environment with little concern shown by the authorities.

Environmental legislation abounds; but as one commentator has put it, there is "a nothing move towards a zero solution."[17] The ministerial functions dealing with the quality of the environment were scattered among no fewer than nine ministries (health, interior, transportation, energy, prime minister's office, defense, agriculture, labor and welfare, industry and commerce). Within each of these ministries small divisions were established to handle aspects of environmental protection which are inherently close to their principal fields of operation.[18] Some of the authority to handle environmental issues is allocated to local authorities. When an ecological accident occurs, which is a recurrent phenomenon, the situation is treated inadequately. The most common activity observed is mutual acrimony—ministries blaming one another for having failed to act. One vivid example of this attitude was the polio epidemic that erupted in September 1987 in the northern part of the country. The interior and health ministries announced that the problem was a local one. The local authorities, for their part, cast responsibility on the ministry of agriculture, which is formally responsible for the water. Everyone involved, it seemed, accused the Treasury of not allocating sufficient resources essential for maintaining the sewage system. The fact of the matter is that the ministries mentioned above have allocations in their budgets for the care of certain environmental problems, but they have done little either to enforce the environmental laws or to police the matter. For example, paragraph 9 of the Water Law enables prosecution of violators. Not once, however, has it been implemented.

A major step toward centralization and coordination of control of Israel's environment was made with the government's decision, on December 1988, to establish a ministry for environmental affairs. The move was taken not because the Israeli leadership finally realized that the country was approaching an ecological catastrophe, but owing to the exigencies of party politics: the need to fulfill a promise to a former aide of Prime Minister Shamir. The establishment of the new ministry was fraught with difficulty. Every minister who readily had passed the buck when an environmental crisis was pending now safeguarded his or her authority and refused to relinquish functions. Intra-ministerial environmental agencies were not easily ceded. Furthermore, the rivalry between the Likud and Labor has added to the hurdles encountered by the new ministry. Objections, too, came from ministries belonging to the designated minister's own party. The squabbles lasted until a firm commitment to establish the ministry finally induced the transfer of some departments.

It is too early at this writing to determine whether the establishment of the ministry for environmental affairs has contributed to any ecological improvement. The limited evidence available is not very encouraging. Israel is still mainly preoccupied with problems of war and peace. Military and defense issues are irrevocably and automatically placed at the top of the national agenda. The setup of the new ministry has also not solved the problem of bureaucratic proliferation, although it did generate some coordination among the numerous actors. A report of the state comptroller in 1989 (483, 501) revealed that there was much (in fact, very much) to be desired with regard to environmental protection in Israel.

In view of this picture, it is little wonder that environmental groups do not meet with any response on the part of the authorities. Admittedly ecological interest groups have had some prominent achievements. They were, as they see it, successful in

blocking the passage of an amendment to the Planning and Construction Law that would have shortened the period for public objections. The victory, however, was erased when the government
later decided to adopt a law termed the "anti–red-tape" bill,
authorizing a small ministerial committee (consisting of the
ministers of finance, interior and housing) to approve plans
without due course to objections.[19] The environmental groups
severely criticized the law, charging the government with evoking
"ecological destruction." The hastiness with which the projects
would have been approved was bound to generate long-range environmental harm. Although some Knesset members branded the
bill as "basically flawed" because of its disregard for environmental outcomes, the general mood was favorable. Finally, however,
legislation was suspended, not because of environmental concerns,
but owing to partisan squabbles over the division of authority.
The skewed government priorities and the diffusion of power
among so many organs thus prevented an adequate response to environmental demands, which, admittedly, were not put forward
with the intensity and vigor characterizing this domain in other
Western societies.

Consumer affairs have also suffered from nonresponse.
Although the Consumers Council operates under the auspices of
the state, the ministry of industry and commerce initiated legislation vesting authority for consumerism with a government official. The Consumer Protection Law, 1981, prescribed the
nomination of a person to be "In Charge of Consumerism" and
whose function was to implement the law, to deal with consumers'
complaints, to initiate and carry out research on consumer affairs,
and to deal with all other issues pertaining to the protection of
consumers. In short, the appointed official rendered the activity of
consumer organizations nil and void. The appointed official,
moreover, criticized the inefficiency of the public associations and
their ongoing rivalry. Alleging that their activities are directed by
considerations other than consumer interests, he was generally unfavorable toward the groups. The associations, for their part,
charged the ministry with ignoring the interests of consumerism.
They cited cases in which the government had yielded to the
pressures of the powerful Union of Banks and the Union of Insurance Companies at the expense of the consumer. A study
undertaken in the late 1970s indicated that 72 percent of the Jewish
population heard about one or another consumer organization; 86
percent were of the opinion that "consumers ought to organize,
and be a powerful factor in order to reduce the prices of products

that are unduly expensive" (Elizur 1979). Despite broad popular support for and rising awareness of the issue, the activity of the organizations responsible for consumer protection has largely lacked any response.

As already noted, the glass of responsiveness is only half empty. Nearly half of the respondents were of the opinion that the political elite does respond to their demands, either fully or through accommodation. The implication of this finding, though inconclusive, is that some interest groups do have a sense of efficacy: they deem their activity to be rewarding in terms of public policy.

Conclusions

The fact that Israel is a party-democracy seems to bear little relevance to interest groups seeking to influence the policy process. Decisions most important to the groups' advocacies are arrived at by the government administration, the less politicized agency among the gamut of state organs. The proportion of those having no contacts with political parties is striking. Even in cases where links have strengthened, parties are perceived as mediators more than as producers of authoritative decisions. Israeli interest groups thus operate in an environment which is not constrained by omnipotent political parties. The examination of contacts between interest groups and state organs in a time perspective reveals that relations with the Knesset, and especially with the government, tend to have become closer. A diffusion of power, with a tendency of concentration in the administrative branch of government is thus evident.

The involvement of interest groups in the policy process is often discussed in terms of their membership in a "policy community" or a "policy network." This criteria was insufficient, in the case of Israel, to distinguish between the three forms of participation in the policy process: the assertive form, where groups have a considerable influence, if they do not hold the lead; a cooperative pattern, where they are partners to policy making; and the exclusivist form, where associations take a limited role in shaping public decisions. The groups' involvement in the policy process was examined through two major questions: the timing of their entrance into the policy process, and their views regarding political responses to their inputs. The following conclusions emerge from the empirical data gathered for this study.

First, the picture is rather gleaming as may have been expected under the circumstances of a party-democracy. If exclusion from the policy process is a reliable indicator for assessing the groups' inclusion in public policy making, Israel does exhibit some elitist tendencies. A sense of exclusion prevails among activists of Israeli interest groups which, perhaps, is not corroborated by the realities of political life, but is eminent in their perceptions. The case of the immigrant associations vividly demonstrates how detrimental, and perhaps irrational, exclusion can be. At the writing of these conclusions the country is flooded with a mass immigration from the Soviet Union. The absorbing authorities were overwhelmed with the unexpected influx of newcomers and were quite unprepared to handle the issue, placed so high on Israel's agenda. Yet, reportedly, the representatives of USSR immigrant associations were prohibited from entering the Ben-Gurion Airport. Their advice was not requested and their help was outrightly rejected. Absorption was monopolized by the officials of the absorption ministry, which was having trouble in controlling the process in face of a mounting inter-ministerial competition over the right to absorb the newcomers. Israel may be advancing toward a new era, but the contribution of those who are not integrated into the mainstream of power is not welcomed, nor is it appreciated.

Second, according to the findings presented in this chapter the policy process is characterized by a high degree of cooperation. This stands in ostensible contrast to a previous conclusion stating that interest groups are, generally speaking, not partners to state agencies in making decisions on who gets what. However, when faced with the alternative of declaring themselves part of the policy process or excluded from it, the majority choose the first one. Cooperation, in this regard, does not imply full-fledged corporatism. The difference between the two patterns has been elaborated in the theory. Indeed, it is not argued that Israel is a corporatist society in the classical sense of the term. The example illustrating cooperation paradoxically reveals the extent to which Israel is not guided by corporatist practices. The introduction of economic planning was followed by extensive cooperation which has not matured into full-fledged corporatism. Yet the likelihood of formulating economic policy without cooperation with the two partners, i.e., the Manufacturers Association and the Histadrut, has considerably decreased. The presence of these actors on the economic scene is undeniable although their links with state authorities are not fully institutionalized.

Third, initiation was found to be surprisingly high. Interest groups can be a source of policy initiatives only under circumstances of extreme pluralism. What is important, especially in Israel, is their sense of being able to raise issues that eventually are placed on the political agenda. The differences between the interest groups in regard to initiation confirm the propositions presented in the Introduction: the party-affiliated organizations, by virtue of their close integration with political parties, are least engaged in initiating policy; the promotional associations, expected to be far removed from party politics, score the highest. Initiation does not necessarily entail domination of the policy process. It merely indicates that interest groups, in approximately a third of the cases, can make their voice heard effectively not at some stage of the policy process, as suggested by Robert Dahl, but in its incipient phase, which may be critical to its subsequent development.

The picture remains ambiguous when examined from the perspective of responsiveness. A total unresponsiveness to group demands was the exception rather than the rule, although the proportion of those stating that endorsement of their requests is mainly lip service was rather high. The parentela nexus was evident when the largest proportion of those stating that response is positive was found among the party-affiliated groups. These groups also exhibited the largest proportion of frustration, which may have emanated from their high expectations. "Other" sectional associations and promotional interest groups hold their hopes at bay; their sense of frustration is thus somewhat lower. They complain, however, of inaction on the part of the state, although response is "positive."

To sum up, the findings of this chapter appear to be inconclusive, even confusing. The answer to the main question regarding the role of interest groups in the policy process remains equivocal. If associations participate in policy communities why do they demonstrate a high sense of exclusion? If, on the other hand, they are excluded, why so many of them do report on inclusion? The answer may be lying both in the issue under consideration and in the pecularities of the country—the land of political paradoxes. Although a substantial portion of groups reported on "initiation," the political agenda portrays rather fixed priorities. Some issues are simply ignored, causing their promoters much disappointment. The inconsistent attitudes of decision makers, who like in a religious ritual move three steps forward and two steps backward in their relations with interest groups may also be a cause for incongruence. The question still remains open: to the extent associations are embedded into the policy process, what are the reasons for their "success." The answers are the subject of the next chapter.

CHAPTER NINE

Determining Outcomes:
Who Gets What and Why?

The final test of interest groups is their ability to exert influence on decision making and to persuade those responsible for allocating resources and imparting values to respond to their needs, be they sectional-material or promotional-ideological. This chapter will attempt to evaluate the extent of success and the determinants of "influence" exercised by interest groups in the political process. A word of caution is in order. Any assessment of how much influence is wielded by this or the other group is difficult and problematic. In fact, to make a judgment on the outcomes of group activity with regard to the policy process is a risky venture. Even when groups regard themselves as successful, it remains unclear whether or not the groups' impressions are based on solid objective grounds, and whether or not a given result was caused by a groups' activity. The difficulty in linking outcomes to inputs derives from the lack of accurate indicators of influence, a subject that is much discussed by the literature. As Wilson (1987: 221) has observed: "Even the fact that a whole body of government policy seems to be in harmony with the interests of a specific group does not mean that that group actually influenced the policy. It may be simply a coincidence that the interests of a group correspond with the government calculation of that national interest at any given time." Furthermore, the government may utilize groups, especially under elitist circumstances, to disseminate its values and implement its policies, the objectives being not those of the group but of the party in control of state organs.

Bearing in mind these difficulties, the following discussion will center on the magnitude of influence and on its determinants. Two questions are under concern: first, what is the scope of influence exerted by interest groups? Second, what are the factors responsible for the influence presumably obtained? The power of the veto was selected as an indicator for the quantity of influence. Since all groups usually report on being "successful," the problem was tackled from its negative aspects. The question addressed to interest group activists did not focus on their ability to advance an issue but rather on their experience in blocking an undesired policy. It was believed that displaying efficacy in regard to the power of the veto reflects "success" more accurately than the ability to attain "positive" objectives. To investigate the determinants of success, respondents were presented with questions enumerating possible factors without reference to the actual result, defined in the vague term of "success." The emphasis in this discussion, as in many other parts of the research, is on the associations' activists' evaluations. Their statements may reflect wishful thinking, far remote from reality. Their perceptions, however, subjective as they may be, tell the true story, as seen by interest groups, of the division of power in Israeli society among voluntary associations, state, and political parties.

The Power of the Veto

The power of the veto has been described by pluralists (e.g., Wootton 1985) as one of the major instruments available to interest groups in a democratic society. In pluralist societies associations hold both ends of the rope: they *initiate* the policy process by articulating demands; they are also able to *terminate* the outcome if it is incongruent with their wishes. How do Israeli interest groups fare in bringing a policy process to an end?

In previous research conducted by the author, over half of the groups surveyed stated that they deemed their activity to be "very successful" in producing results; the rest were of the opinion that their activity was "partially successful" (Yishai 1987a: 179). None of the interest group activists admitted being partially or totally "unsuccessful." If subjective criteria have any meaning, then the interest group arena is rich with winners. Almost every association presented a story of total or partial success. For example, the industrialists have obtained tax benefits and subsidies, which have proved costly to the national budget.[1] The Association of

Development Towns has secured legislation granting generous financial aid to their residents. The Histadrut's achievements are too numerous to be mentioned in this short paragraph. The teachers' organizations induced the minister of education to submit a law to restore classroom hours that had been reduced by budgetary cuts. Naamat was extremely effective in introducing labor legislation protecting women's rights. Even the Black Panthers, poor in resources, proved to be instrumental in affecting the determination of national priorities.

The picture is different when groups were asked about their ability to block a policy process, that is, to induce decision makers to shelve a policy proposal, or to introduce drastic changes that will empty it of its original intention. To the question, "Did your group ever succeed in blocking a policy proposal (legislation or an administrative decision)?", respondents were presented with three options: "(a) Yes. You cannot enforce a decision in face of fierce group opposition; (b) No. There is no need to use veto, since decisions are arrived at by accommodation; (c) No. Only under very special circumstances can a voluntary association thwart an official policy." In aggregate, the answers (presented in table 9.1) contradict the previous finding which revealed a high degree of success. In the late 1980s Israeli interest groups exhibit a low sense of efficacy regarding their ability to block public policy. A majority of all respondents postulated that a veto is possible only under very special circumstances. Even the powerful industrialists conceded that "once the government makes up its mind, we can do very little to change its mind. You have to anticipate in advance, you need a thousand eyes and ears. If you skip the train, you will never get to your destination." Promotional associations are even more skeptical than their counterparts in the sectional sector. Over 60 percent of issue-oriented associations held the opinion that veto is possible only under exceptional circumstances. Their low sense of efficacy is hardly surprising in view of their organizational vulnerability and shortage of resources. When judged by the yardstick of success, Israel still tilts toward elitism. The highest efficacy was found among economic associations. Even within this category the proportion of those displaying disbelief in the power of the veto was over 50 percent. Thus although groups do manage to secure material benefits for their members, to obtain access to the power structure, and to capture media and public attention, this has to be done early on, before the key figures have made up their minds on a given issue. Once they do, and more importantly, once they have reached agreement among themselves, getting them to change the decision is extremely difficult, if not impossible. Examples abound. The Chamber of Commerce, a prestigious and powerful group by all accounts, could not have vetoed the far-reaching regulations restricting imports; the less powerful Association of Artisans and Small Industry failed to change the latitude shown by the government toward imports of merchandise produced in the Far East. The Association of Landlords could not block the proposed legislation protecting tenants from rent hikes; the gas companies were forced to comply with the reform in the gas market imposed despite their vociferous objections; and opponents to university tuition hikes cannot stop the government from carrying out its intention. Even the Union of Bankers, one of the most influential economic groups in the country, had no choice but to bend and yield to state decrees following the 1983 bankshares crisis.

The inability to halt policy decisions is also a common weakness among promotional groups. Peace Now is genuinely unhappy with the generous state funds flowing into West Bank settlements and with the defense ministry's policy in the occupied territories. It can demonstrate and mobilize public opinion; it cannot veto the policy. The Movement Against Withdrawal from Sinai conspicuously failed to thwart the policy that left the Sinai in Egyptian hands. Even the threat to resist with whatever force the movement had and to stage a "civil war"—a highly threatening event in the Israeli political culture—was not sufficient to induce even the smallest concession. The political authorities remained firmly committed to their decision to return Sinai to Egypt within the framework of the peace process. The Israeli defense forces withdrew from the area; Yamit was turned into a heap of stones. It it little wonder that only 13.9 percent of the promotional groups believe that "you cannot enforce a decision in the face of fierce group opposition."

Table 9.1
The Exercise of Veto over State Policy (Percent Reporting)

| | Interest group category | | | |
	Party-affiliated	Economic	Other	Promotional
There is no need to veto	25.9	9.4	11.1	24.0
Veto is possible only under exceptional circumstances	45.1	56.2	61.1	62.1
A decision cannot be enforced in the face of group opposition	29.0	34.4	27.8	13.9
N	31	32	18	37

A pessimistic outlook regarding a group's ability to obstruct the policy process was found also among prestigious and resourceful interest groups. The Association of Hotel Owners did its utmost, in 1989, to block a ministerial decree to regulate hotel prices. The regulation was prompted by what was viewed as exorbitant rates charged by local hoteliers. The fact that Israel was found to be the fifth most expensive country in the world for tourists provided the catalyst for the tourism minister to enforce the regulation. Although the minister became the target of much verbal abuse from the president of the hotel association, he did not veer from his course. Only after the decree imposing a price reduction was issued were the hotel owners willing to come to terms with the minister and hoped to reach some sort of compromise. The skill of pressure, however, is to reveal the extent of the determination prior to making efforts to challenge a ministerial decision.

About one-tenth of the economic interest groups and a quarter of the party-affiliated organizations were of the opinion that "there is no need to veto because decisions are arrived at by a mutual consent." The uselessness of the veto is evident in cases where a common interest binds decision-making authorities and a voluntary association. Among the groups representing this case were the travel agents, who have cooperated with the transport ministry in regard to regulations prohibiting airlines and agents from giving passengers a reduction on tickets. The ban was issued in 1986 in response to the sharp competition that had developed among the airlines and agents and that caused some agencies, including those with a wide clientele, to go bankrupt. The regulations were issued with the full cooperation of the interest group concerned. The need to veto did not arise. In the majority of the cases, however, interest groups failed once again to pass the test of corporatism. Particularly surprising is the wide rejection of the "mutual consent" option among economic interest groups, described in this work as the herald of group-state cooperation. As already suggested, the lines between the two modes of cooperation appear to be clear and distinct. Ignoring the economic interest groups is probably impossible in the late 1980s. Allowing them to thwart an official decision is, however, a different story.

The pluralist version ("you cannot enforce a decision in the face of fierce group opposition") was endorsed by somewhat a higher percentage, especially in the sectional category. Associations advocating material benefits appear to have a higher sense of efficacy than those promoting issues. More than twice the percentage of sectional groups than of their promotional counterparts reported that a veto had been exercised, and felt that in Israel the state cannot "compel" a decision in the face of fierce objection. The successful campaign launched by the Bar Association against a reform in the judicial system, proposed by the justice ministry in June 1988, may serve as an illuminating example. The bill provided for an eventual amalgamation of the magistrates and district courts into one court of first instance. It was intended eventually to create an appellate court to stand between the lower court and the Supreme Court, so that the latter could be freed to hear only appeals of outstanding public or legal importance. The reform was well intended. It was purported to find solutions for the problems of the understaffed, underpaid, underequipped (and undercomputerized) court system. The proposal, which originated in a 1980 report of a select committee headed by the then deputy-president of the Supreme Court, ran up against the opposition of seventy-six (of eighty) of the country's district court judges, who were unable by virtue of their judicial status to mobilize public opinion against the proposed reform. The Bar Association did launch a campaign attempting to halt legislation. Its argument was that the proposed reform was decided upon hastily and without due consultation. The tacit reason for the lawyers' opposition, however, was a fear that radical changes in the judicial system may be detrimental to practitioners of law. Although the press applauded the proposed reform,[2] the decision was vetoed, without much difficulty, by the bar, and never materialized. In fact, the justice minister did not even put it to a Knesset vote.

Even less powerful groups, such as the Union of Post-Elementary School teachers, have showed proficiency in vetoing government decisions. This group successfully blocked an intended reform of the vocational schools that aimed at "preparing students for the technological and scientific changes in society and the economy in the coming century."[3] The reform called for abolishing outdated courses taught in vocational schools and replacing them with new subjects suited to the advances in science. Fearing that many teachers unqualified for this type of training would be fired, the union successfully exercised a veto over the plan. These examples illustrate the potential of the veto power and the ability of interest groups to exercise it. The low frequency of the phenomenon, however, reveals that interest groups have not acquired a strong sense of efficacy and have not internalized the norm that a government cannot act (except under special circumstances) in the face of a vociferious and adamant opposition. The activists of Israeli associations seem to agree with Nordlinger (1981) that the state has a final say in formulating policies and can act—in fact it should act—even in the face of widespread discontent. Veto was exercised when the issue did not entail principles or when support was widely mobilized. A necessary condition, however, was the state's equivocation, without which blocking a policy was hardly plausible.

The Determinants of Power

Although "success" is never a product of one factor, a combination of factors can be grouped under one category which helps to explain the road to influence. These categories fall under the pluralist, the corporatist, and the elitist headings. Resources of all types and shapes are responsible for success in pluralist regimes. Votes both count and weigh; intimate relations forged between policy makers and policy takers kindle the fire of influence. All forms of direct action also constitute part of the pluralist repertoire. In corporatism the emphasis is laid not on what the group *is* but rather on what it *does*; that is, on its members' functional contribution to society. In elitism the scope is widened to encompass fundamental national goals. Those groups contributing to the fulfillment of these goals are bound to enjoy the benefits of success. In order to table their views on the determinants of their success, interest groups were presented with two sets of questions: closed-ended questions offering them the three alternative explanations congruent with the theory, and an open-ended question—"What, according to your experience, has been the most effective means to influence decision makers?" Their answers, presented in the following tables, cast light on the fundamental perception of Israeli interest groups regarding the determinants of influence.

Social contribution

"Social contribution" was considered to be a virtue in Israel, imbued with collective ideas. A comprehensive socializing network encouraged the Israeli citizen, from cradle to grave, to mold his or her personal wishes to be in line with national goals. Defending the country from its enemies or aiding it in developing its economy are not individual pursuits; rather, they are one link in the long chain toward national independence and sovereignty.

Israelis were socialized to believe that their personal well-being is
tantamount to that of the state. Furthermore, the state itself is required to reckon it is a "haven" for Jewish Diaspora, that it does
not exist only for pursuing the happiness of its own citizens, but is
committed to safeguarding the interests of a wider collective: the
worldwide Jewish community. Principles of foreign and domestic
policy are derived from this commitment, which overrides other
considerations. Forging economic and diplomatic relations with
racist and/or authoritarian regimes, anathema in the world community, was justified by the "Jewish" commitment. The primacy
of collective goals has not dimmed over time, although in many
cases collective language may be used to cover private ends.
Young Israelis still volunteer in great numbers to dangerous combat units engaged in life-risking ventures. The new recruits
demonstrate patriotism and self-sacrifice; they are also attracted to
these units by the halo of bravery and masculinity. This duality is
evident in many spheres of Israeli life. Devotion to the collective is
highly legitimized. The Israelis' dedication to the national cause
has been substantiated by a worldwide poll (conducted in thirty-
two countries) questioning the citizens' readiness to defend their
country. Israel was first, with 92 percent ready and willing to do
so.[4] At the same time personal motives also surface. Interest
groups have not escaped this duality, although their answers lean
heavily toward the collective end, that is, in the terms of this
study, toward the elitist version of interest politics. The secret of
success, according to a sizable (in the case of the promotional
groups, an overwhelming) majority of their leaders lies in a
group's social contribution.

Table 9.2
Most Important Factor Determining Interest Group Influence
(Percent Reporting)

| | Interest group category | | | |
	Party-affiliated	Economic	Other	Promo-tional
Resources	25.9	22.2	29.1	8.0
Functional role in society	19.3	13.9	4.2	12.0
Contribution to national goals	54.9	63.9	66.7	80.0
N	31	36	24	50

"Contribution to national goals" is hard to define. It is based
on a subjective sense of participation in a collective venture, of
giving a hand to a common endeavor. Identification with the
public good provides an association with the opportunity to shy

away from the hybrid meaning of "interest" and "group." Contribution to society has always been valued as a desired quality, as a symbol of good citizenship, as expressing a sense of belonging. As a social trait it demonstrates the fact that despite the divisions that cut across every possible economic or ideological domain, Israelis are united in their pursuit of the common, collective good. The sizable majority of groups adhering to the political model that propagates contribution to national goals as a major virtue indicated that the norms of collectivism were not dead, although practice did vary greatly. Many answers vividly reflected the respondents' steadfast clinging to national goals. "Activity for the sake of the state" and "showing intentions to act in domains pertinent to national importance"—these were among the answers given by respondents as to the determinants of their influence.

The attempt to play down the particularized aspects of group activity is evident in the groups' written objectives and in their leaders' pronouncements. In a previous research study, interest groups were asked specifically whether their major objective was to act as representatives of the respective groups or, alternatively, to advance national causes. The distribution of answers (Yishai 1987a: 131) reflected a near equal division between the two alternatives (39.8 percent and 42.5 percent, respectively). It is hardly surprising that the Council for a Beautiful Israel, the Civil Rights Association or the Feminist Movement endorsed collective goals. Adherence of the Association of Writers, the teachers' groups, and the farmers organizations to national objectives is also understandable in view of their historical role in the process of nation building. But the Manufacturers Association, the Union of Bankers, and the Association of Truck Drivers, for instance, have also joined the collective-oriented club.

A cursory glance at the regulations, constitutions, and proclamations of national conventions of a range of interest groups verifies this tendency to emphasize a concern for society at large. The Society for the Protection of Nature, whose major purpose is to bolster the linkage to the land of Israel, defines its goals thus: "to nurture a love of the country, knowledge of the country, including its nature, its animal stock, its plants, and its landscape" (par. 2.2). The society's secretary-general wrote that being familiar with the country's landscape was a prime national-Zionist tenet:

> The universal attributes of nature protection are especially important for the people of Israel, who are attempting to renew their roots in the landscape of this country. Can we imagine our

enduring survival in Israel without being familiar with its nature and landscape? . . . The success of the Zionist enterprise and the consolidation of the Jewish People's hold over their homeland go hand in hand with deepening the attachment to nature and, obviously, with its protection.[5]

Summing up thirty years of activity the society's secretary-general did not mention any advocacy strategy exercised by pressuring authorities; he sufficed with enumerating the associations's numerous contributions to the national cause. Sectional interest groups also widely endorse collective ends. The Histadrut, one of the major proponents of ideological politics, inscribed in its constitution a commitment to establish a welfare society in Israel. These goals were not subscribed to only in the early 1920s. A leader of one of the trade unions maintained during the interview for this research that his goals were primarily national. To back up his statement, he gave an example of a plant whose workers were unorganized. Being an extension of a United States firm, the mother company prohibited unionization and threatened to close the Israeli branch if it were unionized. The national imperative to provide employment and to increase production were more important to the union leader than advancing the interests of the association. He said: "First and foremost, I am a Zionist, only later am I a socialist." "Zionism" implied downplaying the interests of the group and giving first priority to the ends of the collective. Recruiting additional members to the union was less important, in his view, than contributing to the development of Israel's economy.

The manufacturers have not lagged behind their counterparts. Their president stated: "Our particular interests ought to be shoved off to the far horizon. We should be concerned with the future of the national economy, not only with the fate of industry." These comments were pronounced in a closed meeting and were not intended for public hearing. Collective goals are shared by the farmers and by the contractors: the major concern of the former is the redemption of land; the latter's goal is its habitation and development. The doctors proclaim their overriding concern to be public health; the engineers are self-proclaimed guardians of the nation's technological development. Still, adherence to national goals has not been universal. The Teachers Federation, for example, gave priority to the "organization of teachers in one Federation, the protection of members' rights, improving their working conditions, and advancing their professional and economic interests." When necessary, though, this group was quick to jump on the collective wagon. Its secretary-general conceded that adherence to "private" goals demanded a high toll:

> In recent years we refrained from dealing with state issues. Instead we were preoccupied with trade unionism and narrow educational problems. Hence, we were left aside and our voice was not heard. Did we improve our image in the public view? On the contrary, we were pictured as a narrow-minded trade union whose major interest is to secure benefits for its members. Does this image reflect what we really are?[6]

The vital importance of a group's "contribution to national goals," or at least of their self-perception in that regard, is well summed up in those plaintive remarks. The preponderance of the collectivist orientation is, however, not unanimous. In fact the variation between the categories of interest groups is revealing. Contrary to expectations it was precisely the party-affiliated associations that demonstrated the least adherence to "national goals." Their linkage with political parties has attenuated over time, but compared to other categories of voluntary groups they still hold the lead in parentela arrangements. The contacts with parties, however, have not spilled over to values and perceptions regarding the determinants of success. Adversely, promotional associations, expected to exhibit norms congruent with pluralist regimes, do foster collectivism in a proportion far higher than the material-oriented interest groups.

Functional role

Israel's technological development has much benefited from the functional role of interest groups and their members. The contribution of the business community and the professionals both as individuals and as organized groups to Israel's economy has been widely discussed in the course of this work. It remained to be seen whether the activists of these associations appreciate their role in advancing Israel toward modernism as a main factor for their "success." Has this functional role entitled them, according to their own view, to a larger portion of the economic pie? The answer is mostly negative.

The percentage of respondents who choose the "corporatist" explanation for a group's success was the lowest, compared to the two other alternatives. It is hardly surprising that promotional interest groups do not regard "functional contribution" as an important factor inducing success. Commentators on the corporatist theory (e.g. Wilson 1983; Magagna 1988) have noted that public interest groups are generally absent from the scene. Promotional groups can obtain access to decision makers. They are not expected, however, to contribute their expertise to the formulation of state policies.

The low percentage of those selecting the corporatist option among the sectional groups is hard to explain in view of their substantial contribution to implementing policy. Jack Hayward (1964) has noticed the output role generally played by interest groups. Israeli associations are no exception. The Center of Contractors and Builders aids the state in enforcing certification laws by, among other things, detecting unregistered contractors. The travel agents enforce regulations on flight prices, the Bureau of Accountants provides guidelines to its members to acquaint them with the ever-changing currency and tax laws, and the IMA guards the public against medical activities performed by unqualified practitioners. This contribution to the implementation of public policy is not prompted by altruistic motives, however. Rather, it is the competition of unlicensed individuals, the fear of internal rivalry, or the need to provide vital information to members that lies behind the groups' functional contribution. The meshing of private and public ends is brightly exposed in the activities of the MA. The manufacturers' functional contribution is prominent, not only because their activity is essential to advance economic growth and to encourage employment (Vogel 1987), but because they carry out specific campaigns (under the slogan "Buy Blue-White") to encourage the consumption of local goods. Needless to say, the objectives of this campaign are tailored to increasing the industrialists' profits, not just to promoting national goals. The MA also aids the government in enforcing price control, a measure of great public significance but one that also curbs internal competition. The Teachers Federation has enthusiastically implemented the ministry of education's guidelines on dismissing private tutoring in the public school system (the so-called "gray education"). The most striking example of an output role geared to public purposes is provided by the Union of Advertisers, which once launched a "national educational campaign" under the aegis of the prime minister's office for the purpose of "strengthening national pride." The project, entitled "Who, if not I?", was initiated by the union in the late 1980s against a background of low public morale, the Palestinian uprising in the territories, and persisting inflation—the combined effect of which was bound to tempt Israelis to emigrate.[7]

Interest groups play another functional role: they provide the state with information regarding their particular domain of concern. The large economic groups operate highly developed data-gathering machinery. Although state officials insist that the ministry is autonomous with regard to securing information, the informational material presented by groups provides a major supplement of, if not a substitute—despite the official claim to independent sources of knowledge—for the pool of data available to state use. The statistical departments of the major economic groups are invaluable sources of such information. The fact that "functional contribution" was diverted to the sidelines by all categories of interest groups (although somewhat less so by the party-affiliated organizations) thus does not necessarily imply that it does not exist.[8] It reveals, however, that interest group activists do not regard their role in implementing public policies as giving them a claim for influence.

Political and economic resources

The pluralist attributes of the Israeli society enable the use of diversified resources as a means of influence. The electoral system, however, hinders an effective use of the power of the ballot. Voters do not elect representatives; they cast their vote for political parties. These were either surrounded by their own satellites, or wooed nonassociational groups such as the dwellers of development towns, the poor, or peace lovers. Under these circumstances it is difficult to establish a linkage between vote and influence. Studies have shown that in election years the budget reflects the priority of welfare expenditure over other items (Sharkansly 1987). This preference, however, is not linked to a specific organized group activity. That votes count but resources decide (Rokkan 1966) is a widely believed assertion. As elaborated in chapter 7, Israeli interest groups take frequent recourse to strategies identified as pluralist. Although they are reluctant to exercise direct action, all other means of influence, characterized by more subtle forms of pressure, abound. The pluralist version, linking success to groups' resources, was nevertheless widely rejected by interest groups leaders.

Among the promotional associations only a fraction (8.0 percent) attributed their success to the power of resources; among the sectional groups the percentage was far higher, but was still less than a third of all respondents. The highest proportion of those regarding "resources" as a major determinant of their success was among the "other" sectional groups, which were found in the course of this study to be the least rich with organizational and political assets.

The endorsement of elitist-oriented views was far less evident in the answers to the open-ended question looking into the actual experience of group activists in their attempts to influence decision makers. The answers, coded under each of the three analytical categories employed in this research, reflect a clear tendency to choose strategies associated precisely with pluralist politics: pressure tactics, economic and organizational resources, electoral clout, extensive use of media, lobbying activity in the Knesset, and personal contacts with decision makers were mentioned as key resources of influence (see table 9.3). The word "pressure" was frequently used both in the interviews and in the mail questionnaires. Group leaders unequivocally described the merits of adversity. Here are some typical expressions to which these leaders gave vent: "Do not let them sleep in peace"; "He who has might is also considered right"; "To raise a fist against them is the only effective means"; "If you want to see any results you have to nag them incessantly."

Table 9.3
Most Effective Factor of Influence (Percent Reporting)

| | Interest group category | | | |
	Party-affiliated	Economic	Other	Promotional
Pressure	59.4	57.1	47.3	58.9
Cooperation	37.5	39.3	52.6	41.0
Integration	3.1	3.6	—	—
N	32	28	19	39

The variation between the answers describing the theoretical determinants of success and those summing up the associations' past experience (presented in figures 9.1 and 9.2) may reflect the gap between vision and reality. Thus, when confronted with ideal-type situations, groups invariably confirmed that "contribution to national goals" was a major asset for influence. When their answers reflected their experience in exerting influence, the majority of groups acknowledged, in line with the pluralist tradition, that the higher the pressure the better were the group's chances of influencing authorities to comply with its demands and yield to its pleas. Answers to the open-ended question (tabling practical experience) gave much more credit to the corporatist determinants of success than the closed-ended ones (depicting ideal-type factors). The proportion of answers regarding the link with a political party as a major determinant of success was negligible. Not even the party-affiliated associations, still organizationally (if not ideologically) attached to partisan institutions and resources, did not regard this linkage as a source of influence on decision makers.

Fig. 9.1. The Effect of Group Pressure in Theory and Practice (Percent Reporting)

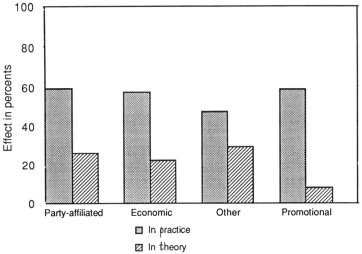

Fig. 9.2. The Effect of Group Integration in Theory and Practice (Percent Reporting)

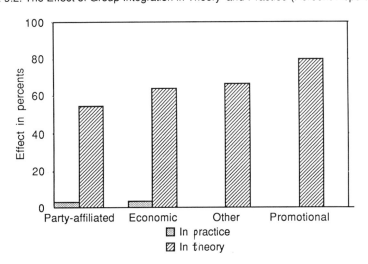

Thus in one respect Israeli interest groups are no different from their counterparts in other democratic societies. Israeli doctors stage strikes with a relatively high frequency (Bar Zuri and Bazri 1988), and the teachers do not lag far behind. Closing kindergartens, schools, or universities on account of a labor dispute or a protest against excessive tuition fees is part of Israeli life. Hardly a year goes by without a disturbance in the country's educational system. The workers of the Israeli Electricity Company can easily compete with British railway employees in causing public inconvenience. Although in comparison to other means of influence demonstrations and strikes do not comprise a major group tactic (see chapter 7), their impact is considered by their instigators to be substantial. Yet there is a special Israeli version of success that amalgamates the three fundamental components of power, the power of pressure, the power of participation, and the power of integration with the political elite. The case of Gush Emunim (between 1974 and 1977) amply demonstrates this type of success.

In the period under consideration, Gush Emunim was highly structured. It commanded resources of all types, including a wide membership devoted to the cause of Greater Israel and the settlement of its lands. The group suffered no serious problems of organizational cohesion. On the contrary, its members, most of whom were trained and bred in religious learning institutions, were united around the group's goals. Gush Emunim was successful in soliciting both private and semi-public funding for its settlement endeavors. Although the movement lacked a firm institutional basis, the attributes that make for organizational effectiveness (i.e., authoritative leadership, devoted membership, material resources, and internal cohesion) were largely available. The strategies employed by the group added to its strength. Gush Emnuim excelled in creating a "nuisance impact" (Milbrath 1967), that is, the power to disrupt society (Finer 1973: 393). Acquiring a nuisance impact, in Israel, implies a combination of pressure, cooperation, and integration. Pressure is applied by mass protests and other forms of direct action; cooperation is exercised by fulfilling a role instrumentally contributing to a mission placed high on the national order of priorities; integration is obtained through reference to fundamental national values.

Although unlike, say, the bus drivers, Gush Emunim could not upset the routine of life in the country, it did exert pressure by taking throngs of people to the street, and by repeating the settlement acts in the occupied territories. It also skillfully used the rift within the political elite to pressure its advocacies and to win attention. A major part of Gush Emunim resources was its broad public expansion. The establishment of the movement provided the religous constituency, or at least its Zionist elements, an opportunity to join the mainstream of Israeli society and to share in some of the glory associated with early pioneering. Not being full-fledged partners to the struggle that had brought about national independence and not enjoying the concomitant prestige bestowed on those who did, the national-religious youth, through Gush Emunim, joined the honorable club of the nation's heroes. By virtue of its "pioneering" activities, which in fact were totally different in nature and scope from pioneer activity in the early days of Jewish settlement in Palestine, Gush Emunim also captured the support of some elements of the Labor camp. By virtue of its ideology, Gush Emunim, naturally, also developed close links with the right-wing camp which espoused the settlement of Greater Israel.

Gush Emunim did perform a function highly valued in Israeli history: it inhabited the land with Jewish settlers. The group was not a full-fledged institutional partner of government in matters relating to the occupied territories. Its activists, however, made the movement eligible for at least a tacit partnership mainly because it played a functional role in settling the lands. furthermore, Gush Emunim was recognized as the legitimate representative of the cause it articulated, and was therefore granted the status of "official advocate" for the case of Eretz Israel. All this added up to what may be termed a case of "weak corporatism" (Keeler 1987: 10).

Finally, Gush Emunim excelled in playing on the most delicate cords of national sentiments and made it extremely difficult for the government to ignore its demands. By "establishing facts" instead of presenting theoretical demands, the group forced the government to pay heed and, eventually, to yield. The high appeal of this issue-oriented association to broad sections of the Israeli political map enabled it to establish close links with political parties, to secure representation both in the Knesset and in the government, and to enjoy the privileges conferred in Israel on party-related interest groups. Gush Emunim advocates occupied seats in every decision making forum whose aid to the promotion of its cause was invaluable (Yishai 1987b).

The integration does not imply that Gush Emunim did not have to fight hard in order to obtain success. On the contrary, the electoral platform of the Alignment, the governing party when this movement burst onto the scene, rejected Jewish settlement in densely populated Arab zones. These were precisely the target of Gush Emunim settlement efforts. The Prime Minister, Yitzhak Rabin, and many other ministers publicly denounced the movement. They derogated its activities, describing them as harmful to both Israel's internal fabric and its external relations. In his memoirs the premier asserted that the movement was "a cancer in the body of the Israeli democracy" (Rabin 1979: 551). Yet the influence of the group was successful; it actually modified the course of the government and introduced changes that later proved to be dramatic. Between 1975 and 1977 it put up four settlements in an area that until then had been closed to Jewish settlement, forcing Israel into a head-on collision with the Palestinian population and the ensuing bloodshed in the occupied territories.

The case of Gush Emunim demonstrates the effectiveness, in terms of policy results, of the combination of the three major strategies available to interest groups: the accumulation of resources, cooperation with and legitimation by the elite, and integration with decision makers. The story of Gush Emunim provides contemporary proof of the ability of an interest group to enter the political arena, to mobilize resources, to acquire status recognized by foes and friends, and to integrate into a political network. Admittedly, Gush Emunim operated under extremely congenial political circumstances: the country was plagued by the trauma of the October war and yearned for national heroism; the Labor Alignment was vulnerable to outside influence; public discontent reached one of its peaks in Israeli history. The government was also riven by deep internal rivaly and factional strife. It is difficult to estimate Gush Emunim's influence on a more cohesive and popular party in government. Yet, the erection of Jewish settlements in the densely Arab-populated area serves as a remarkable example of an Israeli success in the interest domain.

Interest Groups and Society: The Legitimation of Pressure

The outcomes of interest groups' activities may be perceived also by perceptions of their role in society. In order to assess the general contribution of interest groups to society, the leaders were presented with three theoretical alternatives: interest groups contribute to democratic life; interest groups contribute to the functional aspects of governing; and interest groups contribute to the fulfillment of national objectives. They could also maintain that

"Interest groups do not contribute to public life." The picture that emerges from the answers (presented in table 9.4) is illuminating. Once again the attitudes of activists in Israeli interest groups reveal the absence of a "corporatist" mood. The majority of all respondents (55.4 percent) thought that the role of interest groups in furthering collective goals was their most important contribution. Among the promotional associations the proportion of adherence to this elitist strand was far higher than among the party-affiliated and the economic groups.

Slightly more than a third of all surveyed emphasized the democratic aspects. Here again the difference between the promotional and two of the sectional categories is striking. The proportion among the issue-oriented groups praising associational activity on ground of pluralistic norms was considerably lower than among the economic associations, including those affiliated with political parties. Adoption of a democratic rationale for interest group activity was thus much more prevalent among sectional groups than among issue-oriented associations. On the other hand, the belief that the major contribution of interest groups lay in the fulfillment of national, collective objectives was considerably more widespread among the promotional associations. The leaders of the issue-oriented groups, more than their sectional counterparts, did adhere to the values of the "past," which for them had a paramount contemporary significance.

Table 9.4
Perceived Interest Groups' Major Contribution to Society
(Percent Reporting)

	Interest group category			
	Party-affiliated	Economic	Other	Promo-tional
Contribution to democratic life	40.5	46.0	33.3	28.2
Contribution to the efficiency of governance	10.8	5.4	3.7	3.8
Contribution to the fulfillment of national goals	46.0	46.6	63.0	66.0
Do not contribute	2.7	2.7	—	1.9
N	37	37	27	53

Adherence to the past does not mean that interest groups feel out of place or have qualms about their activity. The research referred to the groups' legitimacy by asking their leaders the following question: "It is often postulated that public organizations advance the selfish interests of their members and disregard the needs of society at large. Do you agree with this assumption?"

The answers (presented in table 9.5) were mainly negative. Relatively few were willing to endorse such a stipulation. The lowest proportion of leaders who totally rejected this assertion was found, in line with previous findings, among promotional associations. They do seem to be more uncomfortable with their advocacies, although they are presumably targeted at public ends.

Table 9.5
Opinions Regarding Interest Groups' Goals (Percent Reporting)

| | Interest group category | | | |
	Party-affiliated	Economic	Other	Promo-tional
Fully agree	16.2	11.1	11.1	17.0
Partially agree	27.0	33.3	14.9	33.3
Disagree	56.8	55.6	44.7	74.0
N	37	36	47	27

Conclusions

This chapter revealed a paradoxical picture of interest politics in Israel. On the one hand the associations' activists demonstrated a widespread lack of belief in the power of the veto. Only a minority asserted that a group can change a decision once it has been made. Israeli government does make decisions, many of which seriously affect interest groups. Not being able to reshape the course of such decisions, groups remain quite helpless in the face of a powerful authority. On the other hand interest groups do seem to possess a sense of efficacy, regarding their attempts at influencing public policy as "successful."

The second paradox is reflected in the incongruity between perceptions that may be termed "theoretical," and assertions based on real life situations. When asked what, in the respondents' view, is the major determinant of success, the elitist strand is unmistakable. Interest groups strongly believe in the late 1980s that contribution to the fulfillment of national objectives is still an asset wielding influence. The pursuit of collective goals remains a major, although not a sole, venue for success. One of the striking findings of this chapter is that issue-oriented associations, including environmental groups, consumer organizations, protest groups in defense affairs, and women's movements, endorse values associated with traditional Israeli politics with more enthusiasm than their "conservative" economic counterparts. They even outbid, in this respect, the organizations mostly associated with Israeli elitism—trade unions and agricultural groups. The collective orientation of Israeli interest groups is reinforced by their self-image. Associations' leaders see no "selfish" motives in their organization's activities. In the same breath, however, activists of interest groups highly value pressure as a means of influence and record (in response to an open-ended question) a variety of strategies associated with pluralist politics.

The paradox of interest politics in Israel demonstrates the growing gap between perception and reality. Clinging to the glory of the past is still widely preached, although pioneering and self-sacrifice are much less practiced. Behavior has changed immensely. At the writing of these conclusions violent demonstrations are being staged at different parts of the country. The settlers of Galilee moshavim urge the government to subsidize their poultry; the workers of Koor, verging on bankruptcy, threaten to occupy the Histadrut headquarters and disrupt work. Discontent is demonstrated by burning tires and blocking roads. The pressure on decision makers is direct and massive. Lip service is nevertheless paid to collectivism: members of moshavim argue that their well-being is essential for defending Israel's vulnerable northern border; Koor workers are concerned with the future of Israel's industry. The disharmony between declared advocacies and practiced strategies is one of the paradoxes of the Israeli polity.

CHAPTER TEN

Israeli Interest Groups between Party and State

The case of interest politics in Israel affords a dual opportunity to examine both a complex political reality and the validity of a theory. Reality requires a model to explain the unique characteristics that on the surface provide a sound basis for three possible configurations of interest politics. When this reality is matched with the theory, however, serious deviations are evident. The scope of these deviations, their postulated reasons, and their time sequence comprise the first part of the analysis summing up the Israeli case in this last chapter. The discussion will then proceed with an examination of Israel in a comparative perspective. It will conclude by offering some theoretical implications deriving from the Israeli case.

Reality vs. Theory: The Israeli Case

The elitist model

As a party-democracy, with a strong tradition of party dominance, Israel was expected to exhibit characteristics congruent with the elitist model of interest politics. The evidence to this effect is highly equivocal. To be sure, the organization of the group arena does reflect strong elements of partization, particularly within the sector that was traditionally affiliated with political parties. Israel's political parties are widely perceived as powerful, although much of their power may now have been eroded. One of the most important symptoms of this erosion is reflected in the reduced colonization of state agencies by party staff. The organs of the state may be manned by protégés of influence-peddling politicians, but the state has turned too large, too decisive, and too powerful to be "colonized" by any one party. In fact, one wonders whether it is not the "state" (i.e., people occupying high-level positions in the administration) that at present colonizes the party.

If organizational criteria are applied to Israeli interest groups, marked differences may be found between party-affiliated groups and the other categories of the associational arena. It is mainly the former that show the imprint of political parties. Thus, both trade unions and agricultural groups present party lists that compete in the internal elections of these associations. Their interaction with party institutions and personnel is extensive, and their membership shows an overlap with party leadership. This latter attribute, on the other hand, is not confined to party-affiliated associations but is actually spread across the board of Israeli interest groups.

If the linkage between interest groups and political parties does not manifest itself directly in the organizational arena, it does present itself through the "direct lobby," whereby Knesset members and party politicians represent specific constituencies seeking to promote their individual interests. In all Western democracies there are members of parliament who identify with causes advocated by interest groups. They do so, however, because they were recruited by these groups, because they were persuaded by professional lobbyists, or because they were convinced that their own electoral prospects could thereby be enhanced. In Israel, the lobby phenomenon is unique in the sense that it is not an individual phenomenon, nor is it confined to interest groups traditionally represented in the legislature (e.g., trade unions). Rather, lobbying is a group phenomenon, cutting across party lines. The electoral system also precludes direct electoral rewards for members of such lobbies. The fact that wide constituencies are represented by a group of individual MKs rather than by a party caucus reveals the changing characteristics of Israeli elitism. Influence is secured from within, rather than by lobbyists acting from the outside; however, party lines are crisscrossed by associational interests. The parliamentary lobby, including party leaders, operates independent of party institutions.

The elitist configuration of interest politics is thus undergoing change. Political parties loom large in the background, invisible actors breathing down the necks of all actors. From an empirical perspective, their impression on associational life is modest. Israeli interest groups do not regard political parties as worthy targets of influence. Making contact with the parties is placed far down in the order of strategic priorities. Analysis of the policy process in Israel also refutes assumptions derived from the elitist model of politics. Interest groups are free to push their advocacies; they are not subservient to political parties, their leaders, or their institutions.

Elitism, however, does present itself in a set of values although not in actual behavior. It is in this realm that the components of elitism are clearly evident. Israeli interest groups widely subscribe to national, collective goals and attempt to downplay their particular interests. Their members may burn tires and block roads, but not because their plight demands immediate attention and action; they do so more because they ostensibly wish to defend the national cause. The settlers of the Galilee take such measures to prevent the "arabization" of this region; the workers of the Aviation Industry to continue Israel's technological advancement; and the nurses, to safeguard public health. From a normative perspective, then, influence in the elitist configuration emanates only from good Samaritans, excelling in their contribution to the fulfillment of collective goals. Elitism is thus more evident in norms than in practices; and it is more characteristic of associations that are traditionally affiliated with political parties.

The corporatist model

There is strong evidence in support of the organizational aspects of liberal corporatism in Israel. A recapitulation of the corporatist syndrome presented in the Introduction to this book demonstrates that great similarity exists between theory and the Israeli reality.

The centralization, power, and intrusiveness of the state have been widely illustrated in this work. The Israeli state is certainly not just "another interest group" with which associations have to compete. The state is manipulative, its authority extending octopus-like over interest groups. The Associations' Law (1980), although not strictly applied, is one of the clearest manifestations of the state's involvement in the life of the country's interest groups. The law enables the state, should it so desire, to pry into the intricate details of associational affairs. By enacting this law, the state attempted to grasp the rope at each end, i.e., to ensure the freedom of association and to control the group arena. The absence of a similar law in many other democracies, however, highlights the prominence of the state in the Israeli context. The state was authorized by its early founders to overcome the divisions which beset the Jewish people in the Diaspora, and which allegedly arrested their progress toward political independence. The clamor to overcome divisive tendencies was not apparent on the partisan arena; it found expression in the "state," which was important and dear to all, regardless of their political color and shade. The state was thus ordained to rise above all sectional differences. Its claim to legitimacy was high, especially because of the precarious security situation that it faced. As sole guardian of defense, the state assumed responsibility for many spheres of life that in other democracies are left to the free play of social powers.

Interest groups also exhibit characteristics congruent with the corporatist configuration. Almost every interest area is represented by one single association. In fact, many a group even monopolize its domain of interest; so the number of operating groups is limited. Furthermore, the degree of internal fragmentation within sectors is extremely low. Hierarchies have emerged among associations and they subordinate and coordinate the activities of entire economic sectors. The Histadrut perhaps offers the prime example: a roof organization of all trade unions, it still to a large extent subordinates the activities of its separate units, despite their growing autonomy. The Histadrut does this through a centralized decision-making apparatus, its Trade Union Department, whose head is second in importance to the secretary-general of the Labor Federation. Hierarchy is evident also in the business arena. The activities of the economic organizations is coordinated by the Coordinating Office; though discipline over its subunits may be more tenuous compared to the Histadrut, it still limits the choices available to individual members.

Corporatist features are highly visible in the internal structure of Israeli interest groups. Although membership in associations is, except in one case (the Bar Association), officially voluntary, density is very high. A wide range of de facto as well as de jure arrangements exist, both to bind members to "their" association and to prevent the emergence of competing groups. This description, which was offered by Schmitter (1982: 160) in a different context, may define the Israeli reality. The one major device that enhances interest group control over the members and that binds them to their association is the government's recognition of "representative organizations." Possessing such an official status, a group's membership can hardly nurture the idea of defection, since this group already dominates the particular interest arena by virtue of having secured state recognition. Although this recognized status does not entail government subsidies, it does lead to improved access to government offices and to a say in policy formation. The status of "representative organization" is highly desired by fledgling groups and is not easily granted by the state. Both the government and interest groups regard this status as a privilege, yet it is one that does not seem to compromise the autonomy of groups so conferred. The data show that grassroots participation in the organizational life of the interest groups is rather low and that internal opposition is neither intensive nor vocal. Challenges to leadership constitute a rare practice. Factional strifes on the associational level appear to be low-keyed compared to those taking place within Israel's political parties. The perceived harmonious relationship in the interest group arena thus furnished another important corporatist ingredient.

The major vulnerability of corporatism in Israel is the sharing of power with the authorities. Interest groups, by and large, do not share joint responsibility for public policy formation, not to mention policy implementation. Admittedly interest groups do fulfill important roles in carrying out public policies. This characterization is especially true in regard to the economic organizations. The relationship of the Histadrut and the Coordinating Office to the state is not fashioned along the lines of structured corporatism; however, some form of partnership certainly prevails. The Labor Federation is expected to restrain the workers in regard to wage demands; the employers are expected to control their members' penchant for raising prices. By the same token, the physicians have a devolved authority to safeguard the medical standards of the profession, and the accountants to implement the ever-changing tax laws. Such contributions to implementing policy, however, do not entitle groups to "integrated participation." Although representatives of interest groups do occasionally participate in forums sponsored by the state, they can by no means be considered institutional partners to its decisions. The state is solely responsible for devising policies, not only because of its own choice, but also because interest groups largely prefer to remain outside rather than to integrate into the state machinery. The state is much admired as a conceptual entity, but the love affair between interest groups and the government appears to be platonic—in line with the wishes of the two potential partners. One vivid example of an interest sector wishing to free itself from partnership with the state is provided by the agricultural groups, which operate in a domain that achieved the highest degree of corporatization. The nightmare of corporatism—i.e., rank-and-file revolt against over-structured, over-planned, over-centralized, and over-disciplined associations—has become true in Israel. Farmers attempting to tear themselves from the grip of the agricultural councils has become a commonplace event.

Although interest groups feature many organizational attributes derived directly from the corporatist model—such as high centralization, monopolization, internal discipline, state recognition—they wish to be granted an official status short of integration with the state. In other words, they want to influence the state rather than to become part of it themselves. The corporatism picture is thus marred by three factors: the lack of institutional integration between state and groups, the diminutive image of "implementation" as a source of group success, and the lack of forums enabling the forging of institutionalized cooperation between interest groups and state agencies.

The pluralist model

The elitist characteristics of interest group politics in Israel were found mostly in the normative domain; corporatism was found to predominate the organizational domain; pluralism is mostly evident in the behavioral domain. Some attributes of the pluralist model are clearly missing from the Israeli scene. The state is by no means a "cash register" collecting the input of private associations and adding it up to a balance. The interest group arena is not, in its sectional part, atomized; political parties appear to play a minimal role in mediating between associations and decision-making authorities. Although interest groups are autonomous insofar as their organizatonal resources, their autonomy is only partial. By granting formal recognition to an interest group (as a "representative organization"), the state makes it much easier for this association to solicit funds. Yet for all these lacunas, groups do exhibit unmistakable pluralist characteristics. First and foremost, Israeli interest groups enjoy a high degree of access to the centers of power. The representatives of associations are welcome in the Knesset and in all government ministries. The intensity of interaction between group activists and the formal organs of the state reveals the scope of this access. Furthermore, the state is largely perceived as being responsive to groups' demands. Associational leaders do not face closed doors, nor do they have to make their way to decision makers by using violent means. In fact, the incidence of demonstrations and strikes among Israeli interest groups is quite low by Western standards. Instead, contacts are carried on in an orderly fashion, whether through appeals to the bureaucracy (as a major strategy) or through informal contacts with decision makers. Interest groups are thus offered ample opportunity to exert influence. Although they do not play a leading role in initiating a policy process, which emanates mainly from the elite, associations do make their voices heard in the elaboration of the policy.

The preponderance of pluralist pressure tactics also manifested itself in groups' evaluations of the determinants of results. Strategies associated with the pluralist paradigm were perceived by a sizable proportion of interest groups to be the most effective means to secure influence, more effective than channels identified with either the corporatist or elitist models. When writing a manual for behavior, interest groups recommend adoption of "elitist" strategies; when writing their memoirs, associations recall pluralist designs.

Some Explanations

The use of political pressure tactics in Israel, a highly structured, concentrated society guided by collective-oriented goals, poses somewhat of a riddle to a political scientist attempting to fanthom the chemistry of this particular blend of polity. Three postulates may be put forth to account for the complexity: a cultural explanation, a psychological explanation, and a political explanation.

The cultural explanation

Israel is a Jewish state. Its politics reveal distinctive features that derive from Jewish tradition and heritage. The political scene in Israel is imbued with evocations connecting the state, Israel, with the whole of Jewish history, where the roots of Israeli politics should be sought. The Jewish political culture provides one of the keys to understanding the unique intermixture of the three models of interest group-state relationships, for the three strands originated in first and second commonwealths and evolved over two millenia of frustrating exile.

To begin with, Jewish tradition is not "liberal" in the modern sense of the term. Jewish *Halacha* (religious law) subjugates all Jewish people to Divine authority. Religious laws and rulings are perceived as having ultimate validity. They cover all spheres of

human behavior from beliefs to emotions. Religious commandments prescribe forms of dress and nutrition; they dictate when to
rest and when to have sexual relations. Religious tenets oblige
Jewish people to respect their parents and to treat their fellow
citizens as their brothers. From early morning rising to bedtime at
night, a Jew is ordered how to behave and how to live a particular
way of life. From a secularist-liberal perspective, little may seem left
to individual initiative. Although the source of religious laws is
transcendental, they are given a mundane voice: the rabbis, who
traditionally played a dominant role in the political as well as the
religious life of Jewish communities in the Diaspora. The community rabbis, by virtue of their knowledge, were the interpreters
and conveyors of Divine authority; though they did not always
speak with one voice, their rulings were respected and obeyed.
The spiritual leadership of the rabbis and their wide scope of influence tainted Jewish political life with elitist shades.

Important elements of the corporatist theory are also readily
identifiable in Jewish tradition. The Jewish ethos is underpinned
by the idea of a covenant between God and His people. In their
seminal article on Jewish political thought, Don Yehiya and Susser
explicated the nature of that covenant as follows:

> [It] is a comprehensive, all-embracing cooperation which is
> not confined to a specific domain; neither is it instrumental. It
> integrates all those sharing the deep and over-arching loyalties
> and solidaric links, displayed in all domains. The covenant is
> holy, eternal and inalienable. It is established, however, on the
> basis of consent and free choice. It includes elements of
> reciprocity, cooperation and equality, even though the partners
> are not equals. (1989: 34)

No definition found in modern political science literature
could give a better account of the fundamental idea of corporatism
than this short description of the covenant between the Jewish
people and their God. The "covenant" (*Brit*, in Hebrew) affirms
the cooperation between ruler and ruled; it highlights the mutual
responsibility necessary for maintaining the reciprocal relationship
of the partners; it emphasizes the equality between participants
who are in effect unequal in power; and finally, it underscores the
stability of the relationships under concern.

The idea of the covenant has been so central to Jewish
political thought and practice that a leading scholar defined the
history of Jewish politics as the history of the covenant in its many

forms and expressions (Elazar 1983). He further postulated that Jewish political culture is federal in its essence, that is, it is a product of a series of covenants (or partnership agreements) derived from the great covenant that created the Jewish poeple. This culture reaches down to the immediate compacts that create specific communities within the Jewish body civic or politic and that affirm the essential equality of the partners as well as the authority of the institutions they establish (1986: 187).

Paradoxically, the Jewish religion also puts emphasis on the individual "soul" and reveals many liberal trends. Authority in the Diaspora, especially in the Jewish communities in Europe, was based on a general right of participation. Eisenstadt (1985: 46) referred to "the basic 'democratic' or rather egalitarian premises of the Jewish tradition, premises of basic equality and of equal participation and access of all Jews to the centers of the sacred realm." Apart from this, there was a proliferation of groups of all types: artisan guilds, mutual aid societies, cultural groups, defense organizations, saving and loan associations, charitable groups, burial societies, and even rudimentary forms of trade unions (Katz 1963). The presence of these variegated organizations served to increase the diffusion of power and to sustain opposition to the formal community rule. Bargaining among contending centers of power was habitual. These practices were reinforced by a long, well-established Jewish tradition of opposition to political authority, which legitimized resistance to any formal decision that might be reached (Segre 1981: 300–301). The style of politics was highly contentious (Dowty 1988: 9). Not in vain was the Talmud termed "The Book of Controversy" (Don Yehiya and Susser 1989: 33). While any breach of accepted rules was met with severe sanctions, tradition legitimized more than one version and acknowledged the prevalence of more than one truth. Beit Hillel, the school of Hillel, promoters of more compromising solutions, co-existed with Beit Shamai, a school that propagated more rigid rulings.

The separation between "state" and society constitutes another facet of modern pluralism. In the Jewish political culture, the role of the community in dealing with human needs was perceived to be substantial, but never all-embracing. That is to say, "politics is not conceived to be the all and end all of life, or its architectonic principle. Rather, politics is perceived to be an important means for creating the good society necessary for living the good life" (Elazar 1986: 187). This instrumental attitude toward politics, and the clear demarcation between politics and other spheres of life in the Jewish community, are typical pluralistic attributes. The voluntary aspects of community life, the proliferation of influence, the necessity of bargaining, the contentious mood—all this marked Jewish life in the European Diaspora. These elements were also incorporated into the Israeli political culture.

The psychological explanation

Israel's contemporary political culture provides a combination of deep insecurity necessitating reliance on superior authority, a dire need for immediate and visible accomplishment, and a sense of brotherhood. Each of these psychological strands provides an incentive for the development of a different pattern of interest politics.

Many Israelis evinced a deep and profound sense of insecurity. The Jews carry on their backs two millennia of persecution, which has been only moderately reduced during forty years of independence. The "siege mentality" has had many expressions and has been nurtured by the media and by the educational system. The political establishment, too, has shared this suspicion of the outside world. One striking example of this mentality was provided by Abba Eban, when he was Israel's foreign minister, who recalled the experience of the period preceding the Six Day War in these words: "As we looked around us we saw the world divided between those who were selling our destruction and those who would do nothing to prevent it" (Eban 1977: 392). The siege mentality is not a feature of the past. A study conducted in the summer of 1988 indicated that more than half of all Israelis believe that "the Whole World is Against Us."[1]

The siege mentality has generated pressures for unity, which is necessary for thwarting external threats. Israelis are consistently urged to disguise controversies and to denounce those who breach harmony. Israelis have been implored by their president to learn the lesson of the destruction of the Temple: "We have to rise above dissensions and disagreements and to nurture unity. Unity is imperative in our struggle for the survival of our State."[2] The senior administrators interviewed in the course of the research for this work also referred to unity as a justification for their reluctance to share authority with representatives of interest groups. One of the most derogatory words in Hebrew is that for defectors (*porshim*), a term used to describe those Jewish underground groups during the British Mandate that did not cooperate with the defense forces of the *yishuv* leadership, the Hagannah. The paramount importance attributed to unity constitutes a major hindrance to the development of pluralism in Israel.

The development of structured corporatism is thwarted by the psychological need for short-term accomplishments. Corporatism is, inter alia, a product of the need to forecast economic developments and to introduce a measure of stability into the political and economic systems. This need offers one of the major inducements for the state to devolve part of its authority to interest groups. Israel is geared toward the tangible present more than it opts for the unforeseeable future. The "unplanned" administrative culture of Israel has been subject to much scholarly comment (e.g., Akzin and Dror 1966; Caiden 1970; Sharkansky 1987; Dror 1989). In contrast to Great Britain, where issues "stew" until the right solution emerges (Rose 1980), problems in Israel demand immediate solutions. The term "now" was adopted by the peace movement in order to signify the urgency in negotiating for the end of belligerency and to demonstrate a readiness to relinquish territories occupied in the Six Day War in return for peace. The spirit of "now" (*achshavizm* in Hebrew), however, represents a major deterrent to corporatist arrangements. The orientation toward the present, toward what is visible rather than toward what is forecast, is evident in many spheres of Israeli life. Peace Now demands immediate progress toward peace, but Gush Emunim demands security now. The industrialists ask for a devaluation as an immediate relief, development town dwellers insist on employment now. This emphasis on the present is also reflected in the priorities determined by public policy:

- Infrastucture in transportation and communication in Israel lags far behind the pace of the country's economic development. The telephone network is inadequate, suffering from perpetual shortages and overload. The main reason for this situation is the inability to forecast the rapid development of commercial enterprises, which development results in greater demand for modern communication.

- Investments in industry are not initiated by state bodies, which serve only as a clearing agency for subsidy and funding. Little attempt has been made to attract industries on the basis of long-term priorities. Those projects that can supply prompt solutions to impending economic problems, first and foremost those that can provide immediate relief to the excruciating problem of unemployment, are the first to be granted state aid.

- The educational system is not geared to cope with long-term national trends. The division of resources among the numerous claimants (such as the universities, the vocational school system) is determined either by the needs of the moment or by the effectiveness of the pressure that is applied. The elementry school system has been flooded with computers to keep up with the most advanced educational systems in the Western world, but little attempt has been made to train teachers how to use the equipment and how to instruct their pupils to take advantage of this modern technology.

- Israel has been caught totally unprepared for the fulfillment of its dream and vision: immigration. No contingency plans were available to absorb the mass immigration from the Soviet Union that began to flow to the country in the late 1980s. Problems of housing and employment surfaced, but appropriate solutions, based on long-term planning, were not offered.

The inability to install a mechanism for rational, calculated strategic planning constitutes one of Israel's major political maladies (Dror 1989). It is a problem brought on not by a shortage of qualified manpower, but by the urge to finish the business of the day, to exhibit short-term success and not to await results. Has this impatience been caused by the experience of the long, frustrating exile that lurks in the collective consciousness, and especially its most recent and perhaps ultimate manifestation, the Holocaust? Or is it a product of urgencies produced by contemporary exigencies? The answer is probably both. The outcome of this attitude, in any case, is a basic reservation regarding long-term planning.

The final aspect of the psychological explanation is grounded in the orientation toward community life. That Israel is a collective-oriented society needs no repetition. The roots of this collectivism lie in the deepest layers of the Jewish tradition as well as in the structures of nation building in prestate Israel. The Jewish faith is based on the community, rather than on the individual. Despite the subscription to the value of human life and despite the importance attached to each and every individual, the center of religious life is the synagogue, where one interacts with fellow persons to worship God in common. Indeed, certain prayers cannot be recited unless a quorum of ten men are present, this number being an imperative set by tradition for forming a "community." The prayers, too, are rarely formulated in the first person but employ the collective "we."

The importance of the community in the Zionist endeavor in Palestine cannot be overestimated. Until the 1930s, practically every immigrant came to the country in the framework of an organized immigration. Prospective immigrants were first trained in special training camps set up abroad by the political parties and their affiliated organizations; they were also taught the Hebrew language, and then sent to Palestine as a group. The number of individuals who arrived on their own, unaided either economically or psychologically by the organized institutions of the *yishuv*, was minuscule. The mass immigration that flooded the country in the aftermath of independence was also community oriented. The European refugees of the Holocaust were brought to Israel by "emissaries" (*shlichim*) of the Israeli political establishment, who took care of their financial and other material needs. The immigrants from Arab-speaking countries, such as from Yemen, Iraq, Morocco, were also brought to Israel in organized communities and, what is more, were settled in homogeneous ethnic localities. Indeed, the Israelis' orientation toward their community, as Liebman (1988) has remarked, is stronger than their affiliation to the state. The latter is based on impersonal, universal standards of conduct and governance; the former evokes a familial identity based on primordial symbols and ties.

This need for belonging and comradeship is also spurred by the identity crisis evinced by many Israelis. The identity of the Israeli has not yet fully crystallized. The citizens of Israel are not sure whether they are Middle Eastern, by virtue of the geographical location, or whether they are Western. Westernization is sustained by an economic affiliation with the European community, the source of the heritage of perhaps half of the country's Jewish population, as well as by the perennial hostility of the Arab world to Israel's existence. The identity of Israelis is furthermore blurred by a split between their Jewishness and their "Israeliness." Since Israel is largely a secular society, many people, especially among the younger generation, feel unsure about their Jewishness. At the same time, however, their roots in Israel are not deeply inculcated. One refuge that Israelis seek in order to cope with these uncertainties is to identify with "the community" rather than with the state and its institutions. In a state so pervasive as Israel the strong community orientation is but one aspect of the political paradox; it also impinges upon interest politics.

The political explanation

Political practices in Israel can supply ample reasons for the country's unique blend of interest politics. Elitism, as this title implies, entails a special relationship between a party elite, which by definition is narrow based and restricted, and selected interest groups, chosen on the basis of ideological proximity, tradition orientation, or personal affiliation. The interest group arena in Israel may now take the form of widening circles; but located in the middle of these circles are the parentela groups which enjoy most of the available benefits. The structure of these circles as well as the location of groups in them have not remained static, however. Government intervention in both the economy and the social life of the country have made many interest groups rich. These benefits have not been conferred only on members of the partisan family. Among those who have enjoyed some of the cream have been the members of agricultural settlements, the importers, the industrialists, the small artisans, the pilots, and the hotel owners. The income-generating effect of government expenditure has also raised the income of poorer sections of society. In fact, it is difficult to envisage an interest group which did not secure benefits for its members at one time or another. Following the rules of Wonderland, every one, not only Alice, won a prize. To be sure, there are certain rules defining one's eligibility to take part in the game and to reside in Wonderland; but once a "team" is accepted, it is bound to be rewarded some time, in some form. The share-all rewards system introduced elements of pluralism into the polity.

The fluidity of the Israeli political arena also acts as a check on elitism. Alliances and ad hoc coalitions are constantly being formed and dissolved. The system is neither "hierarchically ordered," its apex insulated from the people, nor vertically arranged, with parentela alliances. Rather, government ministers, civil service officials, members of Knesset, partisan leaders, activists of organized interest groups, and adherents of unorganized associations act together to promote an objective on which they happen to agree. Such alliances, having no formal structure, lead to a strengthening of personal links among those who devote their time to public affairs. No "triangle" of any sort can be traced. The system is more open than those occupying prominent positions in the state administration would like to admit.

The corporatist incentive is offered by a tradition of coalition that was already evident in the prestate era. The extreme proportional electoral system, which has remained intact since the inception of statehood, made coalition government an inherent part of the political structure. No one single party has ever won a majority in the national elections, and the chances of any party's doing so in the foreseeable future are quite remote. The rules governing a coalition regime are also valid for corporatism: mutual guarantees, shared responsibility, regular and institutionalized consultation, and reciprocity. Coalition governments in Israel have been subject to much criticism for their stagnating nature, and for their inability to represent the voters' interests. The need to form a coalition in order to rule the country allegedly invites minority parties to extort benefits from the plurality party that wants to reign. Despite these faults, the system of government by coalition appears to be appropriate for contemporary Israel.

The political explanation for elitism may be concisely summed up in the phrase "the generation of the wilderness." Israel has passed its fortieth anniversary as a state, but its people are still the "generation of the wilderness" whose absorption in the Promised Land has not yet been completed. The year 1989–1990 was declared the "Year of the Hebrew Language." The idea was to commemorate the 100th year since the rebirth of Hebrew as a spoken language in the land of the Hebrews. Another intention was to purify the language from foreign elements that allegedly cripple it and destroy its authenticity. The project of nation building appears to be continuing despite the fact that the Zionist endeavor in Palestine started a little over one hundred years ago. The Israelis are, as it were, mobilized into a giant army that is preoccupied with both protecting the land and carrying on the mission of the national revival. Although there is in Israel a genuine clamor for "normalization," a major effort at advancing national goals proceeds apace. Among leading Israeli scholars there are those (Dror 1989) who believe that the state of Israel cannot, at its current stage of development, be a "normal" state, one in which individuals can express their desires and articulate their needs through the system of associational activity. The Jews of Israel carry on their backs, perhaps against their most sincere desires, the burden of all the miseries of the Jewish people that were, it was hoped, to be relieved within the framework of a national sovereign entity. This frame of reference acted as the major catalyst for the development of an elite, but it is an elite that at times seems to be too enthusiastic in operating a democracy for the people rather than by them.

A Time Perspective: Whither Israel?

During its forty-odd years of independence, Israeli society has witnessed dramatic changes. The underlying question is whether these changes have also affected the interest group arena and in which way. Implicit in this question is the assumption that an interest group system is shaped by the environment in which it operates and that certain forces within that environment prove to be particularly significant, even if not exclusively so. In the Israeli polity, these forces are said to be, first, the rapid economic development of the country, which turned Israel into a technological society; and second, a change of values, which may have shifted Israel to the post-materialistic era. The ensuing discussion of changes in the interest group arena will focus on the purported contribution of interest group to three areas: the intensification of internal political conflict, the problem-solving capacity of the government, and political participation.

Interest groups and the intensification of political conflict

The underlying question in this area has to do with Israel's adherence to the model of a party-democracy. Are the country's political parties still the sole—or at least the major—actors, fulfilling the role of the invisible hand pulling the strings of all political and social processes? The answer that emerges from this study is equivocal. Partisan leaders still determine the course of politics, they still possess enormous economic powers; and they are the most visible actors on the political scene. But they are no longer the sole actors and they no longer exclusively dominate the scene. The Israeli society has changed since 1948. Important social institutions have been extricated from the parties' grip and "nationalized," as it were, to a greater or lesser degree. The judicial system, free of partisan color, has turned into an important source of policy decisions. Even the state bureaucracy is probably less politicized than in the past. These changes have had clear repercussions on the strategies chosen by interest groups. The idea that the interest group system offers an index of the structure of power in a nation is a recurrent one in the literature (e.g., Pross 1989; Macridis 1961). The preferences of Israeli interest groups may thus serve as a litmus test for the might of the political parties in the polity and their ability to exert influence on relevant policy decisions. The information gathered in this study clearly exposes the vulnerability of the parties to changing times. Contacts with them have lost pace compared with contacts with the other power centers. Interest groups interact more intensively with numerous political authorities. Absent from their list of targets are the political parties.

The contribution of interest groups to the mitigation or, conversely, to the intensification of political social conflict is affected by both the dominance of the parties and the structure of the party system. Since 1977, Israel has undergone two major transformations in the structure of its partisan map. First, the dominant Labor party was replaced by its rival, the Likud; second, the two traditional contenders formed a National Unity government. The first development exacerbated internal political tensions; the second had a moderating effect. Interest groups were involved in both processes. The Likud victory in 1977 represented a milestone in Israeli history, since it marked the country's first major change of guard. Many factors were responsible for Labor's downfall, and not the least of them was the dramatic success of Gush Emunim in influencing the government to yield to its demands. The group did not topple the party in power, but it did uncover its vulnerability, and therefore precipitated its decline.

Owing to the putative strong links between parties and groups, changes might have been expected to spill over into the associational arena. This has hardly been the case. Interest group politics during the Likud era turned out to resemble very closely the patterns that had emerged during the Labor party's control. Initially the Histadrut and the newly formed right-wing government were pitted against each other, but it soon became evident that cooperation was indispensable. The advent of the age of the Likud generated a "disjunction" (LaPalombara 1987: 217), that is, a severance of the connection between formal institutions and public policy making. The Likud controlled the political institutions, but the Labor party, through the Labor Federation, held much of the economic power. Labor also enjoyed the support of the media and the intellectual community. This disjunction may have been detrimental to Israel's economy, but it enabled the transfer of power without commotion, without adversarial group politics.

The ascendancy of the Likud also opened the way for the rise of new associational contenders affiliated with what was termed "second Israel"—the residents of development towns and inner urban neighborhoods. The choices made by the new government effected opportunities for what had been peripheral groups to enter the policy arena. The incorporation of the Sephardim into the locus of power gave vent to repressed hostilities, especially against the kibbutzim. This incorporative process, however, also mitigated social conflict by turning "outsiders" into "insiders." With its legitimation as a political power the Likud generated a new political orbit, with new circling stars. Interest groups that had been closely associated with the past regime were not entirely eclipsed, however. The Histadrut, possessing virtual control of the labor scene, was not excluded from the policy process. The Likud may not have been as friendly to the Labor Federation as was its predecessor, but the realities of political and economic life necessitated some form of collaboration. Interest politics proved, in the end, to be superior to party politics.

The establishment of the National Unity government in 1984 posed another problem for the polity. This time, a disjunction occurred between the election results and the resultant government. The wide gap between the two major partners of the coalition government made it very difficult to determine policies and to decide on priorities. The compromise that enabled the establishment of a two-pronged cabinet nearly choked its ability to shape an agenda. The deadlock in the cabinet was symptomatic of a delicate division of power: the government was on the verge of collapse whenever a major decision was at stake. This stalemate triggered a diffusion of power among other state organs. The Knesset shared some of the spoils,[3] as did the local governments and administrative state agencies. Consequently, interest groups had a wider variety of game at which they could target their arrows. The formation of a National Unity government thus aided, even if indirectly, in broadening the scope of the Israeli political milieu. It shifted power from a cumbersome government apparatus to other decision-making institutions; it expanded the size of the associational constituency; and it contributed to the mitigation of social conflicts. The spirit of unity, even if born of necessity, may have also intensified an already-prevailing harmony in the interest arena. The virtual cooperation between the Histadrut and the employers prevented a class conflict, the weakness of public interest groups prevented a serious challenge to corporate rule shared by Labor. It may be concluded, then, that interest groups have served to mitigate social tensions rather than exacerbate them.

Interest groups and problem-solving capabilities

Is Israel moving toward more corporatism as it progresses in economic development? Events certainly point in a positive direction in answer to this question. For a corporatist system to exist, key organized groups must control their domain of interest; they also must be hierarchically ordered and internally disciplined. The degree of organizational concentration in Israel is perhaps the highest in the democratic world. The corporatist model is a highly technocratic one. Primary influence and responsibility for the formation and implementation of public policies fall into the hands of specialists. In each policy domain, government officials and representatives of the most relevant organized groups get together to decide on policy, or at least to determine the options. In such a system, the experts became the de facto governors (LaPalombara 1987: 219). The advent of the professional and economic groups is usually accompanied, and often set off, by a discernible decline in the power of the legislature, whose policy-making (or "problem-solving") capacity seems to be crippled. The data collected for this work testify, at least partially, to this effect. Interest groups are indeed attracted to the government, and they do forge agreements without parliamentary intervention. There is, however, a fly in this ointment: for liberal corporatism to prevail, the administrative elite must be willing to share power with nongovernmental actors. This prerequisite is not being fulfilled. The hurdles to corporatism in Israel are grounded not only in the alteration of the power structure. Schmitter (1981: 292) has noted that corporatization has tended to develop primarily in politics where the strength or reformist tendencies of social-democratic parties has been the greatest and most protracted. There are exceptions to this rule: France, for example, shows that a strongly interventionist center-right government can produce an anomalous form of "corporatism without labor" (Keeler 1987: 17). In Japan, as Pempel and Tsunekawa (1979: 258) have demonstrated, this "curious anomaly" can be explained largely by the fact that the left has been excluded from governing coalitions since the end of World War II. Corporatist relations have developed, however, between big business and agriculture, the "key sectoral components" of Japan's ruling Liberal Democratic party.

Israel's slow movement toward corporatism was caused neither by the decline in the Labor party's power nor by the advent of a non-Labor party. The chances for the development of a government-by-experts appear to be remote in any party-democracy. In Israel, corporatist practice is much less tangible than it may appear on the surface. The wrong inference may be drawn from the great influence exerted by the major economic groups on wage and income policies. At the turn of the decade, 1990, it appeared that the leading economic ministers might bring organized labor and big business together in a corporatist mode of policy making. But much smoke and very little fire has characterized Israeli corporatism. Interest groups may be part of the policy process, but they are not partners to it. As predicted in the literature, the integration of the economic sectors into the policy process in Israel is evident mainly during crisis situations,

When their agreement is most needed. In this respect, associations do indeed play a major role in advancing the state's problem-solving capabilities. Obviously no economic policy can possibly be concluded without agreement among the major economic actors. Relations, however, remain unstructured. Interest groups in Israel stay on the outside, because the administrative elite so wishes it, and also because they themselves prefer such a posture.

Experts have been gaining increased entrance to the policy process, not as group representatives but as individuals. Israel appears to be advancing more toward the pattern of "policy networks" (Richardson and Jordan 1979) than toward structured corporatism. The differences between a policy network and corporatist structure lies in the degree of stability, continuity, restriction, insulation, interedependence, and shared responsibility for policy implementation. The example of the various Social-Economic Councils demonstrated that the quality of durability has largely been missing, that insulation was virtually impossible and that shared responsibility was shunned by both decision makers and group representatives. Interest groups, thus, do not fare well—or, to be more precise, could have fared better—in contributing to the problem-solving capabilities of the country. This arena is limited to the major economic groups and to a few privileged professional associations, whose contribution is usually confined to technical professional issues rather than to general problems of public policy. The potential of interest groups for making a contribution to the functional effectiveness of government and to its ability to solve the complex problems of a technological society does not seem to be exploited to its fullest extent.

Interest groups' contribution to political participation

One of the principal questions guiding this book dealt with Israel's possible shift toward the post-materialistic era, with a concomitant uprise in the activity of promotional associations. Here, too, the evidence is mixed. On the one hand, political participation has become, since 1967, a regular component of the Israeli political repertoire. The number of interest groups, always relatively large, is much larger now than in the past. Promotional interest groups have not only proliferated in number; they have also attracted attention to issues that heretofore were largely ignored both by public opinion and the authorities. These issues extend to all areas of public policy: the fate of battered wives and children, the components of Jewish identity, the quality of life. The emergence of these groups refutes the assumption that Israel is a country where "there is a lack of free-floating issues" (Arian 1985: 189). The introduction of issues to the agenda is no longer monopolized by the established, sectional interest groups. Issue-oriented associations credit themselves with evoking interest, capturing attention, and rallying support for advocacies that might have stayed submerged under the formal agenda. Promotional interest groups are less fortunate, though, in their ability to push the issues forward and to complete the policy process. One of the striking findings of this study is that in their search for influence, promotional groups have not adopted Western-style pluralistic strategies, but remain "more of the same." They attempt to be more pious than the pope—or, in Israel's case, one might better say, more orthodox than the rabbinate—and to prove they are more loyal to collective ends than their sectional counterparts.

The major findings relating to promotional interest groups may be summed up as follows:

- Promotional associations play a distinctively larger role in initiating issues and attracting public attention to their existence than they did in the past. They are considerably less effective than their sectional counterparts in exercising veto over policy decisions.

- Promotional associations are further removed from the core of power than are their sectional counterparts, they are consulted less in the policy process, and are less involved in solving "technical problems"; they participate less in joint state-group bodies. They also have less informal contacts with decision makers than do sectional associations.

- Therefore, to advance their cause, promotional interest groups target their efforts more at the public than at authorities; they regard the media as a major means of influence.

- Yet, promotional interest groups are also linked to the "old regime" by virtue of three major attributes; first, many of their leaders are also activists in their respective parties; second, they regard "contribution to national goals" as a major raison d'être. Finally, and perhaps most importantly, the activists of promotional associations, more than their counterparts in the sectional category, reject the notion that interest group activity is a sine qua non of a democratic way of life.

Promotional groups, thus, do not seem to play their expected role in shifting Israel toward pluralism. This conclusion does not imply that from a normative perspective, Israel should be moving in this direction; or, from an instrumental perspective, that it stands to gain from such a shift. It does suggest that despite the existence of congenial conditions for post-materialism (enumerated in the Introduction), any predictions about Israel's progress on the road to the post-material era are still premature. In other Western societies, post-materialist movements emphasize the growing importance of the individual in a society controlled by huge organizations and national institutions. The general aim of public interest groups in these societies is to advance the "public" good, but the ultimate goal is to improve the life quality of the individuals in that society. In Israel, the issue-oriented associations adopt a different strategy. In the short term, they do subscribe to ends that fall within the individual domain; their final goal is, however, collective-oriented. In a sense, Israeli promotional associations form the conservative force in the society as they strive to retrieve the halo of ideology rather than to influence Israel to eschew its traditional values. The modest expansion of associations promoting genuine issues of "new politics" may serve as an indication that Israel is basically undergoing a process of "de-westernization." It is moving in a direction opposite to the general trend: from a nonmaterialist society to a materialist one. Post-materialism is awaiting its turn, after the basic requirements of physical and emotional security are fulfilled.

Israel's Interest Group System: A Comparative Perspective

A comparison of national systems of interest groups is a tedious job, since, as Lehmbruch has observed (1983: 154) "interest organizations lend themselves much less to systematic cross-national comparison than political parties and party systems—or elections of parliaments—do." The problem, he pointed out, seems to be due primarily to methodological difficulties. Standardized measurements for a cross-national comparison of party systems are relatively easy to establish; by contrast, systems of interest groups constitute complex configurations that are subject to cross-cultural and cross-national variability. Nevertheless, an attempt will be made in the following pages to place Israel in a comparative perspective in order to reveal in which respects it resembles or, alternatively, differs, from other democratic societies so far as its interest group system. Although any such comparison has obvious limitations—paying attention to but one of an almost endless number of variables can easily distort the picture—the utility of a cross-cultural comparative perspective warrants the effort.

At the outset of this book, it was argued that Israel exhibits strong attributes of three configurations: pluralist, corporatist, and elitist. This unique blend enables comparison to other national configurations. The United States, which has been termed an "Interest Group Society" (Berry 1984), is the classic pluralist country. Historically the interest mediation system was marred by the Madisonian dilemma: the apprehension that factions would pursue their own selfish interests in a manner that would endanger the political system at large. The solution was found, not in prohibiting the right to organize self-interested "factions," but rather in constructing a "pluralist" society in which no one faction (i.e., interest group) could ascent to oppress others. The great variety of interests competing for influence would be a safeguard against the tyranny of the minority. The distribution of power in the interest group arena threatened Madison's formula, since powerful groups were found to have a disproportionate influence on government. The advent of public interest groups, however, widened the scope of representation and imparted increased legitimacy to interest group activity. The call for "balance" (Berry 1984: 213) attempted to rectify some of the injustice caused by the very nature of pluralism.

Israel is, in many respects, diametrically opposed to the United States; it is a small, highly centralized country with a unified system of government imbued with ideology. Yet, the pluralist grain is readily identifiable. Israel, like the United States, has been a melting pot, having taken in an assortment of immigrants; Israel, like the United States, is a pioneering, achievement-oriented society, in which performance and initiative are prime virtues. Both countries were "prairie"countries in which wilderness was turned into blooming gardens. Yet, the flow of power in Israel took a different direction. In the United States, individual initiative, sustained by prosperous group activity, fueled socioeconomic development. The American answer to the question, "Who governs?" was interest groups do. In Israel, despite its pluralistic propensity, this answer would in most cases be unacceptable. Its interest group configuration developed in a totally different, one could say converse, pattern from that of the United States.

The Israeli interest group system may be more akin to the British pattern. In fact, Israel's parliamentary regime was largely molded by British tradition through the British Mandate. If the structure of government bears an influence on the structure and behavior of the representational arena, similarities would be expected to prevail. As in Britain, interest groups in Israel target their activities more at the executive than at the legislative branch of government. Here, however, similarities end. The two fundamental attributes of interest group politics in Great Britain are conspicuously lacking on the Israeli scene: order and compromise. A foreign observer highlighted some of Britain's most exquisite political features in these words:

> . . . the British accommodate conflict through anticipatory adjustment. No one is expected to deny differences, but these are carried on within the overall expectation that each actor will work out his position so as to take account of the vital interests of others. Consultation is the mechanism to allow anticipatory adjustment: it allows a subtle change of desired and acceptable positions. (Wildavsky 1975: 14)

Jordan and Richardson (1987) suggested that policy makers in both government and groups share an interest in avoiding deep rifts and in seeking an acceptable solution. The "logic of negotiations" (Jordan and Richardson 1982: 108) emanates from the British inclination to moderation and the general realization that not much will be accomplished by imposition. Self-restraint is also based on a belief that consultation has a higher legitimacy than uncompromising control. Israeli authorities may be reluctant to engage in outright confrontation, but the spirit of moderation is generally lacking. The political temperature stays high, and conflict, especially in the foreign domain, has become a way of life. A middle-of-the-road solution may occur in the policy process, but for reasons different from those prevailing in the British Isles. In Israeli politics, compromise is precisely the outcome of conflict, rather than the result of an attempt to avoid friction.

With the Scandinavian countries (especially Norway and Sweden), Israel shares a fundamental attribute: these countries espouse a highly developed welfare system, induced by the continuing dominance of Social Democratic rule. As pointed out by Heclo and Madsen (1987: 23): "The dominance of the Social Democratic movement reflects in part raw political power but also in part the subtle influence of ideas." In Sweden, for example, the party's influence is consolidated by an interlocking nexus with the trade union movement, which, as in Israel, serves as a link between the political elite and grassroots membership. "Integrated participation" is the key to understanding the role of groups in policy making. The low level of conflict, the paucity of physical violence, the mild political temperature, and the spirit of accommodation have produced a very large network of institutionalized joint group-state decision-making forums. The practice of including interest groups in the policy arena is not confined to the economic organizations. "The tendency is that groups who so far have been absent from, or marginal in, the bureaucratic-corporate system are co-opted: artists, pensioned people, Lapps, the handicapped, and so on" (Olsen et al, 1982: 75). The upshot of this development is that political parties have been deprived of their hegemony as intermediary between the people and the government, while the locus of public policy making has moved from a parliamentary to a bureaucratic-corporative arena (Rokkan 1966; Heisler and Kvavik 1974).

In Israel, neither the priciples of the welfare society nor the past hegemony of the Labor party induced the institutionalization of corporate structures. The fusion of the party with its affiliated organizations had rendered these structures superfluous. On the other hand, the electoral decline of the Labor movement did not give impetus to the corporatist drive. New groups were given entry into the policy arena. But eligibility for inclusion was still, to a large extent, determined by an ideological litmus test or by electoral prospects. Corporatist structures do not constitute the locus of public policy mating..

West Germany also provides an opportunity for comparison. The Federal Republic of Germany has been known since 1949 as a *Parteienstaat* (a party-state), its political parties enjoying disproportionate influence on public life, including permeation of the state bureaucracy. These parties, however, were not the major actors in forging national sovereignty, but they emerged from the second World War "indisputably as the most 'reliable' institutions with the full support of the Allies" (Dyson 1977: 22). Yet policy making in West Germany is guided by three principles that are for the most part largely lacking in Israel: rationality of an objective through examination of all policy options; order, which relates policy proposals in a rationalistic manner to basic constitutional tenets that are sometimes interpreted as mandating certain policies; and finally, collaboration, which emphasizes the need to accommodate group pressures in order to maintain social peace (Dyson 1982: 44). Needless to say, Israel is quite far from the "rationality" and "order" that depict the German political culture. The style of policy making in the Jewish state is marked by disorganization, spontaneous reactions to critical events, and short-term considerations. The absence of a written constitution and the relentless refusal of the legislature down through the years to enact a constitution despite the growing public concern with the issue provide another indication of the unwillingness of the political elite to commit the country to rigid, long-term arrangements. The Israeli body politic still fears that a written document prescribing the principles of the polity would destabilize the society that presumably has yet to conclude the era of transition and change. Despite the similarities in the role of political parties in West Germany and Israel, their respective impact on interest group politics differs significantly.

Italy and France present attributes that enable a more tenable comparison with the Israeli scene. Like West Germany, Italy is a party-democracy. One of the leading experts on its government, LaPolombara (1987: 215), termed it a "partitocrazia," i.e., a system in which parties are more central than any other governing body. Political parties not only run the operations of most governmental institutions; their role in the system is actually self-sustaining. They have replaced the legislature, the executive, the bureaucracy, and even the courts. The epitome of partitocrazia "involves wheeling and dealing by the secretaries general, and a few other notables, of the political parties. . . . One has the impression of a continuing 'summit meeting' among men who may or may not be cabinet members but who nevertheless exercise powers of life and death over them, and over public policies as well' (LaPalombara 1987: 216). This description could almost have been applied to the Israeli polity, except for several important differences. To begin with, Italy does not present the centralized features of the Israeli democracy. The organizational interests of both the Italian trade unions and Italy's employers are largely fragmented; the country is not united by an overall consensus. Nor is Italy fighting for its survival. Another major difference is the weakness of the cabinet, whose short life span has become a hallmark of the Italian regime.

The strong state is the one major attribute that lends itself to a comparison of France and Israel. The active role played by the state in the political process constitutes the major feature of French politics. The power of the executive of the Fifth Republic gives its personnel the dominant role in policy making. This configuration has a marked influence on interest politics, described by Wilson:

> The remote and sometimes authoritarian executive places important limits on interest-group influence. The executive is aloof from the pressure of everyday politics and is very powerful. Just as it has often restricted the policy-making role of the parliament, it can and does limit the involvement of groups in

the decision process on issues where the government had made a major commitment. The government can choose which groups to hear and whether or not to give heed to the warnings or pleas of the groups. (1987: 249)

This description neatly fits the Israeli scene. Furthermore, the French, like the Israelis, have a deep suspicion of sectarian interests and of the self-serving advocacies that contrast with the "general will." The denunciation of fragmentation is rooted in France's historical experiences. The French assert that division paralyzed and destroyed the Fourth Republic and that the purpose of the institutions of the Fifth Republic is to govern above these interests. The Israelis' abhorrence of factionalism goes further into the past. They believe that they lost their ancient sovereignty because of internal squabbles. Differences between the French and Israeli polities are, though, clearly visible. France is characterized by a conspicuous absence of consensus, which is apparent both on the national scene and in the interest group arena. Ideological and personality clashes prevent the emergence of any single group to represent the interests of most social categories. Rival associations are in conflict with one another, both within sectors and between categories. As Wilson pointed out: "They must devote much of their limited resources to these internecine battles, reducing the time and energy they have to try to influence government" (1987: 246). This is hardly the situation in Israel, which is characterized by a high degree of centralization and monopolization and by little rivalry both within and between social categories.

Finally, Israel is also, in some respects, a developing country, especially in terms of its population composition (more than half originated in Third World societies), but also in terms of the objective set by its political elite: to generate a structure enabling the achievement of both economic development and national integration at one and the same time. In this respect, Israel might be compared with India and Turkey, whose systems of interest groups have been extensively studied. Interest politics in these two countries feature a delicate balance between the democratic right to express demands and the inability of the state, weighed down with excessive problems, to respond to those demands. The two states portray totally different features regarding almost all aspects of social and political life—Turkey and India differ markedly. The latter is crisscrossed by linguistic, ethinc, religious, and social cleavages that pose a grave problem to its integrity. It has, however, been governed (until 1989) by a hegemonic party, thus providing stability to the federative political structure. Turkey, on the other hand, is more homogeneous from a social perspective, but is torn by intense political friction and a polarized party system. Both nations faced the challenge of economic development and the dilemmas attendant on such development. Since both states were basically committed to democracy, they attempted to resolve, in a relatively non-coercive fashion, certain tensions in political development that arose owing to the rapid emergence and diffusion of associational interest groups. The solutions found in each of the two states, however, were different. In India, the government attempted to direct its relationship with organized groups such that they would not make demands at all but would, instead, lend their support to development programs. This was done, inter alia, by socializing the groups into a public philosophy that preached limits on demands through "an awareness of what is possible." Interest groups, Weiner has argued, "must learn to consider the effects of their demands upon others; and they must make demands within the rules of a democratic system" (1968: 227). In Turkey, the government has relied less on philosophy and more on political measures, including discriminatory legislation and state coercion, to confine access in the functional arena to controllable corporatist groups and to limit the maneuverability of more militant, pluralist groups, particularly in the matter of plebiscites (Bianchi 1984: 372).

Israel shares with both Turkey and India the challenges of rapid economic development; it, too, has evinced discernible changes in many facets of life. Yet it still presents an interest configuration different from that of both Turkey and India. On the one hand, Israel has a tradition of democratic rule that long antedates its independence as a modern state. More than these two developing societies, furthermore, Israel has incorporated into its polity and society the ideas and norms of Western liberal societies. It does face internal dangers, but these are caused not as much by domestic friction, as they are by the small state's external problems.

The foregoing comparative analysis highlights what Israel shares with other countries. It also highlights the peculiarites of the scene which give rise to Israeli interest politics. These were brightly exposed in the enunciation of one of its political leaders, who wrote the following in reference to Mancur Olson's thesis on the contribution of interest groups organized in a "coalition of distribution" to diminishing economic growth: "Indeed, what the Israeli economy needs is a 'coalition of growth'. Divisive lobbies are certainly not lacking in the Knesset—lobbies whose purpose it is to accord benefits to a specific group or interest, without indicating where the means are to come. The Knesset needs a lobby for the state, not only for individual sectors."[4]

A review of the major points of comparison (shown in figure 10.1) indicates that Israel may be unique only in the specific *combination* of attributes presented by interest group politics. This blend, however, calls for possible refinement of the available theories.

Fig. 10.1. Israeli Interest Groups in a Comparative Perspective

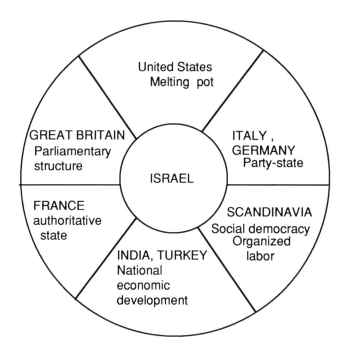

The Israeli Case and Interest Group Theory

Drawing generalizations and reviewing theories on the basis of a single case study is of marginal benefit. It is possible, however, to show how this particular case of Israel fits with broader theories and, on the basis of its deviation, to posit some hypothetical propositions. After delineating the peculiarities of the

Israeli case, this final section will attempt to re-evaluate existing theory on the basis of three variables: sequential development, internal coherence, and conclusiveness.

The uniqueness of the Israeli case

Israel does not conform to any of the models outlined at the beginning of this book and largely deviates from patterns prevailing in other democracies, which served as an empirical basis for constructing the theories. Israel's major deviation from these models is manifested in an incoherence among the components of the interest group configurations, as follows:

- The *structures* of the Israeli body politic are basically corporatist. The state is highly centralized, and so are its major (and even minor) interest groups. High membership density, lack of diversification, near monopoly over domains of interest, high internal discipline, official state recognition ("representative status"), and semi-voluntary membership compose the interest group parameters that place Israel extremely high on the scale of corporatism. When the role of the state as a key public actor is added, the picture of corporatism is almost untainted.

- The *behavior* of Israeli interest groups, however, is far from fitting the corporatist model. Pressure was found to be a major strategy of influence. Israel interest groups interact with public authorities, and do so intensively; but neither their leaders nor senior public administrators (representing the "state") share a sense of mutual responsibility and reciprocal commitment. On the contrary, the relationship is tainted with much rivalry rather than cooperation, which is by no means institutionalized.

- Pluralist practices of interaction between interest groups and the authorities in Israel may be exhibited, but they are not sustained by pluralist *norms and values.* On the contrary, the major values guiding interest group behavior are derived from the elitist configuration: the predominance of the national interest over the needs of the individual; the commitment to pursue the welfare of the nation and to make individual sacrifices in order to advance collective ends. "My country, right or wrong" is still an accepted tenet in Israel society, of which interest groups form an integral part.

The combination of corporatist structures, pluralist behavior, and elitist norms is illustrated graphically in figure 10.2. It has been suggested that some confusion may arise in applying an interest group model if parameters consists of generalizations based on empirical evidence derived from micro- or even meso-level analysis (Wassenberg 1982: 84–85). The evidence presented in this work, however, based as it is on data collected from a national sample covering all sectors, cuts across these levels, and therefore enables some cautious generalizations. What implications do the idiosyncrasy of the Israeli case hold for interest group theory?

Fig. 10.2. Characteristics of Israeli Interest Group Politics

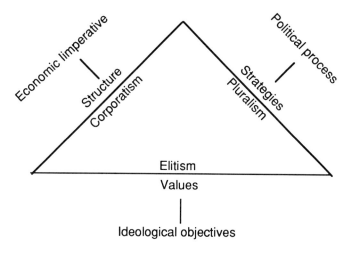

Sequential development

The development of interest politics was said to be caused by transformations of society and the economy: increasing social complexity, shifts in the economy that alter relations among economic sectors, an increased role played by the state in social and economic affairs, the growing inability of political parties to propose coherent programs, and the declining effectiveness of traditional bureaucratic techniques. These are bound to lead to corporatism (Berger 1981: 18–19). A major contention (presented by Schmitter) was that the more voluntarist, fragmented, and unstable pluralist mode of representation corresponded to social and economic systems that have been irreversibly altered. Thus the reallocation of political functions among interest groups, parties, and state reflects changes that are taking place in modern democratic societies. Corporatism has more or less spread to all developed countries, with variations in pace and scope (Schmitter 1981). Its sequential development has been attributed to the deficiencies of pluralism, which assumes a competitive political marketplace, individualism and voluntarism, and, especially as Cawson phrased it, ". . . portrayal of a neutral state which is disengaged from interest conflicts at the same time as it preserves an institutional and ideological boundary between public and private spheres" (1985: 2).

Sequential development might have been expected in Israel, which has advanced in forty-odd years from a stage of rudimentry economic development to advanced industrialization. Corporatist structures have nevertheless failed to follow suit. The law of sequential development is thus invalidated in this case owing to a "missing link" between a structure favoring corporatism and its political outputs, the normative milieu in which these structures develop.

Internal coherence

Both major theories of interest groups, corporatism and pluralism, have been treated as a Gestalt (Williamson 1985: 192; 1989: 187); that is, their use as an analytical tool was most valuable when their various components were examined in terms of interrelationships. The two models were also said to exhibit some form of interdependence among their variables. Schmitter suggested that "the strong hypotheses would be that concertation cannot work without monopolistic, hierarchically ordered, officially recognized, clearly delimited associations and that, inversely, once concertation is established it *must* encourage the development of these properties in collaborating interest organizations" (1989: 65; emphasis mine).

Especially pertinent to the validity of the models is the linkage between structures and modes of behavior; that is, between the ways in which interests are organized and the ways in which decisions are made and implemented. Up to now, studies of interest groups focusing on the corporatist model (e.g., Wilson 1987) regarded the two variables as interrelated. The Israeli case indicates that under certain circumstances—e.g., when norms and behaviors are incongruent—structures and behavioral modes need not co-vary. The fact that interest groups in Israel tend to pressure rather than coordinate their activities with state authorities does not necessarily imply that the system operates according to the principles of a free political market.

Conclusiveness

The two theories of interest group politics that have prevailed until now were each presented as an alternative. As Schmitter pointed out, "One purpose in developing this elaborate general model . . . is to offer to the political analyst an explicit alternative to the paradigm of interest politics which has heretofore completely dominated the discipline of North American political science: pluralism" (1979: 14). Much criticism has been raised against the purported distinctiveness of the corporatist model from the pluralist model (Almond 1983; Jordan 1981, 1984). Grant Jordan, for one, has argued that the lines separating the two are superficial at best. "Corporate pluralism" is, in fact, not easily distinguishable from corporatism (Jordan 1984: 147). The proponents of corporatism nevertheless hold to the claim that the theory "not only provides an alternative, it provides a valuable alternative framework through which to examine organized interests in contemporary liberal democracies" (Williamson 1989: 192). The effort to distinguish corporatism from its pluralist counterpart is not designed to keep a number of corporatist analysts "gainfully employed"; it is meant to impart a recognition that the behavior of organized interests and their relationship with state authorities can be seen from a different position.

The debate between the corporatists and the pluralists is indeed lively and stimulating (for an excellent summary, see Williamson 1989); but the third model, which provides an alternative to both pluralism and corporatism, seems to have received little attention. This book has attempted to offer at least a preliminary contribution to the development of a third option, one based on incongruity among norms, structures, and behavior. The unique blend offered by Israel, where interest groups find themselves torn between *Gemeinschaft* and *Gesellschaft*, speak the language of collectivism, organize in structures of corporatism, and act as though they are competitors in a free market, may offer new insights into interest group theory and research.

APPENDIX A

List of Interest Groups Surveyed

Trade unions (22)

A.M.I. (Union of Israeli Artists)
Federation of Clerks
Federation of Construction Workers
Federation of Diamond Employees
Federation of Hotel Workers
Federation of Metal Workers
Federation of Nurses
Federation of Pilots
Federation of Print Workers
Federation of Retired Employees
Federaton of Technicians
Federation of Wood Craftsmen
Histadrut—General Federation of Labor
Union of Air Controllers
Union of Ceramic Workers
Union of Dental Technicians
Union of Food Workers
Union of Movie Directors
Union of Producers
Union of Sea Workers
Union of State Employees
Union of Writers

Business groups (23)

Association of Artisans and Small Industry
Association of Plastics Producers
Bureau of Insurance Agents
Center of Contractors & Builders
Chamber of Commerce
Electronics Industry Association
Farmers Union
Israel Manufacturers Association
Israel Tour Operators Association
Lahav (Association of Self-Employed)
Organization of Suppliers
Union of Advertisers
Union of Bankers
Union of Customs Agents
Union of Garage Owners
Union of Hotel Owners
Union of Insurance Companies
Union of Investment Administrators
Union of Israeli Ship Owners
Union of Landlords
Union of Merchants
Union of Movie Owners
Union of Nature Shops

Professional associations (19)

Association of Optometrists
Association of Orthodox Scientists
Association of Physiotherapists
Association of Tourists' Guides
Association of Writers
Bureau of Accountants
Bureau of Engineers
Engineers Federation
Federation of Academics in Humanities and Social Sciences
Federation of Microbiologists and Chemists
Federation of Pharmacists
Israel Bar Association
Israel Dental Association
Israel Medical Association

Teachers Federation
Union of Interior Architects
Union of Pharmacists
Union of Post-Elementary School Teachers
Union of Social Workers

Farmer and settlement organizations (15)

Amana (Gush Emunim settlement organization)
Gardening and Landscape
Kibbutz Artzi
Moshavim Movement
Organization of Banana Growers
Organization of Herut Settlements
Organization of Nursery Owners
Takam
Union of Agriculture Workers
Union of Fish Growers
Union of Flower Growers
Union of Fruit Growers
Union of Land Cultivators
Union of Vegetable Growers
Yesha (Council of Settlements of Judea, Samaria, and Gaza)

Categoric groups (17)

Association of Vegetarians
Cystic Fibrosis Society
Klaf (Association of Lesbians)
Men for a Decent Divorce
Multiple Sclerosis Society
Organization for the Protection of Tenants
Organization of People Sensitive to Gluten
Organization of Prisoners of the Nazi Regime
Organization of the IDF Handicapped
Organization of the Nazi Persecution Handicapped
Roof Organization of the Handicapped
Shema (Organization of the Deaf)
Society for Diabetes
Society for Individual Rights
Students Union

Tzevet (Organization of Officer Veterans)
Union of Veterans

Immigrant associations (12)

Alliance of Immigrants from Buchara
Association of American and Canadian Immigrants in Israel
Association of Brazilian Immigrants
Association of British Immigrants
Association of Dutch Immigrants
Beta Israel (Association of Ethiopian Jews)
Federation of French and North African Immigrants
Union of Ethiopian Immigrants
Union of Iranian Immigrants
Union of Latin American Immigrants
Union of Rumanian Immigrants
Union of Soviet Russian Immigrants

Public interest groups (22)

A.L.E. (Prevention of Emigration)
Civil Rights Association
Consumers Council
Consumers Union
Council for a Beautiful Israel, The
Council for Prevention of Traffic Accidents
Efrat (Pro-Life Association)
Eli (Association for Child Protection)
Malraz (Noise and Air Pollution Prevention)
Movement for Rebuilding the Temple
Naamat
Orientals for Peace
Peace Now
Shedula (Women's Lobby)
Shutfut (For the Advancement of Arab-Jewish Understanding)
Society for Better Housing
Society for Family Planning
Society for Prevention of Cruelty to Animals
Society for Prevention of Smoking
Society for Protection of Nature

WIZO
Woman to Woman

Welfare associations (19)

Akim (Society for Rehabilitating the Retarded)
Al Sam (Anti-Drug Association)
Alkan (Society for Learning Disabilities)
Alut (Society for Autistic Children)
Association for Prevention of Alcoholism
Association for Soldiers, The
Association for the Deaf
Association for the Prevention of Sexual Abuse
Cancer Society
E.D.I. (Society for the Advancement of Organ Transplants)
Hand to Hand
Heart to Heart
Keshev (Society for the Hard of Hearing)
Maas
Micha (Society for Educating the Deaf)
Nitzan (Association for Learning Disabilities)
Society for the Protection of Children, The
Yad Sarah (Surgical Appliances Aid)
Zehavi (Association for Large Families)

Sports, cultural, and religious associations (13)

Akum (Society for Preserving the Rights of Composers and Musicians)
Association for Diving
Association for Progressive Judaism
Association of Bridge Players
Bnei Akiva
Chess Union
Israel Basketball Association
Israel Sport Association
Lapid (Movement for Teaching the Lessons of the Holocaust)
Maccabi
Olymic Committee
Society of Friends of the Hebrew University
Union of Parents

APPENDIX B

The Interest Group Questionnaire

1. Year of Founding
2. Number of members/volunteers
3. Percentage of members of those eligible for membership
4. Number of employees in central office
5. Annual budget (1988) in shekels
6. Does the state/Jewish Agency fund the association? No; Yes
7. Does a political party fund the association? No; Yes
8. What is the internal electoral system? Personal; Lists affiliated with parties
9. Has the general meeting been convened on its designated date? No; Yes
10. How long is the incumbency of the present chairperson? Under 8 years; Over 8 years
11. Is there any limit to a chairperson's incumbency? No; Yes
12. How would you rate membership participation? Low; Medium; High
13. Are there major divergencies within the association? Hardly; To some Extent; Many
14. How are controversies settled? Majority vote; Compromise; Imposing discipline
15. What is the degree of centralization? Low; Medium; High
16. Have there been incidents of a serious challenge to leadership? Rarely; Some; Many
17. Is the opposition granted a voice in your publication? Rarely; Occasionally; Often
18. Does your association operate under the auspices of a roof organization? No; Yes

19. What is the frequency of interaction with other groups? Low; Medium; High
20. Do you regard other groups as competitors? No; To some extent; Yes
21. What is the major objective of your association? (a) To advance the interests of its members; (b) To contribute to society
22. Is your organizaton represented on a state council/board/committee? No; Yes
23. What is the major function of such a body? (a) Solving technical problems; (b) Attaining agreement of policy issues; (c) Implementing policy
24. Do government officials consult with your association regarding an issue pertinent to its interests? No; Almost never; Occasionally; Almost always
25. To what end is such consultation aimed? (a) Seeking opinion; (b) Seeking agreement; (c) Seeking retroactive consent for decisions already adopted
26. Have you ever encountered the refusal of a state official to meet with you? No; Yes
27. Have you ever encountered the refusal of a cabinet minister to meet with you? No; Yes
28. Have you met with a cabinet minister in the past year? No; Yes
29. Have you requested to meet the minister? No; Yes
30. In the past decade how have contacts with government ministries changed? (a) Weakened; (b) Remained the same; (c) Strengthened; (d) No contacts with a government ministry
31. Have you been approached by an MK in the past year? No; Yes—once; Yes—several times
32. Have you appeared before a Knesset committee in the past year? No; Once; Several times
33. Have you ever been denied the right to appear in a Knesset committee? No; Yes; Never requested to appear
34. Is there a "lobby" acting on your organization's behalf in the Knesset? No; Yes
35. Is an MK a member of your board? No; Yes
36. In the past decade, how have contacts with the Knesset changed? (a) Weakened; (b) Remained the same; (c) Strengthened; (d) No contacts with the Knesset
37. Did you appeal to a political party in the course of the last election campaign in an attempt to include a plank in its platform? No; Yes
38. Has any political party appealed to you during the past year with an offer or a request? No; Yes

39. Is any member of your leadership a member of a party central committee? No; Yes
40. Is any member of your leadership a senior state official? No; Yes
41. Does your association elect (or select) a candidate for one of the political party lists? No; Yes
42. In the past decade, how have contacts with political parties changed? (a) Weakened; (b) Remained the same; (c) Strengthened; (d) No contacts with political parties
43. Do you agree with the assumption that political parties are the source of power in the country? Disagree; Agree with reservation; Unequivocally agree
44. In your opinion, in what body are the decisions most important to your association arrived at? (a) Cabinet; (b) Knesset; (c) Civil service; (d) Political party; (e) Organization itself; (f) Other

Please state the frequency with which you have resorted to the following strategies during the past 3 years:

	None	Low	Medium	High
		Frequency		
45. Demonstrations or strikes				
46. Appeal to court				
47. Personal meeting with elite members				
48. Deliberations in joint state-group bodies				
49. Mass media				
50. Appeal to a member of Knesset				
51. Appeal to a state official				
52. Appeal to a partisan leader or institution				
53. Other				

54. What do you prefer to do when you encounter unresponsiveness? (a) Appeal to the public; (b) Appeal directly to decision makers; (c) There is no use in appealing to anybody; (d) Did not encounter unresponsiveness
55. Is your association a "representative organization"? No; Yes
56. If not, do you request such a status? No; Yes
57. The policy pertinent to your interests has been formulated (a) Owing to the association's initiative; (b) Cooperation with authorities; (c) Despite the association's objection; (d) The policy predated the group's formation
58. Does the association contribute to implement government policy? No; Yes
59. According to your experience, what has been the reaction of the authorities in most cases to your appeals? (a) Fully responsive; (b) Willing to arrive at a joint solution; (c) Favorable attitude that is not followed by action; (d) Unresponsiveness

60. Has your association been successful in exercising a veto over a policy proposal? (a) There is no need to veto, since decisions are arrived at in cooperation with the association; (b) No, veto is posible only under exceptional circumstances; (c) Yes, a decision cannot be enforced in the face of the group's adamant opposition

61. Please state the most important factor determining the association's success. (a) Association's resources; (b) Functional role the association plays in society; (c) Association's contribution to the fulfillment of national goals

62. It is often asserted that interest groups act selfishly, disregarding the interests of society at large. Do you agree with this assertion? No; Somewhat; Yes

63. What is the major contribution of interest groups to society? (a) Interest groups contribute to democratic life; (b) Interest groups contribute to the efficiency of government; (c) Interest groups contribute to the fulfillment of national goals; (d) Interest groups do not contribute anything to society

64. What, according to your experience, has been the most effective means to influence decision makers?

APPENDIX C

Questionnaire to Senior Government Officials

1. Please identify the principal source of influence on policy making. (a) The minister; (b) Ministry director-general; (c) Political party; (d) Interest group; (e) Professional advisor; (f) Other

2. Interaction with interest group representatives: (a) Frequent; (b) Rare; (c) Non-existent

3. Purpose of most interactions with interest groups is:
(a) Acquire views or opinions on a proposed policy;
(b) Attempt to reach concurrence;
(c) Bring notification of a decision already adopted;
(d) Other

4. What, in your opinion, is the major contribution of interest groups to the ministry's daily activities?
(a) Interest groups play a major role in setting the agenda;
(b) Interest groups aid the ministry to deliver its programs and implement its policy;
(c) Interest groups mobilize their members to support the ministry's programs;
(d) Other

5. What, in your view, is the major disadvantage of contacting interest groups?
(a) Encourages too much pressure on the bureaucracy;
(b) Leads to favoring certain groups over others;
(c) Prevents the bureaucracy from advancing the national interest
(d) Other

6. What, in your opinion, is the major advantage of consulting interest groups?
(a) consultation is indispensable in a democratic form of government;

(b) Leads to a more rational policy;

(c) Enables effective mobilization of support;

(d) Other

7. As you see it, should interest groups be regularly consulted in the process of policy making? Yes; No; Yes in principle, depends on . . .

8. How would you characterize relationships between the ministry and interest groups in the past decade? (a) Weakened; (b) Remained the same; (c) Strengthened

Notes

Chapter One. The Israeli Polity

1. For example, for the elections to the 12th Knesset (1988), the Labor party granted representation on its Knesset list to seven constituencies: Tel Aviv, Haifa, Jerusalem, Moshavim, Kibbutzim, the northern region, and the southern region. The National Religious party (NRP) divided its list among its four organized factions. Even the small party of the Independent Liberals divided its five realistic places among different constituencies.

2. *Jerusalem Post*, December 27, 1979.

3. Ibid. March 21, 1975.

4. After resigning from premiership, Ben-Gurion settled in a surprise move in a Negev kibbutz (Sde Boker). He explained his withdrawal from office by the need to take a repose from political life.

5. The Lavon Affair that originated with the capture of an Israeli-led intelligence network in Egypt (1954) caused a crisis in the Israeli defense establishment. It brought about the resignation of Defense Minister Lavon, who was charged with having the responsibility for the ill-advised order to activate an Israeli-led intelligence network to carry out acts of sabotage in Egypt, in an attempt to delay the evacuation of the British Army from that country. The establishment of a judicial inquiry commission did not clear up the issue and did not reveal the culprits. Ben-Gurion resigned when his call for renewed and thorough investigation of the affair was rejected by Mapai's leadership. A comprehensive analysis of the Lavon Affair may be found in Yanai (1969).

6. The number of Knesset mandates gained by the Labor party (Alignment) in the 1973 election to the 8th Knesset dropped from fifty-six in the 1969 elections to fifty-one.

7. Although the documentation relating to party finance is sparse, testimonies of those involved (e.g. Asher Yadlin, a former Labor party's leader) indicate that the "system" (i.e., diverting public funds for party

needs) has long been in operation. A word of caution is in order: Yadlin's evidence should be taken with reservation, since he was convicted of fraud and held a grudge against his co–party-members (Labor) who allegedly deserted him despite his life-long devoted service.

8. Before the final agreements with the EEC were concluded in 1987, 70 percent of imports to Israel required licensing (*Free Economy* 1988).

9. *Haaretz,* July 21, 1989.

10. The government companies included, among others, the Israeli Electricity Company, the national airline El Al, Israel Chemicals, Israel Aviation Industry, the Dead Sea Works, Mekorot and Tahal (water resource planning and distribution).

11. The phenomenon, of course, is not unique to the Israeli economy. See Arian 1985: 31.

12. *Haaretz,* September 15, 1989.

13. *Jerusalem Post,* July 8, 1985.

14. The porfolios granted authority to enact emergency regulations in 1948 were: defense, finance, commerce and industry, agriculture, transportation, interior, immigration, and the prime minister's office. In 1967 the ministry of labor was added; in 1976, the ministry of health; in 1979, the ministry of energy and infrastructure (Mironi 1983: 7).

15. The lists were: Agudat Israel, the NRP, Etz Hatora, Shas, Meimad (a dovish national religious splinter party), and Yahad Shivtei Israel (Yemenite defectors from Shas). The two last lists have failed to secure a mandate.

16. One recent example is the blocking of the attempt to enact a civil rights law (in November 1989). Future prospects of coalition alignment with religious parties opposing the law impeded legislation that enjoyed a wide consensus among Knesset members of the two major blocs.

Chapter Two. The Universe of Interest Groups

1. *Maariv,* March 13, 1989.

2. *Haaretz,* April 5, 1989.

3. In 1986, 68 percent of the Arabs and Druze workers in Israel were members of the Histadrut (Histadrut 1986: 4).

4. In the early days of the association, an employer of at least six workers was eligible to join the ranks of the MA; subsequently, the

minimum was raised to twenty in order to demarcate between "manufacturers" and the owners of small businesses. The development of personal computer and computer software industries in the 1970s necessitated re-evaluation of membership eligibility, which at present is determined by a special committee.

5. For example, the private sector was originally underrepresented in the Bureau of the Employment Service, established in 1959. They were also adversely affected by legislation regarding inheritance tax, enacted in the early 1960s.

6. These include a religious association, which focuses on protecting the interests of the observant, and an independent Consumers Union, which despite its title is said to be affiliated with the Liberal party. The third group was formed by a former American physician, who has tried to emulate, albeit with very little success, consumer societies operating in his country of origin. Finally there is a group, MIDA, that represents the interests of the merchants themselves; rather than fighting the consumer organizations, those selling the products have decided to join them. This particular type of association is engaged mostly in treating complaints regarding defective merchandise.

7. *New York Times*, November 6, 1988.

8. Peace Now institutionalized by setting up permanent headquarters and for the first time hiring an administrative staff. The purpose of these moves was to expand the movement's operations outside the big cities and to lobby the Knesset more effectively (*Jerusalem Post*, April 4, 1989).

9. The most active of these groups are Enough to Occupation (Dei Lakibush), the 21st Year, A Red Line, A Women's Tribe, and Women in Black. All these protest groups were formed after the inception of the *intifada*. Their members, many of whom are writers and artists, reject the occupation and Israel's policy toward the Palestinian population.

10. One of these groups—Yesh Gvul—has invigorated its activity during the *intifada*. It called for conscientious refusal to serve one's military duty in the occupied territories. Some of its members were jailed for violating army orders by refusing to serve there. In the past the few incidents of refusal to do reserve duty were intermittent. Yesh Gvul for the first time presented an organized challenge to military authorities, although extremely limited in scope.

11. Zahavi operates through a national office and twenty-three branches scattered around the country. Its board of directors includes famous national figures.

12. The orthodox community also abounds with hundreds of learning institutions, registered as associations whose purpose is to solicit

funds. These are outside the purview of this study, which focuses on those associations acting for political purposes.

13. Yad Leachim has twelve branches across the country; its annual budget runs to over a million dollars.

14. There is one exception to this rule: the Union of Post-Elementary School Teachers withdrew in 1958 from the Teachers Federation and operates autonomously, outside the confines of the Histadrut.

Chapter Three. Interest Groups and Political Parties

1. One of the devices adopted by Labor in order to safeguard its power was to change the electoral rules. In 1988, kibbutz and moshav members were entitled to vote for urban local councils and thus tipped the scale in favor of Labor-affiliated parties. Until then, kibbutz and moshav members had voted in the national Histadrut elections, but not for local councils. The Likud remonstrated against this blatant gerrymandering but to no effect (*Jerusalem Post*, May 12, 1989).

2. The exception is Mapam, half of whose membership comes from the Kibbutz Artzi movement.

3. It is not always easy to determine which minister was actually a kibbutz or moshav member, since some Israeli senior politicians have been known to stretch the truth a little with such a claim. The most noted of these was Levi Eshkol, Israel's premier from 1963 to 1968, who avowed he was a member of Degania, located at the southern tip of Lake Kinneret, although he lived in Jerusalem most of his life.

4. Haim Oron, secretary-general of Kibbutz Artiz, *Hedim*, 122, November 1985.

5. *Maariv*, September 28, 1988.

6. Yitzhak Raz, *Engineers and Architects*, October 1988.

7. the percentage of the Labor vote in Gur's hometown, Ashdod, actually declined from 26.2 in 1984 to 23.4 in 1988. *Results of elections to the 12th Knesset*. Central Bureau of Statistics. Special Series no. 855, p. 62.

8. For example, the Labor-backed members in the student union have only one representative in the party's central committee, 1,200 members, and four representatives in the party's assembly, which is comprised of some 3,000 delegates.

9. Until 1985, there were no legal restrictions on a list's objectives. In July of that year, the Knesset approved an amendment to the Basic Law whereby a list is denied participation in the elections if its goals or

activities include explicit or implicit refusal to accept Israel as the state of the Jewish nation, a rejection of Israel's democratic features, and/or an incitement to racism. Only one list (Kach, led by Meir Kahana) has since been denied (after losing an appeal to the Supreme Court) the right to contest for the election.

10. An exception was a list for the 11th Knesset in 1984: the Integration of Immigrants from India.

11. For each year of employment, a worker who belongs to the pension scheme accumulates 2 percent of his or her pension rights; thus after thirty-five working years, one retires with 70 percent of the last salary. But all benefits and allowances, such as telephone, a car mileage, special insurance payments, etc. are not figured in; in reality, therefore the pension may amount to no more than 42 percent of the last salary. The pension, furthermore, is paid on the basis of the last rank before retirement; this rank remains fixed although standards of ranking are constantly changing.

12. Moledet secured 1.9 percent (44,174 votes) of the total vote in the 1988 elections.

13. One notable example of a promotional group's appealing to a political party is Yesha's request presented to Herut's center to undermine the government's 1989 peace initiative. *Haaretz*, May 25, 1989.

14. At the time of this writing, the minister of agriculture, a member of a Negev kibbutz, dismantled Tnuva-Export, an agricultural export company owned by the kibbutz movement, whose mismanagement and severe financial losses were not covered up by loyalties based on a parentela relationship.

Chapter Four. State and Groups

1. *Divrei HaKnesset* (Minutes of the Knesset), December 6, 1954 (17): 254.

2. Ibid., p. 250.

3. Ibid, p. 257.

4. Generally speaking, Arabs were not members of Zionist parties, except for Mapam. See Yishai 1982b.

5. SCJ 253/64 *Jiryis* vs. *District Commissioner*.

6. Ibid., p. 679.

7. The minister of justice, Dov Yoseph, explained this exclusion by stating that "it is inappropriate to limit parties' activity by excessive formalities" *Divrei HaKnesset*, March 23, 1965 (42): 1643.

8. Ibid., April 6, 1965 (42): 1789.

9. Ibid., p. 1796.

10. Ibid., December 3, 1979 (87): 719.

11. Ibid., p. 733.

12. Ibid., July 28, 1980 (89): 4128.

13. The appointment of an audit of religious association first required consultation with the director-general of the ministry of religious affairs.

14. *Jerusalem Post*, June 13, 1989.

15. It might be noted that three of the officials interviewed demonstrated an outright rejection of a group's "contribution" to the ministry's activity.

16. One of these came from the ministry of transportation and another from the ministry of energy, each of which ministry is exposed to extremely powerful and continuous pressures: from the oil companies, the Electric Company, and the public transport companies. The two others showed derogatory attitudes toward promotional interest groups (in the welfare and environmental categories).

17. This stands in contrast with a study of the Dutch civil service. Only less than 15 percent disapproved of close collaboration between administrators and interest groups (Eldersveld et al. 1975: 140–150).

18. The share of the electronic industry in the research and development budget amounted, in 1985, to 67.3 percent, compared to 26.4 percent in West Germany, 20.3 percent in Sweden, and 16.2 percent in Denmark. *The Industrialists*, December 12, 1989.

19. Yehezkel Flumin, *Haaretz*, January 12, 1988.

20. One of the questions presented to officials related to the ability of interest groups to block policy decisions. An overwhelming majority (81.8 percent in the economic ministries and 90.3 percent in the service ministries) stated this is never or only rarely the case.

21. In 1988, the proportion of groups reporting frequent contacts initiated by an MK declined to 17.3 percent.

Chapter Five. The Organization of Interest Groups

1. *Haaretz*, January 27, 1989.

2. Ibid., January 24, 1989.

3. See Wilson 1987: 122–123 for a similar situation in France.

4. *Shtilon*, June-July 1986.

5. Among the respondents twenty-one associations presently attempt to secure state recognition in the form of "representative group."

6. *Haaretz*, August 11, 1989.

7. *See* for example *Budget Proposal*. Ministry of Education and Culture 1989: Special Grant 30.

8. *Maariv*, December 27, 1985.

9. The stated reasons for the measures taken against the teachers were as follows: a public breach of the organization's guidelines; creating an impression that the organization's leadership does not enjoy the full backing of its members; introducing a demoralizing mood (*Meida*, November 1988).

10. On a split in the French Teachers Association, see Clarck 1967.

11. V. Raz, *Hamachar*, 1986.

12. *Haaretz*, January 10, 1989.

13. *Jerusalem Post*, September 4, 1989.

14. Ibid., September 7, 1988.

Chapter Six. Interest Groups and State

1. *Haaretz*, April 5, 1984.

2. *Jerusalem Post*, August 5, 1988.

3. *Ibid.*, January 4, 1989.

4. It is worth noting that the promotional branch of the handicapped associations (i.e., those advancing the welfare for other underprivileged) score much higher on the scale of participation: 42.1 percent compared to 23.5 percent of the categoric groups.

5. *Haaretz*, January 27, 1988. For more details see ibid., January 8, 1988; July 12, 1989.

6. *Jerusalem Post*, December 23, 1988.

7. *The Industry*, 1960/61, 12.

8. Protocol of the SEC session, August 25, 1989.

9. *Haaretz*, May 26, 1989.

10. Ibid., April 12, 1989.

11. Ibid., September 25, 1989.

12. In 1968, a reform designed by the minister of education was meant to change the structure of elementary and post-elementry education from an 8+4 system to a 6+6 system, dividing the post-elementary school into a non-selective junior high school and a selective senior high school. The 1988 reform, proposed by the director-general of the ministry of education, proposed, among other things, to abolish kindergartens and junior high schools, to start primary education at age four, and to end secondary school at age sixteen. *Jerusalem Post*, April 13, 1989.

13. Dr. Kaplinsky, IMA's national council, March 1, 1971.

14. Once a Likud MK, Yosef Tamir represented the Council for Beautiful Israel. The void created by his removal from the Likud list has not been filled.

15. *Haaretz*, April 18, 1989.

16. A lobby headed by a female MK defends the rights of pensions and promotes legislation on behalf of senior citizens. Another lobby wages war on the proposals to change legislation regarding minimum wage. *Davar*, January 23, 1988.

17. *Haaretz*, March 7, 1988.

18. In some certain respects the zones compete for the same resources. In the winter of 1989, for example, a campaign was launched to attract public attention to the problems of the Negev. In the summer of that year, the residents of the Galilee attempted to advance the interests of their region to the top of the national agenda.

19. The Knesset's balcony was once reported to be packed with development town residents from all over the country who had been brought there by their legislative delegates to watch in person how the Knesset pays homage to their cause. See A. Ben-Vered, "Development Towns—the Power of the Masses," *Haartz*, March 7, 1988.

20. Lobbying activity is also carried out on a regional basis. In December 1988, eight MKs, residents of the Galilee representing four parties (Labor, Likud, Hatehiya, and NRP), organized a lobby to act on behalf of their regional constituency. *Davar*, December 25, 1988.

Chapter Seven. Strategies of Influence

1. *Jerusalem Post*, November 13, 1988.

2. Ibid., December 9, 1988.

3. Ibid., March 27, 1989.

4. Comparative data provided by eight medical associations in Western democracies (United States, Great Britain, Canada, Sweden, Norway, Denmark, West Germany, and Holland) demonstrate the low frequency of medical strikes. The respondents were requested to report on the number of medical strike days during the past ten years. The Swedish Medical Association reported on forty-nine days; the Norwegian Medical Association reported on one day. In the remaining countries physicians have not held one single strike in a decade.

5. Yesh Gvul has resumed its protest activity during the Palestinian uprising in the territories. It is the major, in fact, the only, proponent of conscientious objection to military reserve service in Judea, Samaria, and the Gaza Strip.

6. The demonstration was staged in October 1982, when some 400 thousand people (comprising approximately 20 percent of the Israeli adult population) gathered in Tel Aviv to urge the government to establish an inquiry committee to investigate the circumstances for the massacre in the Palestinian refugee camps of Sabra and Shatilla.

7. Moseh Nissim, *Jerusalem Post*, July 12, 1988.

8. Ibid., March 15, 1988.

9. *Haaretz*, September 6, 1989.

10. The sum entitled to every MK was increased from 207,000 shekels per year to 320,000 shekels.

11. Tal Shahaf, "Behind Every Budget You Can Find a Member in the Finance Committee," *Maariv*, April 25, 1989.

12. Ibid.

13. The present research did not cover rank-and-file membership, but my impression is that the practice of circumventing the association is limited to the members of the prestigious economic associations, that is, industrialists and big importers. The impact of this phenomenon, as well as its frequency, on a group's status and power merits additional research.

14. Shimon Peres had a penchant for regular consultations with organizations outside the formal political domain. After his inauguration as minister of finance in 1988, Peres held a get-acquainted meeting with about 150 of the country's top industrialists and businessmen. Its stated purpose was to outline future programs and to obtain some feedback from the audience *Jerusalem Post*, January 10, 1988. During the previous finance minister's tenure such overtures to the business community rarely, if ever, were made.

15. Ibid., August 9, 1989.

16. It is amazing how one little ad can be so instructive with regard to Israeli political culture. Those who published the ad took the trouble to specify that "every appeal would be answered, either orally or by a letter."

17. The association represents men paying alimony allegedly higher than their means and men tricked into fatherhood by single prospective mothers.

18. It should be remembered, though, that empirical studies have an inherent pitfall. A response rate of 58 percent to a mail questionnaire may be satisfactory on methodological grounds, but the remaining 42 percent unreturned questionnaires, and therefore not interviewed population, may include precisely those groups that suffer the greatest amount of alienation.

19. *Haaretz*, February 21, 1989.

20. Files of the Bar Association, February 27, 1989.

Chapter Eight. Interest Groups in the Policy Process

1. *Haaretz*, June 29, 1987.

2. Demonstrated completion of medical studies at a medical school listed by the World Health Organization entitled a person to a one-year license in general practice. At the end of the year, a permanent license was awarded on the basis of positive peer evaluation of professional performance.

3. *Haaretz*, October 13, 1988.

4. *Jerusalem Post*, June 12, 1989.

5. Protocol of the meeting of the MA's presidency, August 24, 1984.

6. Ibid., March 10, 1985.

7. *Jerusalem Post*, December 14, 1986.

8. Ibid., December 26, 1986.

9. Yoel Markus, "This Is What We Have and Nothing But," *Haaretz*, January 16, 1987.

10. Ibid., December 19, 1986.

11. *Jerusalem Post*, November 20, 1987.

12. Under the Histadrut-Treasury accord, the finance minister had agreed to establish a NIS 200 million fund to aid firms facing financial difficulties. In return the Histadrut waived part of the compensation that

was due to the country's salaried employees under the cost-of-living allowance accord. Ibid., June 2, 1989.

13. Ibid., July 24, 1989.

14. Ibid., December 22, 1988.

15. Ibid., August 11, 1989.

16. The mideast is not immune from these developments. In Egypt a strong ecological group was reportedly emerging on the political scene. *Haaretz*, January 12, 1989.

17. Dvora Ben Shaul, "Last Chance for the Environment," *Jerusalem Post*, January 18, 1989.

18. The subunits are: Environmental Protection Service (interior), Institute for Environmental Health (health), Nature Reserves Authority, Kinneret Administration (agriculture), Information Center for Toxic Materials (defense), the Meteorological Service (transport), Geological Institution and Oceanographic and Limmological Institute (energy), and National Parks Department (prime minister's office).

19. The authorization covered a limited number of projects (100) allegedly delayed because of bureaucratic hurdles. The purpose of the law was to provide immediate relief for the unemployed and, especially in regions heavily stricken by unemployment, considered to be a major social disaster. *Haaretz*, September 5, 1989. An intra-cabinet strife gave the proposed law a kiss of death. It has never reached the Knesset agenda.

Chapter Nine. Determining Outcomes

1. The governor of the Bank of Israel once asserted that the manufacturers should "stop milking the budget." *Haaretz*, June 5, 1989.

2. See, for example, ibid., June 29, 1988.

3. Ministry of education spokesman, ibid., June 13, 1988.

4. The results of the poll were reported by the Danish daily *Berlinska*, and quoted by *Haaretz*, August 29, 1989.

5. *Report*. 30 Years to the Society for the Protection of Nature, 1983.

6. *Hed Hachinuck*, August 11, 1984.

7. *Yediot Ahronot*, May 8, 1989.

8. The reason for the underestimation of functional contribution by the groups themselves may be technical. In order to avoid the answer

of "everything is important," which is also common when respondents are asked to rank answers, the groups were requested to select the single most relevant answer.

Chapter Ten. Israeli Interest Groups between Party and State

1. *Haaretz*, June 23, 1989.

2. *Maariv*, July 22, 1988.

3. Since 1984 the Knesset enacted a law providing for a minimum wage income, it introduced legislation pertaining to gender equality, it adopted the Development Towns Law providing Israel's peripheral zones with large benefits, and the Discharged Soldiers Law. The Knesset also showed it was highly responsive to demands of the agricultural sector by enacting the Compensation Law.

4. *Jerusalem Post*, June 2, 1989.

Bibliography

Aharoni, V. 1979. *Government Companies in Israel and the World.* Tel Aviv: Cherikover (Hebrew).

Akzin, B. 1955. "The Role of Parties in Israeli Democracy." *Journal of Politics* 17: 509–533.

Akzin, B. and Y. Dror. 1966. *Israel: High Pressure Planning,* Syracuse: Syracuse University Press.

Almond, G. A. 1958. "A Comparative Study of Interest Groups and the Political Process." *American Political Science Review* 52: 270–282.

Almond, G. A. 1983. "Corporatism, Pluralism, and Professional Memory." *World Politics* 35: 245–260.

Almond, G. A. and B. Powell, Jr. 1966. *Comparative Politics: A Developmental Approach.* Boston: Little Brown.

Almond, G. A. and S. Verba, 1963. *The Civic Culture. Political Attitudes and Democracy in Five Nations.* Princeton: University Press.

Anderson, C. W. 1979. "Political Design and Representation of Interests," in Schmitter and Lehmbruch.

Anton, T. J. 1980. *Administered Politics: Elite Political Culture in Sweden.* Boston: Nijhoff.

Arian, A. 1985. *Politics in Israel. The Second Generation.* Chatham, N. J.: Chatham House.

Aronoff, M. J. 1977. *Power and Ritual in Israeli Labor Party.* Amsterdam: Van Goreum.

Atkinson, M. A. and W. D. Coleman, 1989. "Strong States and Weak States: Sectoral Policy Networks in Advanced Capitalist Economics." *British Journal of Political Science* 19: 47–67.

Avneri, A. 1976. *Sapir.* Givataim: Peleg (Hebrew).

Bachrach, P. and M. Baratz. 1962. "Two Faces of Power." *American Political Science Review* 50: 947–952.

Bar Zuri R. and R. Bazri. 1988. "Strikes in the Economy." *Economy and Labor* 5: 31–34 (Hebrew).

Bar-On, M. 1985. *Peace Now. The Portrait of a Movement.* Tel Aviv: Hakibbutz Hemeuchad (Hebrew).

Barkai, H. 1964. *The Public, Histadrut, and Private Sectors in the Israeli Economy.* Sixth Report 1961–63. Jerusalem: Falk Institution.

Bartal, G. 1989. *Histadrut: Structures and Activities.* Tel Aviv: Histadrut Executive (Hebrew).

Bauer, R., I de Sola Pool and L. A. Dexter. 1968. *American Business and Public Policy.* New York: Atherton.

Beer, S. H. 1969. *Modern British Politics.* London: Faber.

Beer, S. H. 1958. "Group Representation in Britain and the United States." *The Annals of the American Academy of Political and Social Science* 119: 130–140.

Beilin, Y. 1988. *Roots of Israeli Industry.* Jerusalem: Keter (Hebrew).

Bell, D. 1973. *The Coming of Post Industrial Society.* New York: Basic Books.

Ben-Meir, D. B. 1988. *Voluntary Work in Israel. Theory and Practice. Jerusalem: Karta (Hebrew).*

Ben-Avram, B. 1976. *The Association of Kvutzot.* Tel Aviv: Am Oved (Hebrew).

Ben-David, J. 1970. "Professionals and Unions in Israel." in S. N. Eisenstadt, R. Bar-Yosef, and C. Adler (eds.), *Integration and Development.* Jerusalem: Israel University Press.

Benewick, R. 1973. "Politics without Ideology," in R. Benewick (ed.), *Knowledge and Belief in Politics.* London: Allen and Unwin.

Ben-Gurion, D. 1971. *Memoirs.* Tel Aviv: am Oved (Hebrew).

Ben Gurion, D. 1974. *From Class to Nation.* Tel Aviv: Am Oved (Hebrew).

Ben-Porath, Y. 1986. "Patterns and Peculiarities of Economic Growth and Structure." *The Jerusalem Quarterly* 38: 43–63.

Bentley, A. F. 1908. *The Process of Government.* Chicago, Ill.: University of Chicago Press.

Berger, S. 1981. "Introduction," in Berger.

Berger, S. 1981. *Organizing Interests in Western Europe. Pluralism, Cororatism and the Transformation of Politics.* Cambridge: Cambridge University Press.

Bernstein, D. 1979. "The Black Panthers. Conflict and Protest in Israeli Society." *Megamot* 25: 65–79.

Bernstein, J. and A. Antonovsky. 1981. "The Integration of Ethnic Groups in Israel." *Jewish Journal of Sociology* 23: 5–24.

Berry, J. M. 1977. *Lobbying for the People. The Political Behavior of Public Interest Groups.* Princeton, N. J.: Princeton University Press.

Berry, J. M. 1984. *The Interest Group Society.* Boston: Little Brown.

Bianchi, R. 1984. *Interest Groups and Political Development in Turkey.* Princeton, N. J.: Princeton University Press.

Boim, L. 1972. "Financing of the 1969 Elections," in A. Arian (ed.), *The Elections in Israel 1969.* Jerusalem: Jerusalem Academic Press.

Bracha, B. 1980. "Addendum: Some Remarks on Israeli Law Regarding National Security." *Israel Yearbook on Human Rights.* 10: 289–298.

Brenner, M. J. 1969. "Functional Representation and Interest Group Theory." *Comparative Politics* 2: 111–134.

Brum, A. 1986. *Always Controversial.* Tel Aviv: Yad Tabenkin (Hebrew).

Bruno, M. and S. Fischer. 1984. *The Inflationary Process in Israel: Shocks and Accommodations.* Jerusalem: Falk Institution.

Budget Proposal. 1987. "For the Fiscal Year 1987." Presented to the 11th Knesset, January (Hebrew).

Caiden, G. E. 1970. *Israel's Administrative Culture.* Berkeley: Institute of Governmental Studies, University of California.

Cawson, A. 1985. "Varieties of Corporatism: The Importance of the Meso-level of Interest Intermediation," in A. Cawson (ed.), *Organized Interests and the State.* London: Sage.

Cawson, A. 1986. *Corporatism and Political Theory.* Oxford: Blackwell.

Clarck, J. M. 1967. *Teachers and Politics in France: A Pressure Group Study of the Federation de L'Education Nationale.* Syracuse: Syracuse University Press.

Clarck, P. B. and J. Q. Wilson. 1961. "Inventive System: A Theory of Organizations." *Administrative Science Quarterlys* 6: 129–166.

Cobb. R., J. K. Ross, and M. H. Ross. 1976. "Agenda Building as a Comparative Political Process." *American Political Science Review* 70: 126–138.

Cobb, R. W. and C. D. Elder. 1972. *Participation in American Politics. The Dynamics of Agenda Building.* Baltimore: Johns Hopkins University Press.

Cohen, E. 1972. "The Black Panthers and Israeli Society." *Jewish Journal of Sociology.* 14: 93–102.

Cohen, Y. and F. Pavoncello. 1987. "Corporatism and Pluralism: A Critique of Schmitter's Typology." *British Journal of Political Science* 17: 117–122.

Coleman, W. and W. Grant. 1985. "The Organizational Cohesion and Political Access of Business: A Study of Comprehensive Associations." *European Journal of Political Research* 16: 467–487.

Collier, R. B. and D. Collier. 1979. "Inducements versus Constraints: Disaggregating 'Corporatism'" *American Political Science Review* 73: 967–986.

Converse, P. E. and R. Pierce. 1986. *Political Representation in France.* Cambridge: Balknap.

Crouch, C. 1983. "Pluralism and the New Corporatism: A Rejoinder." *Political Studies* 31–452.

Czudnowski, M. M. 1968. "A Salience Dimension of Politics for the Study of Political Culture." *American Political Science Review* 62: 878–888.

Czudnowski, M. M. 1970. "Legislative Recruitment under Proportional Representation in Israel: A Model and a Case Study." *Midwest Journal of Political Science* 14: 217–248.

Daalder, H. 1966. "Parties, Elites and Political Development," in J. LaPalombara and M. Weiner (eds.), *Political Parties and Political Development.* Princeton, N. J.: Princeton University Press.

Dahl, R. A. 1956. *A Preface to Democratic Theory.* Chicago, Ill.: University of Chicago Press.

Dahl, R. A. 1961. *Who Governs? Democracy and Power in an American City.* New Haven: Yale University Press.

Dahl, R. A. 1971. *Polyarchy, Participation and Opposition.* New Haven: Yale University Press.

Dahl, R. A. 1984. "Polyarchy, Pluralism and Scale." *Scandinavian Political Studies* 7: 225–239.

Dalton, R. J., P. A. Beck and S. C. Flanagan. 1984. "Electoral Change in Advanced Industrial Democracies." in R. Dalton (ed.), *Electoral Change in Industrial Democracies: Realignment of Dealignment?* Princeton, N. J.: Princeton University Press.

Dayan, M. 1982. *Story of My Life.* 2nd ed. Jerusalem: Edanim (Hebrew).

de Tocqueville A. 1954. *Democracy in America.* 2 vols. New York: Vintage Books.

Deshen, S. 1978. "Israel Judaism: Introduction to the Major Patterns." *International Journal of Middle East Studies* 9: 141–169.

Deutsch, K. W. 1980. *Politics and Government. How People Decide Their Fate.* 2nd ed. Boston: Houghton Mifflin.

Don Yehiya, E. and B. Susser. 1989. "Continuity and Change in Jewish Political Thought." *State, Government and International Relations* 30: 19–50 (Hebrew).

Doron, G. and B. Tamir. 1983. "The Electoral Cycle: A Political Economic Perspective." *Crossroads* 10: 141–152.

Dowse, R. E. and J. Hughes. 1977. "Sporadic Interventionists." *Political Studies* 25: 84–92.

Dowty, A. 1988. "Expressions of the Jewish Political Tradition in Contemporary Israeli Politics." Paper Presented at a workshop on University Teaching of Jewish Civilization. Jerusalem, July 18–27.

Dror, Y. 1989. *Memorandum for the Israeli Prime Minister. To Build a State.* Jerusalem: Academon (Hebrew).

Duverger, M. 1954. *Political Parties.* London: Methuen.

Dye, T. R. and H. Zeigler, 1970. *The Irony of Democracy. An Uncommon Introduction to American Politics.* Belmont, Cal.: Wadsworth.

Dyson, K. F. 1977. *Party, State and Bureaucracy in Western Germany.* Beverly Hills: Sage.

Dyson, K. F. 1982. "West Germany: The Search for a Rational Consensus," in Richardson.

Eban, A. 1977. *An Autobiography.* New York: Random.

Edelman, M. 1985. *The Symbolic Uses of Politics.* 2nd ed. Urbana: University of Illinois Press.

Ehrmann, H. W., ed. 1958. *Interest Groups on Four Continents.* Pittsburgh: Pittsburgh University Press.

Ehrmann, H. W. 1968. "Interest Groups and the Bureaucracy in Western Democracies," in R. Bendix (ed.), *State and Society. A Reader in Comparative Sociology.* Boston: Little Brown.

Eisenstadt, S. N. 1954. *The Absorption of Immigrants.* London: Routledge and Kegan Paul.

Eisenstadt, S. N. 1967. *Israeli Society.* London: Weidenfeld and Nicolson.

Eisenstadt, S. N. 1972. "The Social Conditions of the Development of Voluntary Associations: A Case Study of Israel." *Journal of Voluntary Action Research* 3: 1-14.

Eisenstadt, S. N. 1977. "Change and Continuity in Israeli Society; Dynamic Conservatism vs. Innovation." *Jerusalem Quarterly* 2: 3-11.

Eisenstadt, S. N. 1985. *The Transformation of Israel Society. An Essay in Interpretation.* London: Weidenfeld and Nicolson.

Elazar, D. 1983. "Covenant as the Basis of Political Tradition," in Elazar.

Elazar, D., ed. 1983. *Kinship and Consent: The Jewish Political Tradition and its Contemporary Uses.* Washington, D.C.: University Press of America.

Elazar, D. 1986. *Israel. Building a New Society.* Bloomington: Indiana University Press.

Eldersveld, S. J., S. Hubee-Boonzaaiger, and J. Kooiman. 1975. "Elite Perceptions of the Political Process in the Netherlands, Looked at in Comparative Perspective," in M. Dogan (ed.), *The Mandarines of Western Europe. The Political Role of Top Civil Servants.* New York: John Wiley.

Elizur, D. 1979. *The Public Awareness of the Activity of Consumers' Organizations and its Preparedness to Fight Rising Prices.* Jerusalem: Israel Institute for Applied Social Research, pub. no (s) DE 1762/H (Hebrew).

Elon, A. 1971. *The Israelis, Founders and Sons.* London: Weidenfeld and Nicolson.

Elvander, N. 1974. "Interest Groups in Sweden." *Annals of the American Academy of Political and Social Science* 41: 27-43.

Eschen, D. V., J. Kirk and M. Pinard, 1969. "The Conditions of Direct Action in a Democratic Society." *Western Political Quarterly* 22: 309–325.

Etzioni, A. 1962. "The Decline of Neo-Feudalism: The Case of Israel." Papers in Comparative Public Administration. University of Michigan.

Etzioni, A. 1970. *Demonstration Democracy.* New York: Gordon and Breach.

Etzioni Halevi, E. 1975. "Protest Politics in Israeli Democracy." *Political Science Quarterly* 90: 497–520.

Fein, J. J. 1967. *Politics in Israel.* Boston: Little Brown.

Finer, S. E. 1958. *Anonymous Empire.* London: Pall Mall.

Finer, S. E. 1970. *Comparative Government.* London: Allen Lane.

Finer, S. E. 1973. "The Political Power of Organized Labor." *Government and Opposition* 8: 391–406.

Free Economy. 1988. Tel Aviv: Israel Chamber of Commerce (Hebrew).

Freidson, E. 1970. *Profession of Medicine.* New York: Dodd and Mead.

Friedman, M. and R. 1980. *Free to Choose. A Personal Statement.* New York: Harcourt Brace Jovanovich.

Friedrich, C. 1963. *Man and His Government.* New York: McGraw Hill.

Galnoor, I. 1978. "Water Policy Making in Israel." *Policy Analysis* 4: 334–367.

Galnoor, I. 1982. *Steering the Polity. Communication and Politics in Israel.* Beverly Hills: Sage.

Gamson, W. A. 1968. *The Strategy of Social Protest.* Homewood, Ill.: Dorsey.

Gilat, N. 1988. "The Thundering Silence. Parents Against Silence." Unpublished MA thesis, Haifa University, Department of Political Science.

Gilb, C. 1966. *Hidden Hierarchies.* New York: Harper and Row.

Gitelman, Z. and D. Naveh. 1976. "Elite Accommodation and Organizational Effectiveness: The Case of Immigrants Absorption in Israel." *Journal of Politics* 38: 963–986.

Gronau, R. 1988. "Privatization." *The Economic Quarterly* 39: 16–20 (Hebrew).

GottLieb, A., E. Yuchtman Yaar. 1983. "Materialism, Post Materialism, and Public Views on Socioeconomic Policy. The Case of Israel." *Comparative Political Studies* 16: 307–335.

Gurr, T. R. 1970. *Why Men Rebel.* Princeton, N. J.: Princeton University Press.

Gutmann, E. 1971. "Religion in Israel Politics," in J. M. Landau (ed.), *Man, State and Society in the Contemporary Middle East.* New York: Praeger.

Gutmann, E. 1977. "Parties and Camps: Stability and Change," in M. Lissak and E. Gutmann (eds.), *The Israeli Political System.* Tel Aviv: Am Oved (Hebrew).

Halevi, N. and R. Klinov-Malul. 1968. *The Economic Development of Israel as a Case Study.* Jerusalem and New York: Praeger with the Bank of Israel.

Hareven, S. 1988. "The First Forty Years." *The Jerusalem Quarterly* 48: 3–28.

Hayward, J. E. S. 1966. *Private Interest and Public Policy.* London: Longman.

Hayward, J. E. S. 1979. "Interest Groups and the Demand for State Action," in J. E. S. Hayward and R. N. Berki (eds.), *State and Society in Contemporary Europe.* Oxford: Martin Robertson.

Hayward, J. E. S. 1984. "Pressure Groups and Pressured Groups in Franco-British Perspective," in D. Kavanagh and G. Peele (eds.), *Government and Politics.* London: Heinemann.

Heclo, H. 1975. "Frontiers of Social Policy in Europe and America." *Policy Sciences* 6: 403–421.

Heclo, H. and H. Madsen. 1987. *Policy and Politics in Sweden: Principled Pragmatism.* Philadelphia: Temple University Press.

Heisler, M. and R. Kvavik. 1974. "Patterns of European Politics: The 'European Polity Model'," in M. Heisler (ed.), *Politics in Europe.* New York: McKay.

Hine, D. 1987. "Parties and Party Government under Pressure," in A. Ware (ed.), *Political Parties, Electoral Change and Structural Response.* Oxford: Basil Blackwell.

Histadrut. General Federation of Labor in Israel. 1986. Tel Aviv: The Executive Committee (Hebrew).

Hoffman, S. 1966. "Obstinate or Obsolete: The Fate of the Nation State and the Case of Western Europe." *Daedalus* 95: 862–915.

Hogwood, B. W. 1987. *From Crisis to Complacency?* Oxford: Oxford University Press.

Horowitz, D. and M. Lissak. 1977. *The Origins of the Israel Polity.* Tel Aviv: Am Oved.

Houska, J. J. 1985. *Influencing Mass Political Behavior.* Berkeley: Institute of International Studies, University of California.

Huntington, S. P. 1968. *Political Order in Changing Societies.* New Haven: Yale University Press.

Huntington, S. P. and J. M. Nelson, 1976. *No Easy Choice. Political Participation in Developing Countries.* Cambridge, Mass.: Harvard University Press.

Hurewitz, J. C. 1969. *Middle East Politics: The Military Dimension.* New York: Praeger.

Hurwitz, I. 1971. "An Index of Democratic Political Stability: A Methodological Note." *Comparative Political Studies* 4: 41–67.

Isaac, R. 1976. *Israel Divided. Ideological Politics in the Jewish State.* Baltimore: Johns Hopkins University Press.

Jiryis, S. 1969. *The Arabs in Israel 1948–1966.* Beirut: The Institute for Palestine Studies.

Jordan, A. G. 1981. "Iron Triangles, Wooly Corporatism and Elastic Nets: Images of the Policy Process." *Journal of Public Policy* 1: 95–123.

Jordan, A. G. 1984. "Pluralistic Corporatism and Corporate Pluralism." *Scandinavian Political Studies* 7: 137–151.

Jordan, A. G. and J. J. Richardson. 1987. *Government and Pressure Groups in Britain.* Oxford: Clarendon Press.

Jordan, G. and J. Richardson. 1982. "The British Policy Style and the Logic of Negotiations," in Richardson.

Katz, J. 1963. *Tradition and Crisis. Jewish Society in the Late Middle Ages.* Jerusalem: Mosad Bialik (Hebrew).

Katzenelson, B. 1946. *Ktavim.* Tel Aviv: Mapai (Hebrew).

Keeler, J. T. S. 1987. *The Politics of Neo Corporatism in France. Farmers, the State, and Agricultural Policy Making in the Fifth Republic.* New York: Oxford University Press.

Keisar, Y. 1989. *Tendencies in the Economy and Society. Developments in Wage and Social Service Domains in Israel.* Tel Aviv: The General Federation of Labor (Hebrew).

Martin, R. 1983. "Pluralism and the New Corporatism." *Political Studies* 31: 86–103.

Medding, P. Y. 1972. *Mapai in Israel. Political Organization and Government in a New Society.* Cambridge: Cambridge University Press.

Meir, G. 1975. *My Life.* Tel Aviv: Maariv (Hebrew).

Meishar, Y. 1984. *Investment Patterns in Israel.* Jerusalem: Falk Institution.

Mendilow, J. 1988. "Israel's Labor Alignment in the 1984 Elections. Catch-All Tactics in a Divided Society." *Comparative Politics* 20: 443–460.

Michael, A. and R. Bar-El. 1977. *Strikes in Israel* Ramat Gan: Bar Ilan University Press (Hebrew).

Michels, R. 1958. *Political Parties.* Glencoe, Ill.: Free Press.

Milbrath, L. W. 1967. "Interest Groups and Foreign Policy," in J. N. Rosenau (ed.), *Domestic Sources of Foreign Policy.* New York: Free Press.

Milbrath, L. W. and M. Goel. 1977. *Political Participation.* et al. Chicago: Rand McNally.

Mironi, M. 1983. *Returning to Work Orders: Government Intervention in Labor Disputes through Emergency Regulations and Work Injunctions.* Tel Aviv: The Institute for Social and Labor Research, University of Tel Aviv (Hebrew).

Modai, Y. 1988. *Eliminating the Zeroes.* Tel Aviv: Edanim (Hebrew).

Moe, T. M. 1980. *The Organization of Interests: Incentives and the Internal Dynamics of Political Interest Groups.* Chicago: University of Chicago Press.

Nachmias, D. and Rosenbloom, D. H. 1978. *Bureaucratic Culture: Citizens and Administrators in Israel.* New York: St. Martin's Press.

Negbi, M. 1985. *A Paper Tiger. The Struggle on the Freedom of Press in Israel.* Tel Aviv: Sifriat Poalim (Hebrew).

Negbi, M. 1987. *Above the Law. The Crisis of the Rule of Law in Israel.* Tel Aviv: Am Oved (Hebrew).

Nordlinger, A. E. 1967. *The Working Class Tories.* Berkeley: University of California Press.

Nordlinger, A. E. 1981. *On the Autonomy of the Democratic State.* Cambridge: Harvard University Press.

Ofer, G. 1967. *The Service Industries in a Developing Economy. Israel as a Case Study.* New York: Praeger and the Bank of Israel.

Offe, C. 1981. "The Attribution of Public Status to Interest Groups: Observations on the West German Case" in Berger.

Olsen, J. P. 1981. "Integrated Organizational Participation in Government," in P. G. Nystrom and W. H. Starbuck (eds.), *Handbook of Organizational Design*, vol. 2. New York: Oxford University Press.

Olsen, J. P. 1983. *Organized Democracy. Political Institutions in a Welfare State-The Case of Norway.* Bergen: Universitetsforlaget.

Olsen, J. P., P. Roness and H. Saettren, 1982. "Norway: Still Peaceful Coexistence and Revolution in Slow Motion?" in Richardson.

Olson, M. 1968. *The Logic of Collective Action.* Cambridge, Mass.: Harvard University Press.

Olson, M. 1982. *The Rise and Decline of Nations.* New Haven: Yale University Press.

O'Sullivan, N. 1988. "The Political Theory of Neo-Corporatism," in A. Cox and N. O'Sullivan (eds.), *The Corporate State. Corporatism and the State Tradition in Western Europe.* Hants: Edward Elgar.

Oz, A. 1979. *Under this Blazing Light.* Tel Aviv: Sifriat Poalim (Hebrew).

Pempel, J. T. and K. Tsunekawa. 1979. "Corporatism without Labor? The Japanese Anomaly," in Schmitter and Lehmbruch.

Peres, Y. 1976. *Ethnic Relations in Israel.* Tel Aviv: Sifriat Poalim (Hebrew).

Peres, Y. 1987. "Most Israelis are Committed to Democracy." *Israeli Democracy.* February 16–19.

Peri, Y. 1986. *Between Battles and Ballots. Israeli Military in Politics.* Cambridge: Cambridge University Press.

Pizzorno, A. 1981. "Interests and Parties in Pluralism," in Berger.

Pross, A. P. 1986. *Group Politics and Public Policy.* Toronto: Oxford University Press.

Pross, A. P. 1989. "The Mirror of the State: Centralist and Decentralist Tendencies in Canada's Interest Group System." Paper presented at the Annual Meeting of the American Political Science Association, Atlanta, September 1.

Putnam, A. 1975. "The Political Attitudes of Senior Civil Servants in Britain, Germany and Italy," in M. Dogan (ed.), *The Mandarines of Western Europe. The Political Role of Top Civil Servants.* New York: Wiley.

Rabin, I. 1979. *A Service Diary,* vol. 2. Tel Aviv: Maariv (Hebrew).

Reuveny, J. 1974. *The Israel Civil Service.* Ramat Gan: Massada (Hebrew).

Richardson, J. J. (ed.). 1982. *Policy Styles in Western Europe.* London: Allen and Unwin.

Richardson, J. J. and G. Jordan. 1979. *Governing under Pressure.* Oxford: Martin Robertson.

Richardson, J. J. G. Gustafsson, and G. Jordan. 1982. "The Concepts of a Policy Style," in Richardson.

Riggs, F. W. 1970. *Administrative Reform and Political Participation: A Theory of Dynamic Balancing.* Beverly Hills, Ca.: Sage.

Rokkan, S. 1966. "Numerical Democracy and Corporate Pluralism," in R. A. Dahl (ed.), *Political Oppositions in Western Democracies.* New Haven: Yale University Press.

Rose, R. 1980. "Government against Subgovernment," in R. Rose and E. Suleiman (eds.), *Presidents and Prime Ministers.* Washington, D.C.: American Enterprise Institute.

Rose, R. 1984. *Do Parties Make a Difference?* 2nd ed. London: Macmillan.

Rubinstein, A. 1967. "Law and Religion in Israel." *Israel Law Review* 3: 380–414.

Rubinstein, A. 1980. *The Constitutional Law of the State of Israel.* Tel Aviv: Schocken (Hebrew).

Safran, N. 1973. "Party Politics in Israel." *Keshet* 15: 125–144.

Sager, S. 1985. *The Parliamentary System of Israel.* Syracuse: Syracuse University Press.

Salisbury, R. H. 1969. "An Exchange Theory of Interest Groups." *Midwest Journal of Political Science* 13: 1–32.

Salisbury, R. H., J. P. Heinz, E. O. Lanmann, and R. L. Nelson. 1987. "Who Works with Whom? Interest Group Alliance and Opposition." *American Political Science Review* 81: 1217–1234.

Sartori, G. 1966. "European Political Parties: The Case of Polarized Pluralism," in J. LaPalombara and M. Weiner (eds.), *Political Parties and Political Development* Princeton, N. J.: Princeton University Press.

Sartori, G. 1976. *Parties and Party Systems: A Framework for Analysis.* Cambridge: Cambridge University Press.

Schattschneider, D. E. 1975. *The Semisovereign People.* Hinsdale, Ill.: Dryden Press.

Schlozman Lehman, K. and J. T. Tierney. 1986. *Organized Interests and American Democracy.* New York: Harper and Row.

Schmitter, P. C. 1974. "Still a Century of Corporatism?" *Review of Politics* 36: 85–131.

Schmitter, P. C. 1979. "Models of Interest Intermediation and Models of Societal Change in Western Europe." in Schmitter and Lehmbruch.

Schmitter, P. C. 1981. "Interest Intermediation and Regime Governability in Contemporary Western Europe and North America," in Berger.

Schmitter, P. C. 1982. "Reflections on Where the Theory of Neo-Corporatism has Gone and Where the Praxis of Neo-Corporatism May be Going," in Lehmbruch and Schmitter.

Schmitter, P. C. 1983. "Democratic Theory and Neocorporatist Practice." *Social Research* 50: 885–928.

Schmitter, P. C. 1989. "Corporatism is Dead. Long Live Corporatism." *Government and Opposition* 24: 54–73.

Schmitter, P. C. and G. Lehmbruch, eds. 1979. *Trends toward Corporatist Intermediation.* London: Sage.

Schweitzer, A. 1984. *Upheavals.* Tel Aviv: Zmora Bitan (Hebrew).

Sefer Hachukim. Israel Book of Laws. Jerusalem: The Government Printer. (Hebrew).

Segal, Z. 1988. *Israeli Democracy. Governance in the State of Israel.* Tel Aviv: Ministry of Defense (Hebrew).

Segev, T. 1984. *1949. The First Israelis.* Jerusalem: Domino Press (Hebrew).

Segre, D. V. 1983. "The Jewish Political Tradition as a Vehicle for Jewish Auto-Emancipation," in Elazar.

Seliktar, O. 1986. *New Zionism and the Foreign Policy of Israel.* London: Croom Helm.

Sella, A. and Y. Yishai. 1986. *Israel. The Peaceful Belligerent 1967–79.* London: Macmillan.

Shalev, M. 1984. "Labor, State, Crisis. An Israeli Case Study." *Industrial Relations* 23: 362–385.

Shapira, R. and E. Etzioni-Halevy. 1973. *Who is the Israeli Student?* Tel Aviv: Am Oved (Hebrew).

Shapiro, Y. 1976. *The Formative Years of the Israeli Labor Party.* Beverly Hills: Sage.

Sharkansky, I. 1979. *Wither the State? Politics and Public Enterprise in Three Countries.* Chatham, N. J.: Chatham House.

Sharkansky, I. 1987. *The Political Economy of Israel.* New Brunswick, N. J.: Transaction.

Sharkansky, I. 1988. "Too Much of the Wrong Things." *The Jerusalem Quarterly* 45: 3–26.

Sherman, N. 1980. "The Agricultural Sector and the 1977 Knesset Elections," in A. Arian (ed.), *The Election in Israel 1977.* Jerusalem: Jerusalem Academic Press.

Shetreet, S. 1984. "A Contemporary Model of Emergency Detention Law. An Assessment of the Israel Law." *Israel Yearbook of Human Rights* 14: 182–220.

Shilhav, J. and Friedman, M. 1985. *Growth and Segregation—The Ultra Orthodox Community of Jerusalem.* Jerusalem: The Jerusalem Institute for Israel Studies.

Shimshoni, D. 1982. *Israeli Democracy. The Middle of the Journey.* New York: Free Press.

Shirom, A. 1983. *Introduction to Labor Relations in Israel.* Tel Aviv: Am Oved (Hebrew).

Shuval, J. T. 1983. *New Comers and Colleagues: Soviet Immigrant Physicians in Israel.* Houston: Cap and Brown.

Shuval, J. T. 1985. "Social Functions of Medical Licensing. A Case Study of Immigrant Physicians in Israel." *Social Science & Medicine* 20: 901–909.

Shuval, J. T. 1988. "Medical Manpower in Israel: Political Processes and Constraints." Paper delivered at the International Conference on "The Political Dynamics of Physician Manpower Policy," London: May 24–27.

Shuval, J. T. 1989. "The Structure and Dilemmas of Israeli Pluralism," in B. Kimmerling (ed.), *The Israeli State and Society. Boundaries and Frontiers.* Albany: State University of New York Press.

Smooha, S. 1978. *Israel: Pluralism and Conflict.* Berkeley: University of California Press.

Soffer, A. 1988. "Population Projection for the Land of Israel." *Middle East Review* 20: 43–49.

Sorauf, F. L. 1976. *The Wall of Separation.* Princeton, N. J.: Princeton University Press.

Sprinzak, E. 1986. *Every Man Whatsoever is Right in His Own Eyes: Illegalism in Israeli Society.* Tel Aviv: Sifriat Poalim (Hebrew).

State Comptroller. *Annual Report.* Jerusalem: The Government Printer.

Statistical Abstract of Israel. Jerusalem: Central Bureau of Statistics.

Stewart, J. D. 1958. *British Pressure Groups.* Oxford: Clarendon Press.

Stone, R. 1982. *Social Change in Israel. Attitudes and Events.* New York: Praeger.

Streeck, W. and P. C. Schmitter. 1985. "Community, Market, State—and Association? The Prospective Contribution of Interest Governance to Social Order," in W. Streeck and P. C. Schmitter (eds.), *Private Interest Government.* London: Sage.

Suleiman, E. 1974. *Politics, Power and Bureaucracy in France.* Princeton: Princeton University Press.

Suleiman, E., ed. 1984. *Bureaucrats and Policy Making: A Comparative Overview.* New York: Holmes and Meier.

Susser, B. and E. Don-Yehiya. 1983. "Prolegorama to a Study of Jewish Political Theory," in Elazar.

Syrquin, M. 1986. "Economic Growth and Structural Change in Israel: An International Perspective," in Y. Ben-Porath (ed.), *The Israeli Economy. Maturing Through Crises.* Cambridge, Mass.: Harvard University Press.

Tarrow, S. and A. Levite. 1983. "The Legitimation of Excluded Parties in Dominant Party Systems: A Comparison of Israel and Italy." *Comparative Politics* 15: 295–328.

Toffler, A. 1982. *The Third Wave.* 7th printing. New York: Bantam.

Tokatly, R. 1979. *Political Patterns in Labor Relations in Israel.* Ph.D. diss., Tel Aviv University.

Truman, D. 1951. *The Governmental Process.* New York: Knopf.

Valenzuela, A. 1984. "Parties, Politics, and the State in Chile. The Higher Civil Service," in E. Suleiman (ed.), *Bureaucrats and Policy Making. A Comparative Overview.* New York: Holmes and Meier.

Verba, S., N. H. Nie and J. O. Kim. 1978. *Participation and Political Equality. A Seven Nation Comparison.* London: Cambridge University Press.

Verba, S. and N. H. Nie. 1972. *Participation in America. Social Equality and Political Democracy.* New York: Harper and Row.

Vogel, D. 1981. "The Public Interest Movement and the American Reform Tradition." *Political Science Quarterly* 95: 607–627.

Vogel, D. 1987. "Political Science and the Study of Corporate Power. A Dissent from the New Conventional Wisdom." *British Journal of Political Science* 17: 385–408.

Vose, C. E. 1981. "Interest Groups and Litigation." Paper presented at the American Political Science Annual Meeting.

Ware, A. 1987. *Citizens, Parties and the State. A Reappraisal.* Cambridge: Polity Press.

Wassenberg, A. F. 1982. "Neo-Corporatism and the Quest for Control: The Cuckoo Game," in Lehmbruch and Schmitter.

Weiner, M. 1968. *Politics of Scarcity.* Chicago: University of Chicago Press.

Weiss, S. 1970. *Typology of Local Elected Officials and the Question of Stability in the Local Government in Israel.* Jerusalem: Academon (Hebrew).

Weiss, S. 1988. *Parliamentary Diary.* Haifa: Renaissance (Hebrew).

Weiss, S. and G. Ben-Dor. 1973. "Activists, Bureaucracy and Political Institutionalization in Israel." *Social Research Quarterly* 5: 9–31 (Hebrew).

Weizman, E. 1981. *The Battle for Peace.* New York: Bantam.

Wildavsky, A. 1975. *Budgeting: A Comparative Theory of Budgeting Processes.* Boston: Little Brown.

Wilding, P. 1982. *Professional Power and Social Welfare.* London: Routledge and Kegan Paul.

Wilks, S. and Wright, M. 1987. "Conclusions: Comparing Government-Industry Relations: States, Sectors and Networks," in S. Wilks and M. Wright (eds.), *Comparative Government-Industry Relations.* Oxford: Oxford University Press.

Williamson, P. J. 1985. *Varieties of Corporatism: A Conceptual Discussion.* Cambridge: Cambridge University Press.

Williamson, P. J. 1989. *Corporatism in Perspective. An Introductory Guide to Corporatist Theory.* London: Sage.

Wilson, F. L. 1983. "Interest Groups and Politics in Western Europe: The Neo-Corporatist Perspective." *Comparative Politics* 16: 105–123.

Wilson F. L. 1987. *Interest Group Politics in France.* Cambridge: Cambridge University Press.

Wilson, G. K. 1985. *Business and Politics. A Comparative Introduction.* London: Macmillan.

Wilson, J. Q. 1973. *Political Organizations.* New York: Basic Books.

Wolfsfeld, G. 1988. *The Politics of Provocation. Participation and Protest in Israel.* Albany: State University of New York Press.

Wootton, G. 1985. *Interest Groups. Policy and Politics in America.* Englewood Cliffs, N. J.: Prentice Hall.

Yaacobi, G. 1980. *The Government.* Tel Aviv: Am Oved (Hebrew).

Yadlin, A. 1980. *The Testimony.* Jerusalem: Edanim (Hebrew).

Yanai, N. 1969. *Split at the Top.* Tel Aviv: Levin Epstein (Hebrew).

Yanai, N. 1981. *Party Leadership in Israel. Maintenance and Change.* Ramat Gan: Turtledove.

Yanai, N. 1987. "Three Forms of Kibbutz-Party Relationship." *Meassef* 17: 105–122.

Yaniv, A. and F. Paskal. 1980. "Doves, Hawks and other Birds of Feather. The Distribution of Israeli Parliamentary Opinion on the Future of the Occupied Territories, 1967–1977." *British Journal of Political Science* 10: 260–267.

Yehoshua, A. B. 1980. *In Defense of Normalcy. Five Essays on Zionist Problems.* Jerusalem: Schocken (Hebrew).

Yishai, Y. 1976a. "Interest Groups and Legislators: The Case of Israel," unpublished paper.

Yishai, Y. 1978b. "Women's Political Representation in Israeli Parties." *Megamot* 24: 238–251.

Yishai, Y. 1981. "Factionalism in Israeli Parties." *Jerusalem Quarterly* 20: 36–48.

Yishai, Y. 1982a. "Israel's Right Wing Jewish Proletariat." *Jewish Journal of Sociology* 24: 87–98.

Yishai, Y. 1982b. "Politics and Medicine: The Case of Israel National Health Insurance." *Social Science and Medicine* 16: 285–291.

Yishai, Y. 1984. "Responses to Ethnic Demands: The Case of Israel." *Ethnic and Racial Studies* 7: 283–306.

Yishai, Y. 1985a. "Israeli Annexation of East Jerusalem and Golan Heights: Factors and Processes." *Middle East Studies* 21: 45–60.

Yishai, Y. 1985b. "War and Legitimacy: The Case of Israel." Paper delivered at the 1985 Annual Meeting of the American Political Science Association, New Orleans, August 30–September 1.

Yishai, Y. 1987a. *Interest Groups in Israeli Politics: The Test of Democracy.* Tel Aviv: Am Oved (Hebrew).

Yishai, Y. 1987b. *Land or Peace. Whither Israel.* Stanford: Hoover Institution Press.

Yishai, Y. 1990. *The Power of Expertise: The Israel Medical Association.* Jerusalem: The Jerusalem Institute for Israel Studies (Hebew).

Zidon, A. 1964. *The Knesset—Israel's Parliament.* Jerusalem: Ahiasaf.

Ziegler, L. H. and G. W. Peak. 1972. *Interest Groups in American Society.* 2nd ed. Englewood Cliffs, N. J.: Prentice-Hall.

Index

411